Shakespeare Performed

R. A. Foakes (photo by the editor)

Shakespeare Performed

Essays in Honor of R. A. Foakes

Edited by
Grace Ioppolo

Newark: University of Delaware Press
London: Associated University Presses

© 2000 by Associated University Presses, Inc.

All rights reserved. Authorization to photocopy items for internal or personal use, or the internal or personal use of specific clients, is granted by the copyright owner, provided that a base fee of $10.00, plus eight cents per page, per copy is paid directly to the Copyright Clearance Center, 222 Rosewood Drive, Danvers, Massachusetts 01923. [0-87413-732-2/00 $10.00 + 8¢ pp, pc.]
Other than as indicated in the foregoing, this book may not be reproduced, in whole or in part, in any form (except as permitted by Sections 107 and 108 of the U.S. Copyright Law, and except for brief quotes appearing in reviews in the public press).

Associated University Presses
440 Forsgate Drive
Cranbury, NJ 08512

Associated University Presses
16 Barter Street
London WC1A 2AH, England

Associated University Presses
P.O. Box 338, Port Credit
Mississauga, Ontario
Canada L5G 4L8

The paper used in this publication meets the requirements of the American National Standard for Permanence of Paper for Printed Library Materials Z39.48-1984.

Library of Congress Cataloging-in-Publication Data

Shakespeare performed : essays in honor of R.A. Foakes / edited by Grace Ioppolo.
    p.   cm.
Includes bibliographical references and index.
ISBN 0-87413-732-2 (alk. paper)
1. Shakespeare, William, 1564–1616—Stage history—To 1625. 2. Shakespeare, William, 1564–1616—Stage history—1950-3. Shakespeare, William, 1564–1616—Dramatic production. 4. Shakespeare, William, 1564–1616—Film and video adaptations. 5. Theater—England—History—16th century. 6. Theater—History—20th century. I. Ioppolo, Grace, 1956- II. Foakes, R.A.
PR3091 S367   2000
792.9'5—dc21   00-024208

PRINTED IN THE UNITED STATES OF AMERICA

Contents

Preface GRACE IOPPOLO	7
Acknowledgments	11

Part I: Shakespeare Performed in His Time:
Theatre, Text, and Interpretation

Shakespeare's Foolosophy JONATHAN BATE	17
Shakespeare's Sense of Direction M. M. MAHOOD	33
Commerce and Patronage: The Lord Chamberlain's Men's Tour of 1597 PETER DAVISON	56
Stage Directions for Music and Sound Effects in *2–3 Henry VI*: "No Quarrel, but a slight Contention" PETER M. WRIGHT	72
"Misconstruing Everything": *Julius Caesar* and *Sejanus* IAN DONALDSON	88
Standing Back from Tragedy: Three Detachable Scenes ALEXANDER LEGGATT	108
"Tenders and True Pay": Representing Falsehood PHILIP EDWARDS	122
The First Performances of Shakespeare's *Sonnets* E. A. J. HONIGMANN	131

Part II: Shakespeare Performed in Our Time:
Theatre, Film, Text, and Interpretation

Writing About Shakespeare's Plays in Performance JOHN RUSSELL BROWN	151
Unfolding and Cutting: *Measure for Measure* at the Old Vic in 1957–58 G. R. PROUDFOOT	164

The Performance of Text in the Royal National Theatre's
1997 Production of *King Lear* 180
  GRACE IOPPOLO
Possessing Edgar: Aspects of *King Lear* in Performance 198
  MICHAEL HATTAWAY
Designs on Shakespeare: Sleeves, Gloves, and Helen's Placket 216
  CAROL CHILLINGTON RUTTER
Australian Shakespeare 240
  ALAN BRISSENDEN
Cutting Women Down to Size in the Olivier and Loncraine
Films of *Richard III* 260
  MARLISS C. DESENS
Film Editing 273
  PETER HOLLAND
Afterword 299
  STANLEY WELLS

Selected Bibliography 306
Notes on Contributors 308
Index 313

Preface

ALTHOUGH PETRUCCIO PROCLAIMS TO HIS GOOD FRIEND HORTENSIO IN *The Taming of the Shrew* that "twixt such friends as we / Few words suffice," the contributors to this volume of essays come together with more than a few words to celebrate R. A. Foakes—"Reg" to his friends—not only for his outstanding scholarship and publications but for his role as dedicated and generous teacher and mentor to all of us, his undergraduate and graduate students, collaborators, and colleagues.

Reg completed his Ph.D. at the University of Birmingham and was one of the three original Fellows of its Shakespeare Institute in Stratford-upon-Avon. In a long and distinguished career, he also taught at the University of Durham, Yale University, the University of Toronto, the University of California, Santa Barbara, the University of Kent, Canterbury, where he founded the Department of English and American Literature and served as Professor and as Dean of Faculty, and finally at the University of California, Los Angeles, where he also held a Professorship. Whether teaching Shakespeare and Renaissance drama or the Romantics, his other major field of study, his lectures were infused with a brilliant command of an astonishing range of material that captivated his audience, and his seminars and tutorials with that endless energy, quizzical look, and quiet authority that made his students want to work very hard to keep up with him. In and out of the classroom he was a superb and demanding teacher, never satisfied until his students demonstrated that they could match his own breadth of knowledge of every field that contributed to the study of literature and drama, whether Renaissance or Romantic, medieval or modern.

His publications in the field of Shakespeare and Renaissance drama stretch from his landmark 1961 edition with R. T. Rickert of *Henslowe's Diary* (and later on his own the two volume *The Henslowe Papers*, much prized by book collectors) through to his numerous critical editions, produced over five decades, of the plays of Shakespeare and his contemporaries, including *The Revenger's Tragedy, The Comedy of Errors, Henry VIII, Much Ado About Nothing, A Midsummer Night's Dream, Mac-*

beth, Troilus and Cressida, and the recent *King Lear,* to his books *Shakespeare: the Dark Comedies to the Last Plays: from Satire to Celebration, Marston and Tourneur, Illustrations of the English Stage, 1580–1642, The Columbia Dictionary of Quotations from Shakespeare* (co-authored with his late wife, Mary), and his powerful modern cultural history of Shakespeare, *Hamlet versus Lear: Cultural Politics and Shakespeare's Art.* His publications in other fields, particularly his brilliant two volume edition of S. T. Coleridge's *Lectures 1808–19: On Literature* as well as his books *The Romantic Assertion, Romantic Criticism,* and *Coleridge on Shakespeare,* would in themselves have more than guaranteed his reputation as a major literary scholar and critic. Yet his examinations through textual study and editing, theatre history, and performance criticism of how Shakespeare's plays were received by his audience in his own time and in our time have helped create and shape our modern notions and conceptions of Shakespeare and his texts.

Throughout his teaching and publishing career, Reg insisted that a dramatic text should first be seen as a *performing* and *performative* text and second as a *literary* and *reading* text. What Reg has offered to his audiences is the imagination to envision the theatrical world of a play. It should not be surprising then that Reg taught, trained, mentored, and collaborated with textual critics *and* editors *and* theatre historians *and* performance critics, for he has been insisting on the interdependence of these fields since the 1950s. The rise in the 1970s of the new revisionism and the overwhelming interest in textual study have encouraged Shakespearian scholars to insist that textual study, editing, theatre history, and performance criticism should be linked. But what has not been recognized before the appearance of this volume is that Reg had been working to integrate these fields for many years.

In this volume, we hope to demonstrate that because of the impact and influence of Reg Foakes, and of his colleagues and his students, modern theatre performance critics are now collaborating with or working from the ideas of Renaissance theatre historians and textual scholars and bibliographers in order to re-examine what Shakespeare as performed in his own time can tell us about Shakespeare as performed in our time. For the first time, performance critics are becoming theatre historians, theatre historians are becoming textual scholars, and textual scholars are becoming performance critics, and vice versa, particularly in their research into the "stability" of the Shakespeare text.

The essays in this collection, divided into two groups, "Shakespeare Performed in His Time" and "Shakespeare Performed in Our Time," share a concern, to use Peter Holland's perfectly conceived notion, with the "invoked authorizing presence" of Shakespeare. Many of the contributors, E. A. J. Honigmann, Philip Edwards, M. M. Mahood, G. R. Proudfoot, and Stanley Wells among them, have been, like their colleague Reg Foakes, those most centrally involved in examining, establishing, and sometimes questioning the critical dominance of the stable Shakespeare text, particularly as a result of performance. These essays, then, reflect the current state of Shakespeare study in all its breadth, richness, and diversity, ranging from the traditional poetical and theatre history inquiries of E. A. J. Honigmann, Peter Davison, and M. M. Mahood, through the bibliographical examinations of Ian Donaldson and Peter Wright and the critical interpretations of Jonathan Bate, Philip Edwards and Alexander Leggatt, to the performance, film, and theoretical criticism of John Russell Brown, G. R. Proudfoot, Grace Ioppolo, Michael Hattaway, Carol Chillington Rutter, Alan Brissenden, Marliss Desens, and Peter Holland.

What the varied and multi-disciplined authors of these essays remind us is that these old and new fields do not merely coexist but must work concurrently and interactively. For example, Peter Davison's intriguing essay on the 1597 touring performances by Shakespeare's company, the Lord Chamberlain's Men, in Marlborough tells us much about Elizabethan actors' ability to adapt and reshape Shakespeare's plays in performance. Davison thus provides an excellent foundation for Alan Brissenden's essay on modern actors' ability to politicize and reclaim colonial and post-colonial Shakespeare in performance. And the theoretical inquiries of Jonathan Bate and Alexander Leggatt, for example, remind us first that text creates performance which creates interpretation which creates text, in that order and sequence, and second that text, performance, and interpretation create each other *simultaneously*, without any order or sequence.

All Shakespearian criticism is cyclical and circular. Shakespearian theatre history, textual, and performance scholars and their fields of inquiry must cross over rather than become isolated and fixed; read in juxtaposition these essays enrich our understanding of the continuing evolution *through performance* of Shakespeare the Author and Shakespeare the Text. These essays demonstrate that literary and theatrical boundaries are not closed off or contained but move effortlessly outside their critically-imposed margins as literature, as theatre, and as performance. For many of these open boundaries we can thank R. A. Foakes. If the swaggering Petruccio does not seem the most appropriate person to quote in declaring our devotion, we can call on the most loyal and steadfast of friends, Kent in *King Lear*, and offer this volume with gratitude to our "great patron," Reg, whom we have ever "honored," "loved" and "followed."

Acknowledgments

THE EDITOR WISHES TO THANK THE FOLLOWING PEOPLE: ALAN BRISSENden for his suggestion, some years ago, that she "think about doing a *Festschrift* for Reg," and for his encouragement ever since; Peter Beal, Stanley Wells, and the staff at Associated University Presses for advice on the manuscript; and, above all, Jay Halio for his support and for his dedication to this volume.

Shakespeare Performed

I
Shakespeare Performed in His Time: Theatre, Text, and Interpretation

Shakespeare's Foolosophy

Jonathan Bate

SHAKESPEARIAN CRITICISM AT THE END OF THE TWENTIETH CENTURY IS IN a state which could be equally well described as lively pluralism or strategic disarray. Armies of new historicists and cultural materialists, feminists and queer theorists, psychoanalyzers and deconstructionists, textual scholars and performance historians clash with confused alarms of struggle and flight. A rough survey of the overall terrain suggests that the majority of critics belong to one of two camps: those whose primary interest is *ideas* and those whose primary interest is *performance*. The idea—or ideology—camp put a high premium on theory, while the performance camp, being more interested in the nuts and bolts of theatre, respond more to practice. Idea-logues ask how we may link Shakespeare's plays to theories of gender, sexual orientation, race, class, history, nationhood, "alterity" and so forth. Performers ask seemingly more mundane questions: in what ways did Shakespeare draw on an inherited set of theatrical conventions and traditions? How may we apply the evidence which has been gleaned from an archaeological discovery such as the excavation of the Elizabethan Rose theatre or a practical experiment such as the reconstruction of the Globe on Bankside? What is the relationship of the early printed texts of Shakespeare's plays to the promptbooks kept in his theatre? Did Shakespeare and his company revise the plays before reviving them? What may we learn about the plays, and about cultural change, from the performance history of individual works in the time between their original production and the present?

The bifurcation between the study of ideas and that of performance, between theory and practice, would have puzzled Shakespeare himself. In the closing chapter of a recent book, I argued that insofar as he had a theory or leading idea of his own, that theory or idea was inextricably linked to practice and indeed to theatrical performance.[1] Here I want to set my thinking about Shakespeare's "philosophy of performance" in the context of the intellectual history of the sixteenth century. In particular I will be reading *King Lear* in terms of what the scholar Hiram Haydn calls the "counter-Renaissance,"[2] a tradition which embraces Michel de Montaigne, the writer who most eloquently rejected the claims of theory for those of experience and of practice, and Erasmus's *Praise of Folly*, the book which provides the best precedent for Shakespeare's fascination with that consummate performer, the wise fool. Although I will be raising questions at the level of history and theory, the answers—insofar as there are any answers—coming back from Shakespeare and the counter-Renaissance tradition are always at the level of performance and practice. *Lear* is my leading test case because it is the play most commonly regarded as the apex of the Shakespearian vision of the world.

I want to start with the question of "history" which, since the "new historicism" of the 1980s, has made much of the running in *fin de siècle* Shakespeare studies:

> Of history, that is, the true narration of things, there are three kinds: human, natural, and divine. The first concerns man; the second, nature; the third, the Father of nature. One depicts the acts of man while leading his life in the midst of society. The second reveals causes hidden in nature and explains their development from earliest beginnings. The last records the strength and power of Almighty God, and of the immortal souls, set apart from all else.[3]

So begins the first chapter of Jean Bodin's *Method for the easy Comprehension of History*, written in 1565 and published in Latin in Paris the following year. According to Bodin, natural and divine history follow an "inevitable and steadfast sequence of cause and effect," whereas "human history mostly flows from the will of mankind, which ever vacillates and has no objective." For this reason, human actions are invariably involved in *new errors*. The function of history is to guard against such errors by means of an analysis of past human actions and the rules governing them. Bodin thus abandons divine history to the theologians and natural history to the philosophers. By chapter three of his *Method*, he has narrowed his definition of the word history down to "the activities of men only" and "the truthful narration of deeds of long ago."

Bodin's secularisation of history is a typically Renaissance humanist move. Although the humanist historiographer speaks of human errors, by confining the object of study to the activity of human subjects he implicitly makes man the master of all things, or at the very least explicitly measures all things by the standards of man rather than nature or God. The same may be said, despite its self-description as an anti-humanism, of the so-called new historicism which shook up Renaissance studies in the 1980s. Like all forms of postmodernism, that movement was premised on the Nietzschean deconstruction of metaphysics: God is dead and there is no such thing as nature unmediated by human ideology.

Several leading strands in the modern criticism of *King Lear* have been concerned with questions of history. Three kinds of historical approach to the play have become common: (1) analysis of the play's use of the *human past* and in particular the chronicles of early (semi-mythical) British history by means of which it explores questions of national identity; (2) analysis of the play's relationship to its *human present*, its own historical moment—in other words, an interrogation of the specifically early Stuart inflections given to the Lear story, by way of reflection on the significance of a play about the harmful effects of the division of the kingdom of Britain being staged in front of King James VI and I at Whitehall shortly after he had united the kingdoms of England and Scotland or of the meaning of Tom o'Bedlam's demonic possession in the light of the King's treatise on demonology; and (3) analysis of some aspect of the play's place in what from Shakespeare's point of view would have been the *human future*, that is to say a consideration of its theatrical and critical life in relation to later history (examples of this kind of work would be Michael Dobson's treatment of Nahum Tate's infamous rewriting of *Lear* in relation to the Exclusion Crisis, my own investigation of what happened to the play when England really did have a mad king during the period of the Regency Crisis, and R. A. Foakes's suggestion that *Lear* took over from *Hamlet* as Shakespeare's most highly regarded play in the 1960s because it was the nearest thing to a Shakespearian apocalypse and that was what fitted the mood of the Cold War).[4]

It seems to me that all work of this kind follows Bodin in abandoning the divine and the natural. At the same time, it seems to me that of all Shakespeare's tragedies and historical plays, *Lear* is the one which is most concerned with matters of natural and divine history, the one in which and for which secular humanism is most wanting. For Bodin, human history depicts the acts of man while leading his life in the midst of society: the starting-point of *King Lear* is a rejection of society. Lear's abdication signals that the play will be about what happens to a man when he departs from the midst of society, when he goes alone—or nearly alone—back to nature. In accordance with Bodin's definition of the second kind of history, natural history, the play asks what are the "causes hidden in nature." At its center are such questions as Lear's "Is there any cause in nature that makes these hard hearts?" (3.6.74–75). What is the answer to that question? Bodin would find one by moving to his third category, divine history, but in the case of Shakespeare's play, Christian providence (Bodin's "strength and power of Almighty God") is notably absent—at least on the surface.

I would suggest, then, that the kind of history with which we should be concerned when thinking about *King Lear* is the second, Bodin's *natural* history. As I have said, he regarded this kind of history as the province of the philosophers, an opinion which serves as a reminder that what he calls natural history was also generally known in the sixteenth century as *natural philosophy*. I therefore think that the central question which *we* need to ask about *King Lear* is not "what is the play's position on matters of secular human history?," but "what is its implied natural philosophy?"

Did Shakespeare have a "philosophy of life"? Do his plays have a consistent philosophical vision? What did he know about philosophy and what did he think of philosophers? We need to be wary of such questions, given Shakespeare's frequent use of other people's ideas and his variety of forms. We cannot say that he had an optimistic view of life when he wrote comedies and a pessimistic one when he wrote tragedies. Nevertheless, it is surely a question worth investigating. A good beginning will be to look at the occasions on which Shakespeare uses the word "philosopher." These are surprisingly few: there are just ten occurrences in the concordance.

In *The Merchant of Venice* (1.2.42), one of Portia's suitors, a melancholy man, is compared to "the weeping philosopher," Heraclitus, who wept at how people gather up treasure for themselves while neglecting to take care to bring up their children well. The philosopher, then, is someone who anatomizes human folly and hypocrisy. Jaques in *As You Like It* answers well to the description. But *As You Like It* plays the melancholy man off against the Fool. Where Jaques weeps, the Fool anatomizes folly through laughter; paradoxically, it is the man of folly who perhaps has the true wisdom. The word "philosopher" is used twice in *As You Like It*. Touchstone describes Corin as "a natural philosopher" (3.2.28), in response to Corin's down-to-earth wisdom ("the property of rain is to wet and fire to burn"—a very philosophical statement). Here the word "natural" has a double sense: from Touchstone's point of view it means foolish (a village idiot was known as a "natural"), but to the audience it also suggests that Corin speaks the truth of nature—which is the opposite to that of the court. The truth of nature, as opposed to the flattery of the court, is exactly what Lear has to learn: the structural movement of his play is strikingly similar to that of *As You Like It*. Lear goes to the country with his Fool, a Touchstone, but he is also exposed to the plain wisdom and virtue of the low-born (such as the Old Man who follows Gloucester).

The second reference in *As You Like It* is to "the heathen philosopher." It occurs immediately after the saying "The fool doth think he is wise, but the wise man knows himself to be a fool" (5.1.29–30). This is the most famous saying of Socrates. In the sixteenth century, it had become proverbial; it was quoted in the widely known *Adagia* of Erasmus. The longest of the adages concerns the "Sileni of Alcibiades": a Silenus was a kind of box which was hideous on the outside but revealed a deity when opened. Socrates, Erasmus said, was like a Silenus box, with his snuffly nose and peasant face; on the surface, he was a blockhead bumpkin who used simple language and had no care for appearance, but within, there was deep wisdom, his wisest insight being that he knew nothing. Christ was also seen as a Silenus, because of his humble exterior, his poverty, his rejection by the elite, his time in the wilderness. According to Erasmus, the real truth of things is the most profoundly concealed, not easily detected by the many, certainly not by those with wealth and rank—these are just externals. Socrates's paradoxical wisdom, Christ's ethos of love which proposes turning the other cheek instead of the superficially reasonable requital of an eye for an eye—these are inversions of expected values. Erasmus's word for this is "praeposterum," a rhetorical figure of reversal. The English translation of this adage aptly uses the word "topsy-turvy."[5] Remember Lear in his madness which is his time of greatest sanity: "What, art mad? A man may see how this world goes with no eyes. Look with thine ears. See how yon justice rails upon yon simple thief. Hark in thine ear: change places and handy-dandy, which is the justice, which is the thief?" (4.6.146–50).

Sight only gives you the superficial appearance: the robes of the Justice and the rags of the thief mark out their allotted roles. But close your eyes and listen, and the railing voice of the justice is as much an affront to the law of love and forgiveness as any act of theft could be. Robes and furred gowns hide all. *Lear* is about the deceptiveness of appearance and dress; it does not respect those who have power in history or ideology. When Lear takes off his finery, he opens the Silenus box of wisdom.

Touchstone's adage about knowledge and ignorance is an indication that Shakespeare's plays are sceptical of the claims made by conventional rationalizing philosophy. They are more interested in the paradoxes of "wise folly." That scepticism is apparent from the fourth use of "philosopher" in the comedies. In *Much Ado about Nothing*, Leonato is distraught that the honor of his daughter and his family name have been besmirched by Claudio's accusation of sexual infidelity. He refuses to listen to the "counsel" of his brother: passion overrides rational advice. People always advise "patience" to those who are in sorrow, but they are not able to apply the advice to themselves when suffering. Leonato says:

> I will be flesh and blood,
> For there was never yet philosopher
> That could endure the toothache patiently,
> However they have writ the style of gods,
> And made a pish at chance and sufferance.
> (*Much Ado*, 5.1.34–38)

The irony here is specifically directed against Stoicism, the philosophy which preaches "patience" in the face of adversity and recommends that we aspire to be like the gods who are above suffering, that we try not to be influenced by fortune. A testing of the limits of Stoicism is one of the principal motifs of the Roman plays.

Of Shakespeare's ten uses of the word "philosopher," four occur in the comedies and none in the histories. The other six are confined to two tragedies, written in close proximity to each other. They are two tragedies which follow a similar pattern of a man going from high to low estate, out from city or court to forest or stormy place where there's scarce a bush. In this "outside" space, the protagonist is filled with fury at his fellow humans.

One of these two plays is *Timon of Athens*. Jaques may fancy himself as a philosopher, but this play includes the only professional philosopher in Shakespeare: Apemantus. He is an extreme embodiment of the philosophy embraced by Jaques: Cynicism. A Cynic takes the Stoic rejection of worldliness to an extreme; a Cynic, the saying had it, was a Stoic without a tunic. The paradigm was Diogenes, who rejected "civilization," returned to the "natural" life, became a vagabond, was outspoken and without shame. Apemantus is "the philosopher" in Shakespeare. Yet for Apemantus, as for Jaques, Cynicism is a pose, a performance—they both actually rather enjoy company and food. It is Timon himself who becomes the real Cynic. In act 2 of *Timon*, the Fool goes off with Apemantus: "I do not follow lover, elder brother, and woman: sometime the philosopher" (2.2.115–16). As on many occasions in *Lear*, a line spoken by the Fool is at a deeper level applicable to the main character. Timon is the one who follows the way of the philosopher instead of the lover. He becomes a Diogenes, rejecting all worldliness, dying in his cave by the seashore.

And so to *King Lear* itself. The three occurrences of the word "philosopher" are clustered together in the hovel: "First let me talk with this philosopher. / What is the cause of thunder?" (3.4.150–51); "Noble philosopher, your company" (3.4.168); "I will keep still with my philosopher" (3.4.172). To these we should add, in the same passage, "I'll talk a word with this same learned Theban" (3.4.153): since philosophy began in ancient Greece, "Theban" is a synonym for "philosopher." The allusion may even be specifically to a Diogenes-like philosopher from Thebes, Crates the Cynic.[6] So who is Lear's philosopher? He is of course poor Tom o'Bedlam. Why does Lear call an apparent madman his philosopher? What other kinds of "philosopher" are there in the play? To what is Tom an alternative?

Gloucester blames it all on the stars: "These late eclipses in the sun and moon portend no good to us" (1.2.103–4). Edmund disputes this: "An admirable evasion of whoremaster man, to lay his goatish disposition on the charge of a star" (1.2.126–28). He argues that things often regarded as the "natural order" are in fact "custom"—for him, primogeniture and the stigmatism of bastardy would come into this category. The position articulated here is close to that of Michel de Montaigne in the closing section of his "Apology of Raymond Sebond": any custom abhorred or outlawed by one nation is sure to be praised or practised by another. But if you have nothing save custom, no divinely sanctioned hierarchy, then where does your value-system come from? Edmund commits himself to "nature" as a principle of survival and self-seeking. In this, he has been seen as a proto-Hobbesian philosopher, espousing a doctrine of raw competition. Montaigne argues instead for Christian love and humility. Perhaps this is what Edmund moves towards at the end of the play, with his last attempt to do some good and his discovery that he was beloved.

Gloucester's philosophical orientation, meanwhile, turns towards the Stoic idea of finding the right timing for death. After his mock suicide he says: "Henceforth I'll bear / Affliction till it do cry out itself / 'Enough, enough' and die" (4.6.75–77). But he can not sustain this position: in 5.2, when Lear and Cordelia lose the battle, he is in "ill thoughts again," wanting to rot. Edgar responds with Stoic advice: "Men must endure / Their going hence even as their coming hither. / Ripeness is all" (5.2.8–10). But this idea of good timing does not work out: by mistiming the revelation of his own identity to Gloucester, Edgar precipitates his father's death.

The pattern, then, is of Stoic comfort not working: in 4.1 Edgar reflects on his own condition and cheers himself up with thoughts about the worst, then his father comes on blinded and he's instantly confounded—things are worse than before. If the case of Edgar reveals the deficiency of Stoic comfort, that of Albany demonstrates the inadequacy of belief in divine justice. His credo is that the good shall taste "the wages of their virtue" and the bad drink from the poisoned "cup of their deservings" (5.3.301–3). This scheme works for the bad, but not for the good. In the closing scene, Albany tries to orchestrate events, to make order out of chaos, but each of his resolutions is followed by new disaster: he greets the restored Edgar, then immediately hears the news of Gloucester's death, then the news of the two queens' deaths; then Kent comes on, dying; then in response to the news that Cordelia is to be hanged, Albany says "The gods defend her" (5.3.254), only for Lear to enter with her in his arms already hanged—the gods have not defended her. Then Albany tries to give power back to Lear—and he promptly dies. Then he tries to persuade Kent and Edgar to divide the kingdom, and Kent promptly goes off to die.

The final speech of the play suggests that Albany or Edgar has learnt that Stoic comfort won't do, that it's better to speak what we feel than what we ought to say. I regard the Folio ascription of this speech to Edgar as superior to the Quarto's to Albany, on the grounds that Edgar's stripping down in act 3 is an exposure to feeling, occurring in conjunction with Lear's feeling with and for the poor, which makes him the character better prepared to voice this sentiment.

So the Stoic philosophy fails. One aspect of Poor Tom as philosopher is to offer an alternative, extreme position. The idea is similar to that in *Timon*: the truest philosopher is the most Cynical. Timon and Tom—is there purpose in the resemblance of names?—take the philosophical idea of rejecting worldly goods, clothes etc., to an extreme. They are Cynics, Stoics without tunics. Note here the most famous saying of Diogenes, which was mediated to Shakespeare via Montaigne's "Apology of Raymond Sebond," in the translation of John Florio:

> Truly, when I consider man all naked (yea be it in that sex, which seemeth to have and challenge the greatest share of eye-pleasing beauty) and view his defects, his natural subjection, and manifold imperfections; I find we have had much more reason to hide and cover our nakedness, than any creature else. We may be excused for borrowing those which nature had therein favoured more than us, with their beauties to adorn us, and under their spoils of wool, of hair, of feathers, and of silk to shroud us.[7]

Compare Lear: "Is man no more than this? Consider him well. Thou ow'st the worm no silk, the beast no hide, the sheep no wool, the cat no perfume. Ha? Here's three on's are sophisticated; thou art the thing itself. Unaccommodated man is no more but such a poor, bare, forked animal as thou art" (3.4.101–6). He then starts taking off his clothes to follow Tom's example.

The influence of Montaigne's essay, I suggest, is the key to the play's critique of Stoicism. What is man like, asks Montaigne:

> Let us now but consider man alone, without other help, armed but with his own weapons, and unprovided of the grace and knowledge of God, which is all his honour, all his strength, and all the ground of his being. Let us see what hold-fast or free-hold he hath in this gorgeous and goodly equipage. . . . Is it possible to imagine any thing so ridiculous, as this miserable and wretched creature, which is not so much as master of himself, exposed and subject to the offences of all things, and yet dareth call himself Master and Emperor of this Universe? In whose power it is not to know the least part of it, much less to command the same. (258)

Lear's mistake is that he tries to command that which he does not know. The weather, the "admirable moving of heaven's vault" in time of storm, is not controlled by man, not for his benefit. Montaigne's essay is an attack on those who argue that reason is our highest faculty and a sign of the power of the human—the historical—subject: "Presumption is our natural and original infirmity. *Of all creatures man is the most miserable and frail, and therewithal the proudest and disdainfulest.* . . . When I am playing with my cat, who knows whether she hath more sport in dallying with me, than I have in gaming with her?" (260). Man is the only animal whom God has left "naked on the bare earth," "having nothing to cover and arm himself withal but the spoil of others" (262)—other animals have their shells, hair, wool, hide and feathers. Furthermore, "Generation is the chiefest natural action: we have a certain disposition of some members, fittest for that purpose" (271)—yet we are the one animal disgusted by the sight of genitals. The disgust cited by Montaigne is expressed by Lear in his infamous disquisition on the sulphurous pit. Lear's words do not come from some personal disgust at women on Shakespeare's part: they are in an historically identifiable philosophical, or rather *anti*-philosophical, tradition.

Montaigne's work is a perpetual critique of abstract wisdom in the name of experience. As the passage about the philosopher and the toothache in *Much Ado about Nothing* suggests, Shakespeare had been engaging in a similar critique throughout his career. He always finds theory wanting in the face of action. He is more interested in how people perform than in what they profess. He was, after all, a performer himself. His reading of Montaigne in Florio's translation some time before the writing of *Lear* gave him a more philosophically articulated basis for his long-standing practice.

"What do I know?" asks Montaigne. I know experience, he replies to himself in his final essay. At the end of the "Sebond" essay, he suggests that all we can do is fall back on divine grace, on God: "Whatsoever we attempt without his assistance, whatever we see without the lamp of his grace, is but vanity and folly" (321). Again, the attack is specifically upon Stoicism. We will be saved by "our Christian faith," not "Stoic virtue." Sebond had argued that you could infer God from the order of created nature and from the reason. The "Apology" in Montaigne's title is ironically meant: the essay comprehensively refutes Sebond's natural religion and says that what you need instead is blind, irrational faith.

I suggest that *King Lear* comes to a similar conclusion, but that it does so not through thinking, in the manner of Montaigne, but through enactment—through performance. It moves from a theoretical and philosophical inquiry into deep causes to a practical faith in the surface truth of human actions and a trust in the wisdom to be gained from immediate experience. Albany says:

> If that the heavens do not their visible spirits
> Send quickly down to tame these vile offences,
> It will come:
> Humanity must perforce prey on itself,
> Like monsters of the deep.
>
> (4.2.47–51)

He is instantly mocked by the news that Gloucester has been blinded and Cornwall slain. Albany regards the servant who kills Cornwall as an agent of divine justice, but he can not make sense of Gloucester's blinding. Edgar, though, tries to do so in the final scene, in a notably cruel "eye for an eye" judgment: "The dark and vicious place where thee he got / Cost him his eyes" (5.3.170–71). But this notion of divine justice certainly can not account for Cordelia's death. We should recall here Shakespeare's two major alterations to his source, the old anonymous play of *King Leir*: its happy ending was removed, Cordelia being wantonly killed, and the whole of the action was displaced from a Christian to a pagan setting. Albany's lines quoted above are close to the source:

> Oh just *Jehova*, whose almighty power
> Doth governe all things in this spacious world,
> How canst thou suffer such outrageous acts
> To be committed without just revenge?[8]

This sentiment is voiced by the play's Kent-figure as he and Leir are about to be killed by a murderer sent by Gonorill and Ragan. But then there is a benign divine intervention (in Bodin's term, an "outstanding miracle of God"—the exceptional occurrence in which divine history overlaps with human): it thunders, the murderer quakes and drops his knife. By the end of *Leir*, justice does come: Gonorill and Ragan are defeated, Leir and Cordella restored.

Remove the Christian values and structure: what do you then have? You have humanity as monsters, preying on each other. You have no value structure or sure knowledge. You have something very much like the "Apology of Raymond Sebond" without its Christian ending.

But it seems to me that in Shakespeare's strand of "wise fooling," a kind of divine history is smuggled back into the raw natural world of *Lear*. The key additions to the old *Leir* play are the characters of the Fool and Poor Tom. They force us to turn from the "Apology of Raymond Sebond" to another "counter-Renaissance" text. Socrates's saying that he is the wisest of men because he knows he is the most ignorant was quoted by Erasmus not only in his *Adagia* but in his *Praise of Folly*.

Erasmus's Folly's first claim is that only she brings joy. Proof: your face lights up when she comes forward to speak; you were gloomy before, you perk up when she comes on stage. Isn't this what happens with the Fool in a play? Don't you feel good the very moment Lear's Fool appears? Orators attempt to clear the mind of troubles and sorrows by means of elaborate speeches; Folly achieves this in a flash simply by making an appearance. The Fool's one-liners make more sense of Lear's predicament than do the Stoic rationalizations of Gloucester and Edgar.

This is the attraction of the court fool: he is fun and he speaks the truth, whereas wise rhetoricians invert the truth. Only the fool is allowed to speak the truth without incurring displeasure. With Folly, no art is needed to find the mind's construction in the face: "For in me (ye must think) is no place for setting of colours, as I cannot say one thing, and think another: but on all sides I do resemble myself."[9] People who disguise themselves always unwittingly reveal their true identity. In the play's opening scene we are invited to contrast the plain speakers with those who say one thing and think another: Cordelia and Kent are pitted against Goneril and Regan. The tragedy of the court is that you can only gain advancement there through false speaking. Plain-speaking Kent is forced into disguise as servant Caius.

Biology is an affront to rationalizing philosophy. Everybody, even the Stoic philosopher, has to do the same undignified thing in order to make a baby. Life itself does not come from the respectable parts of the body, but from the part so foolish that it cannot be mentioned without a snigger. So says Erasmus's Folly, in the same (anti-)intellectual tradition as Lear's "Let copulation thrive." Folly notes, too, that we like babies, who lack wisdom. Growing old is a return to childishness. Lear is happiest on the heath and in the reunion scene when he has lost his grip on reality.

The Stoic philosopher tries to be ruled by reason rather than passion. But for Erasmus the notion that to be wise you must suppress the emotions is inhuman. The most important thing is to "feel"—as Gloucester has to learn, to see the world not rationally but "feelingly" (4.6.145). Folly points out that friendship is among the highest human values, and it depends on emotion. The people who show friendship to Lear (Fool, Kent as Caius, Edgar as Poor Tom and then as Peasant) and to Gloucester (Servants, Old Man) are not the wise or the rich.

We are ruled by our passions and our bodies; we go through life performing a series of different roles of which we are by no means in control. In Folly's eyes, "all this life of mortal men, what is it else, but a certain kind of stage play" (Chaloner, 38). History and theory are so much mere breath; they are no more than part of the brief and often risible performance that is human life. "When we are born we cry that we are come / To this great stage of fools" (4.6.178–79). "What sport and pastime the Gods themselves have at such Folly of these sely mortal men" (Chaloner, 68). In the great theatre of the world, with the gods as audience, we are the fools on stage. Under the aspect of Folly, we see that a king is no different from any other man. The trappings of monarchy are but a costume: this is both Folly's and Lear's discovery.

Folly tells us that there are two kinds of madness—one is the thirst for gold, lust and power. That is the madness of Regan, Cornwall, Edmund and Company. Their madness is what Lear and Timon reject. The second madness is the desirable one, the state of folly in which "a certain pleasant raving, or error of the mind, delivereth the heart of that man whom it possesseth from all wonted carefulness, and rendreth it divers ways much recreated with new delectation" (Chaloner, 52). This "error of the mind" is a special gift of the goddess Folly. Thus Lear is happy when his mind is free, when he's running around in his madness like a child on a country holiday. "Look, look, a mouse: peace, peace, this piece of toasted cheese will do't" (4.6.88–90). That brings a smile to our faces, not least because the mouse isn't really there. In the Folio text, Lear repeats his "look, look" at the end of his life. Cordelia is dead, but he deceives himself into the belief that she lives—that the feather moves, that her breath mists the looking-glass. His final words are spoken in the delusion that her lips are moving—"Look on her: look, her lips, / Look there, look there!" (5.3.309–10). Her lips aren't moving, just as there isn't a mouse, but it's better for Lear that he should not know this. Philosophers say that it is miserable to be deceived; Folly replies that it is most miserable "not to be deceived" (Chaloner, 63), for nothing could be further from the truth than the notion that man's happiness resides in things as they actually are.

We are far from the pursuit of conventional wisdom now, from Bodin's high humanist view of the admonitory function of history. Deception may conceivably be a good thing, says the play. "I would fain learn to lie" (says the Fool at 1.4.171). Lying is destructive in the mouths of Goneril, Regan and Edmund at the beginning of the play, but Cordelia—the Fool's double—has to learn to lie. At the beginning, she can only tell the truth (hence her banishment), but later she lies beautifully and generously when Lear says that she has cause to do him wrong, and she replies "No cause, no cause" (4.7.75).

The closing section of Erasmus's *Praise of Folly* undertakes a serious praise of Christian "madness." Christ says that the mystery of salvation is hidden from the wise and given to the simple. He delighted in simple people, fishermen and women. He chose to ride an ass when he could have mounted a lion. The language of his parables is steeped in simple, natural things—lilies, mustard seed, sparrows. We might compare Lear's language of wren, dog and garden waterpots in act four. The fundamental folly of Christianity is its demand that you throw away your possessions. Lear pretends to do this in act 1, but actually he wants to keep "the name, and all th' addition to a king" (1.1.137). Only when he loses his knights, his clothes and his sanity does he find happiness.

But he also becomes kind. Little things show us this: in act 1, he's still always giving orders. Even in the storm he continues to make demands: "Come, unbutton here" (3.4.107). But in the end he learns to say *please* and *thank you*: "Pray you undo this button. Thank you, sir" (5.3.308). He has begun to learn true manners not at court but through the love he shows for Poor Tom, the image of unaccommodated man, the image of himself ("Didst thou give all to thy daughters? And art thou come to this this?"—3.4.48–49). True wisdom comes not in Gloucester's and Edgar's words of Stoic comfort or Albany's hapless faith in divine providence, but in moments of folly and love, as in this exchange:

> EDGAR Bless thy five wits!
> KENT O pity! Sir, where is the patience now
> That you so oft have boasted to retain?
>
> (3.6.56–58)

Patience is the boast of the Stoic. It is a retainer like the hundred knights. To achieve true wisdom, you must let it go. You must let even the wits, the sanity, go. What you must keep are the *pity* and the *blessing*. Pity and blessing seem to me the very heart of *King Lear*, though we do not hear much about them in "historicist" readings. Pity means the performance of certain deeds, such as showing kindness to strangers. Blessing is a performative, in the sense of the philosopher J. L. Austin: a performative is an utterance that effects an action by being spoken or by means of which the speaker performs a particular act. Typically, blessing is accompanied by a small but forceful *gesture*, a kind of action that is of vital importance on the bare boards of the Shakespearian theatre.

For all the inventiveness of their language, both Montaigne and Shakespeare are fascinated by an aspect of humanity that is anterior to language. In his "Apology of Raymond Sebond," Montaigne notes that animals can express emotions: a dog will bark in one way and a horse will know that he is angry, he will bark in another way and it will be clear that he is not perturbed. We do not actually need educated speech in order to articulate our emotions and to communicate with others. There is an expressive language even of the eyebrows and the shoulders. And as for the hands,

> What do we with our hands? Do we not sue and entreat, promise and perform, call men unto us, and discharge them, bid them farewell and be gone, threaten, pray, beseech, deny, refuse, demand, admire, number, confess, repent, fear, be ashamed, doubt, instruct, command, incite, encourage, swear, witness, accuse, condemn, absolve, injure, despise, defy, despite, flatter, applaud, bless, humble, mock, reconcile, recommend, exalt, show gladness, rejoice, complain, wail, sorrow, discomfort, despair, cry out, forbid, declare silence and astonishment? (Florio's Montaigne, 261)

Montaigne's list of emotions, actions and desires that may be performed by the hands is like a litany of the processes through which Lear has to go in the course of his play. The actor, with the gestures of his hands and the other parts of his body, is able in the most literal sense to *perform* the full gamut of human being.

The progression from command to questioning to entreaty is one of Shakespeare's most striking developments of the character of the

King in the old *Leir* play. In *King Lear* the exterior trappings of Christianity which characterize the source-play are emptied out and replaced by a processual, performative approach to being. But in despite of the pagan setting, those essentials of the Erasmian and Montaignian—that is to say the counter-Renaissance—Christian vision, are still there: folly and love.

Fool and Tom teach us to split apart the idea of *philo-sophy*. The word is derived from Greek *philos*, love, and *sophos*, wisdom. The natural history of *King Lear* rejects the law of *sophos* in the name of *philos*. Erasmus' great mock-encomium had a neat word for the folly of those who pursue wisdom. But by the end of the *Praise*, with its discovery that true wisdom is paradoxically to be found in folly, the word is no longer to be mocked. It is one of the Greek coinages that Erasmus slips into his Latin text, partly in homage to his friend, Sir Thomas More: "Morosophos."[10] "Moros" is Greek not only for the name "More," but also for "foolish" (hence our "moron"). The compound word may, it seems to me, be attached most aptly to the Shakespeare who wrote *King Lear*. He was not a historian. He was not a philosopher. He was a FOOLOSOPHER.

Notes

1. "The Laws of the Shakespearean Universe," chapter 10 of my *The Genius of Shakespeare* (London: Picador, 1997 and New York: Oxford University Press, 1998).

2. See Haydn, *The Counter-Renaissance* (New York: Scribner, 1950).

3. Bodin, *Method for the Easy Comprehension of History*, ed. and trans. Beatrice Reynolds (New York: Columbia University Press, 1945), chapter 1.

4. Dobson, *The Making of the National Poet: Shakespeare, Adaptation and Authorship, 1660–1769* (Oxford: Clarendon Press, 1992); Bate, *Shakespearean Constitutions: Politics, Theatre, Criticism 1730–1830* (Oxford: Clarendon Press, 1989); Foakes, *Hamlet versus Lear: Cultural Politics and Shakespeare's Art* (Cambridge: Cambridge University Press, 1993).

5. "Sileni Alcibiadis," *Adagia* (1515), 3.3.1, trans. Margaret Mann Phillips, *Erasmus on his Times: A Shortened Version of the Adages of Erasmus* (Cambridge: Cambridge University Press, 1967), 77.

6. See R. A. Foakes's note to this line in his third series Arden edition of *King Lear* (Walton-on-Thames: Thomas Nelson, 1997), 283. The "good Athenian" at line 176 would then be Diogenes himself.

7. "An Apology of Raymond Sebond," in *The Essayes Or Morall, Politike and Millitarie Discourses of Lo: Michaell de Montaigne. . . . First written by him in French. And now done into English*, trans. John Florio (London: Edward Blount, 1603), 280. Spelling modernized in quotations.

8. *King Leir*, lines 1649–52, quoted from *Narrative and Dramatic Sources of Shakespeare*, ed. Geoffrey Bullough, 8 vols. (London: Routledge and Kegan Paul, 1957–75), 7:377.

9. Erasmus, *Moriae Encomium* (in Latin, 1509), trans. Thomas Chaloner (1549), *The Praise of Folie*, ed. Clarence H. Miller (London, New York and Toronto: Oxford University Press for The Early English Text Society, 1965), 10. Spelling modernized in quotations.

10. Translated by Chaloner (10) as "foolelosophers."

Shakespeare's Sense of Direction

M. M. MAHOOD

1

"A PLAY READ, AFFECTS THE MIND LIKE A PLAY ACTED." THE CONFIDENT tone of Johnson's statement suggests that he was gifted with an unusually alert theatrical imagination. For those of us, however, whose reading habits have been formed by narrative fiction, mounting a thought production as we read a play can be as arduous as the setting up of a thought experiment is for the physicist. Yet the effort has to be made if we are to reanimate the text with even a modicum of its original theatrical life. We may, rather secretively, have recourse to visual aids. "Discovered in his [or her] study," the Shakespearian scholar can sometimes be found shifting chessmen or spice jars around the desktop, in an attempt to work out entrances and exits. If these prove logically and logistically viable, and in particular if they do not result in avoidable "broken" entrances whereby a character enters through a door from which another character has just exited, they merit preservation in our working copies. My own notation for exits and entrances in Shakespeare's plays is here the starting point for an exploration of the very distinctive sense of direction that I believe Shakespeare shared with his audience and his fellow actors.

It is a simple notation, consisting of "ID," "OD" and, very rarely, "?CD" The infrequency of the last does not imply assent to the theory that the public stages for which Shakespeare wrote had only two doors. Rather it reflects the belief that Shakespeare, when he wrote a play, hoped it would be performed at Court and at the same time knew that it might on occasion be acted in a great hall such as the Inns of Court could provide, or be taken on tour for performance in provincial town halls, private houses, and the largest available rooms of inns. Conditions even at Court could be cramped—all that could be provided for the three companies that performed the Christmas plays at Richmond in 1588 was a stage fourteen feet by fourteen[1]—and whatever the Globe and the Blackfriars may have offered, it is unlikely that Shakespeare could count, elsewhere, on more than two entrances. To put the point unfashionably: I believe that Shakespeare habitually *thought* in terms of two ways on and off the stage. With David Bradley, I see these means of access as "the systole and diastole of the great heartbeat of the Elizabethan stage as it fills and empties, fills and empties."[2] The "D" of my notation stands indifferently for a door or a curtained aperture or any other means of access, such as a short flight of steps. The "I" and "O" are what really matter. They represent my belief that in the Elizabethan theatre there operated upon playwrights, actors and audiences alike an unvoiced and almost unconscious distinction between "outward" and "inward" entrances and exits, especially in interior and urban scenes. We may play a little with the flexibility of English prepositions to put the theory this way: through OD, characters either come on in or go off out; through ID they either come on out, or go off in. Because of this long-held conviction, it was hugely satisfying to find Tim Fitzpatrick, in "Shakespeare's Exploitation of the Two-Door Stage: *Macbeth*," arguing that "in cases where the stage can be seen as an intermediate place between an off-stage place which is 'further inwards' and another off-stage place which is 'further outwards' *it is always the same stage door* which leads 'inwards,' the other door always leading 'outwards,' "[3] and illustrating this practice from a strikingly clear example, the sequence of scenes in *Macbeth* which culminates in the discovery of the murder (1.5–2.3).

In the absence of any indication of right and left hand doors in the playtexts and the Plots of the period, such "triangulation" (as Fitzpatrick calls it) would have provided actors with a default setting for entrances and exits which, unlike the convention proposed by Bernard Beckerman of characters always entering by one door and leaving by the other,[4] was spatially logical. On account of this and other theatrical implications, the theory would appear to merit extensive testing, not only by a scrutiny of playtexts (was it, for example, a generally followed convention, or is it more evident in the plays of one company than in those of another?) but also by examination of extant promptbooks to discover how far it has prevailed in past productions, and by consultation with living directors over the kind of spatial awareness that guides them in today's productions. This is enough scope for investigation, surely, to keep several people busy for some time to come.[5] My purpose here is to put forward some ideas which may conceivably prove relevant to such inquiries. One is that a steady awareness of the conventions of Elizabethan domestic architecture and of the social significance of space which they embody is essential to our understanding of the manner in which interior scenes are orientated in Shakespeare's plays. Another, to which we are led by the persistence into external scenes of the inward-outward orientation, is that the adoption of this binary, or one-dimensional, system is a rule of the dramatic game, and one moreover which an audience is helped to keep by reason of its affinity with some real-life situations. A third is that Shakespeare exploits what may have been an instinctively-applied convention, as he does other theatrical conventions, to brilliant dramatic effect.

2

Architectural awareness is expected of all Western theatrical and film audiences. When the curtain went up on one of his domestic dramas, Ibsen could count upon the spectators being familiar with the normal layout of a middle-class Scandinavian home—which subtly differed from an English interior of the time, as did both from the ground plan implicit in a play by Chekov. When, at the beginning of a English television play, the camera affords a long downward shot of a narrow town-house hallway, viewers know precisely the directions in which lie living rooms, kitchen, bedrooms and street. In like fashion, the layout of a sizeable sixteenth-century house was printed on the consciousness of Shakespeare's early audiences. The main circulation space of such a house was also a hall, but a "great hall." There were two ways out of such a space. One (my OD) was through the screen and thence either through the various doors connecting the hall with the domestic offices—buttery, pantry, kitchens, servants' quarters; or else through the main entrance door of the house. By Shakespeare's time this last was often protected by a substantial storied porch, though in older houses it might give onto a courtyard surrounded by lodgings and terminated, on the side opposite to the main door to the hall, by a gatehouse. The plan is still evident in a number of Cambridge colleges. Beyond porch or gatehouse lay the exterior world of journeys and warfare. The other way (my ID) led from the upper end of the hall to what Burghley once described in a letter as "the stately ascent from your hall to your great chamber."[6] Adjacent to the great chamber, which was the center of family activities, there was usually a withdrawing chamber, and on the inward side of this lay one or more bedchambers. Probably the average playgoer of the time had only a vague notion of the layout of these upper rooms. But when a play was to be performed in the great chamber, the withdrawing chamber, in which it was usual for personal servants to sleep, would have furnished a space in which the actors could "make ready" more comfortably than they were able to do in the kitchen—which Shakespeare's fellow actor Armin implies was the practice when a play was acted in the hall itself.[7]

I have rather willfully introduced players into this brief recall of Elizabethan domestic architecture in order to point out one confusion (for so it seems to me) which needs to be cleared up before we can consider the relevance of this architectural tradition to Shakespeare's interior sequences. The assumption is sometimes made that because, first, the *scaenae frons* of the public theatres resembled the screen of a great hall, and because, secondly, such a screen would literally form the background to any play performed in a large house or a town hall, an Elizabethan audience would view a hall scene as one *taking place* at the lower end of a hall. An instance of this would be Dover Wilson's stage direction for *Coriolanus* 4.5: "A hall in Aufidius's house, with three doors, one right leading to the outer gate, one left leading to the buttery, etc.; the third centre opening into the great chamber."[8] Unfortunately no known Elizabethan or Jacobean house has such an arrangement of its spaces. When there was a central opening in the back wall of the hall, behind the screen passage, it led to the kitchen, not the great chamber. The assumption is in fact based on shaky premises and a no less shaky conclusion. There is no hard evidence that the *scaenae frons* was modelled on a hall screen, however much it may have resembled one; and although we know that plays were sometimes acted at the lower end of a hall, there would have been difficulties about using the two ways through the screen as equivalent to the two doors onto a playhouse stage. If the actors had been provided with a platform the openings might prove too low, and in any case latecomers might ruin a scene by walking into the middle of it. Finally, Shakespeare and most of his fellow dramatists appear to have regarded the facade behind the actors simply as the interface between the backstage space and the stage itself. Only Ben Jonson, who knew more than the rest of them about the Roman theatre, looked at the *scaenae frons* of the newly-built Globe and was struck by its resemblance to an interior elevation—not however of a hall, but of the the west end of St Paul's Cathedral. Even so, he had to enlist the help of a choral character to point out the similarity.[9]

Shakespeare may once, rather late in his career, have attempted this kind of scene-setting, when he visualized the stage as the poop of Pericles' ship viewed from the main deck. By and large however, he is content to do no more than indicate, by means of dialogue or the movements of supernumeraries, that his characters are in some kind of circulation space which they enter from two, or rarely from three, directions. Once an audience had begun to conceive of this space as an interior, and so most probably a hall, they would infer that the opening on one side of the stage gave access to the exterior and to the domestic offices (through the screen, as it were) and that the opening on the other side gave access, as from the upper end of the hall, to the great chamber and other family rooms. This is the setting established in *Romeo and Juliet* 1.5, when the maskers, having "marched about the stage," come to a standstill well down on the OD side. That they are now to be thought of as inside the hall is made clear by the servants who hurry from ID to OD with empty dishes and by other servants, summoned to their aid, who are moving from OD towards ID when the Capulets and their guests enter from that door as from dinner in the great chamber.[10] Comparison of this scene with one which seems to echo it in *The Fair Maid of Bristow*,[11] a Globe play of 1604, shows just how functional is Shakespeare's deployment of Capulet's servants. Lacking such a device, the later play leaves us confused as to where we are.

Subject then to the proviso that we should experience a scene of indoor concourse as analogous with, though in no way homologous with, the great hall as the main circulation space of an Elizabethan house, it is possible to return to the murder sequence in *Macbeth* and discover that an awareness of the layout of the rest of the building makes the allocation of entrance and exits even more consistent and straightforward than they are shown to be in Tim Fitzpatrick's analysis.

From the shift in locale that occurs between 1.4, when Macbeth departs OD[12] from Forres with Duncan hard on his heels, and 1.5, when Lady Macbeth's ID entrance establishes, by the process which Fitzpatrick calls "wipe and re-set," that we are now in Macbeth's castle, we are orientated in a way that lends a projectile-like inevitability to the murderers' purpose. During five scenes, the action remains on an invisible line between the gatehouse and the family apartments. For one of these we are moved briefly down the line in the outward direction: Duncan's "This castle hath a pleasant seat" has the air of being spoken in a courtyard. But immediately Duncan has entered the building we in our turn are brought under Macbeth's roof by means of the procession of supper dishes across the stage from OD to ID—a locating device similar to the movements of the servants in *Romeo and Juliet* 1.5. Today's directors often cheat us of this spectacle. In addition, however, to its having been enjoyable in itself to a Globe audience (a similiar bit of pomp and circumstance enlivens another Globe play, *Thomas Lord Cromwell*),[13] the procession serves to move us on in time as well as place: the torches, a normal element of the ritual on a winter evening,[14] indicate that the hall is now in darkness. This accords well with the moral darkening of the ensuing scene between Macbeth and Lady Macbeth, which is what Fitzpatrick calls a "loop" scene: first one, then the other, enters from ID, letting out the sounds of the feast as they do so, and at the end of the scene they return to the royal presence through the same door.

Banquo emerges from that door at the start of 2.1. His dialogue with Fleance indicates that time has passed since the end of 1.7, but there is nothing in it to make us aware of a change of place, and early editors located the scene in "a hall." It was Johnson who objected that this could not be an internal scene because "Banquo sees the sky." So he could do—by glancing out from the interior of a dark hall through the usual lofty oriel. He has just escorted the old king to bed; not perhaps in the great chamber itself, as would have been the custom a generation or two earlier, but in the bedchamber beyond it. His host and hostess, having vacated the great chamber complex for the king, his sons and his bodyguard, have presumably retired to other family rooms behind ID. It is because hosts and royal guests together with the grooms of the chamber can all be assumed now to be "shut up" in the inner part of the castle that Banquo is so quick on the draw when he and Fleance hear footsteps approaching from outside at the lower, screen end of the hall. The gesture seems somewhat exaggerated if, as Fitzpatrick supposes, Banquo in going to his bedroom merely encounters Macbeth coming away from his. The torch which Fleance holds in place of the more usual taper by which an individual would get around indoors (and of which effective use will be made later) can be taken to imply that Banquo, as a courtier in the king's entourage, has been given a lodging in the courtyard—in which case he has fared better than the other thanes, who have been relegated to lodgings outside the castle. To conceive of bedrooms on both sides of the intermediate space, as Fitzpatrick would have us do, is an abandonment of the dominant in-out orientation and one that suggests that the layout of a modern house has been superimposed on our sense of an Elizabethan interior.

At the end of the scene Fitzpatrick has Macbeth, who has sent the servant off OD with the message that Lady Macbeth should "sound upon the bell" when his drink is ready, respond to the signal by exiting ID in the direction of Duncan's bedchamber. The anachronistic image of a twentieth-century landing, with a number of bedrooms opening off it, would appear still to haunt his staging here and also in the next scene, in which he has Lady Macbeth enter OD and exit at the end OD with Macbeth, as towards their bedroom. Since Macduff must come from outside through the same door this arrangement lands the critic in acute difficulties and he has to have recourse to a double "wipe and re-set" actually *within* 2.3: "During the twenty lines of the Porter's address to the audience DR [my OD] becomes another door leading to another place [i.e., we are removed to the south entry]; and twenty lines later it reverts to being the door it once was, leading to the various bedchambers [i.e., we are back on the landing where Fitzpatrick sets 2.2]" (211). While the strangely disorientating effect of the porter's comic turn has to be recognized, it is perfectly possible to contain the action of 2.2 and 2.3 within the same neutral space. We are helped to do this if we ask a question which may seem to belong more to Thurber's *Macbeth* than to Shakespeare's. Where is Lady Macbeth during Macbeth's "dagger" soliloquy? Holinshed indicates the answer: she is in the withdrawing chamber just outside the room where Duncan lies already asleep, and is pressing one last, laced drink on the grooms. The bell sounds in 2.2 from the ID side; Macbeth exits towards its summons, and Lady Macbeth then emerges from ID at the beginning of another loop scene, which ends with the couple retreating to their own chamber among the family apartments reached through ID.

Nor, for 2.3, do we need any change of locale to the south entry. By now Macduff and Lennox, arriving from whatever storm-swept lodging they have found outside the gatehouse, have gained admittance there (Macbeth could have more than one security man) and are thundering on the exterior door to the hall itself, which lies beyond OD. The Porter, not being quite himself, requires a bit of time before he feels able to resume his duties; there is therefore nothing surprising about his emergence by OD as if from his cubby hole near the exterior door or from the servants' quarters, before he returns through the same entrance to admit, via the unseen exterior door, the thanes whom he follows back onto the stage with a whine of "I pray you remember the porter." An entrance through the discovery space curtain would, in the public theatre, have been even more striking, and in line not only with the Fool's traditional style of entry but also with an earlier porter scene, at the beginning of *Henry the Fourth, Part Two*. In that, a character is admitted, OD, to Northumberland's castle by a porter who can have come out of the discovery space as if from his lodge near the door, or as if through the door in the back wall of the hall which led to the servants' quarters, while Northumberland enters ID as from his orchard, which we can imagine as in the inner court reached through a facing door—a setting that corresponds exactly to the screen passage of many Elizabethan houses.

Macbeth 2.3, then, can take place in the circulation space we have been in ever since the sewer led his procession across the stage. Macduff and Lennox enter OD from outside the castle; Banquo comes in by the same entrance from his forecourt lodging; Macbeth, Lady Macbeth, Donalbain and Malcolm all emerge ID from the direction of the state apartments.

There are possible objections to my localization of this whole sequence in the hall of the castle. Where does the servant go after delivering Macbeth's message to Lady Macbeth? (he will not be the first in Shakespeare to fail to return from an errand, but if need be he can pass unobtrusively back from ID to OD during Macbeth's soliloquy). Why does the bell not wake Duncan? (perhaps it does; a conscious victim increases the horror of the act). Why, at 2.3.134, does Macbeth not tell the thanes to meet "*here* i' the hall"? (Shakespeare chooses to keep the visible theatrical space fluid and unspecific). A more serious objection to my visualization of the sequence is that it adds a further broken entrance, between Macbeth's exit ID at the end of 2.1 and Lady Macbeth's entrance by ID at the start of 2.2, to the two (near the beginning of 1.7 and between 1.7 and 2.1) already present in Fitzpatrick's account. It is however open to question that Elizabethan spectators experienced the sense of panic which is felt by the members of a modern audience when, individually isolated in darkness, they face a brightly-lit vacant stage and wonder if the systole and diastole of entrances and exits has given way to cardiac arrest. On the contrary, Shakespeare's original spectators may have welcomed, especially as Macbeth moves off to do the deed, an opportunity to comment among themselves on the action, just as an African or Indian audience does today under lighting conditions similar to those of the Elizabethan playhouse. In any case there are means, such as the noises off after the sewer's procession has exited ID, of maintaining continuity. At the start of 2.1, Fleance (too juvenile to have been present in the great chamber) can come with his torch from OD and cross to ID before Banquo emerges from the state room side. It may be, however, that a marked pause is called for here to suggest a lapse of time in which Macbeth has gone outside the building, since his entrance in this scene is from OD. In the Blackfriars theatre, the pause could even have been long enough to fill with interact music, though this might not have corresponded with Shakespeare's intentions. Too long a pause would rob Macbeth's OD entrance, to which I shall return, of some of its power to startle.

The assumptions I have been making about the ground plan of Macbeth's castle apply to more modest interior settings in Shakespeare's plays, such as Ford's house in *The Merry Wives of Windsor* (the action at the house of the more open-natured Page appears to take place in a forecourt), and to the scenes set in the Garter Inn in the same play, as well as to the Eastcheap scenes of the two *Henry the Fourth* plays. In these hostelries, the circulation space appears to be on an upper floor, and so represents the first-floor hall which survives in some old inns today. The aristocratic great hall remains, however, the basic image behind many of Shakespeare's interior scenes. As such it has implications which go beyond the simply logistical. The two stage doors not only indicate an outward and an inward direction in relation to the visible stage space, they also signal the possibility of movement upwards or downwards. That movement would, to some degree, be literally up and down. Most of the family rooms in a great house were reached via the main staircase, while the access to its outer door or to the porch at the other end of the hall was usually up a number of steps; so too, by Jacobean times, could be the access from the kitchens, which builders and architects were beginning to place below ground level. But the distinction, which leads us still to speak of the lower and the upper ends of a hall even when there is no dais, was primarily a social one. The hall was neutral territory between the household "downstairs" and the household "upstairs"—"the place where 'state' and 'service' met in the day-to-day life of the house."[15] Because of this distinction it would feel right to the actors, and look right to an audience, if servants or messengers customarily came on stage OD, through the door leading to the domestic offices and the outside world. Since the other door led towards the family rooms, audiences would expect the head of the household to come in from ID except when he was returning from a journey or from outdoor pursuits. The inward-facing door would also be the normal means of entry for any actor playing a female role, whether as a member of the family or as one of the comparatively few female attendants in a wealthy household. The women's sphere of activity was contained in the part of the house which lay beyond ID, and this separation of the women's space from the men's space could be rigid, especially in a household with strong social pretensions such as that of Sir Francis Willoughby. The ladies of his great house at Wollaton were expected to take their outdoor exercise on the rooftops and were denied free access even to the hall.[16]

If I am right in believing that the usual convention pertaining to entrances on the Elizabethan stage was that servants and messengers came in from the door which connected with a conceived outer space, and that women came in from the door which connected with a conceived inner space, the consequences such a convention would have for theatrical practice are indeed striking. Of the three divisions of an Elizabethan acting company, the hired men playing the small male roles, reinforced on occasion by backstage staff and even by the gatherers, would assume, unless they were told otherwise, that their entrances would be OD; the boy actors, together with any adult players of women's roles, would assume their entrances to be from ID, on the other side.[17] Only the sharers and the more experienced hired men who, between them, played substantial roles with which, given the repertory system, they might have become familiar over the course of years, would enter and leave the stage by either door according to the course of the play's action and the spatial logic that action imposed. Such an organization of the cast perhaps brings us as close as we can get to a rule of thumb for entrances and exits. It has the additional merit of distributing the company over the backstage area where room for movement, especially on tour, must sometimes have been very limited.

3

Though the rule of thumb here suggested for entrances and exits derives in the main from the ground plan of a large Elizabethan house and the social divisions that such a plan reflects, it would be fully serviceable only if the same inward-outward orientation could be felt to operate also in scenes that are to be thought of as taking place out of doors. Fitzpatrick has shown in detail that this is the case with *Macbeth*, and his study of other plays leads him to conclude (as does my own) that it holds for at least ninety per cent of scenes in Shakespeare's plays. It is particularly evident in plays with an urban setting, where it takes the form most familiar today as the contrasted road signs, "Out of Town" and "Town Center." Thus in *The Merry Wives of Windsor*, where a two-way spatial awareness is very strong in the three indoor or before-door locales, it persists in the play's two outdoor sequences, 2.3 to 3.3 and 5.2 to 5.5. The series of brief scenes 5.2, 5.3, and 5.4 is an especially effective piece of wipe-and-reset staging as three successive groups of characters sweep with great determination of purpose across the stage from the direction of Windsor town (ID) to the direction of the Great Park (OD). By the time that Falstaff appears, also from ID, as Herne the Hunter, we scarcely need the faint chimes of the Windsor bell to confirm the distance that our imaginations have put between the town and Herne's Oak. Without these scenes of exodus, the Quarto's transfer of the action to the Great Park is uncomfortably abrupt.

Other plays with a strongly defined inward-outward orientation have a seaport setting. *The Comedy of Errors* is exceptional among Shakespeare's plays in that it requires the use of three onstage "houses," but there is also a need for two side exits, the one leading downwards to the harbor and thence out to sea, the other inwards and upwards to the Duke's palace.[18] This last arrangement prevails also in *Twelfth Night*, in which first Viola and then Sebastian and Antonio arrive from the seaward side before heading for the palaces and inns of the Illyrian seaport. In like manner the chief characters of *Othello*, on their arrival in Cyprus, enter from OD, the harbor side, and go off ID in the direction of the castle, which is the seat of government and the highest strategic point. This persistence into outdoor scenes of an inward-outward orientation tempts me to seek a more all-embracing explanation for it than the architectural one I have ventured to put forward for indoor scenes—even though to hazard such an explanation is bound to produce, in myself no less than in the reader, the sensation of skating over very thin ice.

The phenomenon of orientation has been widely studied by historical geographers, anthropologists and psychologists, but as a feature of daily life rather than of the creative writer's projected world. A single literary critic, John Barrell, has concerned himself with "the sense of place" in poetry and painting, arguing that a circular spatial awareness (similar to the ethnocentricity of medieval maps) persisted in John Clare's village-centred vision of an unenclosed landscape, even while his contemporaries looked out on a world made rectilinear by roads and hedges and the frames of landscape paintings.[19] Shakespeare's sense of direction can be presumed however to have been not that of a peasant, but of a well-read and comparatively well-travelled man of the Renaissance, familiar with the net of longitude and latitude cast upon the globe since "the augmentation of the Indies." Moreover, the orientation of his scenes as I have tried to describe it is not radial, as might be that of a landscape poet surveying the world round him. Because it is imputed to the characters on stage by the audience and associated by them with the two doors to the rear of the stage, it is of necessity linear and binary, offering a choice of "this way" and "that way." This extreme simplification has an aesthetic advantage: it helps to conserve our imaginative energy for the other claims made on it in the course of the theatrical experience. (One reason for Fitzpatrick doubting the existence of a third stage entrance is that such an entrance would make an inordinate mental demand on us, after each change of place, to postulate *three* unseen new spaces.)[20]

But does such a simplification ever apply in real life? There are indications that it does in the sense of direction shown by the inhabitants of small islands. Until Great Blasket was abandoned, the equivalent of "in" and "out" in the Irish of its inhabitants meant "onto the island" and "onto the mainland." The same basic distinction served in the Pacific for the Tileopia, whose spatial references are said to have been limited to the words for "inland" and "seawards."[21] But neither group of islanders could have survived without having recourse to more complex systems of reference for their fishing, and in fact there are Pacific communities who take their navigational bearings from as many as thirty points of reference. It would appear that in some real-life situations we instinctively narrow down our spatial awareness to a linear, inward-outward orientation. As a geographer has put it: "All individuals and groups use more than one mode of thought to evaluate space and its properties, and even to evaluate a single form, shape or place. Although some modes are more distinctive and developed in one society than in another, all normal human beings have the potential to express themselves in each of the modes."[22] One situation which is strongly relevant to the ley line that we mentally lay down for the characters in a play is the experience of visiting a strange town as a tourist. At the point of our arrival—car park or station—we begin to plot the straightest line we can to the palace or cathedral which is the object of our visit, and any deviations we make will be pictured in our minds as deviations from that invisible axis; for the purpose of our visit, we have assumed temporarily an orientation system quite different from that we make use of when we stand at our front gate.[23]

This example is relevant to Shakespeare's seaport settings and in particular to those of the two comedies. *The Comedy of Errors* derives directly from Plautus, and shares with *Twelfth Night* a Mediterranean perspective, the Plautine wanderer's view of the harbor where he will land and the high-set town center that he will make for after landing. It could even be that this affinity between the theatrical sense of direction and that of the Mediterranean traveller originated in something more than a mere analogy. Whereas the action of a play in the Theatre of Dionysus took place between a literal outer distance, which was the open country visible to the audience on their left hand, and a literal, closer, "inner" distance, which was the Athenian market place and the harbor of Piraeus visible on their right hand, the Greek comedies that were dispersed through the Mediterranean by travelling actors and were the basis of Plautus's work were set in an imagined intermediate space between, on the spectator's left, a harbor and the open sea and, on the right, the market place.[24] Slight though the change is from the Athenian convention, it brings the spatial awareness of Plautus's plays nearer to the actual experience of landfall at an island in the Aegean or the Adriatic. The seafarer seeks a safe harbor and on landing climbs to the highest point. The straight-line orientation we impose upon a dramatic character is closely analogous to the basic, straightline orientation which results from the forward drive, accompanied by wariness, of the real-life traveller. In both Ephesus and Illyria the behavior of the natives is unreliable and, in view of what happens to Egeon, Antipholus of Syracuse does well to keep open his way of retreat to the sea.

The inward-outward orientation continues, I believe, to operate in even the most geographically wide-ranging of Shakespeare's plays. The space that we see in the individual scene or sequence of scenes may be indeterminate, but it is nearly always to be thought of as intermediate. As distinct from this perceived space, the space beyond it to the one side is conceived as open country, or as a route to the sea and perhaps to lands beyond the sea; on the other side it is conceived as any permanent or temporary settlement—city, stronghold, farmstead, camp. Sometimes however we do lose our bearings, and suspect that we are meant to lose them. Do characters go in to, or out to, the wood near Athens? Within the wood a sense that ID is the interface with feminine space perhaps holds. We expect Titania to emerge from her bower, much as in Arden we expect Rosalind to appear from her cottage, on the ID side of the stage. But at other times we have to admit, with Lysander, to being completely lost. It was a production of *A Midsummer Night's Dream* which in fact first brought home to me how closely analogous the theatrical experience is to a voyage of discovery, whether that of a seafarer in the ancient world or of today's tourist. It took place on a small island near Helsinki.[25] The audience arrived, or came in, by sea, and assembled first at a stage near the shore, as in the rational world of Athens. From there, while the sky darkened, they moved literally stage by stage into the wooded center of the island and the heart of the play's confusions; retreated thence to the seat of power, now open to a haunting irrationality; and finally, to the fading strains of the bergamask, sailed out again into their own lives.

Is every worthwhile theatrical experience a kind of landfall? The question itself invites a exploration of unfamiliar territory, but one best left to those with expertise in the problems of aesthetics. Discretion brings me back to a safer middle ground between such quicksands and the practical rule of thumb with which we began: namely, to the dramatic, as distinct from the purely theatrical, consequences of the inward-outward orientation here postulated.

4

Shakespeare's dramatic exploitation of the sense of direction he shares with his actors and his audiences may have an overall or a local effect. The changing meanings we attach to the unseen space behind each of the two main exits can color our response to the play in its totality, while a powerful dramatic strike can occur when a character appears from, or exits by, what the spectators feel to be the "wrong" side. I turn to examples of both processes.

Ambivalence, that prime source of dramatic riches, is a recurrent feature of the out-and-down/in-and-up antithesis created by Shakespeare's use of exits and entrances. Banishment, rejection or dismissal culminates in an OD exit. On occasion, however, the victimized character can rightly claim to be going to liberty and not to banishment. Similarly, a character may go off ID to accept or seize a position of dignity and power, even as the audience realizes that he or she is entering a trap. Such is Duncan's fate, and such eventually the fate of Macbeth at Dunsinane; and at 4.3 of the same tragedy a further ambivalence comes into play when the unseen space from which the usurper has emerged to give orders to kill is reset in our minds as the presence chamber of the lifegiving Edward. The opening scene of *Measure for Measure* also confirms that the conceived space behind ID is the seat of power, a power which the Duke relinquishes by his exit OD and Angelo assumes by his exit the other side. But before long our awareness, aroused by changes of location, of other unseen enclosures behind the same door—a friary, a prison, a nunnery, the cells within a prison, a moated grange—builds up into the play's overall claustrophobic atmosphere. The associations of the OD exit also become ambivalent. In 1.2 it admits characters from a city that, the opening scene has informed us, is becoming a sink of iniquity. But because it is the side from which the disguised Duke habitually appears, and because we soon discover that there is iniquity in plenty in the seat of power itself, we begin to look to OD for both liberation and liberalization: for the setting free, once the Duke has returned to Vienna in his own person through this entrance, of imprisoned characters such as Claudio and Juliet and of self-imprisoned ones such as Mariana and Angelo.

The positioning of the play's women strengthens this thematic use of an inward-outward orientation. Mistress Overdone makes her entry in 1.2 appropriately enough from the side which her dialogue with Lucio and his friends (who have also entered from the red light district) quickly establishes as the libertine side, and thus helps to define Juliet's status, when she enters, guarded, from the same direction, as that of a "loose" woman in the eyes of the world. Isabella's first appearance, from what is normally the women's side and in the company of a nun, forms a strong contrast to these entrances. In its turn, it heightens the startling effect of her appearance from the "wrong" side and with no more reputable an escort than Lucio when, in 2.2, she comes to Angelo to plead for her brother's life. In the theatre, the boldness of this stage action does something to counteract the initial reticence and hesitation of her pleading. Her second appearance before the Deputy, completely alone, is even more reckless, and her assumption of a nun's habit suggests an attempt to play down this audacity.[26] The change of costume, together with the fact that all her subsequent entrances are from OD, also has the effect of placing her symbolically as well as literally on the same side as the Duke in their visits to the prison and to the moated grange. But when, at the end of the play, he leads her off ID into what we are now to think of as a palace of justice liberalized by mercy, we are perhaps left with some uncomfortable memories of that exit's association with confined and repressive spaces in earlier scenes.

Though it is not easy to mount a two-entry thought production of *Measure for Measure* without giving rise to broken entrances, a contrast between OD as the route to liberty of thought and action and ID as the way to literal and mental incarceration is an essential part of the play's total effect. The same holds true of *Hamlet*, though here the use of a third door such as the Globe in all probability provided, and the uncertainty such an additional way off the stage creates as to what lies beyond it, can add to our sense of Elsinore being both an architectural and a spiritual labyrinth. Less use is made of the outward-orientated door than of the door, or more probably two doors, that lead to the recesses of the court. But the basic outer-inner dichotomy persists. The fourth scene begins with characters emerging from the palace into an atmosphere that bites, nips, and devours ("eager"), as if of itself playing an active role in the action and so preparing us for the Ghost's chilling exposure of the truth. During the events that follow, the association of certain characters—the Ghost, Horatio, the Players, Fortinbras, the Sailors, the English Ambassador and increasingly Hamlet himself—with the outward-orientated door maintains our sense of that exit as the direction from which come both enlightenment and the action that a conviction of enlightenment makes possible. From OD come the Ghost's affirmations of revealed truths about the afterworld; through it too lies the world of intellectual enquiry represented by the universities of Wittenberg and Paris.[27] Claudius's refusal to allow Hamlet to return to this world condemns the hero to the prison of Elsinore where he must rely on those who come from the "real" world without: on the incorruptible Horatio for moral support (the movements of Rosencrantz and Guildenstern show how quickly they are sucked into court intrigues) and on the Players for an exposure of Claudius's guilt.

As with other plays, scenes in *Hamlet* which give the effect of taking place in a great hall provide the setting for a confluence of outside and inside worlds. Here, where the two worlds also represent candor and truth on the one hand and deception and lies on the other, two thronged scenes inevitably culminate in exposure. The structure of the Play Scene lends itself to the enactment of The Mousetrap on the OD side of the stage, as if at the lower end of the hall, and to the grouping of the court on the ID side, from whence Claudius flees into the state rooms. An outer-to-inner flow of entrances and exits in the ensuing scenes carries Hamlet, and with him the audience, deep into the center of corruption. But he passes by the opportunity for a revenge that is now known to be just, and heads for the Queen's closet which is both the heart of the palace and the focus of his own anguish—itself a form of corruption. One of the play's most dramatic OD entrances occurs here, as the Ghost appears from the side of truth in an endeavor to release Hamlet from the rival haunting of his own obsessions.[28] A contrary, outward flow of the action now begins, from which we finally emerge with Hamlet in open country and on his way to England: doomed and powerless in Claudius's eyes, but actually out at last in the world of freely chosen action. He is to make his final entrance OD as from that world, determined on exposure and vengeance, only to be halted, thanks to Claudius's machinations, in the intermediate space of a hall scene. The last confrontation is to take place in this meeting place of values. For both opponents it is a fight to the death, but Horatio survives to relate the truth, Fortinbras and the Ambassadors arrive through the outward door to confirm that this truth will be disseminated, and Hamlet is borne out by the same door into the cold air from which, throughout the tragedy, truth has emanated.

In the pattern of entrances and exits on which the above is based, most characters appear through or leave by the door which the audience feels to be appropriate to their roles in the action. It is not until the fourth act that Shakespeare tellingly breaks this order of things. Until then, Gertrude's acquiescence and Ophelia's submissiveness have resulted in both women keeping to the inward side, "looping" on and off the stage through ID or possibly on occasion through a central door representing access to another place at court, such as Polonius's quarters. But at the end of her first mad appearance in 4.5, Ophelia's call for her coach suggests that she goes out OD. This action, as Claudius sees ("Give her good watch"), renders her a desperately vulnerable figure— alone, unkempt, and accosting all and sundry with her bawdy songs. Her re-entry OD in this state is all the more shocking to Laertes because it implies she has been wandering the public streets. She finally exits in the same direction, but what at this point is of most interest is Gertrude's response. Unwilling as always hitherto to face facts, the Queen has begun this scene by refusing to see Ophelia. An exit OD with her waiting women, made either in Ophelia's wake or, after visible hesitation, at the end of the scene, as Claudius leads Laertes off to private talk through ID, and made moreover in the direction of an angry crowd, implies nothing less than a change of heart. The move forms a fitting preliminary to Gertrude's most dramatic appearance, alone and from the outside, at 4.7.163. "But stay, what noise?" asks Claudius. As he and Laertes are now in an inner room, the noise cannot be the crowd. In all likelihood it comes from the waiting women and is the traditional tragic outcry that prepares us for the news of a death. Gertrude has come in by the door through which we might expect a messenger, rather than the Queen of Denmark, to make a solitary appearance. Instead of uttering any outcry (and the closet scene has made us sceptical of such cries of distress on her part), she in fact takes on the role of messenger and delivers, from what we have come to think of as the side of the truth, a narration that is the more moving in that it is formal and impersonal. It is as if Ophelia's death has forced her to see things as they in truth are—something that all Hamlet's reproaches failed to do—so that, speaking with a voice that transcends her nature as we have hitherto known it, she gains a new stature.

Love's Labour's Lost is another play which displays both a thematic use of the inward-outward axis and great dramatic skill in its handling of entrances from, or exits into, an unexpected direction. Much of its unique quality derives from a daring reversal of the courtly love conventions which its southern and aristocratic setting appears to demand. Comedies of love are traditionally built around a siege laid to the castle of chastity. Whether the means to this are seemly—Cesario's ambassade to Olivia, the delegated courtship of Hero—or unseemly, like the subterfuges of Bianca's suitors, they nearly all work out in spatial terms as a drive by the male characters from OD towards ID, checked by the occasional reverse but concluding in a triumphal two-by-two exeunt ID in the direction of the bridal bed. In the playhouse this exeunt may have been through the central opening, for Andrew Gurr's theory that this was one function of the third entrance is very attractive.[29] Once the play was over, the exposure of the backstage area, which has always seemed to me to tell against the repeated use of a third way onto the stage, would no longer be of any account, and such an exeunt would imply that the battle of the sexes had concluded not in outright victory but in peace with honor.

In *Love's Labour's Lost* however, these procedures are reversed. The castle of chastity still lies somewhere behind ID, but it is the King and his companions who have chosen to immure themselves inside it. The women, having embarked on the traditionally male activity of a political mission, make a highly striking first appearance from the "wrong" side. Though their diplomatic overtures are courteously received, their exclusion in some pavilion understood to lie beyond OD completely reverses the usual direction of a comic plot. This palace-park-pavilion triangulation, with the usual male and female placings reversed, persists throughout the play. Even when the men have admitted their real objectives to one another and set about their wooing in earnest, the guardians of the pavilion successfully repel their sorties from the masculine stronghold, and the play ends with "You that way; we this way": Shakespeare's through-the-looking-glass comedy has flaunted all the conventions of sexual space on the stage.

Shakespeare plays variations too upon the social implications of his two main means of access. OD is a route for the down-and-out, ID offers a chance to the upwardly mobile. In the opening scene of *As You Like It* everything that Orlando has to say concerning his brother's behavior is given countenance by the facts that his confidant is a servant and that the two of them have entered from OD. Beyond that door lie the byres ("stalling of an ox"), stables ("his horses are bred better") and the accommodation of the outdoor workers ("he lets me feed with his hinds"). His brother, who appears through ID, treats him as a trespasser—"What make you here?" We learn we are in the orchard, which was customarily regarded as a very private pleasance; it could be reached, as Orlando has reached it, by walking through the screen passage from the main door or from the domestic offices (hence Oliver's "Get you in" later in the scene), but was also often accessed from the family apartments.[30] By such means, together with Orlando's enforced departure through OD first from the court and then from his brother's house and the flight through the same door of Rosalind, Celia and Touchstone, the dramatist builds up to the moment, highly satisfying to the audience, when Oliver is thrust out OD from the court and stripped of his patrimony.

A brotherly inequality is also reversed in the course of *King Lear* but with tragic consequences. Before all bearings are lost in the disorientations of blindness and madness, this play shows a pronounced outward-inward orientation, especially in the scenes located in some intermediate space—hall or courtyard—of the three great houses belonging to Lear, Albany and Gloucester. The comings and goings of Edmund, Edgar and their father serve to reinforce these spatial effects. When, at the start of the play, Kent and Gloucester emerge ID as from the royal presence, Edmund is hovering near the outward exit and knows he is in some danger of being sent off through it: "away he shall again." In his father's house, which is the setting of the next scene, he enters OD, as into the hall, to hiss his imprecations against "legitimate Edward" across in the ID direction. Gloucester's emergence confirms that this door leads to the family rooms, and his "Edmund, how now? What news?" implies a belief that his bastard son would have ventured thus far with a paper in his hand only if he had a message to deliver. After sowing suspicions about Edgar in his father's mind, Edmund duplicitously offers his brother shelter, and the scene shifts to the vicinity of Edmund's lodgings in an outer courtyard. Edmund and Curan come on "severally"—Curan ID, because he has been with Gloucester, Edmund OD or CD as from his lodgings.[31] After the put-up fight and Edgar's OD disappearance, Edmund's position is transformed not only in his father's eyes but in those of the newly arrived Cornwall. As he accompanies them ID into the main part of the house, the actor can convey his assurance that the flourish of trumpets is as much for himself as it is for the noble guests. Only one obstacle now remains between him and the title. Its removal begins in 3.3, when Gloucester goes out OD to find and help Lear, and Edmund exits ID to report this to Cornwall. It is completed in 3.5 when Cornwall leads Edmund off ID to present him to Regan as the new Earl of Gloucester.

A reversal of social position through jealous machinations, such as forms the subplot of *King Lear*, is at the heart of *Othello*, and here too Shakespeare gives it visual expression through his manipulation of theatrical space. After the arrival in Cyprus, Cassio's promotion over the head of Iago, of which we heard much in the opening scene, is brought home to us almost as sharply as it is to Iago when the lieutenant accompanies Othello and Desdmona in their exeunt ID to the castle, leaving the ensign behind with instructions to go back to the harbor—that is, downward and outwards by OD—and see to the luggage. After a proclamation has indicated the passing of time, the scene is reset in some hall-like space in the castle, intermediate between the court of guard (beyond OD) and the governor's private rooms (behind ID). An entrance from this inner side in the company of Othello and Desdemona emphasizes Cassio's privileged position. He has been dining with them on what Othello's words later in the scene are to remind us is their long-delayed wedding night. But when Cassio is dismissed, there can be no obvious crossing-over as of the two brothers in *King Lear*, because it is important to the ensuing action that ID should primarily be seen as the way leading towards Desdemona's bedchamber. So when at the end of 3.3, the first long temptation scene, Othello tells Iago "Now art thou my lieutenant" he does not lead him into the private rooms from which Desdemona is about to appear, but draws him off OD, outside the castle, to help him find "some swift means of death / For the fair devil." Oxymoron and stage movement together underline Othello's inability to distinguish his good angel from his attendant fiend. The point of Iago's machinations is not that they result in Cassio's fall and his own advancement, but that they enable him to drag down Othello.

This sketch of some episodes in which Shakespeare finds brilliantly meaningful use for the "inward" and "outward" significances of his two main ways onto the stage may appropriately conclude with two hall scenes, both already touched upon, in which a character makes an entrance that strikes the audience as misplaced. The first is Coriolanus's entry into Aufidius's house in Antium (4.5). As in *Romeo and Juliet*, the shift from outside the house, which Coriolanus has just entered (from our view, exited into) ID with the words "if he give me way / I'll do his country service," is indicated first by the sound of music and then by the eruption of two servants from the same door, which we now understand to represent the way to the great chamber from the upper end of the hall. Each man shouts for service through OD before hurrying back to his duties at the dinner table. OD however leads to the main door of the hall as well as to the kitchens and buttery, and through it comes, not the expected servant, Cotus (who will emerge a little later to take part in the dialogue as "3 Servingman"), but—in a powerful visual echo of the word "service" in the last line of 4.4 and the first line of 4.5—Coriolanus. The effect is not just that this proudest of heroes has been brought low and that we are once again witnesses to the fall of princes. What happens is much more in accordance with the nature of Renaissance tragedy. It is a recognition by the audience of the fact that Coriolanus, in seeking service with Aufidius, is self-destructing, going against his own nature: a recognition, fed by the scene with the servants that follows and not effaced in those later moments when he holds Volumnia silently by the hand, that this entrance to Aufidius's house represents the exact moment of tragic choice.

For my last instance I return to the murder sequence in *Macbeth*. One striking incongruity in the exits and entrances that I outlined earlier is Macbeth's appearance in 2.1 from OD—the entrance that so much startles Banquo. What is he doing outside at this hour? Answers half form in the spectators' minds. He has lost his nerve and fled, as he did at the beginning of the previous scene. But then he has returned, so he must still be resolved to kill the king. Perhaps he has escorted his other guests to the gatehouse to make sure that the coast is completely clear. If so, he has shown them more courtesy than he has shown Duncan: and here perhaps is the clue to the incongruity of the entrance. Macbeth has been in the wrong place before now. In a grave lapse of protocol that leads Duncan to ask "Where is the Thane of Cawdor?" he has left his wife to receive their royal guest. On that occasion the thought that he may be washing off the blood of battle only heightens our sense of the huge deception that is to be performed in the effort he will make to conceal his murderous thoughts beneath a mask of welcome, an effort he temporarily abandons during the feast, where his absence is once again noted. Ultimately, thanks to the regicide, the usurper Macbeth establishes himself in the wrong place, and the Thane of Cawdor, that loyal champion, is no longer to be found. The contribution that the play's language makes to this effect of incongruity and misplacement has long been recognized. That the playwright's handling of a play's seen and unseen spaces and the entrances and exits which result from this handling also contribute to the total effect of this and other plays by Shakespeare has been the theme I have touched upon here, in the hope that it may lead to deeper and more informed exploration.

Notes

All Shakespeare line and scene references are to *The Riverside Shakespeare* (Boston: Houghton Mifflin, 1974).

1. Glynne Wickham, *Early English Stages, 1300–1600*, 2 vols. (London: Routledge, 1959), 2:2:181.

2. David Bradley, *From Text to Performance in the Elizabethan Theatre: Preparing the Play for the Stage* (Cambridge: Cambridge University Press, 1992), 29.

3. *Theatre Research International* 20 (1995): 214.

4. "Theatrical Plots and Elizabethan Stage Practice," in *Shakespeare and Dramatic Tradition: Essays in Honor of S. F. Johnson*, ed. W. R. Elton and William B. Long (Newark, Del.: University of Delaware Press, 1989), 115–16.

5. An in-depth investigation of Shakespearian exits and entrances is currently being undertaken by Mariko Ichikawa. I am grateful to Andrew Gurr for drawing my attention to her project and to Fitzpatrick's article. Hanna Scolnicov, in "Theatre Space, Theatrical Space, and the Theatrical Space Without," in *Themes in Drama 9: The Theatrical Space*, ed. James Redmond (1987), has valuable things to say, from an angle different from mine, about the significance in the theatre of unseen, or conceived, space.

6. Quoted by Mark Girouard, *Life in the English Country House: A Social and Architectural History* (New Haven and London: Yale University Press, 1978), 83. The remainder of this chapter is one of the best surveys of Elizabethan country house architecture. Because many English castles had been transformed into comfortable and unfortified country houses during the Elizabethan building boom, the phrase "Macbeth's castle" would not have evoked, early in the seventeenth century, the Scottish Baronial image that it does in the mind of anyone reading Holinshed today.

7. Peter Davison, ed., *The First Quarto of King Richard III* (Cambridge: Cambridge University Press, 1996), 47.

8. J. Dover Wilson, ed., *Coriolanus* (Cambridge: Cambridge University Press, 1960), 90. Compare R. B. Parker, ed., *Coriolanus* (Oxford: Clarendon Press, 1994), 90.

9. *Everyman Out of his Humour*, 2.1.260–62.

10. Old Capulet's various orders to the servants at 1.5.26–28 are a means of getting them off the stage so as to leave plenty of space for the dance. The "room" is probably not the hall, but the great chamber which the company has just left; compare *2 Henry IV*, 2.4.13–14.

11. *The faire maide of Bristow* (London: T. Pavyer, 1605), A2[r-v].

12. I have substituted OD and ID for Fitzpatrick's DL and DR. In my visualization, stage right is the OD side, whereas Fitzpatrick sees stage left as the outward exit. This difference is not significant, though experience of plays of all kinds and periods suggests some preference on the part of directors for positioning an outward door stage right and an inward door stage left.

13. *The true chronicle historie of . . . Thomas lord Cromwell* (London: W. Jones, 1602), B3[r].

14. See for example the Willoughby household orders of 1592 in Alice T. Friedman's *House and Household in Elizabethan England: Wollaton Hall and the Willoughby Family* (Chicago: University of Chicago Press, 1989), 185–87. Torches also figure in the opening stage direction to the previous scene, but this is probably a misplacement originating in a prompter's note for the procession of 1.7 to assemble. See Nicolas Brooke's note in his edition (Oxford: Clarendon Press, 1990), 115.

15. Maurice Howard, *The Early Tudor Country House: Architecture and Politics, 1490–1550* (London: G. Philip, 1987), 78.

16. Friedman, 49–50.

17. The stage direction, *Enter* Maquerelle *knocking at the Ladies door*, in Marston's

The Malcontent (London: W. Apsley, 1604), prompts the question "Was this the theatrical term for one of the doors?" The direction, however, is more likely to be fictional than theatrical—to make use of Richard Hosley's distinction.

18. R. A. Foakes's argument in his edition (London: Methuen; Cambridge, Mass: Harvard University Press, 1962) for only one side entrance plus three "houses" seems to me to overlook the need for the Duke to appear in act 5 as if from *his* (unseen) house, which would be at the inmost and highest point of the town. T. S. Dorsch (*The Comedy of Errors*, Cambridge: Cambridge University Press, 1988, 23–24), postulates two side entrances in addition to the three houses, but he thinks that at the Gray's Inn performance in 1594 these were provided by the two outer arches of the arcaded screen. In fact these were not doors. Like most screens, which were made to exclude, not create, draughts, the Gray's Inn screen had only two doors.

19. John Barrell, *The Idea of Landscape and the Sense of Place, 1730–1840: An Approach to the Poetry of John Clare* (Cambridge: Cambridge University Press, 1972), 103 especially.

20. Fitzpatrick, 208–9.

21. Maurice O'Sullivan, *Twenty Years A-Growing: Rendered from the Original Irish* (London: Oxford University Press, 1933); Kevin Lynch, *The Image of the City* (Cambridge, Mass: MIT Press, 1960), 129.

22. R. D. Sacks, *Conceptions of Space in Social Thought: A Geographic Perspective* (London: Macmillan; Minneapolis: University of Minnesota Press, 1980), 23.

23. Lynch, 129, cites in translation Pierre Jaccard's *Le Sens de la Direction et l'Orientation Lointaine chez l'Homme* on the behavior of French commercial travellers visiting a series of strange cities: "They assert that they pay little attention to names or landmarks, but simply keep a continuous mental record of the direction back to the railway station, and strike out for it directly when their work is done."

24. See Niall W. Slater, "Transformations of Space in New Comedy," *Themes in Drama 9: The Theatrical Space*, ed. James Redmond (1987), 1–10.

25. 1994, directed by Ralf Longbacka.

26. Andrew Gurr, "*Measure for Measure*'s Hoods and Masks: the Duke, Isabella, and Liberty," *English Literary Renaissance* 27: 89–105, argues for Isabella being masked rather than dressed as a nun in this scene.

27. See Hanna Scolnicov, "The Undiscover'd Country: Theatrical Space Without in *Hamlet*," in *Actes du Congrès 1984: Lieu et Temps*, ed. J. Fuzier (Paris: Société Française Shakespeare, 1989).

28. Andrew Gurr, in his 1996 British Academy Shakespeare lecture, "Traps and Discoveries at the Globe," *Proceedings of the British Academy* 94: 97, sees the Ghost as exiting by the central opening. But though one meaning of "portal" is an impressive arched doorway such as the stage's central opening might well represent, the Queen's closet is unlikely to have had such a feature. Another meaning of "portal" in Elizabethan English was "a space within the door of a room, partitioned off and containing an inner door" (*New English Dictionary, sv* 2); in fact the sort of barrier which might be built between a private room and the more public space outside, as the dictionary's example—"a portall Dore to the upper studdye"—suggests.

29. Andrew Gurr, "Staging at the Globe" in *Shakespeare's Globe Rebuilt,* ed. J. R. Mulryne and Margaret Shewring (Cambridge: Cambridge University Press, 1997), 161–62.

30. The recent surge of interest in garden history should give scope for an exploration of the imagined positioning of the gardens in Shakespeare's plays, and the effect of this on his staging.

31. Edmund's call to his brother to "Descend" at line 19 suggests that the central opening was here used to represent access to a staircase.

Commerce and Patronage: The Lord Chamberlain's Men's Tour of 1597

PETER DAVISON

JUST OVER FOUR HUNDRED YEARS AGO, THE LORD CHAMBERLAIN'S MEN were trudging through the Kent or Sussex countryside to perform in Faversham or Rye. We know, too, that they also visited Dover, Bristol, Bath and Marlborough on that tour. Curiously, every printed account of these visits has, over the past ninety years, been recorded erroneously by scholars as distinguished as J. T. Murray, E. K. Chambers, D. L. Patrick, and Giles Dawson (who omits the visit to Dover). Entries for Faversham for 1596 and 1597 are conflated, amounts given as "rewards" wrongly entered, entries misdated, and accounting years wrongly calculated. Dawson writes of players who toured Kent travelling the main road to Dover, perhaps diverting by the coast round Whitstable and Ramsgate, thence, from Dover to Lydd "and through Rye and Hastings toward Southampton and the West."[1] That "Grand Tour" was firmly fixed in my mind when considering where the Chamberlain's Men might have stopped to perform in 1597 in order to earn sufficient means to meet their touring charges. Thus I had the charming fancy of their playing the Quarto text of *Richard III* in Hastings (despite no visit being recorded) and having Lord William Hastings meeting Pursuivant Hastings in the town of Hastings. The Pursuivant is only named in Q1; in F he is "Sirrah" and "fellow." Surviving records for 1597 for Maidstone, Canterbury, Folkestone, Lydd, New Romney, Southampton, Winchester, Calne, Chippenham, and Malmesbury, where the Chamberlain's Men might have been expected to play had they followed Dawson's route, show that they received no rewards for performing (or even for not performing) in these towns. They also visited Rye before Dover.

Examining the records led to the question: why did more companies visit Marlborough than either Bristol or Bath? Bristol, after London, was the largest or second largest city in England with a population of about 12,000 in 1603. Marlborough's population was perhaps about one-tenth of that and notably ungenerous towards the company with which Shakespeare was associated. In 1594 they gave the company a reward of 2s 8d and in 1597 6s 4d (not the 6s 8d Chambers records), hardly a noble reward to make a visit worthwhile even with what might be gathered from audiences of very poorly paid locals.[2] So: why did so many companies visit the small town of Marlborough and what were the logistics of touring at this time ? And are there any implications we might draw from considering these questions ?

Touring: Provocative Implications

In 1795, Tate Wilkinson described three kinds of touring companies. At the top were those like his, based in York, permanent, all-the-year round, with a regular circuit—Wakefield, Leeds, Doncaster, Hull. Then came a company like that based in Manchester which ran for part of the year and was broken up each year. At the bottom came "runabout scouring troops . . . [which] vaunt, look big, and promise . . . 'But tap 'em and the devil a drop comes out.' "[3] The Chamberlain's Men were akin to Tate Wilkinson's company in that it was permanent but it chiefly performed in London and at Court and much less frequently toured. According to surviving records, in Shakespeare's lifetime the Chamberlain's/King's Men only visited three or more towns in the provinces in 1597 (6), 1603 (6 plus a court performance at Wilton), 1605 (3), 1606 (5), 1607 (3), 1610 (5), and 1613 (5). In some years they seem not to have toured at all. Touring for the Lord Chamberlain's Men was not, therefore, a prime activity as it was for Wilkinson's players. In the next rank came companies like those of Hertford (which, apart from an appearance at Court on 6 January 1592, never played in London) and Pembroke. At the lowest level were runabouts like Richard Bradshaw's troupe which ended up in Banbury jail in 1633, Christopher Simpson's illegal company of Roman Catholic actors in Yorkshire, and Hudson and Lister's company of three men and four children which played at farms and houses on the Yorkshire Moors in the winter of 1615–16.[4] I suspect that the Chamberlain's Men only stirred from London when circumstances pressed. It is notable that when the Chamberlain's Men travelled to Wilton (near Salisbury and thirty miles south of Marlborough) in 1603, they were paid £30 for their "pains and expenses" in venturing so far.[5] The only year they visited six towns other than 1597 was the terrible plague year of 1603, Dekker's *The Wonderful Year*. What was so special about 1597, for it was not a plague year?

On 28 July 1597 all London theatres were closed down following *The Isle of Dogs* scandal. It looked as if the theatres might be permanently closed. The Chamberlain's Men had to do one of three things to sustain themselves. They could sell plays to printers (and they sold *Richard II* to Andrew Wise, who entered it on 29 August 1597); they could pawn or sell props and apparel as Pembroke's Men were "feign" to do according to Henslowe's letter to Edward Alleyn of 28 September 1593 because they could not meet their touring charges;[6] and they could tour.

We know that the Chamberlain's Men did tour in 1597 and we know that by 27 August they had played in Rye and presumably visited Faversham on route, though the date of their visit to Faversham is not recorded. They were in Dover about 3 September and Bristol some two weeks later between 11 and 17 September. We do not know when they visited Bath and Marlborough nor when they got back to London, but Pembroke's Men, who only visited Bath and Bristol in 1597 and had preceded the Chamberlain's Men in Bristol by a week or so, were playing *The Spanish Tragedy* with the Admiral's Men at the Rose on 11 October,[7] the theatres having unexpectedly been allowed to reopen. (The Admiral's Men do not seem to have toured in 1597.) The Chamberlain's Men sold Wise *Richard III* about the time of the reopening of the Rose for he entered it on 20 October. They seem, therefore, to have visited these six towns in about eleven weeks. If they travelled by that "Grand Tour" route (London-Dover-South Coast-Bristol-Marlborough-London) they would have covered something like 475 miles. They could manage about one hundred less if they went to Dover and back and then made a return journey from London to Bristol. It is quite a useful exercise, which I have tried with students, to time and work out the logistics of such tours, getting from A to B, gaining permission for performances, performing enough times and in enough places where earnings were a small fraction of those pertaining in London, regarding Sundays as non-performance days, and taking enough at the door to sustain a company of actors and their support staff (bookkeeper, musicians, stage-hands, gatherers, even though actors could sometimes take on one or two of these tasks), and pay for at least one horse and wagon with which to convey garments and props.

What were wages in London and, say, Wiltshire? The Royal Proclamation of 1589 set these (among many) wages: Carpenters: 7s 0d per week without food; 4s 6d with food; Plumbers: 6s 0d and 3s 4d respectively; Watermen: 3s 0d and 1s 0d. Wages in Wiltshire were far less. By 1655 (after high inflation and Civil War) they had not reached London wages of 1589. Master carpenters and plumbers were not allowed by the Justices of the Peace to be paid more than 1s 0d to 1s 3d a day (depending on the time of the year), without meat and drink; with meat and drink they were paid 6d to 8d a day. Journeymen were paid between 10d and 1s 0d; apprentices only 7d whatever the time of year. Country pennies to attend theatrical performances in 1597 would be hard come by. Actors are not covered by the Proclamation but Henslowe agreed on 17 July 1597 to pay Thomas Hearne 5s 0d a week for his first year; 6s 8d in his second year. On 8 December 1598 he hired William Kendall at 10s 0d a week but at only 5s 0d a week in the country "euerie week of his playing." The country rate might have been because food and lodging were provided on tour or because country prices were lower than in London.[8]

What were the practicalities of touring? First, getting from A to B. The very rich could travel by coach in 1597, at least in London, though from the magnificent specimen presented by James VI and I to Boris Godunov (Tsar, 1598–1605), preserved in the Armoury Museum in the Kremlin, even the best coaches were not highly maneuverable; its front wheels could not turn right or left so the coach had to be lifted round from its back to get round corners. A coach is reported to have been used in the Wells Show on 17 June 1607, though it may have been a wagon or chariot.[9] Andrew Gurr quotes a reference from Faversham records to "a wagon or coache of the Lo. Bartlettes players" in 1597–98. He continues, "To call it a coach, even as a synonym, suggests that it must have been at the least a covered waggon" providing protection from the elements for playbooks and costumes. It might, he says, give shelter at night on longer journeys.[10] Whatever the "coach," more than one would be needed if it were to carry all the actors and supporting staff plus costumes and props. The state of the roads seems to put genuine coaches out of the question and wagons would travel at walking pace. Some journeys might be made by water—by river, say, for the few miles from Bath to Bristol—or, as the company visited Dover after Bath, perhaps by sea from Dover to Southampton, then going overland to Marlborough or Bristol. Tarlton's stories are apocryphal but their settings, like those of quasi-realistic films, may be truer to life than the stories in which they are set. One tells of Tarlton journeying by boat from Southampton to London with his wife in, shall we say, "a Tempest," for a mighty storm arose which endangered the ship.[11] Sailing from Dover westwards would have been easier in 1597 than in most years because the winds that summer blew from the north-east, not the usual prevailing south-west.[12] The visit to Dover after Rye (which meant going out of the direct route) might support a conjecture of a journey by sea.

A wagon and a horse were essential to haul props and apparel. Apart from being a commonsense necessity, Tarlton tells of the Queen's Players coming to a gentleman's house and of their wagon being unloaded of its apparel. As this is only incidental to the jest, it has an authentic ring.[13] More certain evidence is that provided by Drewe Turner's claim before Banbury Justices that he had done no more than "drive the horse and beat the drum."[14] Note, *the* horse. A horse and cart meant as slow a journey as walking. Travel by horse was a possibility. We know Edward Alleyn had a horse. He sent it back from Bristol in 1593 to be sold, but his father-in-law, Henslowe, found Smithfield market so depressed because of the plague then raging that he could get no more than £4 for it and so put it out to pasture in the country.[15] In any case, how many actors could afford to buy a horse and pay for its keep? It cost ninepence to one shilling a day to hire a horse and it still had to be fed;[16] it thus cost at least as much as an actor's pay for a week to hire a horse.

That leaves walking as the principal means of travel. It is no accident that the word "stroller" for a touring actor comes into print in 1608.[17] How far was a day's walk? Shakespeare, in *Richard III*, writes of Tamworth to Bosworth Field as "but one day's march," about 25 miles (5.2.12–13), but I do not know how accurately he knew that distance. John Mackarness, a Puritan escaping the London authorities, set out for Bath and managed the journey in five days, that is twenty miles a day, and he had reason to make haste.[18] Touring meant hard walking. Jonson said actors "walked with their shoes full of gravel . . . after a blind jade and a hamper" to "stalk upon boards and barrel heads."[19]

Takings

Calculating takings from one company and then extrapolating them to another is a dangerous exercise but it must be attempted if we are to examine the logistics of touring. The figures we have are not for the Lord Chamberlain's Men's Theatre but derive from Henslowe's Rose, and the ethos and practices of these two London theatres were different. Henslowe was an entrepreneur and the actors, except for his son-in-law, Edward Alleyn, were employees. Shakespeare and many of his colleagues were sharers in what we might now call a cooperative. Nevertheless, they were the two major companies and worked in the same environment, affected by the same regulatory authorities, and drawing on the same audiences. I have taken out some figures from Henslowe for twenty-five performances given in the seven weeks from 26 January to 14 March 1597 (the year of the tour) and have calculated from "pennies at the door" audience sizes.[20] In brief, £122 2s 11d taken would go to the players, or £17 9s a week. For the 16-cast company posited by David Bradley, and bearing in mind Chambers's argument that as many again of support staff would be required to run a company,[21] that would be a little over £1 *per adult actor* for a company of, say, 20–25; this allows for leaving behind non-essential actors and helpers. Bearing in mind that the top rate for a master craftsman was 9s 0d a week and the sums paid Thomas Hearne and William Kendall mentioned above, these figures make economic sense, especially if one allows for the additional costs of touring (roughly, perhaps, borne for the Chamberlain's Men out of the portion of money that at the Rose went to Henslowe to manage the company). William Ingram has calculated that a company of six required 10–14s a day to survive on tour.[22]

Extrapolation and comparison are suspect, even more so when one compares past and present. The contradictoriness of "evidence" can readily be seen from the fact that Welsh National Opera is granted less because it tours; the Royal Opera, despite its enormous grant, argues it cannot tour without a vast increase in subsidy. Paul Daniel of English National Opera said "touring is a vastly expensive option" and Sir Jeremy Isaacs, former head of the Royal Opera, maintained that "more touring requires far more money." Instead of touring he maintained that Royal Opera needed "a mite" more in grants: this "mite" is the meiosis of the decade.[23] In response, Royal Opera was given a huge increase—not to perform at all in 1999. Thus, applying the 1597 Rose figures to the Chamberlain's Men's tour of later that year is risky. Nevertheless, it is plain that the money received as rewards from the six towns visited, £5 3s in total, would pay no more than a wage for one actor for the eleven weeks of the tour. Further, the average size of audience for the seven weeks examined at the Rose was 870, varying from 40 on 8 February to 2,316 on 12 February, almost a capacity house and twice the population of Marlborough. Bath was probably not very much larger than Marlborough before the coming of the turnpikes in the eighteenth century made it fashionable. In Shakespeare's time it was still mainly within its medieval walls as John Speed's 1610 map shows.[24] I do not know how many people Bristol Guildhall could accommodate (where performances were given) but Alan Somerset calculates that

Leicester Guildhall, which still stands, could accommodate an audience of 300–55.[25] Playing out of doors might allow bigger audiences, but not in Marlborough. Apart from the smallness of the population, the yard behind the White Hart (where now the aptly-named Tudor Tea Rooms is situated) is quite small.

I wish to stress that I am not making a general challenge to Bradley's or Gurr's assumptions about large-size touring companies. There are plenty of records of touring companies of fifteen to twenty. G. E. Bentley lists companies of fourteen in 1611 and 1612; fifteen in 1619 and 1635; sixteen in 1612; and twenty in 1619 and 1624.[26] However, David George found that "there is much evidence that 10 is about the right number" for companies visiting Gawthorpe Manor in Lancashire between 1608 and 1619.[27] I am concerned with *one specific tour.* Putting together my results for doubling *Richard III*, the economic disaster facing London-based companies, and the logistics of touring, I am inclined to think that a ten-cast company (which means ten adult actors plus boys and support staff), which would have allowed the inclusion of all the Chamberlain's Men's sharers, would have been more practicable than Bradley's 16-cast company and its accompanying entourage. It will be recalled that in 1591–92, the Admiral's/Strange's company (which included five future Chamberlain's sharers), petitioned to return early from tour because the size of the company made their touring costs intolerable,[28] and, as already mentioned, Pembroke's Men could not meet their touring bills in 1593. To raise, on the basis of the Rose's £122 for seven weeks, £192 for an eleven-week tour for a 16-cast company would require thirty-nine performances with average audiences, as in London, of 870; average audiences of half that number, 435, would require a performance every day (including Sundays) and no time for travel. It is obvious how conjectural and imprecise such calculations must be, but they should suffice to illuminate the logistical problems. The situation would be easier with a ten-cast company; that would require only something like £120. If fifty percent of the average London audience could be attracted, 435, that would then necessitate forty-nine performances allowing twenty-eight days on the road—thirteen to seventeen miles a day, depending on the route. I doubt very much whether the company could arrange forty-nine performances in the places they visited for the time they seem to have been there and, Bristol apart, populations would hardly provide enough repeat audiences of the size required. There is still, therefore, a considerable financial problem to be resolved, not to mention practical difficulties. They must have been overcome because the tour was completed and the company survived, even if they had to sell the Quarto manuscript of *Richard III* to Andrew Wise immediately on their return to London by 20 October.

How the Chamberlain's Men financed their 1597 tour might be answered by first trying to answer another question. Why did not only they but so many other companies bother calling at Marlborough? Marlborough was visited by more touring companies in this period than either Bristol or Bath: forty-one companies visited Bath between 1592 and 1617 (and in 1617 the Queen's Players did not receive a reward but had to pay to use the Town Hall); the same number visited Bristol between 1593 and 1634 (but at least one account book seems to be missing); but forty-three visited Marlborough between 1590 and 1622. Bath and Marlborough became increasingly Puritan in the seventeenth century; Marlborough supported Parliament and was twice sacked by the Royalists. Shakespeare's father had traded in Marlborough (in 1599 he sued John Walford, Mayor and Chamberlain of Marlborough in the Court of Common Pleas for £21 for twenty-one tods of wool),[29] but it is unlikely that this association drew the company to the town. It was not, as has been sometimes proposed, because Marlborough was on the main road from London to Bath and Bristol. Only one other company beside the Chamberlain's visited all three towns in the same accounting year: the Queen's Players in 1598. Very few companies—seven—even visited both Bath and Bristol, a mere dozen miles apart, in the same year; only twice were Marlborough and Bristol visited in the same year, 1613 and 1621, each time by the Lady Elizabeth's Players. It was certainly not because Marlborough was generous in its rewards; it was frankly mean. Its rewards to the Chamberlain's Men in 1594 were 2s 8d and in 1597 6s 4d, though it offered more in the seventeenth century. In contrast, Hertford's Players had received 15s 0d in 1592, but they were the company under the patronage of a local lord.

The attraction of Marlborough was not the size of the rewards it gave, not its position on the way to Bristol, but, I think, the neighboring great estates, specifically Tottenham House in the Savernake forest (about two miles east of the town), owned by the Earl of Hertford (Sir Edward Seymour), and Wilton, where the Pembrokes entertained James VI and I in 1603, thirty miles to the south, and where the Chamberlain's/King's Men performed for him. This may be confirmed by the date when companies stopped coming to Marlborough: 1622. Both Hertford and the Countess of Pembroke died in 1621. Hertford presented a famous entertainment for Queen Elizabeth at his estate in Hampshire, Elvetham, in 1591. Both families patronized companies of players and the Countess was not only an important patroness of the arts but translator of Robert Garnier's *The Tragedie of Antonie* (1595). The Pembrokes owned Manton estate and mill, now part of Marlborough, and abutting onto Hertford's lands. Henry VIII often hunted in the Savernake and it was at another Hertford/Seymour house, Wulfhall (a little of which still stands—Tottenham House was destroyed by Parliamentary forces) that he met and married Jane Seymour. There is an uncertain reference to players visiting Wulfhall in 1547, or alternatively Beauchamp House in London, with St Paul's choristers.[30] Unfortunately the Pembroke Domestic Accounts for this period were destroyed by fire and at present I only know of Hertford Domestic Accounts from the 1670s.

Visits to Tottenham House and Wilton would have been in line with visits by players to the Earl of Cumberland and Lord Clifford,[31] and those by Dudley's, Derby's, Mounteagle's, Stafford's, and the Queen's Players to Gawthorpe Hall and Manor.[32] The Lord Chamberlain's Men played *Titus Andronicus* for Sir John Harington at Burley-on-the-Hill, Rutland, in 1596.[33] Bradshaw's little runabouts played to Sir Thomas Lucy at Stratford-on-Avon and to Sir William Spencer in 1633,[34] and Hudson and Lester's little band of players worked Yorkshire farmouses as mentioned earlier. What I am suggesting is that the Chamberlain's Men in 1597 visited not only six towns but the estates of the powerful, with whom, through their contacts at Court, they might be expected to have access. This is well-documented practice. What is implied for this tour however, and perhaps for others, is that the focus should shift from playing before the mayor and council for such reward as they deigned to give, to performance in the great houses on route. The lack of a license to perform a memorially reconstructed manuscript of *Richard III* might then prove no problem. The peers who welcomed the players would doubtless know what plays they were asking for and would be in a position to overlook the absence of a license, if, indeed, they bothered to ask to see it.

Some Implications

1. Marlborough was popular, not because of its being sited on the road from London to Bristol, and despite its meanness, but because of the possibility of playing at private houses.
2. It might, therefore, be productive to look at touring routes with an eye on nearby estates. Did the Chamberlain's Men play

at Littlecote, ten miles east of Marlborough (home of Lord Chief Justice Popham)? Or Great Chalford Manor, Westwood Manor, Corsham Court, Clevedon Court, Montacute, Barrington Court, and Longleat, in the library of which is held the illustration of a performance of *Titus Andronicus*?[35] One tiny bit of indirect evidence might prove illuminating. In 1610, the minstrel, John Streating, went from Nailsea to play at "Cleeuedon," three-and-a-half miles away. He realised he had left his "box of string*es*" at home and returned at night unexpectedly to find his wife in bed with a neighbor. This led to a lawsuit which caused the incident to be recorded. But where was he playing in Clevedon, in the village or at Clevedon Court?[36] Clevedon Court still stands and has a fourteenth-century Great Hall. This reference is to a musician, not actors, but it might point to private-house perfomances.

3. We must abandon the idea of a touring route that automatically took in the main places on the Great West Road. It is surely remarkable that only two companies visted Marlborough, Bath and Bristol in the same accounting year between 1590 and the outbreak of the Civil War. I suspect that the London companies especially targeted where they visited. The Chamberlain's Men, with contacts at Court, may have been in a relatively strong position to arrange quickly a tour which took in private houses.

4. There is, I believe, an editorial relationship between the Q1 text of *Richard III*, and the logistics of touring. That might be worth considering with other play texts.

5. We should not assume that the editors of the REED volumes, excellent though their work is, have necessarily dug out all that might be useful to us: they are concerned specifically with the drama. We might sometimes find that the context in which the dramatic references are set will prove revealing. Let me give two examples. The Marlborough records show that the Lord Chief Justice, Sir John Popham, was provided with wine in 1597 (entry 14) and entry 20 shows a payment of £6 7s 9d for his "diet" at the Michaelmas Sessions. Entry 19 is the reward of 6s 4d for the Chamberlain's Men. (Incidentally, entry 22 is payment for constructing a gibbet.) The possibilities are obvious. Did the Chamberlain's Men play before Sir John Popham at Marlborough, or Tottenham House, or at his own house, Littlecote, ten miles to the east of Marlborough? More intriguing, was he the pattern for the Lord Chief Justice of *2 Henry IV*, which Shakespeare was about to write? John Aubrey cannot

wholly be relied upon—he liked a good story—but he says of Popham that he led a wild youth, enjoyed "profligate company, and was wont to take a purse with them."[37] A likeness to Prince Hal springs to mind, especially as Popham experienced a sudden conversion and took to his studies. May this throw light on how the better-informed in the audience saw Hal and the Lord Chief Justice of the play? Even if Aubrey was only retailing gossip, may they also have heard it? The second example is less exciting. Entries 27 and 28 show that Marlborough spent money buying two gifts of sugar-loaf (a "sweetener" if ever there was one) for Hertford and others, costing 16s 0d and £1 16s 5d (in sharp contrast to the 6s 4d for the Lord Chamberlain's Men). These appear in the accounts as the 27th and 28th entries; those for the Lord Chamberlain's Men and Popham are placed 19th and 20th. Entries may not be in chronological order (though the September visit of the Chamberlain's Men and the Michaelmas Assizes are juxtaposed), but it is certainly possible that Hertford was at Tottenham House at the time the Chamberlain's Men visited the town.

6. It is mistaken to think that the size of rewards is related to the size of the town. Clearly a company under the patronage of a local peer might expect to be treated relatively generously; that is natural. But Wilton, smaller even than Marlborough, gave the "kinges seruantes" £6 5s 0d when they played before the Pembrokes and James VI and I.[38] (The Chamberlain's Men became the King's Men by royal patent of 19 May 1603.)[39]

7. Finally, one cannot assume that town accounts are arranged chronologically. Giles Dawson has shown that whereas Dover accounts tend to be current, those for most towns were "copied fair at the years' end."[40] The Bristol accounts are arranged by the week, but some dated accounts cannot be relied upon. One example will suffice. Bath records show that the Queen's Players were paid 13s 4d on 22 August 1593; this is followed by entries for payments to Mounteagle's, Pembroke's, and Strange's Players.[41] However, we know from Henslowe's letter to Alleyn of 28 September 1593 that Pembroke's Men had been back in London for five or six weeks.[42] Allowing for a week's travelling, they would have had to have left Bath by 7 August, three weeks before the payment is dated, if these dates are to hold.

Bibliographical Notes

The most substantial corpus of information on touring is to be found in the Records of Early English Drama published by the University of Toronto Press. So far these have covered six cities (York, Chester, Coventry, Newcastle upon Tyne, Norwich, and Cambridge), and nine counties (Cumberland with Westmorland, Gloucestershire, Devon, Herefordshire with Worcestershire, Lancashire, Shropshire, and Somerset with Bath). It is important to appreciate that they are devoted to drama and so what is not at first sight anything to do with drama—such as the visit of the Lord Chief Justice to Marlborough and the gifts of sugar loaves to the Earl of Hertford in the little extract printed above—are inevitably excluded. Another useful volume of this kind, published by the University of Toronto and Cambridge University Press, 1984, is Ian Lancashire's *Dramatic Texts and Records of Britain: A Chronological Topography to 1558*.

Earlier volumes of records are useful but not always reliable. These include J. T. Murray, *English Dramatic Companies 1558–1642*, 2 vols. (London: Constable, 1910) and E. K. Chambers, *William Shakespeare: a Study of Facts and Problems*, 2 vols. (Oxford: Clarendon Press, 1930). These both incorrectly record details of the Chamberlain's 1597 tour. For example, Chambers records the reward for the Chamberlain's Men as 6s 8d, not 6s 4d, and he and Murray conflate the 1596 and 1597 visits to Faversham. Chambers also takes the Bath accounting year to end at Midsummer, not Michaelmas. However, used circumspectly they contain useful information, for example, on the fate of Bradshaw's touring company at Banbury. Tate Wilkinson's *The Wandering Patentee* (see n. 3) is a mine of information (and often very amusing).

Two books by Andrew Gurr are specially helpful: *Playgoing in Shakespeare's London* (Cambridge: Cambridge University Press, 2d ed., 1996), and *The Shakespearian Playing Companies* (Oxford: Oxford University Press, 1996), especially chapter 3, "Travelling Companies." A general account, with interesting suggestions for Shakespeare's links with Marlborough, will be found in Michael Justin Davis, *The Landscape of William Shakespeare* (Exeter: Webb & Bower, 1987). Of many other books that could be mentioned, three will be found very useful: Ann Jennalie Cook, *The Privileged Playgoers of Shakespeare's London, 1576–1642* (Princeton: Princeton University Press, 1981); G. E. Bentley, *The Profession of Player in Shakespeare's Time, 1590–1642* (Princeton: Princeton University Press, 1984); and Leeds Barroll, *Politics, Plague, and Shakespeare's Theater: The Later Stuart Years* (Ithaca: Cornell University Press, 1991).

Theatre Notebook often discusses aspects of touring. Three articles are especially valuable: David George, "Jacobean Actors and the Great Hall at Gawthorpe, Lancashire" (37, 1983): 109–21, with useful illustrations; John Wasson, "Elizabethan and Jacobean Touring Companies" (42, 1988): 51–57; Philip V. Thomas, "Itinerant, Roguish Entertainers in Elizabethan and Early Stuart Norwich" (52, 1998): 118–29. A very valuable journal article, but less easy of access, is G. W. Boddy, "Players of Interludes in North Yorkshire in the Early Seventeenth Century," *North Yorkshire County Record Office Journal*, 3 (1976): 95–130; this has useful sketch maps. William Ingram discusses "The Cost of Touring" in *Renaissance and Medieval Drama in England*, 6 (1993): 57–62; see especially 59; and Alan Somerset has a very useful illustrated article in *Shakespeare Survey*, 47 (1994): 45–60, " 'How Chances it they Travel': Provincial Touring, Playing Places, and the King's Men"; this has calculations of audience capacity. Malone Society *Collections* are founts of useful information.

Notes

1. See Peter Davison, ed., *The First Quarto of King Richard III* (Cambridge: Cambridge University Press, 1996), 39 and especially nn. 1 and 3; as "Davison, *Richard III, Q1*" hereafter. This edition gives detailed data only summarized here. See also John Tucker Murray, *English Dramatic Companies, 1558–1642*, 2 vols. (London: Constable, 1910), 2:274; as "Murray" hereafter; E. K. Chambers, *William Shakespeare: A Study of Facts and Problems*, 2 vols. (Oxford: Clarendon Press, 1923), 2:321; as "Chambers" hereafter; D. L. Patrick, *The Textual History of Richard III* (Stanford: Stanford University Press, 1936), 32; Giles Dawson, ed., *Collections VII*, Malone Society (Oxford: Oxford University Press, 1965), omits Dover from 48 (as "Dawson, *Collections VII*" hereafter), but it is to be found on Folger Microfilm, Acc 276.3, f. 345. Dawson's description of the routes he believes actors took to the south east and westwards is given on xxviii. Fuller details of errors in recording the various accounts of 1597 are given in Peter Davison, "Of Sugar-loaves and Horsemeat: The Value of Archives and the Limitations of their Printed Forms," in *The Founders' Library, University of Wales, Lampeter: Bibliographical and Contextual Studies* (Lampeter: Trivium Publications, 1997), especially 265–71. I am grateful to Professor Kate McLuskie for suggesting the title of this essay, which was developed from a paper given at the Scaena Conference in 1997.

2. It is impossible to know precisely how many people lived in Marlborough in 1597. A comparison of annual accounts for 1597 for Marlborough, Bath, and Bristol may give some indication of their relative sizes. Accounts for Marlborough have sixty-five entries, of which thirty-seven were payments, ten allowances for unpaid rents, and eighteen for rents lost 'by fyer' (fire then and to this day has been of remarkably frequent occurrence in Marlborough); Bath 250 entries; Bristol 1,145 (excluding totals). Payments for the year were: Marlborouugh £59 3s 11d (with £17 18s for lost rent); Bath £153 12s; Bristol £514 0s 7d. The population of Bristol in 1603 is estimated at 12,000 (compared to 200,000 for London) according to Peter Clark and Paul Slack, *English Towns in Transition 1500–1700* (Oxford: Oxford University Press, 1976), 83. Although the populations of Marlborough and Bath cannot be directly related to the number or amounts of these payments, it is clear that Bristol was far larger than these two towns. Wages in Wiltshire were much lower than in London: see n. 8.

3. Tate Wilkinson, *The Wandering Patentee: A History of the Yorkshire Theatres, from*

1770 to the Present Time, 4 vols. (York: printed for the author, 1795); facsimile in 2 vols. (Ilkley: Scolar Press, 1973), 4:45, 44.

4. An excellent account of these companies is given by G. W. Boddy in "Players of interludes in North Yorkshire in the early seventeenth century," *North Yorkshire County Record Office Journal*, 3 (1976): 95–130. Hudson and Lester's troupe walked some 150 miles over the North York moors in the depths of winter, performing and staying in thirty farmhouses and yeoman's cottages. They do not seem to have walked more than ten miles in a single day.

5. J. Leeds Barroll, *Politics, Plague, and Shakespeare's Theater: The Later Stuart Years* (Ithaca: Cornell UP, 1991), 112, 114.

6. R. A. Foakes and R. T. Rickert, eds. *Henslowe's Diary* (Cambridge: Cambridge University Press, 1961), 280. I am particularly delighted on the occasion of the publication of this volume to be acknowledging a fine example of Reg Foakes's scholarship. Hereafter as "Foakes and Rickert."

7. Foakes and Rickert, 60.

8. For London wages, see Paul L. Hughes and James F. Larkin, eds. *Tudor Royal Proclamations*, 3 vols. (New Haven: Yale University Press, 1969), 3:39–41; quoted by Ann Jennalie Cook, *The Privileged Playgoers of Shakespeare's London* (Princeton: Princeton University Press, 1981), Appendix A, 277–79. For wages in Wiltshire, see *Records of the County of Wilts* (Devizes: 1932), 292–93. For Thomas Hearne's and William Kendall's wages, see Foakes and Rickert, 238 and 268–69 respectively.

9. The various references in the records of the Wells Shows of 1607 are given in James Stokes, ed. *Somerset*, Records of Early English Drama (Toronto: University of Toronto Press, 1996); as REED *Somerset* hereafter. The records are unclear as to what kind of vehicle was used. Diana was either carried on a coach (268), on men's shoulders (370), or both (339), or in a chariot (372). Even by 1836, when the railways were about to take over from stage coaches, which were then driving over maintained turnpike roads, "The Regulator" coach could only average 9.3 mph from London to Bristol, "The Monarch," 8.1 mph, and the General Stage Company's Night Coach, 6.7 mph (Alan Bates, comp. *Directory of Stage Coach Services, 1836*, [Newton Abbott: David and Charles, 1969], 11).

10. Andrew Gurr, *The Shakespearian Playing Companies* (Oxford: Clarendon Press, 1996), 45; as "Gurr" hereafter. Some members of Welsh National Opera's orchestra camp on tour, often in bad weather.

11. *Tarltons Iests* (London: T. Snodham for J. Budge, 1613) D3^v; as *Tarlton's Iests* hereafter. Gurr says, "There is no record of the companies using any other form of transport, but one does wonder whether they did not often travel round the coast by sea" (Gurr, 46).

12. Private communication from the late Hubert Lamb, the distinguished historical meteorologist, 21 July 1994.

13. *Tarltons Iests*, D1^r.

14. Murray, 2:165; for the account of the trial, see 163–67; see also Bradley, 62.

15. Foakes and Rickert, 280. Gurr mentions that "there is surprisingly little correlation between the [London] plague closures and the records of touring" (Gurr, 53). Marlborough records show that in 1608, a plague year in London, when the King's Men visited the town, there were many payments to alleviate sickness, presumably plague. In 1610, when London theatres were closed for several months because of plague and Queen Anne's Players visited Marlborough, there were again payments to alleviate sickness and so many wandering men and women were whipped away that a penny was spent on the provision of new whipcords. (Marlborough Chamberlain's Accounts, Wiltshire Record Office, Trowbridge, call number

G22/1/205/2; these have not yet been printed; herafter as "Marlborough Accounts.")

16. Marlborough Accounts for 1606 show that 18d was spent on hiring two horses to go to Littlecote, ten miles away. The Bath accounts for 1601–2 show that the Queen's Men were given "their Kytchinge bread beare wyne & sugar" at a cost of 8s 0d, plus 3s 2d for "horsemeate" (REED, *Somerset*, 18). The Bath records for 1619 show 2s 0d was charged to hire one horse for two days. This is not recorded in REED *Somerset*; I checked the actual records at Trowbridge, Bath, and Bristol.

17. *OED* records stroller from Dekker's *Lanthorne and Candle-light* (London: G. Eld for J. Busbie, 1608) as "a proper name given to Country-players, that . . . trot from town to town on the hard hoof."

18. Information from Lorelei Williams, Honorary Archivist, The Merchant's House, Marlborough, 8 October 1996.

19. Michael Justin Davis, *The Landscape of William Shakespeare* (Exeter: Webb & Bower, 1987), 55. As "Davis" hereafter.

20. From Foakes and Rickert, 56–57. Full details are given in Davison, *Richard III, Q1*, 42–46.

21. Bradley, 17–20 and 229; for the Admiral's Company in 1597, see 234; Chambers, 2:80–81. The support staff for a modern Shakespeare company is now several times the number of actors.

22. "The Cost of Touring," *Renaissance and Medieval Drama in England*, 6 (1993): 59; quoted by Alan Somerset, " 'How Chances it they Travel': Provincial Touring, Playing Places, and the King's Men" *Shakespeare Survey*, 47 (1994): 51; hereafter as "Somerset."

23. "Today," BBC Radio 4, 4 November 1997.

24. See *Roman and Medieval Bath* and *Georgian Bath* in the Ordnance Survey Historical Maps and Guides series.

25. Somerset, 59; the interior of Leicester Guildhall is illustrated on 51.

26. Bentley, *The Profession of Player in Shakespeare's Time, 1590–1642*, (Princeton: Princeton University Press, 1984), 184–86; quoted by Somerset, 51, n. 24.

27. "Jacobean Actors and the Great Hall at Gawthorpe, Lancashire," *Theatre Notebook*, 37 (1983): 111. As "George" hereafter.

28. E. K. Chambers, *The Elizabethan Stage*, 4 vols. (Oxford, Clarendon Press, 1923), 1:12 and 4:311–12; quoted by Bradley, 69–70.

29. Davis, 52.

30. See Ian Lancashire, *Dramatic Texts and Records of Britain: a Chronological Topography to 1558* (Toronto: Toronto University Press, 1984), 291 and 453.

31. Lawrence Stone, "Companies of players entertained by the Earl of Cumberland and Lord Clifford, 1607–39," *Collections V*, Malone Society (Oxford: Oxford University Press, 1960 for 1959).

32. John Harland, ed. *The House and Farm Accounts of the Shuttleworths of Gawthorpe Hall in the County of Lancaster and Gawthorpe, September 1582–1621*, 4 vols. (Cheetham Society: 1856–58), 4 (as vol. 46), 893–94. See also George, 109–21.

33. *Titus Andronicus*, ed. Jonathan Bate (London: Routledge, 1995), 43.

34. Murray, 2:164.

35. An account of this illustration is given by R. A. Foakes in *Illustrations of the English Stage, 1580–1642* (London: Scolar Press, 1985), 48–51.

36. REED, *Somerset*, 176.

37. Oliver Lawson Dick, ed. *Aubrey's Brief Lives* (Harmondsworth: Peregrine Books, 1962), 309.

38. The Accounts of the Company of Masters and Burgesses of the Borough of

Wilton, 1565–16 are held at Trowbridge Record Office, call number G25/1/91. The money is entered as being laid out "vppon giftes and fees." I. A. Shapiro has suggested to me that by "servants" the whole of those attending upon the king might be intended, not just the players. However, as mentioned above, the journey from Mortlake to Wilton was subsidized to the tune of £30 (see n. 5), so the enterprise appears to have been lavish.

39. Chambers, 2:329.
40. Dawson, *Collections VII*, xix.
41. REED, *Somerset*, 15.
42. Foakes and Rickert, 280.

Stage Directions for Music and Sound Effects in *2–3 Henry VI*: "No Quarrel, but a slight Contention"

PETER M. WRIGHT

READING *THE CONTENTION* AND *THE TRUE TRAGEDY* WE ARE STRUCK BY the plentiful stage directions in these "short" Quarto and Octavo texts. In *The Contention* there is a stage direction of some sort for approximately every eleven lines of dialogue, and in *The True Tragedy*, 1:15; *Antony and Cleopatra* and *Coriolanus* (thought to derive from "authorial" manuscripts) muster only 1:17 and 1:21, respectively.[1] W. W. Greg's categories for literary stage directions are amply illustrated in *The Contention*: attitude ("raving and staring as if he were madde"), physical condition ("that he is drunken"), purpose ("to the Parliament"), costume ("with a white sheete about her"), even new information as in "Duke Humphrey lets it fall." Like little islands of commentary, these often breathless directions ("and then . . . and then") seem to attract the eye's attention on the page as much as does the dialogue and even to overshadow it and they can take longer to read than the action described needs to be performed.[2] Much the same can be said of *The True Tragedy* whose directions, though shorter and less numerous than those in *The Contention*, show equally vivid and specific detail—"Crookback Richard," "Clifford with an arrow in his necke," and even white and red "Roses in their hats." Yet, in contrast with these directions which recreate the staging for us in such detail, cues for sound and music are not only sparse but for the most part are limited to simple noisy effects like "alarum" and the warlike drum. In this essay I would like to examine this apparent discrepancy between the otherwise imaginative staging indicated by the directions in these "short" plays and the strikingly plain sound effects.[3]

In *The Contention* William Montgomery finds evidence of a "large cast of at least 19" and "sophisticated staging facilities," including a platform stage with a trap, an upper acting area, at least two entrances, possibly a discovery space, all suggesting that "the text as reported reflects the full staging facilities of a well-equipped London amphitheatre or hall playhouse"; I would add that these conclusions might also be applied to *The True Tragedy*.[4] Yet even with such ambitious staging marked frequently with vivid detail in the directions, the Quarto and Octavo texts rely almost exclusively on a narrow range of military sound effects like the offstage battle-noises of "Alarum" and its onstage counterpart the marching, beaten drum, even though there exist numerous opportunities for other types of stage music like "Flourish," "Trumpet," "Sennet" and more specific, tonally colored instruments like "Hoboyes" and "Hornes."[5] This apparent imbalance suggests not only a predominantly harsh and clangorous tone for plays with already grim subject-matter, but leads to a comparison with the musical directions in the Folio versions of these plays which in so many other ways resemble their shorter kin.[6] While *2–3 Henry VI* are longer by half and have fewer stage directions per lines of text, the music-directions are not only more numerous in Folio in proportion to other directions, but show much greater variety and color as well.[7]

I can only guess at reasons for the relative paucity and stark quality of the short texts' sound effects, and particularly for the "absence" of other musical cues; perhaps the compiler(s) took for granted a reading audience who could supply the "missing" effects for themselves, or, as is most likely, these short texts were intended for production where the normal resources of the playhouse were unavailable.[8] It is also possible that the sophisticated production evident in *The Contention* and *The True Tragedy* used only the harsher, more stirring sounds of drums and "alarmes," and I suspect that the sound effects marked in the "short texts" were not so much left crude or inadequate but (as I assume for now) were designed to affect the audience in a particular way.[9] The issues I discuss (briefly and speculatively) are all related: first is the completeness and integrity of the short texts' directions for music and noises, and their significance for the production of these texts. The second issue derives from the first, for it is difficult to avoid comparing the short texts with their Folio counterparts, when there are so many moments similar in both texts. So, beginning with *The Contention* and *2 Henry VI*, I shall examine what I find to be a striking difference in the number and variety of directions marked for both music and sound effects, which suggests the performance in the Folio versions of more varied theatrical music and sound effects which were unmarked, eliminated, or differently performed in the "short" texts. At the same time I shall try to consider the possibility that music directions surviving in the short and long texts represent significant differences in the emotional response expected from the audience in performance.[10]

Any one set of differences can be fascinating: *The Contention*'s instruction, "and Duke Humphrey staies all the rest," appears as "Manet the rest" in a Folio text 1.1 where many Quarto directions appear pruned or altered in wording. Do his peers hover round the Duke, joining or even provoking his repressed "greefe," a long conversation which results in the Cardinal's admonition and the Duke's answering flare of rancor (as in the Folio)? Or does Gloucester (as the Quarto suggests) sternly gather them, willing or embarrassed, to hear his "passionate discourse" which immediately provokes Cardinal Beaufort into a hot condemnation of the Protector's envious malice? To what extent does the Duke or Cardinal, abetted by the nobles of his faction, intentionally foment the divisiveness and self-seeking that follow to become the hallmark of this play, themes which John H. Long calls "the decline of feudalism" in the tetralogy as a whole?[11] This is a small difference, but one which highlights the importance of stage directions to both action and tone, and affirms the importance of understanding how any stage directions in both texts affect the audience in performance.

Apart from "alarums" and drums, *The Contention* has fewer simple directions for musical effects than we might expect, given the many royal entries and the military action later in the play. The play's first direction shows King Henry, Gloucester, Somerset, Buckingham, and Cardinal Beaufort entering at one door, while "at the other doore" enter Yorke, Suffolke, Queen Margaret, Salisbury, and Warwick, a technique repeated in the Folio. This formal entry of separate processions at opposite doors might well have been simultaneous, and could perhaps have foreshadowed, were the grouping of each faction more pronounced, the dynastic rivalry of Lancaster and York. This dignity of this stately entry soon disintegrates and then coalesces into the suspicious rivalry suggested by the entry: Margaret and Suffolk, Salisbury and Warwick, Somerset and Buckingham, with York playing a lone hand so far.[12] The King's formal appearance receives no fanfare or trumpet of any kind, but a "sound trumpet" does occur when Margaret is hailed as Queen, "England's happinesse."[13] This isolated trumpet-call could be meant as a hint of the King's future weakness, or as dramatic pointing for Duke Humphrey's reading of the disastrous articles of peace and espousal (perhaps the entrants now drift toward their eventual partners in rivalry); there is a specific direction for Gloucester to "let fall" the paper, but no musical cue for the royal party's exit as

"Duke Humphrey staies all the rest." Apart from an "alarum" hastening the defeated King and Queen's flight from the Battle of St. Albans, the Lancastrian party is given no specifically royal fanfare for any of their numerous exits or entrances in this play.

On the other hand, the Duke of York *is* given, for his victorious entry after the battle, the dignity of an extended musical effect "Alarmes, and then a flourish, and enter," a direction which raises the possibility of an ironic contrast between the fleeing King and the triumphant usurper.[14] Though somewhat scarce in this play, the few music cues and more numerous sound effects actually marked seem thoughtfully placed (e.g., the Commons' offstage denunciation of Suffolk). However, the Quarto does offer a number of different "alarums" during the military action, accompanied by phrases such as "like as it were a fight at sea" (complete with discharged "chambers"), "to the battaille," "againe," and "still." This play shows a potential for sophisticated staging and a lively appreciation for theatrical effects which include complex action in the various Cade broils, the conjuration with thunder and lightning, and in addition, the debunking of the man born blind, a scene accompanied by one of the few directions for "musicke." In contrast, those directions for music marked in the Folio version show us how this ambitious staging might have been reflected in the different musical cues as well, for similar opportunities are there in the Quarto text.

Many of the directions in the Folio text appear to be alike in their Quarto counterparts: the Quarto's "Alarums to the battaille" corresponds to Folio's "Alarums to the fight," but sometimes the minor differences are more interesting. The "curing" of the blind Saunder Simpcoxe in Quarto 1 bears some resemblance to the longer Folio version of *2 Henry VI*; however, the Quarto and Folio stage directions differ in one important respect: Quarto's call for "Musicke" does not appear in the Folio's narrative direction:

> Enter the Maior of Saint Albones and his brethren with
> Musicke, bearing the man that had bene blind,
> betweene two in a Chaire
> (Quarto, C2)
> Enter the Maior of Saint Albones, and his Brethren,
> bearing the man betweene two in a Chayre.
> (Folio, 2.1. 795–96)

One obvious omission from the Folio direction is the phrase "that had bene blind"; the Folio's allusive phrase "the man" must refer to an earlier line of dialogue [790] and indicates close attention to the text by whoever supplied the Folio direction, "a blinde man at Saint *Albones* The Shrine." The Quarto reads much the same: "a man that came blinde to S. Albones." The Folio's only mention of music occurs in the King's sorrowful speech several lines *before* the arrival of "one crying a Miracle": "The Windes grow high, / So doe your Stomacks, Lords: / How irksome is this Musick to my heart? / When such Strings iarre, what hope of Harmony? / I pray my Lords let me compound this strife"; the Quarto has simply "The wind growes high, so doth your chollour Lords." If "music" in the Quarto intended a harmonious consort, then we observe solemn music healing a fraudulent blindness, an ironic commentary on the King's inadequacy and a terrible blow to his faith.[15] For the Folio then, it is also arguable that "music" was omitted to emphasize internecine discord and to highlight the King's weary failure as a peacemaker from whom such harmony and order should flow.[16] On the other hand, if stress is laid on Henry's words "*this* Musick," then, perhaps, a harmonious consort was intended in Folio to introduce the Simpcoxe healing, in direct contrast with the jarring ambitions of Henry's nobles. We would have then a simple omission of a music cue, whose performance would have been taken for granted. Alternatively, both the Quarto and Folio could well have used a consort playing "lowd," "rurall," or any festive music, possibilities that offer a wholly different range of ironic contrasts. Whatever speculative conclusion we reach in reading or performance, the presence of music, whether metaphoric or aural, is essential to the understanding and performance of this very telling scene.[17]

Along with six "alarums" found also in the Quarto, the directions in *2 Henry VI* also contain many more sophisticated terms for musical effects, such as six "Flourishes," three "Sound Trumpets" and two "Sennets" which announce a number of royal entries and exits, as well as two "retreats" and a "Parley," a range of effects not found in the Quarto's "darker" version.[18] The opening scene offers a vivid example of musical effects new to the Folio. While the Quarto calls for no music until Margaret's acclamation as Queen, the Folio begins with "Flourish of Trumpets: then Hoboyes," a remarkably different royal entry, an event usually heralded with the appropriate brass fanfare.[19] Here we have two distinct musical effects, a fanfare for the entry followed by a long and conceivably foreboding tune on the "hoboyes" as perhaps the factions begin to group onstage, "on the one side . . . on the other." Furthermore, if Margaret ("England's joy") and those following her entered slightly later than the King and his party, then it is possible that the "hoboyes" were intended to be a musical comment on her and Suffolk's entry; the

Folio seems to offer not only an "opposing" entry but in addition an aural dimension to enrich the visual spectacle.[20]

Royal entries in the Quarto *Contention* and Folio *2 Henry VI* show other interesting differences, not only in the presence of sound effects but also in their specific nature. For example, Henry's entry in the middle of 1.3 (after Margaret and Suffolk scheme to destroy the Duke and Duchess of Gloucester) has no fanfare in the Quarto (he enters apparently surrounded by the factions "on both sides, whispering with him"), and his first words are consistent with this visual effect ("My Lords I care not who be Regent in *France*, or *York*, or *Somerset*, alls wonne to me") as he presides over the regency of France and all the contumelious wrangling which attends that appointment. The Folio signals the royal entry with a "Sennet" (a longer brass fanfare usually accorded to royalty), giving us a Henry leading the entry, followed by "Duke Humfrey, Cardinall, Buckingham, Yorke, Salisbury, Warwicke, and the Duchesse"; Henry ends this scene with a "Flourish" on a briefly more assertive note. Similarly at 3.1, Quarto gives us a Henry who appears following the Heralds, Buckingham, Suffolk, York, the Cardinal, with the Queen, Warwick and Salisbury behind him, a monarch surrounded by those who would control him, not the climactic appearance of the most powerful person arriving last on the stage. Here also the Folio offers us a royal direction, "Sound a Sennet," bringing on King Henry leading the entry of the Queen, Cardinal, Suffolk, York, Buckingham, Salisbury, and Warwick, the concluding "to the Parliament" the same phrase which opened the Quarto direction. Henry's speech seems here more forceful, three lines rather than Quarto's single line "I wonder. . . ." As at 1.3, we may have here, an equally invidious occasion, a different King; in the Quarto unassertive and manipulated, in the Folio momentarily bold as he presides over the dismissal of Gloucester as Protector.[21] In both Folio examples we could see a contrast between the regal opening of the scene and a King unable to control the discord of his subjects.

On the other hand, "sound trumpets" occurs in the Folio three times in connection with a royal entry, but the more common "Flourish" or "Sennet" is not used in these instances. "Sound trumpets" occurs in scenes where the King (with "State") banishes Duke Humphrey's Duchess (2.3), at the opening of the trial of the just-murdered Duke Humphrey with the repudiation of Suffolk (3.2), and a third time for the appearance of King, Queen and Court "on the Tarras" to judge the noosed and penitent rebels (4.9). All three scenes show us a manipulated and distressed King. Finally, Henry is not given in the Folio (or in the Quarto) any brass fanfare at all when he enters with a "Supplication" along with Margaret cherishing Suffolk's head (4.4); the lack of such a direction may emphasize Henry's futility as a monarch and as a husband. If we accept Long's argument that such specific choices of effect are intentional and *if* the Folio's terminology can be trusted to be precise, then these three entrances given less than a royal "Flourish" would signify a less than effective monarch.[22] For the Quarto, then, it can be argued that Henry's royal dignity was undercut by a *lack* of appropriate royal fanfares. Of course, putting such systematic weight on the inconsistent wording of stage directions is perhaps to erect a house of cards in a gale, but the basic point remains: a contemporary audience hearing a fanfare suggestive of royal authority and dignity would be aware of the ironic inconsistency of this Henry's disastrous vacillation.[23]

Finally, the Folio has six "Flourishes" not in Quarto; the first signals Henry's entrance in 1.1, the second, Margaret's acclamation a few lines later, perhaps ironically foreshadowing the Queen's dominance. The remaining four examples of "Flourish" all signal exits for Henry but not necessarily a cleared stage as well; the last "Flourish" he receives in this play concludes 4.9 after the words "Come wife, let's in, and learne to govern better, / For yet may England curse my wretched raigne," whereas Quarto concludes the scene with "Come let us hast . . . And triumphs of this happie victorie" (with no exit-"Flourish" [G3ᵛ]). If these can bear the significance Long attaches to them, then we have examples (here and in the opening direction) of music used to create a specific tone for the dramatic action, the sort of shading which is both "representational" and "rhetorically" affective in portraying the confused and tragic monarch further developed in *3 Henry VI*, a technique in Folio which markedly emphasizes both the formal panoply and the incessant warfare of this History play.[24]

While there are fewer directions in *The True Tragedy* than in *The Contention,* narrative detail is colorfully noted: "a dead man in his armes," "three sunnes appeare in the aire," the "Maire" with "keies in his hand," Clarence taking his red Rose out of his hat and throwing it at "Father of *Warwike.*" The literary quality of these directions remains prominent, but directions for musical effects are as sparse as those in *The Contention* and are predictably of a military nature. There are no sound effects for Lancastrian royal entries (apart from the ubiquitous "alarmes" and drums), nor are Warwick and the Yorkist usurpers accorded the dignity of royal music, particularly when they enter fresh from their victory at St. Albans (2.6). Similarly, when the King and his royal Lancastrian party enter in 1.1, there is no fanfare when they confront the Duke of York, the "sturdy rebel" who has claimed the "chaire of state." The only sound effect ("Sound Trumpets") comes as York takes his leave, presumably descending from the throne of the reconciled King, whom he has just forced to entail the Crown and disinherit his own son, Prince Edward (A5ᵛ). With so many occasions for specific fanfares not exploited, this lone call for trumpets stands out, again, as at a similar moment in *The Contention*, suggesting an ironic effect: for which "King" is the musical courtesy intended, Henry or Richard? Though *The True Tragedie* has some generally worded sound effects marked in the text, it also has numerous opportunities for varied and colorful music which were more thoroughly exploited in Folio's *3 Henry VI*.

The pattern of expanded musical effects I have described for *2 Henry VI* is even more noticeable in *3 Henry VI* which boasts approximately twenty-six "new," more articulate musical directions ("flourishes," "marches," "alarums," "drums and trumpets," "drums and colours," "sennet," "retreats," and "hornes"), a remarkable range of theatrical effects. "Flourish" in most cases should herald the entry of royalty, presumably the anointed Henry, but here the use seems ambiguous, for it is the usurping "King" Edward Plantagenet who receives a number of triumphant "Flourishes" at the end of the play; these musical cues may herald his current royal legitimacy. Perhaps the best example of Octavo/Folio differences occurs at the opening of the play. Folio *2 Henry VI* concludes with "Alarum. Retreat," a direction which is perhaps reflected in the opening "alarum" of *3 Henry VI*. The Plantagenet family enters first, and after a Folio direction "They goe up" (to the throne or "state"), the Yorkist pretender is confirmed by a "Flourish" ("Resolve thee *Richard*, clayme the English Crowne"). This specific direction (not in Octavo) occurs precisely as the Lancastrian party arrives, and may well ironically herald the entry of the "true" king and highlight the perplexities of civil war.[25] The subsequent direction for Warwick to stamp his foot (Folio only) might reinforce with the "armed men" what the ambiguous entry directions have only hinted, and again suggests the hand of someone intimately aware of the scene's political issues and its dramatic potential. Furthermore, Octavo's generic direction when York vacates the throne ("Sound Trumpets") is in Folio the more specifically regal "Senet. Here they come downe," a difference in the music which, if perceived, would heighten the tragic irony of this scene.[26]

Though the Yorkist faction is given in Folio neither exit nor "Flourish" just before the Queen accosts the sheepish Exeter and timid Henry who wish to "steale away," a "Flourish" does occur for the exit of Henry, Margaret and Exeter, coincident (between 1.1 and 1.2) with the next entry of Richard, Edward and Montague, and after a few more lines their father, the Duke of York. Later in the play throughout act 4, both Edward and Henry are given a "Flourish" for most of their formal entries (except in the heat of battle where some form of "Alarum" appears); the sound cues perhaps suggest the precarious nature of the battle and the rival claims. York's eldest son is variously referred to as "Edward," "the King," or "King Edward" with little apparent reference in the speech-prefix to his political state at a given point during these "tumultuous Broyles," while Henry is called "King Henry" or "The King." However, after the final Lancastrian defeat and the death of Warwick (5.3), the stage direction reads "Flourish. Enter *King* Edward in triumph" (my emphasis). Henry's final entry "Enter Henry the sixt . . . on the (Tower) walles" receives no fanfare, perhaps suggestive of his deposed state.[27] The general care with which these scenes are set out by the stage directions is all the more remarkable, for the Folio omits numerous exits found in the Octavo, traffic cues which are not so important to guide performance as entries.

In addition, the Folio directions for music often occur together in various combinations, such as "A short Alarum within," "Alarum and Retreat," "Flourish. Sound," "Alarum, Retreat, Excursion," and these expansions occur as often at moments closely similar in both texts as in scenes different in Folio. Even simple directions like "alarum" and "march" are often elaborated by "within," "lowd," "short," "afarre off," In fact, the Folio stage directions show as much expansion and alteration as does the Folio dialogue. Although the Octavo directions are remarkably specific ("Clifford grones and then dies," "two keepers with bow and arrowes"), the Folio versions are even more numerous, explicit and sophisticated as they accompany the expanded dialogue. Compare for example two parallel scenes in Octavo and Folio, the audience with Lewis of France (3.3), and the capture of Edward by Warwick (4.3). Although the Folio text of this play is longer by fifty percent, the number of *musical* directions has nearly trebled. Finally, a common direction found in both texts ("Drums and Soldiers") appears in Folio as "Drumme and Colours," a more specific visual and aural effect, and this change becomes something of a trend in *3 Henry VI* where, at 5.1, the siege of Coventry, "Drumme and Souldiers" becomes "Drumme and Colours" four times in less than twenty-five lines.[28]

Taken singly, differences between directions in the "short" or "bad" texts and their Folio counterparts (where they exist) are intriguing enough, but when viewed as a continuous pattern suggest a thoughtful realization of potential musical effects left largely unmarked (or performed differently) in both shorter texts. It is difficult to claim that the directions in Folio have been marked consistently in all respects, but there are enough parallels to provoke further inquiry of similar usages in other Folio texts, which might well yield evidence of contemporary staging and its fuller realization in the Folio versions. For example, the "bad" Quarto of *Henry V*, a text of only 1500 or so lines, has seventy-four stage directions, of which three are for music (mostly "alarum"); the Folio text (3381 lines) has 133 directions, of which twenty-one are for music, a fourfold increase in the Folio for music calls.[29]

Recent scholarship has demonstrated that the "bad" or "short" texts are valid dramatic documents in their own right, and, whatever their provenance, should no longer be considered as the stolen and surreptitious poor relations of the Folio versions, or treated exclusively as quarries for the Great Walls of textual theory and editorial practice. If these "short" texts have been redeemed from disrepute, then, as Montgomery shows, all aspects of their production deserve further scrutiny, particularly the stage directions which must work in harmony with the dialogue which has so far received the most attention. Once we accept that these "short" texts preserve in their stage directions remarkably clear hints of their original production, they should not be carelessly conflated with the Folio versions for the sake of editorial policy, to the confusion of what might be intentionally different effects in both versions. If, as legitimate parts of the whole text, the stage directions preserve for us some inkling of contemporary production whether in London or elsewhere on tour, then equal attention should be paid to the rich and allusive directions for music which are often today slighted in texts or ignored in production. Unfortunately, though critics have begun to take seriously the stage directions, we still have tin ears; any old brass noise is not enough and frustrates the author's purpose, even in seemingly minor effects like military entries and their various sound and music cues.[30] If we would understand how a contemporary audience *saw* a performance, should we also not understand how they *heard* it was well?

When in *3 Henry VI* the Duke of York asks "Why how now sonnes, and Brother, at a strife? What is your Quarrel? how began it first?" Edward answers "No Quarrel, but a slight Contention." There are still a number of unresolved problems in these texts, among which looms large their provenance. I have not attempted here to enter the debate over just what exemplar may still lurk behind both the "short" and Folio versions of these plays, nor can I speculate on the transmission of either text, already performed so well by others.[31] But in spite of such a disclaimer, these questions inevitably arise in our treatment of multiple-text plays, for there is a natural tendency to see in parallel texts some sort of relationship with each other. If only the laws of cause and effect allowed us the comfort of direct kinship between "short" and Folio versions, so many hard choices between legitimate performance directions would be avoided. Some light would be shed on the extent to which the Folio directions were crafted for the educated reader (as Jonson's were in his 1616 *Workes*) or remain clear directives for production. For the moment, I would argue that an examination of Quarto-Octavo/Folio stage directions, here the directions for music and noises, is valid, and when done in a comparative manner, illuminates and enriches our understanding of the staging of these theatrical documents and, perhaps, even of their relationship.

Notes

1. This essay was originally submitted to the Shakespeare Association of America (1994) seminar on "Revision and Adaptation in Shakespeare's Two- and Three-text plays," chaired by Kathleen Irace of UCLA. I am very grateful to her and to Alan Dessen and Guy Hamel for their thoughtful comments before the Albuquerque meeting which have much improved the original paper in its subsequent revision.

2. A. R. Braunmuller comments that "we may remember that Shakespeare's plays were originally edited to benefit the solitary reader, not the actors or theatrical personnel." Furthermore, "it does seem a safe bet that whoever prepared a manuscript for performance use could assume that certain common and ritualized occasions (e.g., royal entrances and battles) would receive appropriate aural accompaniment without specific instructions in the script." See "Editing the Staging / Staging the Editing," in *Shakespeare and the Sense of Performance: Essays in the Tradition of Performance Criticism in Honor of Bernard Beckerman*, ed. Marvin and Ruth Thompson (Newark, Del.: University of Delaware Press, 1989), 139 and 147 n. 11. In his response to this essay at the SAA seminar, Guy Hamel remarked that compositors would set whatever was in their copy, including matter originally meant for the actor or bookkeeper such as stage directions; plays orally reconstructed from memory would contain stage directions for sound and music added by someone familiar with the production in order to make the "short" text conform in appearance to a legitimate book. In other words, a reporter would not invent sound cues [I here summarize Hamel's initial comments]. Or on the other hand, if we accept Irace's argument, then it is conceivable that a compiler/adapter/abridger might leave out certain directions unsuitable for an *ad hoc* production, directions that would then be found in the fuller text represented by Folio. But see below, n. 8 and 10.

3. In the course of his analysis of the annotations in the Folger Quarto of *The Two Merry Milkmaids*, Dessen pertinently warns that an "orderly, meticulous"

promptbook assumed by generations of editors as typical of playhouse manuscripts is perhaps an idealized concept; "to build mosaics from large numbers of stage directions can be highly misleading, for such details are the exception." We can only guess at the fuller theatrical language experienced in performance and "teased" out of printed texts of "playscripts not of our age," "eavesdropping on a conversation being conducted in a language we only partly understand." See "Recovering Elizabethan Staging: A Reconsideration of the Evidence," in *Textual and Theatrical Shakespeare: Questions of Evidence,* (Iowa City, IA: University of Iowa Press, 1996) 44–63. Two important studies are his *Elizabethan Stage Conventions and Modern Interpreters* (Cambridge: Cambridge University Press, 1984), and *Recovering Shakespeare's Theatrical Vocabulary* (Cambridge: University of Cambridge Press, 1995); the first two chapters in both books are especially helpful.

4. Montgomery comments that "the text of *The Contention* as it survives in the first quarto may have been put together *for* a provincial tour, but it must have been put together while the London production of the play was still the dominant memory of its reporters—before, that is, a tour forced the Company to adapt and simplify the plays' staging" (22). See "The Original Staging of *The First Part of the Contention* (1594), *Shakespeare Survey* 41, ed. Stanley Wells (Cambridge: Cambridge University Press, 1989), 13–22. In his "New Cambridge" editions of *2–3 Henry VI* (Cambridge: Cambridge University Press, 1991, 1993), Michael Hattaway reaches similar conclusions about early performances of these plays, observing that stage directions in *The Contention* "recall performance in a London playhouse ," e.g., possible references to a discovery space, noises "within," the three levels of cellarage, "above," and the Tower for Elinor's conjuration, along with a tiring-house, two entrances, a gallery, and walls, for *The True Tragedy.* See further "Dates and Occasion" 60–68, and "Note on the Text" 70–71, a discussion reiterated in his edition of *3 Henry VI.*

5. Simple military sound effects are numerous in the "short" texts. *The Contention* has 10 examples of "Alarum" and *The True Tragedy* 7. Both plays have one or two examples of "Sound" or "Sound Trumpet(s)," but in their martial entry directions, both plays rely heavily on "Drum and Souldiers" (6 in the Quarto, 10 in the Octavo), a form of direction which suggests on-stage performance often called for by the dialogue; there seems little reason to include a drum for visual effect only. On the other hand, there are a number of entries for the various armies simply as "souldiers" or even "a troope of Hollanders"; a number of these directions appear in the Folio text as "March" or "Alarum." The differences in the corresponding Folio directions, and the predominance of this sort of military noise, suggest that a martial noise (whether onstage or offstage) was performed whenever appropriate. Had I considered only sound cues performed on actual musical instruments (one in Quarto, two in Octavo) instead of including "alarums" and drums, the "tonal" contrast between the directions in the "short" texts and the Folio versions would have been all the more remarkable.

6. Statistical evidence can help here: of Quarto's 223 stage directions, 18 are for music/noises, or 8.1%. In *2 Henry VI*, 3355 lines of text yield 160 sds, and 24 of these, or 15%, are for music/noises. For Octavo / *3 Henry VI*, the figures are more interesting: Octavo's text has 2128 lines with 144 directions (18 for music, or 12.5%). As for Folio, *3 Henry VI* shows 3213 lines with 154 sds; 44 or 28.6% are for music/noises. Even allowing for errors in counting, the proportions are remarkable and reflect discernible trends. All Folio references are to Charlton Hinman's facsimile *The First Folio of Shakespeare* (New York: W.W. Norton, 1968), where I used Hinman's "TLN" figures for my total line-count; and for Q and O, I relied upon

Michael J. B. Allen and Kenneth Muir's *Shakespeare's Plays in Quarto* in which I added up the number of lines per page.

7. I am much indebted to the following works: F. W. Sternfeld, *Music in Shakespearean Tragedy* (London: Routledge & Kegan Paul, 1963); and to John H. Long, *Shakespeare's Use of Music: The Histories and Tragedies* (Gainesville, Fla.: University of Florida Press, 1971); *Shakespeare's Use of Music: The Final Comedies* (Gainesville, Fla.: University of Florida Press, 1961); *Shakespeare's Use of Music: A Study of the Music and its Performance in the Original Productions of Seven Comedies* (Gainesville, Fla.: University of Florida Press, 1955). Each of Long's volumes is hereafter referred to by its subtitle.

8. Montgomery admits that some theatrical effects (the cannon, the "fight at sea") may have been performed, but suggests also that the latter phrase "may be the reporter expanding the stage direction for the benefit of a reading audience." A reporter with such a vivid imagination taking such care to insert stage directions would have found it easy to supply more varied and colorful sound cues, especially so if he had been one of the actors witnessing the original musical effects. Had the text derived from a touring production, then the absence of more elaborate musical directions would be understandable. But if *The Contention* (or *The True Tragedy*) with its sophisticated staging originated in a London production, then the comparative absence of more varied musical directions is all the more surprising unless we are to believe that the compiler(s) altered and eliminated the "original" more varied sound and music effects to make the text more suitable for a touring production, which generally speaking is Irace's conclusion. For a convincing summary of her arguments in support of adaptation and abridgment within the context of "the still contested theory of memorial reconstruction," see Kathleen O. Irace's "Conclusion" in *Reforming the "Bad" Quartos: Performance and Provenance of Six Shakespearean First Editions* (Newark, Del.: University of Delaware Press, 1994), 160–72.

9. Long describes "alarum" as "probably the clangor of trumpets, the roll of drums, shouts, clashing arms, neighing horses—all produced offstage" (*Histories and Tragedies*, 79). Furthermore, Montgomery comments that "the phrase, 'like as it were a fight at sea' (line 1464), suggests that there may also have been, in addition to the cannon, particular sound effects relevant to sea battles, such 'as the rattling of chains and hawsers, cries of sailors, and the blowing of the boatswain's whistle' " (22, citing Louis B. Wright in *Anglia*, 51 [1927], 110).

10. Irace argues that Folio may represent versions of the play of which the Quarto/Octavo apparently are memorially reconstructed abridgements and adaptations. See also in Stanley Wells and Gary Taylor's *Textual Companion* to the Oxford edition (Oxford: Clarendon Press, 1987), "Canon and Chronology" 111–12, 175–78, "The First Part of the Contention"; and 197–200, "Richard Duke of York."

11. Long, "The First Tetralogy," *Histories and Tragedies*, 17–32.

12. For C. Walter Hodges' visualization of the stage-grouping of the various factions, see Hattaway's edition of *2 Henry VI*, "Introduction," illus. 9, 35.

13. Hattaway uses the Folio direction, describing "hautboyes" as "probably playing a 'sennet' or processional march"; he describes the details of this opening stage direction as "prescriptive or descriptive, deriving from either foul papers or prompt-book," but that "neither F nor Q . . . divides the entrants neatly into Lancastrian or Yorkist camps. In procession the most eminent person entered last, so it is not possible to argue that either text offers a record of performance," *2 Henry VI*, n.0 sd. 3–4, 79.

14. The different terms "Flourish," "Sound Trumpets," "Tucket" etc. cannot be lumped together as stage shorthand for noisy music. On the essential differences between these and other terms, see Long, *The Final Comedies*, 17.

15. Harold Hobson (*Sunday Times*, 21 July 1963) noted of David Warner's portrayal of the king: "As the fraud is exposed, the King's face is stricken. We see a man's faith, which is all in all to him, momentarily destroyed." Cited by Hattaway, *2 Henry VI*, 50.

16. If this term here demands a harmonious consort—whether stringed or "broken"—as it frequently does in later plays, then we might find in this comic scene an interesting and very early use (1591; Quarto 1594) in a public theater (possibly "The Rose") of a quiet musical effect generally considered characteristic of the private theaters like the Blackfriars. In a private note to the author, Alan Dessen questioned the interpretation of "musicke" as necessarily meaning "elevating or refined" music in Sternfeld's terms: e.g., the healing music in Quarto *King Lear*. When we remember the resolution of the Saunder Simpcoxe episode, the music might well be "*alla burla*" at least after the Beadle's ministrations, even if the scene began with mock-solemnity in Quarto. We may note that the imprisoned Richard II endured music that was "sowre" with broken time "and no proportion kept"; and also that, as Sternfeld points out, the softness of the "aristocratic strings" may have constituted "an acoustical hazard" in a public theater like the Globe, whereas wind instruments might have been more audible (Sternfeld, "III. Pan's Pipes versus Apollo's Strings,") 226–35. With a final statistic, I note that of the more than forty uses of "musicke" in Folio, over half could called "soft" or "solemn," in contexts where sleep, solemnity, healing, visions, banquets, etc., were present with music meant to be marked.

17. Even if the cue was mistakenly omitted, other alterations to the scene, including the King's use (new to Folio dialogue) of the "harmony" metaphor, suggest that the changes might have been intentional, from instrumental music to political disharmony of a more emotional kind. The action and dialogue take over the musical cue; in Folio *King Lear* it is Cordelia alone who heals her father without the aid of Quarto's "louder the music there." Long comments that the sources for the Simpcoxe episode (e.g., Sir Thomas More's *A dyalogue,* 1529) support Quarto's stage direction, which if accepted, directs the irony "toward religious faith instead of political loyalty," the contrast between the "pious fraud" and *Te Deum Laudamus* severely shaking the King's religious faith (*Histories and Tragedies*, 26). While accepting Quarto stage directions, Long finds its dialogue to be "textually corrupt," supporting his judgment with the King's lines from Folio which are not in Quarto.

18. Urkowitz comments (of 5.2) that "the Quarto shows a political order destroyed by men already reduced to primitive fury and blood-feud while the Folio shows the same order destroyed by men still sensitive to nobility and grace. . . . The Folio appears to develop or integrate images not yet fully formed in the Quarto" which "represents . . . a different but coherent state of composition" of scenes common to both Quarto and Folio, rather than any inconsistency of design between the two versions. Cf. " 'If I mistake in Those Foundations Which I build Upon': Peter Alexander's Textual Analysis of *Henry VI Parts 2 and 3*," *English Literary Renaissance* 18 (1988): 230–56, here 248, 250; and "Good News about Bad Quartos," in *"Bad" Shakespeare*, ed. Maurice Charney (Cranbury, N.J.: Associated University Presses, 1988), 189–206. For a response to Urkowitz's views on the origin, relationship and provenance of "Bad" Quartos and Folio texts, see Irace, *Reforming the "Bad" Quartos*, especially chapters 5, 6, and 7. See also John Jowett's review of Irace's *Reforming the "Bad" Quartos* in *Shakespeare Quarterly* 49 (Cambridge: Cambridge University Press, 1996), 330–31. On the stage directions, Irace (97) argues that key stage directions (those which are nearly identical in Q and F) "were included in segments apparently copied from an edition of the quarto when printing-house compositors set type for the Folio."

19. This sort of timed or delayed effect occurs elsewhere in Shakespearean directions: cf. *Hamlet* "after the which" (Folio), and *Richard II* "when they are set" (Quarto), "then" (Folio), for the ordered entry of the armed combatants to their trial.

20. We might also cite the "hoboyes" in Folio *Titus Andronicus* which introduce the Thyestean banquet (5.3), those which precede the ominous Dumbshow in Folio *Hamlet* (3.2), the "hoboyes" which introduce Duncan to Macbeth's castle and accompany the banquet (1.7), and finally the hautboys ("under the stage") which presage the forsaking of Antony by his genius Hercules (4.3). Long makes the point that "hoboyes" generally introduced a procession, or courses of a feast as perhaps they do in *Macbeth*, and need not have a necessarily ominous or tragic effect (in *Henry VIII* they occur at stately moments); but the contexts in the examples chosen show striking similarity in their potential ironic effect. The affective use of instrumental music in Folio can be posited elsewhere, e.g., "cornets" in *Merchant of Venice*, *All's Well*, *Coriolanus*, and *Henry VIII*; cf. Long's discussion of the psychological effects of music in *Twelfth Night* (1.1) found in *A Study of . . . Seven Comedies*, 164; and in *Measure for Measure* (4.1), *The Final Comedies*, 20–23.

21. Kathleen Irace brought to my attention these differing entries, and I am much indebted to her work for clarifying my own views, particularly chapter 4 "Staging, 70–92. See her discussion of this entry in *Reforming the "Bad" Quartos*, 78.

22. On "music as rhetoric," see chapter one, "The Music of Men's Lives," in Long's *Histories and Tragedies*, (1–16).

23. In "The First Tetralogy" Long describes Shakespeare's music as "both broad and subtle" serving many dramatic purposes, whether to enhance ritual and ceremony with pageantry and color, or simply to accommodate the movement of actors and suggest offstage action, or with rhetorical intent, to offer "a kind of dramatic irony in which the feudal and chivalric ideals suggested by the drum roll, the trumpet flourishes, and the solemn processional measures are pointedly in contrast with the plots and treachery of the selfish and proud barons of England, France, and Burgundy, and to an ineffectual Henry VI." See *Histories and Tragedies*, 17–18.

24. I borrow these terms from Mary Chan; see her *Music in the Theatre of Ben Jonson* (Oxford: Clarendon Press, 1980), especially 1–15.

25. Cf. Long, *Histories and Tragedies*, 27–28.

26. "Sennet" occurs almost exclusively in the Folio texts, and is almost always used for royal entries: Agamemnon, and Macbeth "as King," Henry VIII's consistory, Caesar and Antony to the Triumvirs' "banket." The term is also used twice in *Coriolanus*, in 2.1 for Coriolanus's return to Rome "crown'd with an Oaken Garland," and once again in 2.2 for his formal welcome "in the Capitoll"; there is also one usage in *Julius Caesar* for Caesar's exit early in 1.1. The only Quarto example of "sennet" announces Lear's first entry, and reappears in the altered Folio entry-direction.

27. At his appearance "on the Walles" of Flint Castle (in Folio *Richard II*), Richard Plantagenet is given a "Flourish" and another is sounded when the scene ends with everyone removing to London. Richard has no other royal entry after his defeat, nor does Henry Bolingbroke receive a royal "Flourish" (even "to the Parliament") until the very end of the play in 5.5, immediately after the murder of Richard. The Quarto has only the one "The trumpets sound" as Richard "appeareth on the walls," and thereafter is silent, except for "the musike plaies" as Richard muses "Ha ha keepe time, how sowre sweete Musicke is / When time is broke, and no proportion kept" (I4), a moment echoed in the Folio text.

28. The phrase "Drums and Colours" appears *only* in the Folio texts, right along

with "Drums and Trumpets," a term common in the Quartos, which it frequently replaces; "colours" may signify the ensign or standard of the contestants, or even their heraldic devices. In *King Lear* the differences between the various "colours" can be essential, as R. A. Foakes has shown in his edition. In his note to 5.1.0.1., he comments that "Folio calls for martial drums and *colours*, the standards or flags displaying the emblems of two armies; however the badges of Goneril and Albany might be distinguished from those of Edmund and Regan, both presumably would include some indication that they are British, as distinct from the French forces who enter in 5.2" (Thomas Nelson and Sons, Ltd.: Walton-on-Thames, Surrey, 1997) 357, 362. Cf. also C. Walter Hodges's illustrations for this scene in Hattaway's edition of *3 Henry VI*, 22–23.

29. The proportions are interesting: for Quarto *Henry V*, the ration of directions to lines of text is 1:21, with four percent for music; for Folio, the ratio is 1/21, similar to other Folio plays. Of the 133 directions in Folio *Henry V*, those for music account for about sixteen percent.

30. Sternfeld and Long show that musical terms like "flourish" or "sennet" hide from us a wealth of uniquely different "tunes" or formulae immediately recognizable to a contemporary; there was available for playhouse use a large number of different fanfares and trumpet calls of the period. The sound of the trumpet is described in the dialogue of the plays as "sullen, lusty, brazen, loud, angry, dreadful, hideous, braying." See Long's *Histories and Tragedies*, "Appendices I–V—Military and Ceremonious Music," 269–86; *A Study . . . of Seven Comedies*, "Instrumental Music in Elizabethan Drama" 16–50; and Sternfeld, IX "Instrumental Music: Part Two, 'Stringed versus Wind Instruments,' I. Trumpets," 210–14. How well such music works can be seen in the opening moments of Olivier's 1945 Film of *Henry V* (1.2) where the "Ambassadors of France" enter to a long and articulate flourish rather than to a short blast on the brass so common in many productions. Though a stage direction for a "Flourish" here is not in Quarto or Folio *Henry V*, the dramatic effect is appropriate.

31. Two helpful essays on postmodern, poststructuralist Shakespeare textual criticism (the "authorial," textual multiplicity, and hypertext) are Paul Werstine's "Editing after the End of Editing," in *Shakespeare Studies*, XXIV, ed. J. Leeds Barroll, (Cranbury, New Jersey: Associated University Presses, 1996) 47–54; and "The Problem of Shakespeare's Text(s)," in which Barbara Mowat argues that finding a holograph manuscript would not "umproblematize the text," and that "editorial sacralizing of lost authorial manuscripts has made us frame the problem of Shakespeare's texts incorrectly"; given the "idiosyncrasies of manuscript transmission . . . certainty and authenticity will not be guaranteed at the end of a search for the manuscripts that lie behind those plays," in *Shakespeare Jahrbuch* 132, ed. Wolfgang Weiss, (1996): 26–43. For general surveys, see also "Editions and Textual Studies" in *Shakespeare Survey*, ed. Stanley Wells (Cambridge: Cambridge University Press), especially Volume 48 (1995), by H. R. Woudhuysen 268–78; Volumes 49 (1996) 330–33, 50 (1997) 271–78, 51 (1998) 317–34, with commentary by John Jowett.

"Misconstruing Everything":
Julius Caesar and *Sejanus*

Ian Donaldson

MANY PLAYS OF THE LATE ELIZABETHAN AND EARLY JACOBEAN PERIOD, as Anne Barton has suggestively remarked, seem to be curiously linked one to another, as if caught in a kind of imaginary dialogue or conversation.[1] One play proposes, a second play responds; one piece of dramaturgy provokes another; themes from an earlier drama are elaborated, phrases echoed, ideas rebutted. Shakespeare's *Julius Caesar* and Jonson's *Sejanus* are plays which appear to be joined in a conversation of just this kind, as I shall argue in greater detail in the final section of this paper. The conversation between these plays turns in particular on the uses of Roman history, and the interpretation, more generally, of historical and present events. Both plays are explicitly concerned, moreover, in a seemingly self-reflexive way, with the problem of interpretation itself: each presents hermeneutic riddles, showing events and actions that are in some way catastrophically *misunderstood*. Yet there are stark differences also in the manner in which interpretation is regarded in the two plays: differences which seem, in a larger sense, suggestive of the contrasting methodologies of the two dramatists, and the various styles of interpretation which we as readers might want to bring to an understanding of their texts.

Such has been the interest over recent years in the regulation of literature in early modern England that it is tempting to refer problems of interpretation such as these two plays present to the operation of censorship, and to approach the texts in the manner famously advocated by Annabel Patterson in her influential works *Censorship and Interpretation* and *Reading Between the Lines*. In periods during which censorship is routinely practiced, Patterson argues, writers and readers learn to move by stealth, watching the gaps, listening to the silences, reading between the lines, to detect some contemporary allusion: strategies which may in turn be profitably adopted by modern interpreters. Textual indeterminacy, she suggests, is of special significance in these conditions, lexical and narrative ambiguities becoming "functional," bearing vital, though encrypted, clues to meaning. Textual indeterminacy, in Patterson's view, is largely but not wholly in the control of the writer. It may also be produced by historical accident, for a literary work may come to look topical and allusive through the mere passage of time, as Jonson's *Sejanus,* many years after its first performance, came to look as though it was about the fall of James's favorite, the Duke of Buckingham.[2]

For certain sorts of early modern texts this style of reading is brilliantly suited. For other sorts of texts it may seem less appropriate. The obvious problem is to know when the method should be applied and when it should not. "Reading between the lines" is an exhilarating business, which must nevertheless prompt questions about its own hermeneutic limits. For what can you *not* find when you read "between the lines," and how is this oblique and interlinear mode of reading ultimately to be controlled and validated? When does textual indeterminacy cease being "functional," and how various are the functions it can play? Applied to Jonson's *Sejanus,* such a method of reading seems at once apt and highly suggestive. *Julius Caesar,* on the other hand, seems curiously resistant to approaches of this sort, which seek to understand the play's obscurities by reference to contemporary political events.

1

Until very recent times, *Julius Caesar* was not regarded as a play that needed to be read in relation to contemporary English politics. To an earlier and more humanistically minded generation of commentators, *Julius Caesar* scarcely seemed indeed to be about politics at all; it was concerned basically with questions of human nature, of personalities in friendship and conflict. "Shakespeare's primary interest," wrote M. L. Clarke in his book *The Noblest Roman,* "is in the characters, rather than in their political aims, and it is Brutus's character that determines the outcome" of the play.[3] T. S. Dorsch in the long introduction to his 1955 Arden edition of the play makes no reference to contemporary political events in England, to the possible reasons for Shakespeare's treating this theme at this moment or for his general interest at this time in Roman history, and subsequent editors of the play have largely shared his general assumptions.[4]

Richard Wilson's 1992 monograph on *Julius Caesar* takes an entirely different line.[5] For this new historicist critic, *Julius Caesar* belongs "to the poetics of the post-modern," to the mode of *"faction* or 'fact' as 'fiction.' " Through the semi-transparent veils of ancient Roman history, Shakespeare is dealing, so Wilson argues, with political issues that are very much of his own time, in a manner that Wilson sees as subversive and carnivalesque, threatening to orthodoxy and public order. *Julius Caesar* was one of the first plays to be presented at the newly completed Globe Theatre on the Bankside by Shakespeare's own company, the Lord Chamberlain's Men, in September 1599. In 1599, Richard Wilson recalls, Elizabeth's former favorite the Earl of Essex was beginning the maneuverings for power that were to culminate in his abortive rebellion two years later. In the very month in which *Julius Caesar* was performed, Essex returned from Ireland against orders with two hundred swordsmen to parley with the queen, and after bursting into her bedroom at Nonsuch Palace was placed under immediate arrest. Shakespeare's play, in Wilson's view, offers a dramatic account of the extremely hot topic of armed rebellion against a legitimate ruler.

One of the problems with this kind of reading is that it may seem to work rather too hard to establish particular parallels between theatrical and historical narratives, between Roman and English history. Many of the events to which Wilson wants to relate the play are simply too contemporary to allow even such a rapid writer as Shakespeare sufficient time to pen a dramatic response. It may seem pedantic to point out that Essex did not actually arrive at Nonsuch Palace and break into the queen's bedroom until a week after *Julius Caesar* had opened at the Globe, and that when performances began, he was still in Ireland. "Pedantic," because the concept of textual indeterminacy allows critics to think of social and political events that occurred after, as well as before, the composition of the text in question, rather than of precise historical correspondences, and to show how a play might be *caught up in* the politics of the time. But the excitement of Wilson's case and the plausibility of his claims for the radical and subversive nature of this play do rest in part on his presentation of Shakespeare as a kind of front-line journalist, a Truman Capote of the Elizabethan theatre, dealing with highly topical and volatile political material, with this week's news. The correspondences might seem more compelling, though less dramatic, if put in more general terms. For it is reasonable to say that any play concerned with conspiracy, political ambition, and the assassination of a ruler was bound to be of absorbing interest to audiences in England in the late 1590s, who would no doubt have seen some broad resemblances to their own times in the political uncertainties and jockeyings for power of late Republican Rome. Throughout the last years of Elizabeth's reign there had been a succession of plots, scares, and threats to the life and safety of the queen, whose failure to produce an heir, like Calpurnia's barrenness in Shakespeare's play, deepened public anxiety about the question of political succession. *Julius Caesar* would therefore in all likelihood have seemed an *interesting* play to contemporary audiences in 1599, as Wilson's own account makes abundantly clear. But is it more than that; is it also, as Wilson implies, an allusive and subversive text for its times?

It has been suggested that Shakespeare's turning to Roman history in the latter half of 1599 may have been prompted in part by the ban on the printing of English histories imposed on 1 June 1599. This ban was triggered by the publication, earlier in 1599, of the first part of John Hayward's history of *The Life and Raigne of King Henrie IIII*, with its lavish dedication to the Earl of Essex.[6] Hayward's dedication and his account of the deposition of Richard II were interpreted by the authorities as reflecting directly on the present political situation in England. His book was suppressed, and copies were brought before the Bishop of London and formally burnt. A year later, when Essex himself was on trial, Hayward too was charged, interrogated, and remanded to the Tower where he remained throughout the rest of Elizabeth's reign. The parallel between Elizabeth and Richard was of course a familiar one in the period: the three editions of Shakespeare's play of *Richard II* to be printed in Elizabeth's lifetime all appeared without the deposition scene in Act IV. On 7 February 1601, as is well known, Shakespeare's company, the Lord Chamberlain's Men—the company which had performed *Julius Caesar* in 1599—were paid the sum of 40s by followers of the Earl of Essex in order to stage a play about Richard II; whether it was Shakespeare's play or not we just don't know. This was the very day before Essex led his abortive coup for which he and several of his followers were to be tried and executed. The company were said to be reluctant to perform the play because it was an "old" one. Shakespeare's *Richard II* had been first performed about 1595, and by Elizabethan standards that would probably mean that the play was now "old." But whichever play it was, it obviously had not been written specifically with Essex's rebellion in mind, but had evidently been remembered by Essex's men who plucked it from the archives presumably in the belief that a performance at this critical historical moment would help to arouse public sympathy for the imminent uprising. Here, then, is another case of a play that is *politicized*, so to speak, by events susbequent to its composition—like the case of *Sejanus* already mentioned, and of Voltaire's drama *Brutus*, written (with its companion piece, *La Mort de César*) without particular political intent in the 1730s but later closely identified and embroiled with revolutionary events in Paris during the 1790s.[7]

Did Shakespeare in the latter half of 1599 turn to an episode in Roman history because of the pressures of censorship, and was he attempting, through this more distant historical perspective of ancient Rome, to reflect upon events of his own time? Was he, alternatively, writing a less engaged, less consciously topical piece, like Voltaire's *Brutus* or *La Mort de César*, a play that, with the passage of time and the operation of hindsight, came to look as if it had been topically intended? Does *Julius Caesar* reveal Shakespeare's interest in constitutional issues, or give some indication of his political leanings? These questions may seem to lead too deeply into the forests of intentionalism to be worth pursuing, yet they are questions that are worth pondering, and may be answerable, up to a point, from a reading of the text.

2

It is a commonplace of modern historiography that history never exactly repeats itself and that every historical moment is novel, particular, and unique; that what history ultimately teaches us is, paradoxically, that—so far as direct warnings, examples, and precedents are concerned—history teaches us nothing. From such a philosophical position, *the shape of the past*—while by no means wholly chaotic, being governed by particular causes, and subject to rational analysis—is essentially complex, fluid, and ever-changing, difficult to map, never precisely predictive of the shape of things to come. Renaissance views of history and visions of the past were generally of a very different kind. History was often regarded by Renaissance commentators as a cyclical and exemplary process, moving in patterns that tended to recur and were more amenable to formulaic description. Much the same kind of events, much the same kind of people, it could be assumed, returned from generation to generation, from era to era, and the methodical study of past wars, revolutions, conspiracies, negotiations, systems of government, and individual lives might directly illuminate the dilemmas and decisions of the present.[8]

The writings of Tacitus, who believed that through history one might discover the underlying causes and logic of past events which might be of direct value and application in the present, enjoyed a growing vogue with English readers in the 1590s.[9] Tacitus was read with particular attention by the followers of Essex, and indeed by Essex himself. Richard Grenewey's translation of Tacitus's *Annals*, dedicated significantly to Essex, had been published in 1598 in a double volume along with Sir Henry Savile's translation of Tacitus's *Histories,* which carried a prefatory address "A.B. to the Reader," praising the virtues of Tacitean history. Ben Jonson was later to praise Savile's Tacitean qualities and insight in *Epigram* 95, and to inform William Drummond that "Essex wrote that Epistle or preface before the translation of the last part of Tacitus which is A. B."[10] Jonson retained a strong interest, as Martin Butler has recently suggested, in the ideals of Essex and his circle, as he did also in the writings of Tacitus, on whom he was to draw deeply in *Sejanus*.[11]

Though Shakespeare may also have shared this interest in Tacitus in the late 1590s, *Julius Caesar* is not a strongly Tacitean play in the manner of *Sejanus*, and the views of history which the two plays invite us to take are notably different. Both plays, however, are centrally concerned with questions of interpretation: with how one interprets the past, and the present, and their relationship to one another. At significant moments in *Julius Caesar* the characters themselves ponder what I have called *the shape of the past*, and the ironies and circularities of history. Take this episode in act 5 scene 3, for example, when Cassius finally realizes that he faces defeat on the plains of Philippi at the hands of Mark Antony and his army:

Pindarus	Fly further off, my lord, fly further off!
	Mark Antony is in your tents, my lord.
	Fly, therefore, noble Cassius, fly far off!
Cassius	This hill is far enough. Look, look, Titinius!
	Are those my tents where I perceive the fire?
Titinius	They are, my lord.
	Titinius, if thou lov'st me,
Cassius	Mount thou my horse, and hide thy spurs in him,
	Till he have brought thee up to yonder troops
	And here again, that I may rest assur'd
	Whether yond troops are friend or enemy.
Titinius	I will be here again, even with a thought. [*Exit.*]
Cassius	Go, Pindarus, get higher on that hill;
	My sight was ever thick. Regard Titinius,
	And tell me what thou not'st about the field.
	[*Exit Pindarus.*]
	This day I breathed first. Time is come round,
	And where I did begin, there shall I end.
	My life is run his compass. Sirrah, what news?
Pindarus [*Above.*]	O my lord!

Cassius	What news?
Pindarus	Titinius is enclosed round about
	With horsemen, that make to him on the spur,
	Yet he spurs on. Now, they are almost on him.
	Now, Titinius! now some light. O, he lights too!
	He's ta'en! [*Shout*]
	And hark! they shout for joy.
Cassius	Come down; behold no more.
	O, coward that I am, to live so long,
	To see my best friend ta'en before my face.
	5.3.10–35

The day of Cassius's defeat and death at Philippi is the anniversary of his birth; Cassius has mentioned his birthday once before, and now meditates on the irony inherent in this curious patterning of events: "Time is come around, /And where I did begin, there shall I end."[12] The circle of his life draws tighter, like a noose, like that ring of horsemen enclosing Titinius, marking or appearing to mark the necessary end. And we, as observers of the larger action of the play, can notice other symmetries, other ironies, at this moment. Cassius sends Pindarus his bondsman up the hill to act as a lookout, and report what is happening to Titinius on the plains below: "My sight was ever thick," says Cassius. But it was in fact Cassius's "lean and hungry look," we may remember, that so perturbed Caesar in act 1 (1.2.191); it was Cassius whom Caesar characterized as "a great observer" who "looks / Quite through the deeds of men" (1.2.199–200); it was Cassius who spoke scornfully of the fever that Caesar suffered in Spain, when "that same eye whose bend doth awe the world / Did lose his lustre" (1.2.122–23); Cassius who lectured Brutus, with a skilful metaphor drawn from optics, on the need for seeing at times one's own situation through the eyes of others (1.2.50). But now near the close of the play Cassius admits that he himself is a poor observer, "ever thick" in sight, and, at this crucial moment in a matter of life and death, sends another person, Pindarus, to observe the situation for him, a proxy who fatally *misinterprets* what he sees and hears. For the horsemen that he watches are allies, not adversaries; the shout that is heard is not prompted by the capture of Titinius, but by a shared victory. The great interpretative question that has been the undoing of Caesar—how one distinguishes friends from enemies, how to see which is which—finally defeats Cassius himself.

Those distant shouts resemble the shouts from the Forum that Brutus and Cassius have heard in the second scene of the play, whose significance Casca is later to interpret, as Caesar three times refuses the laurel wreath offered to him by Antony. The laurel is an ambiguous token, both of kingship and of victory; in Shakespeare's account (though not historically) Caesar comes to the Lupercalia fresh from his victory over Pompey's son. How the symbol is now interpreted is therefore of crucial importance. In a wonderful moment of ironic repetition in the fifth act of the play, Titinius comes to the dead Cassius, like Antony to the living Caesar, with a wreath in his hand, wishing to crown him as a victor at Philippi, but finding, like Antony, that wish frustrated. He comes, as it happens, not only too late but also too early, for the battle isn't yet over, and will have eventually a different resolution:

> Why didst thou send me forth, brave Cassius?
> Did I not meet thy friends, and did not they
> Put on my brows this wreath of victory,
> And bid me give it thee? Didst thou not hear their shouts?
> Alas, thou hast misconstrued every thing.
>
> 5.3.80–84

Coming as it does in these final moments of the play, Titinius's anguished phrase seems to reflect on more than this single, disastrous act of misjudgement. Viewed in a longer perspective, Cassius may be thought indeed to have misconstrued *everything*, to have tragically misread the political needs of the times. As so often in *Julius Caesar*, the lines take us to the central difficulty of understanding, of interpreting an historical moment, and the perils of relying on the interpretation of others—as Caesar himself, earlier in the play, has relied on the devious skills of Decius Brutus to interpret Calpurnia's dream:

> This dream is all amiss interpreted;
> It was a vision fair and fortunate:
> Your statue spouting blood in many pipes,
> In which so many smiling Romans bath'd,
> Signifies that from you great Rome shall suck
> Reviving blood, and that great men shall press
> For tinctures, stains, relics, and cognizance.
> This by Calpurnia's dream is signified.
>
> *Caesar*   And this way have you well expounded it.
>
> 2.2.83–91

Julius Caesar is a play of almost Mozartian formal beauty, whose themes and motifs elegantly and hauntingly return, just as its central character returns in a literal sense to haunt his murderers. The final suicides of Cassius and Brutus in the name of liberty and freedom seem ironically to mirror the killing of Caesar in the forum, Cassius covering his face as he falls upon his sword, as we have seen the dying Caesar "in his mantle muffling up his face" (3.2.189) and (earlier still) the conspirators meeting in Brutus's house with hats "plucked about their ears, / And half their faces buried in their cloaks" (2.1.74–75). "O Julius Caesar, thou art mighty yet! / Thy spirit walks abroad, and turns our swords / In our own proper entrails." The formal symmetries of the play carry their own historical implications about political causes and consequences, and what I have called the shape of the past: a past that returns constantly to affect and mock the present.

One might expect this kind of drama to be particularly susceptible to contemporary application. The reason that, in my view, *Julius Caesar* is not to be easily read off in terms of English political developments of the late 1590s is that at the heart of this intricately textured play there are interpretative riddles, mysteries, and misunderstandings of the kind just indicated. These kinds of political reasoning, like the covered face of Caesar and the conspirators, can't quite be seen, and like the conspirators' whisperings of act 2 (2.1.100) and the whisperings in the final act of Brutus to Clitus and Dardanius (5.5.5–6, 8) can't quite be heard. Though the play appears to possess an internal logic from which political truths may be derived, it is tantalizingly difficult to say at last what that logic is. This relative absence of political reasoning within the play sharply delimits any possible sense in which it might be described as "subversive."

Typical of the play's procedures is the crucial soliloquy of Brutus in his orchard at the opening of act 2.

>   It must be by his death: and for my part,
> I know no personal cause to spurn at him,
> But for the general. He would be crown'd:
> How that might change his nature, there's the question.
> It is the bright day that brings forth the adder,
> And that craves wary walking. Crown him?—that;—
> And then, I grant, we put a sting in him,
> That at his will he may do danger with.
> Th'abuse of greatness is when it disjoins
> Remorse from power; and, to speak truth of Caesar,
> I have not known when his affections sway'd
> More than his reason. But 'tis a common proof,
> That lowliness is young ambition's ladder,

> Whereto the climber-upward turns his face;
> But when he once attains the upmost round,
> He then unto the ladder turns his back,
> Looks in the clouds, scorning the base degrees
> By which he did ascend. So Caesar may;
> Then lest he may, prevent. And since the quarrel
> Will bear no colour for the thing he is,
> Fashion it thus: that what he is, augmented,
> Would run to these and these extremities;
> And therefore think him as a serpent's egg,
> Which, hatch'd, would, as his kind, grow mischievous,
> And kill him in the shell.

While bearing all the signals of logical argumentation—"then," "but," "since," "I grant," "there's the question," "therefore"—the speech is fatally undercut by hesitations, generalities, hypotheses, and non sequiturs, revealing a process not of political logic but of mental agitation. Brutus adduces no clear argument for joining the conspirators as he drifts ruminatively towards his startling conclusion: *"kill him in the shell."*

The presence of these qualities might perhaps be explained in terms of Annabel Patterson's principle of linguistic indeterminacy and functional ambiguity. These vaguenesses, these whisperings, it could be argued, serve as indices of what cannot directly be said because of the pressures of censorship: Shakespeare cannot afford to give Brutus a fully articulated, persuasively argued speech in favour of killing a legitimate ruler. But ambiguities, to risk a tautology, may function in more ways than one, and what the play more obviously emphasizes is the exceptional difficulty, in psychological and rational terms, of interpreting political events at moments of turmoil like those depicted. It reminds us repeatedly of the opacity of history, and the difficulty of reading the past as well as the present.

Unlike a play such as Brecht's *Mother Courage,* whose episodic structure reflects the interminable nature of the Thirty Years War, *Julius Caesar* is much concerned with notions of genesis and closure, of where and how political actions originate and find their ultimate endings:

> *Caesar*   What can be avoided
> Whose end is purpos'd by the mighty gods?
> Yet Caesar shall go forth; for these predictions
> Are to the world in general as to Caesar . . .
> It seems to me most strange that men should fear,

> Seeing that death, a necessary end,
> Will come when it will come.
>
> 2.2.26–27, 35–37

The end of Caesar is not of course the end of the play; in various forms, Caesar lives on within this drama, through the words and actions of Antony, and his own ghostly reappearances at Sardis and at Philippi. And while the play itself seems to describe one brief but shapely movement of history from the Lupercalia in 44 B.C. to the Battle of Philippi in 42 B.C., from the hatching of the conspiracy to its logical end with the suicides of the two main conspirators, it is also clear that the story Shakespeare chooses in part to depict has a much longer historical trajectory, completing and complementing the story of the rape of Lucretia, that great foundation myth of the Roman republic that had drawn Shakespeare's attention just a few years earlier. That story has its own ironic progression and symmetry, as I have tried elsewhere to suggest.[13] Tarquin rapes Lucretia after threatening her with a dagger; Lucretia turns the dagger to her own breast, and takes her own life; Lucius Junius Brutus plucks the dagger from Lucretia's body, and swears upon the dagger to drive the Tarquins out of Rome. The final turning of the sword against the original aggressor in this story resembles the final turning of the sword against the conspirators, Cassius and Brutus, in *Julius Caesar*, as time performs its slow and circular pavanne. Taken together, the two stories present an even more intricate pattern of historical consequences that deserves closer analysis than can be given here. The historical Marcus Junius Brutus and his brother Decius Brutus claimed, for convenient political purposes, to be descendants of the (probably mythical) Lucius Junius Brutus, and it is known that Marcus Brutus kept a bust of his alleged ancestor in his house.[14] In Shakespeare's play, Cassius suggests to Cinna (1.3.142) that he throw anonymous letters in through Brutus's window, urging him to join the conspiracy against Caesar, and to set up one letter with wax "Upon old Brutus's statue." Shakespeare got this touch from Plutarch. The trick works precisely. The letter is delivered to Brutus in act 2 as he completes the soliloquy just discussed, shortly before the arrival of the conspirators:

> Shall Rome stand under one man's awe? What, Rome?
> My ancestors did from the streets of Rome
> The Tarquin drive, when he was call'd a king.

Pondering at this crucial moment another critical and seemingly analogous episode in Roman history, Brutus is pushed into political action: the note is enough to clinch his resolve to join the conspirators who are even now arriving. This is a morsel of Roman history that has been, quite literally, lobbed in through the window by political agitators in order to encourage Brutus towards an act of political murder. The moment invites us again to consider the uses and abuses of history, and its bearing upon the present.[15]

3

While Shakespeare repeatedly draws us towards such episodes in which interpretation is at once demanded yet shown often to present formidable difficulties to the interpreter, Ben Jonson seems determined to head his readers away from independent acts of interpretation, insisting on the stable and singular meaning of his texts. Time and again throughout his work Jonson castigates that "solemne vice of interpretation," as Probee calls it in *The Magnetic Lady*, that "deformes the figure of many a fair *Scene*, by drawing it awry; and indeed is the civill murder of most good *Playes*" (Chorus after act 2, 34–36). Those who interpret plays after their own manner, Jonson's Horace declares in *Poetaster*, "are the moths and scarabes of a state; / The bane of empires; and the dregs of court" (4.7.44–45). "Application is now, growne a trade with many," Jonson writes again in the Epistle Dedicatory to *Volpone*, "and there are, that professe to have a key for the decyphering of every thing: but let wise and noble persons take heed how they be too credulous, or give leave to these invading interpreters, to bee over-familiar with their fames, who cunningly, and often, utter their owne virulent malice, under other mens simplest meanings" (65–70). Such protestations are those of a writer who had found himself continually in trouble with the authorities, from the earliest to the latest period of his career (as Shakespeare notably had not): committed to Marshelsea for his part in *The Isle of Dogs*, summoned before the Lord Chief Justice to answer questions about *Poetaster*, hauled before the Privy Council on charges concerning *Sejanus*, imprisoned with Marston and Chapman on account of their jointly written comedy *Eastward Ho!* which made fun of royal policies and Scottish accents, and encountering further troubles with *Epicoene*, *The Devil is an Ass*, and *The Magnetic Lady*. Jonson was a writer who had learnt to defend himself in many ways. Converted to Catholicism in 1598 while in jail on charges of manslaughter after killing a fellow-actor, Jonson was in and out of the consistory courts on further charges of recusancy during the early years of James's reign, and it is reasonable to suppose his knowledge of Jesuitical practices of equivocation: practices which tally precisely with those literary techniques of evasion, subterfuge, and finely calibrated ambiguity that Annabel Patterson describes.[16]

For this reason, Jonson's work often demands to be read with a greater degree of conjecture than generally seems appropriate with the work of Shakespeare. Patterson's own Tacitean reading of *Sejanus*—alert to those "oblique" glances (3.404) which the play at once performs and denies—is thus broadly persuasive in its general interpretative approach, for *Sejanus* appears to be at once a highly cryptic and highly allusive play.[17] From Jonson's *Conversations with Drummond* (235) we know that his adversary the Earl of Northampton brought him before the Privy Council to answer charges "both of popperie and treason" in relation to *Sejanus,* but the precise nature of these charges is far from clear.[18] This is partly because of the compression of Drummond's note, partly because of tantalizing gaps in the Privy Council Register at this point of time, and partly because of a crucial uncertainty about the precise dates of the first performance of *Sejanus*. The major difficulty arises from the fact that the original performing text of *Sejanus* has vanished, having been replaced with the elaborate 1605 Quarto text that has evidently been extensively rewritten partly at least in the interests of Jonson's personal safety and those of his original collaborator. The Quarto is a book of immense typographical elaboration, painstakingly Romanized in appearance, with speeches set out in the manner of classical inscriptions, learned annotations erected like doric columns alongside the heavily architectural slabs of dramatic text, surmounted by monumental running heads. It is a book eloquently and emphatically dissociating itself from the experience of the theatre where the play was evidently first performed with spectacular lack of success.[19]

This heavily-guarded fortress of a play is notoriously difficult of access, but arrows fly from its loopholes, seemingly aimed at living subjects. The opening scene of the play, in which Silius and Sabinus deplore the corruption of court life under Tiberius, and measure their distance from it—"this place is not our sphaer": "We have no shift of faces, no cleft tongues, / No soft, and glutinous bodies, that can sticke, Like snailes, on painted walls," etc., 1.2.7–9—must have had a disconcerting effect upon English Court spectators if the play was performed at Whitehall, as perhaps it was in 1603. Yet Jonson's insistence on the play's authentic adherence to Roman history allows him a measure of protection against charges of open libel. The world that Jonson projects in *Sejanus*—of court flattery and royal favorites, of spies and surveillance and informers, where

Agrippina is "wayted on by envies, as by eyes; / And every second ghest your tables take, / Is a fee'd spie, t'observe who goes, who comes" (2.442–45)—is nevertheless one with which he himself was thoroughly familiar; John Jowett has aptly described the play as "Catholic."[20] This is a society in which it is necessary to speak indirectly, by hints and innuendo; where the meaning of words is constantly turned, as Silius declares, through

> Furious enforcing, most unjust presuming,
> Malicious, and manifold applying,
> Foule wresting, and impossible construction.
>
> 3.227–29

Jonson thus depicts in *Sejanus* a political state not altogether dissimilar from the one in which he himself is currently working. It is tempting to see Arruntius's comment on the arrest, imprisonment, and banishment of Nero, Drusus, and Agrippina as charged with memories of Jonson's own recent brushes with Northampton. On what charge were these three taken? "Treason," replies Laco. And Arruntius responds: "O? / The complement of all accusings? that / Will hit, when all else failes" (4.342–44).

In the third act of *Sejanus*, in what Annabel Patterson has seen as a central and self-referential episode, the historian Cremutius Cordus is arraigned before the Senate, and his books taken off by the lictors to be formally destroyed for supposedly reflecting upon the times.[21] This act of textual and political *misinterpretation* has a wider suggestive power within *Sejanus* that is in some ways comparable to those acts of misinterpretation already examined in *Julius Caesar*. To understand the full significance of this episode in *Sejanus* and the reasons for the burning of Cordus's books, however, it may be helpful to align *Sejanus* more closely with *Julius Caesar,* and to ask if Jonson's play is not offering a deliberate response to the earlier and seemingly more successful drama of his great friend and rival.[22]

4

What kind of "conversation" was going on between Shakespeare and Jonson on the topic of Roman history, and how, if at all, are their Roman plays linked? *Julius Caesar* (1599), *Sejanus* (1603–4), and *Catiline* (1611) were all performed by the same company, the Lord Chamberlain's Men (known after 1603 as the King's Men). Burbage and several of his colleagues acted in two and probably all three of these plays. Shakespeare himself performed in *Sejanus*, probably in the role of the Emperor Tiberius. Jonson's tragedy would have been unavoidably in Shakespeare's mind as he went on to write his other Roman plays, *Antony and Cleopatra* (1606–7) and *Coriolanus* (1607–8); Jonson in turn evidently knew *Julius Caesar* very well. Shakespeare's play was apparently popular in the theatre,[23] and would have been just as centrally in Jonson's mind as he sat down to compose his two major Roman tragedies. As early as 1599—the very year in which *Julius Caesar* was performed—we find Jonson in *Every Man Out of his Humour* gently mocking a couple of lines from Antony's Forum speech—"O judgement! thou art fled to brutish beasts, / And men have lost their reason" (3.2.106–7): *"Reason long since is fled to animals,* you know," says one clown knowingly to another in Jonson's play (3.4.33). Shakespeare's lines were evidently familiar enough to parody in this way, and the half-quotation signals Jonson's awareness of the play's popularity. Later in the same comedy when the garrulous Carlo Buffone has his lips forcibly sealed up with wax, his last intelligible words are *Et tu Brute!* (5.6.79)—already obviously a familiar, burlesquable cry at critical moments of this kind.

Some lines attributed to Caesar himself just before his assassination in Shakespeare's play figured centrally and puzzlingly in Jonson's notorious verdict in his commonplace book, *Discoveries,* about the nature of Shakespeare's genius and shortcomings.

> *I remember,* the Players have often mentioned it as an honour to *Shakespeare,* that in his writing, (whatsoever he penn'd) hee never blotted out line. My answer hath beene, Would he had blotted a thousand. Which they thought a malevolent speech. I had not told posterity this, but for their ignorance, who chose that circumstance to commend their friend by, wherein hee most faulted. And to justifie mine owne candor (for I lov'd the man, and doe honour his memory (on this side Idolatry) as much as any.) Hee was (indeed) honest, and of an open, and free nature: had an excellent *Phantsie,* brave notions, and gentle expressions: wherein hee flow'd with that facility, that sometime it was necessary he should be stop'd: *Sufflaminandus erat,* as *Augustus* said of *Haterius.* His wit was in his owne power; would the rule of it had beene so too. Many times hee fell into those things, could not escape laughter: As when he said in the person of *Caesar,* one speaking to him; *Caesar, thou dost me wrong.* Hee replyed: *Caesar did never wrong, but with just cause;* and such like; which were ridiculous. But hee redeemed his vices, with his vertues. There was ever more in him to be praysed, then to be pardoned. (647–68)

The particular example which Jonson cites of Shakespeare's carelessness as a writer has caused perplexity, for nowhere in the earliest text (the 1623 Folio) of Shakespeare's play is Caesar made to say, "Caesar did never wrong, but with just cause." In such an important critique, Jonson could surely not have got the line wrong? Dover Wilson many years ago posited an ingenious solution to this problem: when helping to put together the 1623 Folio, Jonson took the liberty of correcting the line which he pedantically regarded as a solecism. The players, however, continued to use the earlier version of the line, with which they were familiar; and Jonson—galled by the continuing popularity of Shakespeare's work—accordingly went on mocking it, as he does again in *The Staple of News* in 1626, three years after the appearance of the First Folio (*"Cry you mercy, you never did wrong, but with just cause,"* Induction, 36–37).[24] Yet this explanation seems to rely all too heavily on the long-exploded myth of Jonson's malignity towards his great rival, and of his grammatical pedantry. It is more plausible to conjecture that Jonson's point was not primarily linguistic, nor driven by rancour, and that his objection was rather to the political absurdity of the formula "Caesar did never wrong, but with just cause," which he may have seen as a central constitutional proposition within Shakespeare's play.

Certainly in his two Roman plays Jonson takes pains to present Julius Caesar in a far more critical light than is ever shed upon him in Shakespeare's play, and his characterization may well have been affected by the popularity of Shakespeare's play. In *Catiline*, which depicts events occurring in 65 B.C.—twenty-odd years before the assassination of Julius Caesar which Shakespeare dramatizes—Jonson goes so far as to present a younger Julius Caesar who is actually involved in the Catilinarian conspiracy. During Cicero's long indictment speeches in the Senate during the fourth act of the play, Caesar is observed muttering contemptuous asides about Cicero—"cunning artificer!"—and after Catiline's indictment pleads ineffectually for the banishment of the conspirators rather than their death. When Cato and Quintus press for the indictment of Caesar himself, Cicero refuses their request, arguing that the evidence against Caesar is dubious and insufficient. Jonson does not want us, as audience, to conclude, however, that Caesar's complicity was ever in doubt, for the play has already shown his deep collusion with the conspirators.

Jonson's picture of Julius Caesar is very different from the admiring account given by Sallust, and from the account given by, for example, Bacon in his essay "Of Tribute."[25] It presents a remarkable reversal of the by now familiar narrative pattern of Shakespeare's play, in which Julius Caesar is sabotaged and struck down by conspirators. In Jonson's play Caesar is himself presented as a conspirator, and a clear enemy of the Roman state. His final assassination may have seemed to Jonson poetically and politically deserved.

In *Sejanus,* Jonson dramatized events occuring sixty or seventy years after the assassination of Julius Caesar, shifting from the last days of the republic as depicted by Shakespeare to the early years of the Roman empire. The emperor Tiberius is a more sinister, remote, and corrupt ruler than Shakespeare's Julius Caesar, and Rome has slid into a condition of graver degeneracy, to which Jonson offers no obvious political solution other than patient stoicism and personal moral integrity. When Jonson introduces the character of Cremutius Cordus who has been writing the annals of an earlier period of Rome's history, Sabinus and Arruntius observe his entry and comment on the differences between the present time, and the earlier age which Cordus chronicles, when 'god-like CATO' 'durst be good':

> When CAESAR durst be evill; and had power,
> As not to live his slave, to dye his master.
> > Or where the constant BRUTUS, that (being proofe
> > Against all charme of benefits) did strike
> > So brave a blow into the monsters heart
> > That sought unkindly to captive his countrie?
> > O, they are fled the light.
>
> 1.90–97

This account of Caesar's assassination differs dramatically from that of Shakespeare. Jonson's Julius Caesar is presented unequivocally as "evill," as a "monster," while Brutus—the gentle waverer of Shakespeare's play—is "constant," "proofe / Against all charme of benefits" (i.e., uncorruptible by any thoughts of personal advancement). So, far from being a pawn in the hands of Cassius or of Antony, Brutus is now commemorated and mourned as one of the "mightie spirits" in Rome's historic past (1.98), whose presence in modern times is dearly craved. As for Cassius, the "lean and hungry" political opportunist of Shakespeare's play, he now emerges as another national hero, "*Brave* CASSIUS . . . *last of all that race*" (1.104).

It is precisely on account of these notably un-Shakespearian sentiments that the writings of Cremutius Cordus are finally seized and burnt:

> *Natta*   Comparing men,
> And times, thou praysest BRUTUS, and affirm'st
> That CASSIUS was last of all the *Romanes.*
> *Cotta* How! what are we then?

>
> Varro   What is CAESAR? nothing?
> Afer   My lords, this strikes at every *Romanes* private,
>   In whom raignes gentrie, and estate of spirit,
>   To have a BRUTUS brought in paralell,
>   A parricide, an enemie to his countrie,
>   Rank'd, and preferr'd to any reall worth
>   That *Rome* now holds. . . .
>   CAESAR, if CASSIUS were the last of *Romanes*,
>   Thou hast no name.
>
>   3.390–99, 405–6

The view of late Republican Roman history which the scene (like the play more generally) offers is in marked contrast to that in *Julius Caesar*. So too, more fundamentally, is Jonson's vision of how such crucial acts of political misconstruction occur in the first place: of how history happens. In *Sejanus* the available choices are starkly those between moral and political "good" or "evil." Acts of misinterpretation, such as those made by Cremutius Cordus" accusers as they read his annals, derive from wickedness or plain stupidity. Misinterpretation in *Julius Caesar* occurs in simpler and more innocent ways, in which we as audience are often implicated. A shout or gesture or a dream is honestly misunderstood. The past, like the present, retains its hermeneutic puzzles, and its shape, though often glimpsed, is never perfectly understood.

Notes

    1. Anne Barton, *Essays, Mainly Shakespearean* (Cambridge: Cambridge University Press, 1996), 231–32.

    2. Annabel Patterson, *Censorship and Interpretation: The Conditions of Writing and Reading in Early Modern England* (Madison, Wisc.: University of Wisconsin Press, 1984); *Reading Between the Lines* (Madison, Wisc.: University of Wisconsin Press, 1993). There is no agreed view as to how oppressive censorship was, or was perceived to be, in late Tudor/early Stuart England. In Christopher Hill's opinion, Patterson underestimates its severity (*Literature and History*, 12 [1986]; "Censorship and English Literature," *The Collected Essays of Christopher Hill*, [Amherst: University of Massachusetts Press, 1986], 1:32–71). In that of Blair Worden, both Hill and Patterson tend to exaggerate its effects: see A. B. Worden, "Literature and Political Censorship in Early Modern England," in *Too Mighty to be Free: Censorship and the Press in Britain and the Netherlands*, ed. A. C. Duke and C. A. Tamse (Zutphen: De Walburg Pers, 1987), 45–62. A highly selective list of recent discussions of this topic must include the following: Richard Burt, *Licensed by Authority: Ben Jonson and the Discourses of Censorship* (Ithaca, N.Y.: Cornell University Press, 1993); Martin Butler, *Theatre and Crisis 1632–1642* (Cambridge: Cambridge University Press, 1984); Janet Clare, *"Art Made Tongue-Tied by Authority": Elizabethan and Jacobean Dramatic Censorship* (Manchester: Manchester University Press, 1990); Cyndia Susan Clegg, *Press*

Censorship in Elizabethan England (Cambridge: Cambridge University Press, 1997); Richard Dutton, *Mastering the Revels: The Regulation of English Renaissance Drama* (Iowa City: University of Iowa Press, 1991); Philip J. Finkelpearl, " 'The Comedians' Liberty': Censorship of the Jacobean Stage Reconsidered," *English Literary Renaissance*, 16 (1986): 123–38; Margot Heinemann, *Puritanism and Theatre: Thomas Middleton and Opposition Drama Under the Early Stuarts* (Cambridge: Cambridge University Press, 1980); Jerzy Limon, *Dangerous Matter: English Drama and Politics in 1623/4* (Cambridge: Cambridge University Press, 1986); William W. E. Slights, *Ben Jonson and the Art of Secrecy* (Toronto: University of Toronto Press, 1994); and Richard Wilson, "The Kindly Ones: The Death of the Author in Shakespearean Athens," in *Literature and Censorship,* ed. Nigel Smith, *Essays and Studies* (1993).

3. M. L. Clarke, *The Noblest Roman: Marcus Brutus and his Reputation* (Ithaca, N.Y.: Cornell University Press, 1981), 121.

4. T. S. Dorsch, ed., *Julius Caesar* (London: Methuen & Co., Ltd, 1955); all quotations are from this edition.

5. Richard Wilson, *Shakespeare: "Julius Caesar,"* Penguin Critical Studies (1992). For another and very different attempt to read *Julius Caesar* in relation to contemporary events, see Steve Sohmer, *Shakespeare's Mystery Play: The Opening of the Globe Theatre 1599* (Manchester: Manchester University Press, 1999).

6. G. B. Harrison, "Books and Readers," *The Library,* 4th series, xiv (1933): 1–33, especially 15; cf. Patterson, *Censorship and Interpretation,* 47; Anne Barton, *Ben Jonson: Dramatist* (Cambridge: Cambridge University Press, 1984), 338; John Hayward, *The Life and Raigne of King Henrie IIII, the first and second parts,* ed. John J. Manning (London: University College, London, 1991).

7. See Peter Ure's introduction to his Arden edition of *Richard II* (London: Methuen & Co., Ltd., 1956); R. S. Ridgway, *Voltaire and Sensibility* (London: Methuen & Co., Ltd., 1973), 113–17; Robert L. Herbert, *David, Voltaire, "Brutus," and the French Revolution* (London: Methuen & Co., 1972).

8. D. R. Woolf, *The Idea of History in Early Modern England* (Toronto: University of Toronto Press, 1990).

9. Malcolm Smuts, "Court-Centred Politics and the Uses of Roman History, c. 1590–1630," in *Culture and Politics in Early Stuart England,* ed. Kevin Sharpe and Peter Lake (Stanford: Stanford University Press, 1994), 21–45; Ronald Mellor, *Tacitus* (New York: Routledge, 1993); Worden, "Literature and Political Censorship in Early Modern England," 58.

10. *Conversations with Drummond,* lines 368–69, in C. H. Herford and Percy and Evelyn Simpson, *Ben Jonson,* 11 vols. (Oxford: Clarendon Press, 1925–52), 1:142; i/j and u/v spellings regularized. All quotations are from this edition.

11. Martin Butler, " 'Servant, but not Slave': Ben Jonson at the Jacobean Court," *Proceedings of the British Academy,* 90 (1995), 65–93. I have benefited also from Blair Worden's "Politics in *Catiline*: Jonson and his Sources," in *Re-presenting Ben Jonson: Text, History, Performance,* ed. Martin Butler (New York: St. Martin's Press, 1999), 152–73, and the same author's "Ben Jonson's Tragedies: Ancient Rome and Modern England" (unpublished ms).

12. Shakespeare himself is curiously imagined to have been born and died on the same day, though the precise day of his birth is in fact unknown. Such symmetry was admired at the time. Cf. Dekker's account of Queen Elizabeth, who "came in with the fall of the leafe, and went away in the Spring: her life (which was dedicated to Virginitie) both beginning & closing up a miraculous Mayden circle: for she was borne upon a Lady Eve, and died upon a Lady Eve," *The Plague Pamphlets of Thomas Dekker,* ed. F. P. Wilson (Oxford: Clarendon Press, 1925), 17. Robert Ferrar similarly

admired the (now disputed) fact that Kenelm Digby's birthday, victory at Scandaroon, and death all fell on the same day of the year; see R. T. Peterson, *Sir Kenelm Digby: The Ornament of England 1603–1665* (London: J. Cape, 1956), 328.

13. Ian Donaldson, *The Rapes of Lucretia: A Myth and its Transformations* (Oxford: Clarendon Press, 1982).

14. Cicero, *Letters to Atticus*, xiii.40; *Philippic*, ii.26.

15. The example of the past is similarly invoked at other points of the play: e.g., by Cassius at 1.1.80–82 ("for Romans now / Have thews and limbs like to their ancestors; / But woe the while! our fathers' minds are dead," etc.) and by Portia, speaking of her ancestry, 2.1.291.

16. On Jonson and equivocation, see Ian Donaldson, *Jonson's Magic Houses: Essays in Interpretation* (Oxford: Clarendon Press, 1997), ch. 4.

17. Patterson, *Censorship and Interpretation*, 57–66.

18. The evidence is examined by Philip Ayres in the introduction to his Revels edition of *Sejanus His Fall* (Manchester: Manchester University Press, 1990) and by Richard Dutton, *Mastering the Revels*, esp. 10–14.

19. See John Jowett, " 'Fall before this Booke': The 1605 Quarto of *Sejanus*," in *TEXT, Transactions of the Society for Textual Scholarship*, 4 (1988): 279–95.

20. Jowett, " 'Fall before this Booke,' " 291–92.

21. See also Donaldson, *Jonson's Magic Houses*, ch. 12.

22. The two plays have been discussed together, though in very different ways, by Antony Miller, "The Roman State in *Julius Caesar* and *Sejanus*," in *Jonson and Shakespeare*, ed. Ian Donaldson (Atlantic Highlands, N.J.: Humanities Press, 1983), 179–201, and Edward Pechter, "*Julius Caesar* and *Sejanus*: Roman politics, inner selves, and the powers of the theatre," in *Shakespeare and his Contemporaries: Essays in Comparison*, ed. E. A. J. Honigmann (Manchester: Manchester University Press, 1986), 60–78. Anne Barton has wondered whether Shakespeare may not have collaborated with Jonson in the writing of *Sejanus*: see her *Ben Jonson Dramatist*, 93–94.

23. As Leonard Digges's well-known verses prefixed to John Benson's 1640 edition of Shakespeare's *Poems* suggests.

24. J. Dover Wilson, "Ben Jonson and *Julius Caesar*," *Shakespeare Survey*, 2 (1949): 36–43.

25. *Francis Bacon*, ed. Brian Vickers, (Oxford: Oxford University Press, 1996), 26–28. Plutarch gives a hint of Caesar's involvement in the Catilinarian conspiracy, which Jonson develops and Shakespeare chooses to ignore: see *Shakespeare's Plutarch*, ed. T. J. B. Spencer (Harmondsworth, Middlesex: Penguin Books, 1964), 27. Machiavelli in the *Discourses* (i.10) had remarked that Caesar's power was so great in his lifetime that no one dared to criticize him.

Standing Back from Tragedy: Three Detachable Scenes

ALEXANDER LEGGATT

IN 5.1 OF *TITUS ANDRONICUS*, AARON THE MOOR, UNDER QUESTIONING BY Lucius, recounts the action from his own point of view:

> I played the cheater for thy father's hand,
> And when I had it, drew myself apart
> And almost broke my heart with extreme laughter.
> I pried me through the crevice of a wall
> When, for his hand, he had his two sons' heads,
> Beheld his tears, and laughed so heartily
> That both mine eyes were rainy like to his....
>
> (5.1.111–17)[1]

Seen through Aaron's wall, the tragedy, as in *A Midsummer Night's Dream*, becomes a comedy, and tears of grief are countered by tears of laughter. This cruel detachment is Aaron's standard attitude throughout the play, but it also reminds us how easily a tragic action can come to seem ludicrous if seen from a different angle of vision, just as a film, however serious, becomes farcical if speeded up.

Performances of tragedy skirt the edge of laughter, and while there are many moments particularly in Shakespearian tragedy when laughter is legitimate, when indeed the text invites it, laughter in the wrong place is an embarrassment, a sign that the actors (or the audience, or both) have failed. This problem haunts *Titus Andronicus* in particular. Extravagant and grotesque, it constantly flirts with the ludicrous, and its stage history in the modern period is in part a story of the efforts of actors and directors to control the laughter, either by suppressing it or by finding moments to release it without doing damage.[2] Whether this was a problem for the play's contemporaries is by no means clear. Ben Jonson's sardonic reference in the Induction to *Bartholomew Fair* to a taste for *Titus Andronicus* as a sign that one is hopelessly out of date merely shows that the play, once popular, is now (in Jonson's eyes at least) passé. *The Span-*

ish Tragedy, which *Titus* seems to be trying to outdo, became the butt of jokes, but these, like *Casablanca* jokes for the modern filmgoer, play on the familiarity of certain lines in a kind of backhanded tribute to an entertainment at once old-fashioned and fondly remembered. Whatever a modern audience might do, we cannot be sure that the first audience laughed like Aaron when Hieronimo bit out his tongue or Titus chopped off his hand.

But Aaron's account of his own laughter shows the possibility is there, and it may be that the play's creator, looking back at his own work—from what distance we cannot be sure, but it might have been years—saw that possibility himself. The Folio text adds a new scene, 3.2, commonly called the fly-killing scene from its most striking incident. This scene is at once a new contribution to the ongoing action, or rather a new interruption of it, and a retrospective commentary on the play as a whole. It takes its cue from Aaron's boast, following his account of his laughter, "I have done a thousand dreadful things / As willingly as one would kill a fly" (5.1.141–42). Marcus does just that, as casually as Aaron commits his crimes, but he is not allowed to get away with it.

Titus's first reaction to his brother's deed is outrage: "Mine eyes are cloyed with view of tyranny" (3.2.55). Having been through the killings of Alarbus, Mutius, and Bassianus, the rape and mutilation of Lavinia, the self-mutilation of Titus, and the judicial murders of Martius and Quintus, the audience even at this halfway point may be starting to feel the same way. This is a world in which even a fly is not safe. Piling on cruelty, the play has also piled on grief, family grief in particular. Tamora weeps for Alarbus, Titus weeps for Martius and Quintus, and the surviving Andronici gather about Lavinia in protracted, helpless laments. And so Titus's imagination gives the fly a mourning family. Marcus's mild, reasonable "Alas, my lord, I have but killed a fly" triggers an explosion:

> 'But'? How if that fly had a father and mother?
> How would he hang his slender gilded wings
> And buzz lamenting doings in the air!
>
> (3.2.59–62)[3]

Marcus has the answer. In the circling action of revenge tragedy, the roles of victim and assailant are easily conflated. And so the fly, seemingly an innocent victim, "Poor harmless fly" (3.2.63), becomes in Marcus's words "a black ill-favoured fly, / Like to the Empress' Moor. Therefore I killed him" (3.2.66–67). Titus's first reaction, "O, O, O!" (3.2.68) is an open invitation to the actor: anything from a huge cry of rage to a croon of recognition (the sort of noise Eccles used to make on *The Goon Show*) seems possible. He redefines Marcus's act of random violence as "a charitable deed" and commands:

> Give me thy knife. I will insult on him,
> Flattering myself as if it were the Moor
> Come hither purposely to poison me.—
> There's for thyself, and that's for Tamora!
> [*He takes the knife and strikes.*]
> Ah, sirrah!
>
> (3.2.71–75)

His words suggest a rapid series of repeated blows, in anticipation of the finale in which three characters, Tamora, Titus and Saturninus, are despatched in four lines.

With Titus, as with Hieronimo and Hamlet, there is always a question as to how mad he really is. When they come to him disguised as Revenge, Rape, and Murder, Tamora and her sons misread him, and pay the price. What looks like demented hallucination can be bitterly sane irony; what looks like a loss of grip on reality can be critical detachment from it, leading to penetrating insight. We touch on this possibility when Titus, his violence against the fly exhausted, ends with something like a shrug:

> Yet I think we are not brought so low
> But that between us we can kill a fly
> That comes in likeness of a coal black Moor.
>
> (3.2.76–78)

Marcus, as so often, is one step behind his brother, seeing only hallucination: "Alas, poor man! Grief has so wrought on him / He takes false shadows for true substances" (3.2.79–80). But it may be that Titus, knowing perfectly well what he is doing, has been acting out his sense of helplessness, dramatizing the fall of the Andronici with sardonic irony: once a great power in Rome, leading warriors of the Empire, they are reduced to killing a fly.

The fly-killing belongs to a long literary tradition, the grand treatment of a trivial subject: the pseudo-Homeric battle of the frogs and mice, Donne's flea, the rape of the lock. For the play's most recent editor, Jonathan Bate, it is a key passage, and provides the conclusion to his Introduction. Having argued that in his grief for the fly "Titus becomes a human being," he goes on, "But wait: the tragic empathy here is with a fly. Is this an extreme instance of the 'special providence in the fall of a sparrow' cited by Jesus and Hamlet? Or is it a glorious comic parody of tragic empathy? I suspect it is both, and in that lies the greatness of *Titus Andronicus.*"[4]

Let us take the comedy first. Arguably, the two key motives of the play are grief and revenge. The fly-killing scene subjects them both to mock-heroic treatment, showing both grief and revenge as it were through Aaron's wall, deeply serious to those involved in them, ludicrous to us as we watch. For the actors this scene can function as a safety valve, letting the audience release its impulse to laugh where such laughter is legitimate, thus reducing the possibility of unwanted laughter elsewhere. It seems to have functioned this way in Deborah Warner's much-praised 1987 production for the Royal Shakespeare Company.[5] In a production I took part in at the University of Toronto in 1985, the actors used the fly scene deliberately to drain away laughter, laying special emphasis on its comedy at performances where the audience seemed particularly inclined to laugh.

Yet while the scene reflects the play's issues in comically miniaturized form, by that very device it distills them, conveying their essence. Titus's massive swing from grief to murderous rage reflects the general extremity of his reactions, and the feeling that it is all too much is a feeling the play elsewhere conveys quite seriously: no one should suffer this much, no one should kill so pitilessly. Behind the seeming pleasure of the world is lurking violence. The fly who, "with his pretty buzzing melody / Came here to make us merry" (3.2.64–65), turns out to be an emissary of evil, just as the pastime of the emperor's hunt conceals a more terrible hunting and the final banquet, whose overt intent is hospitality and peacemaking, collapses into cannibalism and butchery. No living thing is safe and no occasion is innocent.

As a retrospective on the play, placed not at the end but at the centre, 3.2 also gives the sharpest reflection on the central problem of Lavinia. Losing her tongue and her hands, Lavinia has lost the ordinary capacity for language that we take for granted, and those who can still speak find their own language tainted by her loss. Rebuking Titus for urging Lavinia to kill herself, Marcus uses a perfectly ordinary turn of phrase: "Teach her not thus to lay / Such violent hands upon her life" (3.2.21–22) only to have Titus retort that the expression he has used is now unusable: "What violent hands can she lay on her life?" (3.2.25). Titus himself offers to repair her loss of language by speaking for her, but this reveals an insoluble problem:

> Hark, Marcus, what she says;
> I can interpret all her martyred signs.
> She says she drinks no other drink but tears,
> Brewed with her sorrow, mashed upon her cheeks.
> Speechless complainer, I will learn thy thought;
> In thy dumb action I will be as perfect
> As begging hermits in their holy prayers.
> Thou shalt not sigh, nor hold thy stumps to heaven,
> Nor wink, nor nod, nor kneel, nor make a sign,
> But I of these will wrest an alphabet
> And by still practice learn to know thy meaning.
>
> (3.2.35–45)

As though aware that his first attempt at translation is impossibly detailed, ludicrously overconfident, Titus pulls back and promises only that he *will* learn. But in speaking for Lavinia, will he be conveying her thoughts, or imposing his? At the end of 3.1, in one of the play's most bizarre moments, he put his hand in her mouth; now will he put words in her mouth? "Wrest an alphabet" implies forcing: however sympathetic his intentions, he will coerce her thoughts as Chiron and Demetrius coerced her body.

The problems of language surrounding Lavinia have been acted out from the rape scene onwards. But 3.2 does not just act them out, it reflects on them and comments on the problems more explicitly than any other scene. It is as though Shakespeare, from whatever distance lies between this scene and the original play, is reflecting on what he has done, here with more unqualified seriousness than in the fly episode. And the reflection has a similar tendency: as pity and revenge become absurd, so does language, its basic function of communication hopelessly compromised as one person has to speak for two.

Theatrically the reflection is also a digression, a pause in the action. In the Quarto version of the play, which lacks this scene, we go straight from the family's vow of revenge to their first practical move as Lavinia enters pursuing young Lucius, the latter bearing the books Lavinia will use to name her assailants. We go straight from the vow of revenge to the first gathering of information. But 3.2 cuts across this movement with a scene that lies outside the story proper, and its opening line "So, so. Now sit" calls for a pause in the play's forward movement, a chance to sit (literally) and reflect. It is a surprise after 3.1, and awkwardly joined to 4.1. As Bate points out, it "requires a group of characters to go offstage and come straight back, something that Shakespeare nearly always avoided."[6] Continuity goes awry as Titus ends 3.2 by inviting Lavinia and young Lucius to join him in his closet, where he will read to them, while 4.1 opens with Lucius carrying books, Lavinia pursuing him, and Titus and Marcus entering separately. The books suggest a link which the arrangement of the characters' entrances breaks. Though even heavily cut productions of *Titus* generally use 3.2, it was cut in Edward Ravenscroft's Restoration version, and in a 1991 Cambridge production where the effect, Bate reports, was a gain in pace.[7] In presenting it as a reflection on the play's key issues, I have implicitly argued for its inclusion. But the play originally did without it, and there may be theatrical reasons for cutting it.

It is one of those passages in Shakespeare that are paradoxically both important and disposable. The Folio *King Lear* does without the mad trial, and if a hypothetical text of *Hamlet* lacking "To be or not to be" were presented to a hypothetical reader with no knowledge of the play or the speech's reputation, such a reader would not notice anything was missing. In such a text the dramatic movement would be so logical as not to require comment: Claudius and Polonius hide, Ophelia remains as decoy, Hamlet enters and begins a conversation with her. It is "To be or not to be" that poses a theatrical problem: what is Ophelia to do while Hamlet soliloquizes? Like the fly-killing scene and the mad trial, the soliloquy reflects on the action (rather distantly, in this case) while contributing nothing to its forward movement. "To be or not to be" is there in every version (though differently placed in the First Quarto), but the mad trial may be an authorial cut as the fly scene is likely an authorial addition. The scene that stands back from tragedy is not so much a device Shakespeare is committed to as a device he experiments with.

We do not normally think of the Deposition scene in *Richard II* in these terms. Its absence in the early Quartos is regularly attributed to censorship, and if that conventional wisdom is correct it has no place in this discussion. David M. Bergeron, however, has argued against the conventional wisdom, insisting that there is no ironclad evidence for censorship, that *Richard II* is perfectly playable without the scene, and that it may be a late addition, possibly not written until 1601 or later.[8] He demonstrates not so much that the censorship theory is wrong as that it is not inescapable and the matter should be left open. In that spirit we can consider the possibility that the Deposition scene, like the fly-killing scene, is a reflection on the action added at a later date, at whatever cost to dramatic momentum. Without it, we go straight from Bolingbroke's ascent of the throne to the hatching of the Abbot's counterplot, usurpation triggering an immediate countermove. Without it, the weight of protest shifts to Carlisle, whose denunciation of the usurpation thereby looms much larger (4.1.115–50). With that speech thus emphasized, we may notice more readily how it rewrites the dying Gaunt's vision of England, the crusading nation leaving the infidels at peace as Englishmen fight each other and Eden becomes Golgotha. The Flint Castle scene (3.3) becomes Richard's greatest public moment: his major confrontation with his challenger, his most extended public lament. He then disappears until 5.1, anticipating the long disappearances of later tragic heroes like Hamlet, Lear, and Macbeth (the so-called "Burbage tea break"). Richard's private meeting with his Queen, his first appearance after a long gap, is thrown into high relief instead of appearing, as it does in the familiar text, a somewhat anticlimactic coda to the Deposition. Overall the action is faster, and the sense that Richard is not just deposed but hidden away in the hope that he will be forgotten is stronger. This in turn makes his ability to haunt his successor more striking. In short, without the Deposition scene the play is perfectly workable, and there are some interesting differences of emphasis when we compare this version with the familiar text.

What the Deposition scene adds is what the fly-killing scene adds: a chance to stop the flow of the action and contemplate its significance. Once again the contemplation uncovers absurdity. Pity and revenge seem meaningless when directed against a fly. Passed from hand to hand, the crown of England becomes meaningless, and Bolingbroke's triumph becomes empty: the symbol that makes him king is a symbol that has lost its power. When Richard holds out the crown with the invitation, "Here, cousin, seize the crown" (4.1.182), he is tempting Bolingbroke to reveal the significance of his usurpation by the shocking gesture of grabbing at the symbol as though it were a material object he wanted to steal. "Seize" conveys the violence behind the act. At the same time there is a casualness in Richard's invitation that trivializes the event. The fact that Richard has to repeat his command, "Here, cousin" (4.1.183), like telling a recalcitrant dog to fetch, suggests that Bolingbroke, knowing quite well what game Richard is playing, hestitates. When Richard poses himself and Bolingbroke each with a hand on the crown, he creates a stage picture at once significant and absurd: two bare-headed men, each claiming to be king, and an empty crown between them.[9] The symmetry of the picture triggers Richard's comparison of himself and Bolingbroke to two buckets in a well, a comparison that devalues Bolingbroke's victory. He has risen because he is empty: "The emptier ever dancing in the air" (4.1.187). If Bolingbroke seems weightless, the crown is *mere* weight. At some point Richard seems to have put it back on his own head; he removes it with the words, "I give this heavy weight from off my head" (4.1.205). Behind the obvious reference to the burden of kingship is a more subversive thought: the crown, removed from its true owner, is no longer a crown, merely a nameless thing. It has size and weight but no significance. Bolingbroke's act, by its very nature, has drained itself of meaning: he has not won the kingship, because there is no kingship to win.

As the crown loses its identity, so does Richard. His smashing of the mirror, like Titus's attack on the fly, is a sudden, surprising burst of violence with a touch of the bizarre. Why take it out on a fly? Why take it out on a mirror? Richard claims he is breaking the mirror because it fails to reflect his sorrows truly; the only way to make it do that is to shatter it: "A brittle glory shineth in this face—/ As brittle as the glory is the face" (4.1.288–89). He acts out the loss of identity he has formulated in words earlier in the scene:

> I have no name, no title,
> No, not that name was given me at the font,
> But 'tis usurped. Alack the heavy day,
> That I have worn so many winters out
> And know not now what name to call myself!
> (4.1.256–70)

It is at the end of this speech, having compared himself to a melting snowman, that Richard calls for a mirror "That it may show me what a face I have, / Since it is bankrupt of his majesty" (4.1.267–68), to see in effect if he has any identity left. Identity is as crucial for this play as language is for *Titus*; in each case we confront the nightmare of seeing a central value emptied out.

Without the Deposition scene, *Richard II* shows a transfer of power, and gives us plenty of reason to see the transfer as illegitimate (however justified in practical terms by Richard's behavior) and the position of the new king as insecure. With the Deposition scene, the play cuts deeper. Richard loses his name, and the crown loses its meaning. Bolingbroke's victory entails not just redefining the basis of the office, from divine right to practical power, but draining the office of meaning by emptying out its key symbol. This happens when Bolingbroke touches the crown. It will happen again when his son takes the crown from his pillow as he lies dying. If we take the plays in the normal order, the Deposition scene in *Richard II* anticipates the crown-stealing in *2 Henry IV*. But if we think of the Deposition as written later—written, perhaps, as Shakespeare's final comment on the whole history play sequence, as the fly scene is arguably his final comment on *Titus Andronicus*—then Shakespeare can be imagined as reading back from the end of Henry's reign to the beginning, planting in an early play an image of the desanctification of kingship he has already used in a later one, as though to say, "I have come to realize this is what it meant all along." The method of *Titus Andronicus* is reversed, but we can see an equivalent absurdity: a fly becomes portentous and a crown becomes meaningless.

While the fly-killing scene and (possibly) the Deposition scene are late additions, the bulk of 4.4 of *Hamlet* belongs to an early stage of the text, the second Quarto, and is cut in the Folio. In that later version the scene does no more than give a brief glimpse of Fortinbras as he approaches Denmark on his way to Poland; Hamlet's part of the scene is gone. With it goes what the fly-killing and the Deposition have contributed to their plays: a sharp sense of the absurdity of the action. The passage begins with the Captain's appraisal of the absurdity of his leader's campaign. He speaks as a blunt, practical man:

> Truly to speak, and with no addition,
> We go to gain a little patch of ground
> That hath in it no profit but the name.
> To pay five ducats, five, I would not farm it.
>
> (4.4.18–21)

He goes on to point out that the Poles are as keen to defend it as Fortinbras is to capture it. Why mourn a fly? Why steal a circle of metal no bigger than a man's head? Why fight and die for a small, worthless patch of ground? Responding to the Captain's point about cash value, Hamlet acknowledges the absurdity: "Two thousand souls and twenty thousand ducats / Will not debate the question of this straw" (4.4.26–27). In the soliloquy that follows he sees Fortinbras as

> Exposing what is mortal and unsure
> To all that fortune, death, and danger dare,
> Even for an eggshell.
>
> (4.4.52–54)

This means that the Fortinbras of the Second Quarto is subjected to a critical scrutiny he is spared in the other two texts, and the implications go beyond 4.4 itself. In the other versions it is possible to see Fortinbras at the end of the play as the redeeming hero who will purge Denmark, but in this version he is cast in a sardonic light that undermines such optimism. Far from being purified, Denmark falls into a new and different kind of danger.[10]

The irony affects Hamlet himself. R. A. Foakes points to the paradox of "How all occasions": "the soliloquy demonstrates for us what Hamlet seems not to perceive, the waste and absurdity of fighting for the sake of honour."[11] Having expressed the absurdity of Fortinbras's enterprise as graphically as the Captain has, Hamlet sets out to emulate it. Up to a point the soliloquy runs in parallel to the "rogue and peasant slave" soliloquy: there Hamlet described the absurdity of the player's grief for Hecuba and tried to emulate it with some player-like rant of his own. But he caught his own absurdity and called himself to order:

> Why, what an ass am I! This is most brave,
> That I, the son of a dear father murdered,
> Prompted to my revenge by heaven and hell,
> Must like a whore unpack my heart with words
> And fall a-cursing, like a very drab,
> A scullion! Fie upon't, foh!
>
> (2.2.583–88)

There is no such moment of withdrawal in the later soliloquy. Hamlet begins by seeing action—and this seems to include Fortinbras's action—not as absurd but as the necessary use of a God-given capacity, as the commitment that makes us human:

> What is a man,
> If the chief good and market of his time
> Be but to sleep and feed? A beast, no more.
> Sure he that made us with such large discourse,
> Looking before and after, gave us not
> That capability and godlike reason
> To fust in us unused.
>
> (4.4.34–40)

He goes on to justify Fortinbras, and take him as an example, with only the twisted syntax (the argument requires reading "not to stir" as "not not to stir") betraying a strain:

> Rightly to be great
> Is not to stir without great argument,
> But greatly to find quarrel in a straw
> When honour's at the stake.
>
> (4.4.54–57)

By deciding to emulate Fortinbras, Hamlet in effect equates his own dedication to revenge with quarrelling over a straw or an eggshell. Titus equated his revenge with killing a fly; the difference is that Hamlet seems less aware of the absurdity.

The speech rises to a striking climax, with a touch of the claptrap: "O, from this time forth / My thoughts be bloody or be nothing worth!" (4.4.66–67). This sense of climax is exploited in the Kenneth Branagh film version: Branagh's voice rises, the music soars, the camera pulls back to reveal more and more soldiers, more and more mountains, and one senses the approach of the interval. But as the effects get bigger, the figure of Hamlet gets smaller and smaller.[12] He has just dedicated himself to revenge, while on his way out of the country, virtually under arrest. It sounds as though he is promising bloody deeds; in fact he promises only bloody thoughts. Did Shakespeare remember this moment when he came to write *The Tempest*, where Stephano approaches the climax of his futile plot against Prospero with the words, "I do begin to have bloody thoughts" (4.1.220–21)? Hamlet's revenge is the central action (or non-action) of the play, and the effect of 4.4 is to surround it with irony, to show Hamlet talking himself into an absurdity of which he himself seems unaware. Like the other scenes we have examined, it is unnecessary to the action, even an interruption; it stands back and subjects action itself to ironic scrutiny. As Foakes puts it, the soliloquy "is unnecessary dramatically; but it reveals something of Shakespeare's vision, how critically he saw old Hamlet, and how confused Hamlet becomes in justifying his revenge."[13] Even Hamlet's idealized father, as Foakes observes, is caught in this ironic vision: he too was a warrior-hero who thought it was worth risking his life against the Poles for a patch of land.[14]

If Hamlet's soliloquy casts a sardonic light on the central business of the play, it does the same to the critical activity the play has generated since its first appearance. The business of *Hamlet* criticism begins within the play itself. Everybody scrutinizes Hamlet, everybody has a theory about him (Polonius sticks to his diagnosis of love-melancholy with the stubbornness of a certain kind of academic) and Hamlet himself consciously resists attempts to pluck out the heart of his mystery. Interpretation is a key motif in this play, as language is in *Titus* and identity in *Richard II*; and once again the motif is explored to the point of frustration. As though writing an essay on himself, Hamlet surveys possible motives for his delay, and offers a conclusion in which nothing is concluded:

> Now, whether it be
> Bestial oblivion, or some craven scruple

Of thinking too precisely on th'event —
A thought which, quartered, hath but one part wisdom
And ever three parts coward—I do not know
Why yet I live to say "This thing's to do,"
Since I have cause, and will, and strength, and means
To do't.

(4.4.40–47)

Thinking too precisely is not a bad explanation of Hamlet's problem, and applies particularly to his refusal to kill Claudius at prayer, but Hamlet seems to reject it and conclude, "I do not know." The hostility he expresses to overscrupulous thinking, dismissing it as mostly cowardice, may explain the peculiarity of this soliloquy, in which Hamlet refuses to notice what he is really saying. If he thought too much about what his admiration for Fortinbras really means, he would be stymied again. And so he argues vigorously, but refuses to think.

Without this speech the action is a little tighter, though not by much. Burbage gets a longer tea break, and Hamlet goes from the prickly death-jokes of 4.3 to the cooler, more philosophical death-jokes of 5.1. Arguably, his line of development is straighter, less jagged. G. R. Hibbard calls the soliloquy "redundant" apart from its revelation that Hamlet "has become unrealistic"; his edition accepts the Folio cut.[15] Philip Edwards declares "it is not one of the great soliloquies," finds it inadequate as an account of what has gone before, and suggests it was written at an early stage before the full complexity of Hamlet's character had developed.[16] Giorgio Melchiori takes a very different view, calling 4.4 "the hallmark of true tragedy: catastasis, the retarding moment, when the action is apparently at a standstill and attention is directed instead to the inner meaning, the ideological core of the inextricable knot the characters have been tying." He compares this moment, "apparently irrelevant to the development of the action," to the fly-killing scene in *Titus* and the "night scene" (3.1) of *2 Henry IV*.[17] In his view the Second Quarto, based on Shakespeare's manuscript, is virtually a closet drama, intended for learned readers who would appreciate the effect, as opposed to the acting versions represented by the First Quarto and the Folio.[18] It is tempting to apply the same speculation to the fly-killing scene: given the awkward join between 3.2 and 4.1, was it actually intended for the theatre? It is harder to imagine the Deposition scene in these terms, given its striking theatricality; harder, but not impossible.

Whether intended for readers, audiences, or both, all three

scenes have a quality (in Hamlet's words) of "looking before and after" (4.4.38). They provide the sort of overall reflection one can construct in retrospect when the action is over; two of the three may even have been written later than the main play. Yet they are placed in the thick of the action, in it as well as out of it, stopping the forward movement for a period of thought. What that thought in each case uncovers is absurdity: the absurdity of grief, of revenge, of action; the emptiness of the signs of power and identity; the blocking of language, the frustration of thought. Yet tragedy is not theatre of the absurd, and so none of these scenes has a secure, immovable role in its play. All have textual histories that call their status into question; as they are both in the action and out of it, they are also (in different versions) in the play and out of it. It is not even clear that all these decisions are authorial: the censors may have been at work on *Richard II*, the acting company on *Hamlet*. We need to bear in mind Paul Werstine's caution that in *Hamlet* "there is simply no evidence for determining the authorship of cuts."[19] Throughout this discussion I have been committing the critical heresy of assuming authorial intent. (Critics do this all the time, of course; we just don't like to be caught doing it.) I have to admit the risk this entails. What does register as we examine the textual shifts in each play is a certain uneasiness, taking different forms, over whether a scene that so radically exposes central absurdities in the main action should really be part of the play. The hesitations may be the author's, or they may be those of his theatrical colleagues. Whatever their provenance, they are there, and they are understandable.

To return to Aaron: his brutal laughter as he spies on Titus through the wall would, if it became the controlling view, reduce the tragedy to a bloody farce. We might cease to care about it. There is a similar danger that we will cease to care about the crisis of kingship in *Richard II* if we become too fixed in the idea that kingship is meaningless, and cease to care about Hamlet's revenge if all action is absurd. It is not the business of tragedy to produce that sort of detachment. And yet absurdity has its place in tragedy, though it cannot be a central one. Emotions—pity, rage, grief—can come too easily, can let the audience indulge itself in a simple release of feeling. Tragedy is not absurd, but it is not sentimental or melodramatic either. It needs an edge of irony, even absurdity, to keep its emotions from being too soft, too easy and self-indulgent. We need to feel something of the grim self-awareness Titus shows when he attacks the fly, aware that what he is doing is ridiculous but doing it anyway. It should not be too easy for us to weep at suffering or applaud revenge. We need that critical edge. That tragedy is prepared to skirt the edge of the absurd, even the ludicrous, is part of its honesty. Aaron reports that he laughed, from behind his wall, at the sufferings of Titus in the scene the audience saw as 3.1; what he does not seem to have noticed is that in the same scene Titus was laughing too.

Notes

1. All references to Shakespeare are to *The Complete Works of Shakespeare*, ed. David Bevington (New York: HarperCollins, 1992).
2. See Alan C. Dessen, *Shakespeare in Peformance: Titus Andronicus* (Manchester and New York: Manchester University Press, 1989), 111–12.
3. On the textual problem presented by this passage, see Jonathan Bate's Arden edition (London and New York: Routledge, 1995), 120–21.
4. Bate, 121.
5. Dessen, *Performance*, 63. Dessen also cites a production in Washington, D.C. in 1986–87 that played the entire scene for comedy, including "the frustrations of a handless Lavinia trying to join the other Andronici in their meal of chips and dip" (111).
6. Bate, 117–18.
7. Bate, 98.
8. Bergeron, "The Deposition Scene in *Richard II*," *Renaissance Papers 1974* (Durham, N.C.: The Southeastern Renaissance Conference, 1975), 31–37. Bergeron has been supported by J. Leeds Barroll, "A New History for Shakespeare and His Time," *Shakespeare Quarterly* 39 (1988), 441–64. For recent arguments in favor of the censorship theory, see Janet Clare, "The Censorship of the Deposition Scene in *Richard II*," *Review of English Studies*, n.s. 41 (1990), 89–94; and Cyndia Susan Clegg, " 'By the choise and inuitation of al the realme': *Richard II* and Elizabethan Press Censorship," *Shakespeare Quarterly* 48 (1997), 432–48. The latter argues that the printed text was censored because of the authority it attributed to Parliament.
9. I have discussed this effect in *Shakespeare's Political Drama* (London and New York: Routledge, 1988), 67.
10. Philip C. McGuire, "Which Fortinbras, Which *Hamlet?*," *The Hamlet First Published*, ed. Thomas Clayton (Newark: University of Delaware Press, 1992), 169, 173.
11. Foakes, *Hamlet versus Lear: Cultural Politics and Shakespeare's Art* (Cambridge: Cambridge University Press, 1993), 92.
12. This point emerged in my graduate seminar on Shakespearian tragedy in 1997–98, in a discussion of the scene led by Paulo Horta.
13. Foakes, *Hamlet versus Lear*, 94.
14. Ibid., 93.
15. Oxford edition of *Hamlet* (Oxford and New York: Oxford University Press, 1987), 109.
16. Edwards, Introduction, *Hamlet* (Cambridge: Cambridge University Press, 1985), 17.
17. Melchiori, "*Hamlet*: The Acting Version and the Wiser Sort," *The Hamlet First Published*, 198.
18. "Acting Version," 200.
19. Werstine, "The Textual Mystery of *Hamlet*," *Shakespeare Quarterly* 39 (1988), 2.

"Tenders and True Pay": Representing Falsehood

Philip Edwards

A GOOD DEAL OF ELIZABETHAN DRAMA IS DEDICATED TO THE DETECTION of "seeming," as though the dramatists, those masterful impersonaters and counterfeiters, saw themselves as a special police force to combat counterfeiters and impersonators. Set a thief to catch a thief. The purpose of this paper is to explore some of the problems which arise when the theatrical profession, whose definition is masking, undertakes its self-appointed task of unmasking: of distinguishing the true from the false. Shakespeare is the obvious writer to concentrate on. Society in his plays (and his poems) is continously imperilled by the unseen infection of deceit: by Richard III, by Iago, by Goneril and Regan, by Angelo in *Measure for Measure*. "Rank corruption, mining all within / Infects unseen."[1] During the course of a play the falsehood of the deceivers, which is known to the audience, will be exposed to the characters, who at some cost have learned who is not to be trusted.

But Shakespeare will all the time illustrate the pitfalls in this process of unmasking. Polonius, a notable schemer himself, is confident that *he* knows the difference between sincerity and insincerity, and he castigates Ophelia for not appreciating the difference between "tenders . . . which are not sterling," and "true pay," in regard to Hamlet's profession of his affection (1.3.106–7). But events quickly make him change his mind and he apologizes to Ophelia for casting beyond himself in his earlier opinion: "I feared he did but trifle" (2.1.109). What is the evidence of the sincerity or the insincerity of Hamlet's professions of love? There is the mawkish and graceless letter which Polonius reads out "To the celestial and my soul's idol, the most beautified Ophelia." If ever the English language demonstrated insincerity, it is there. In the nunnery scene we have the following exchange:

Hamlet. . . . I did love you once.
Ophelia. Indeed, my lord, you made me believe so.

> *Hamlet.* You should not have believed me, for virtue cannot so inoculate our old stock but we shall relish of it. I loved you not.
>
> *Ophelia.* I was the more deceived.
>
> (3.1.114–19)

In the graveyard scene Hamlet declares to all and sundry,

> I loved Ophelia. Forty thousand brothers
> Could not with all their quantity of love
> Make up my sum.
>
> (5.1.269–71)

It seems impossible to discern the genuineness of his affection for Ophelia from Hamlet's words.

The root of the problem (as Shakespeare sees it) is the identity of speech (as well as behavior) in both truth and falsehood. There's no art to find the mind's construction in language, any more than in the face.

> Angels are bright still, though the brightest fell.
> Though all things foul would wear the brows of grace,
> Yet grace must still look so.
>
> (*Macbeth*, 4.3.22–24)

So says Malcolm to Macduff. Malcolm's faith that goodness does in fact exist is clouded by the knowledge that you cannot identify it. There is no linguistic code which the virtuous can use to signify that they are the real thing. They can only express themselves in terms which the wicked can easily simulate. The bad may be believed; the good disbelieved. When Isabella has found out the true nature of Angelo, and threatens to "tell the world aloud / What man thou art," the iciness of Angelo's reply—"Who will believe thee, Isabel?"[2]—sends a chill through every happy ending. In order to find out whether Macduff is in fact a spy of Macbeth, Malcolm employs the stratagem of deceit, and pretends to be a villain. He requires Macduff to prove the point he has made, namely, that dissimulation looks like truth. Macduff's credulity in believing that Malcolm is a rogue, and for that reason denouncing him, asserts his own worth.

The identity of truth and falsehood in speech works in more than one way. Sincere speech is easily fabricated by the insincere, but sincere and well-intentioned people may sound very insincere. If we are worried by the artificiality and affected rhetoric of Hamlet's letter to Ophelia, we might take comfort in the thought that it is a common thing in Shakespeare for young men to express genuine and sincerely held emotion in clumsy, stilted, extravagant language.[3] Juliet does not doubt the genuineness of Romeo's affection, but his protestations more than once embarrass her because they sound exaggerated. In *Macbeth*, when Macduff has discovered the murder of Duncan, it is hard not to think that Macduff's baroque imagery registers less genuine shock and horror than the lines spoken by the hypocritical Macbeth.

> *Macduff.* Confusion now hath made his masterpiece!
> Most sacrilegious murder hath broke ope
> The Lord's anointed temple, and stole thence
> The life o' th' building.
> . . . .
> *Macbeth.* Had I but died an hour before this chance,
> I had lived a blessed time; for from this instant
> There's nothing serious in mortality:
> All is but toys: renown and grace is dead,
> The wine of life is drawn, and the mere lees
> Is left this vault to brag of.
>
> (2.3.66–69, 91–96)

The problem posed by not being able to judge the sincerity of the speaker by his or her language was wonderfully put by Sidney in *Astrophil and Stella*:

> What may words say, or what may words not say,
> Where truth itself must speak like flattery?
>
> (35:1–2)

The protestations of love for their father by Goneril and Regan *sound* genuine enough. Cordelia knows that there is nothing that she can *say* to distinguish her truth from what she knows to be their falsehood. So she tries an absence of words: "What shall Cordelia speak? Love, and be silent."[4] But silence is as easily misinterpreted as speech.

It seems that Sidney would line up with Shakespeare in disagreeing with Erasmus's apophthegm developed by Jonson in *Discoveries*: "Language most shows a man: speak that I may see thee."[5] Quite the contrary! "Thou mayst be false, and yet I know it not" (Sonnet 92). The faith of Pericles in Erasmus's dictum when he is speaking to the unknown young woman standing before him is no strong argument for Shakespeare's authorship of the play:

> Prithee speak.
> Falseness cannot come from thee, for thou lookest
> Modest as justice, and thou seem'st a palace
> For the crowned truth to dwell in. I will believe thee.
> (*Pericles*, 5.1.119–22)

We have already—with Malcolm testing Macduff by pretending to be wicked—blurred the simple distinction between good people (who speak sincerely) and bad people (who speak insincerely). Falsehood comes in many guises. Malcolm is one of a whole army of good deceivers in Shakespeare, many of whom adopt a physical disguise as well as a verbal disguise—Rosalind and Duke Vincentio, Edgar and Kent, Paulina and Ariel.[6] One of the many difficulties for readers and actors in this matter of the indistinguishability of falsehood is in the use of irony. Here is the famous declaration of Hamlet to Rosencrantz and Guildenstern:

> I have of late, but wherefore I know not, lost all my mirth, forgone all custom of exercises; and indeed it goes so heavily with my disposition that this goodly frame, the earth, seems to me a sterile promontory; this most excellent canopy the air, look you, this brave o'erhanging firmament, this majestical roof fretted with golden fire—why, it appeareth no other thing to me but a foul and pestilent congregation of vapours. What a piece of work is a man! How noble in reason, how infinite in faculties, in form and moving how express and admirable, in action how like an angel, in apprehension how like a god! The beauty of the world, the paragon of animals—and yet to me, what is this quintessence of dust? Man delights not me—no, nor woman neither, though by your smiling you seem to say so. (2.2.293–310)[7]

I don't know why some people so deeply resent the notion that Hamlet is here speaking disingenuously, that he is using this fine language to mislead Rosencrantz and Guildenstern. How could he be speaking this in all sincerity? He has just made his two supposed friends admit that they are spying for Claudius. The last thing he is going to do is confess the true cause of his distemper and his "transformation." World-weariness he has indeed been suffering from, but there was no "wherefore I know not" in *that*. He teases them to the end: in this splendid parade of spiritual disillusionment, and in his final jest, "I am but mad north-north-west."

The problem of detecting irony is even more serious in *Othello*, in which our understanding of the hero after the murder of Desdemona, and to an extent during the play as a whole, depends on a decision whether two or three remarks of Othello are spoken ironically or not. One of these is his reply to Lodovico's question, "What shall be said to thee?"

> Why, anything:
> An honourable murderer, if you will;
> For nought I did in hate, but all in honour.
>
> (5.2.293–95)

If this is said in all seriousness it is pathetic if not despicable. But if the words are spoken ironically, Othello is condemning the whole ethos of honor and honesty by which he has lived and Desdemona has died. It would be an admission of responsibility unparalleled in Shakespeare's tragedies.[8]

The responsibilities of the actor in delivering these lines of Hamlet and Othello are grave indeed. But before we start discussing them we should consider another observation by Jonson in his *Discoveries*, which Shakespeare might be more in agreement with than with the last:

> I have considered, our whole life is like a play: wherein every man, forgetful of himself, is in travail with expression of another. Nay, we so insist in imitating others, as we cannot (when it is necessary) return to ourselves.[9]

That phrase "forgetful of himself" needs qualification. Self-dramatization can be deliberate and purposeful. Whether it is wilful or unwitting, it is worth considering as a form of falsehood. Bolingbroke certainly considers it so, as he listens to Richard drawing out the scene of his deposition with the breaking of the looking-glass:

> Mark, silent king, the moral of this sport,
> How soon my sorrow hath destroyed my face.

To this Bolingbroke replies:

> The shadow of your sorrow hath destroyed
> The shadow of your face.
>
> (*Richard II*, 4.1.290–93)

Detecting the 'insincerity' of self-dramatization, and then fashioning its presentation on the stage, is, with the detection and presentation of irony, the actor's most burdensome, almost unendurable, responsibility: in Brutus, for example, "with himself at war." It is fortunate indeed when a character such as Hamlet or Berowne, is conscious of stepping outside himself and calls attention to it. Both of them (at least some of the time) recognize when they are, to use Berowne's words, "blown . . . full of maggot ostentation." But the extreme edge of the difficulty in reading self-dramatization in Shakespeare's characters is in identifying the self they are supposed to be dramatizing. "Forgetful of himself," "we cannot . . . return to ourselves," wrote Jonson. What self? What selves? Oh, for the confidence of Polonius: "To thine own self be true!" Strindberg wrote that "Shakespeare renders people, in all their facets, as inconsistent, self-contradictory, fragmented, and forever fragmenting, conflicting, ultimately unfathomable, as human beings are."[10]

In the final stages of *Antony and Cleopatra*, the queen finds a language to raise and exalt the dead Antony. In doing that she raises and exalts herself. Where her "true self" resides becomes a difficult and perhaps a foolish question. In the earlier love-tragedy, when Juliet mocks Romeo for the exaggerated wording of his protestation of love, she contrasts it with "conceit," her inner thought, which is "more rich in matter than in words."[11] The idea that there is a protected inner area of the self, where thoughts or feelings (be they good or bad) lie in pure form awaiting birth into the distortions of language, is common in Shakespeare and may suggest a certain naiveté in the speaker. "I have that within which passes show," says Hamlet at the beginning of the long trek to discover what is indeed within. When Parolles comes to the lines, "Simply the thing I am / Shall make me live,"[12] we may think him honest but naive, and may wish to compare his faith in a true inner self with that of the continuously self-inventing Troilus when he says,

> I am as true as truth's simplicity,
> And simpler than the infancy of truth.
> *(Troilus and Cressida*, 3.2.169–70)

The treachery of language (as urged by Shakespeare) is intolerably complicated by the instability of the self. The *Sonnets* are there to demonstrate the complication. "O let me, true in love, but truly write," beseeches the sonneteer (21), who in a hundred and fifty poems finds his poetry pulling away from the truth not only about the youth and the woman but about his constantly dramatized self:

> Most true it is that I have looked on truth
> Askance and strangely.
> (110)

But, in insisting on the refusal of language to face up to the situation, is he talking about language in general or the language of poetry? Most certainly the language of poetry, whatever the implications may be for language in general. By definition it is artificial.

In all that we have been saying about the inscrutability of language in Shakespeare's plays, about the impossibility of distinguishing sincerity from insincerity, truth from falsehood, are we talking about language in general, or the language of drama? The difficulty of distinguishing fabricated emotions and misrepresented reports from honest attempts to tell the truth is bad enough in life—in court cases and television interviews as well as in personal encounters—but at least there is a real distinction to be made and to be sought. But in drama all the speeches are insincere, in that they have been manufactured by the dramatist to express not his or her feelings but those required by the fiction. Both truth and falsehood in the language of characters in a play demand the same degree of artfulness and contrivance. Given the conventions of poetic drama in a distant Elizabethan age, our criteria for recognizing false emotion from true emotion are very insecure, despite the confidence of critics who, working from their knowledge of the story, feel able to indicate those stylistic features of (say) Claudius's speeches which brand him insincere. An actor may be forgiven for thinking that almost any intense speech in Shakespeare is exaggerated or beyond the requirement of the moment, and shaping his/her interpretation of the character in the light of this perception.

But Shakespeare (it may be said) has an unmatched ability for differentiating characters by the speech he fashions for them. Who could confuse the speech of Hotspur and Falstaff, or Coriolanus and Menenius? If he was able to make such distinctions to indicate differences of temperament, could he not also have made distinctions to indicate speeches that are meant to deceive? The answer is, he doesn't. It was his own belief that truth and deceit speak the same language. Shakespeare forged a language to make real an invented or imagined character on the stage. Drama has no voice that is not assumed. How *can* the disguising of true feeling be unmistakaby represented if all is disguise?

Shakespeare rejoiced in the problem. I think of works as different as *Love's Labour's Lost* and the *Sonnets* as declarations of the inadequacy of poetry as a faithful vehicle of experience, and of its unrivalled value as a substitute for experience. What happens when we couple with this the fact that Shakespeare's plays are awash with deceit, and that as prominent as those characters whose lives are tragically altered by misrepresentation are those whose lives are permanently changed for the better by well-intentioned deceit? Benedick and Beatrice come together because of Don Pedro's practical joke; Angelo and Mariana, Bertram and Helena are brought together by means of the "bed-trick." Above all these is the special case of King Lear, who is brought to a belief in the true nature of mankind by the spectacle of Edgar acting as Tom o' Bedlam. Misrepresentation comes in all forms and for all reasons: as magic (with Oberon and Prospero) or disguise; for justice (Portia), for obedience (Viola), for survival (Edgar and Rosalind), and for mischief (Don Pedro). In demonstrating, as it so often did, that all the world's a stage, the Elizabethan theatre was obviously performing a valuable service. But was this the service that Shakespeare was offering in his dramatic representation of a world afloat on falsehood?

Initially, the province of "seeming" belongs to bad people, who assume the garb and speech of virtue to advance themselves and destroy others. But it quickly becomes apparent that seeming, deliberate or unwitting, is universal; it is the common mode of life for all, the bad, the good, the middling sort. A self comes in a language, and most Shakespearian characters try out selves like suits of clothes. Life becomes a contest in deception. "Craft against vice I must apply," says Duke Vincentio.[13] "O 'tis most sweet," says Hamlet, "When in one line two crafts directly meet" (3.4.209–10).

Eripitur persona, manet res, said Lucretius. In time of great affliction, or at the approach of death, he wrote, the mask we all wear is torn aside and reality is exposed;[14] so it is in the theatre. At the end of a tragedy, the deceptions of an Edmund, an Iago, a Claudius are exposed, the perpetrators defeated and subdued, though the damage they have done is irreversible. At the end of a comedy, the well-intentioned deceivers reveal themselves or are revealed, but either their victims are meant to deserve what they have got, as with Malvolio or Shylock, or it turns out that the falsehood has done a lot of good, as with Katherina, or the couples I mentioned before, Benedick and Beatrice for example. In tragedy and in comedy, misrepresentation ends as the play ends, even though the effects endure. It is therein that drama strays into true falsehood.

A police force that not only connives at wrongdoing but actively contributes to it is not unknown. And that is the analogy for Shakespeare's theatre viewed as an agent to detect imposture. It is compromised because it is substituting one imposture for another: the enduring falsity of poetic language for the opacity of the language of life. Set a thief to catch a thief. Its exposure of malefactors is factitious, its confidence in knowing them is subverted by the testimony of the plays themselves on the inscrutabilty of imposture. As language is manufactured for the creatures of fiction, it becomes apparent that the argument that pretence can clean up pretence is a pretence. Shakespeare recreates the confusion of life. The sharp edge of the conflict between right and wrong, true and false, good and bad becomes hopelessly blurred in the representation of misrepresentation. Shakespeare's plays are always arguing against their own right to exist. "It is not good to stay too long in the theatre," said Francis Bacon,[15] but, as his essay on simulation and dissimulation so convincingly demonstrated, there is nowhere else to go.

Notes

1. *Hamlet*, 3.4.148–49. Quotations and line references for Shakespeare's plays are from the Riverside Shakespeare.
2. *Measure for Measure*, 2.4.153–54.
3. See my essay, "The Declaration of Love," in *Shakespeare's Styles*, ed. P. Edwards, I-S. Ewbank and G. K. Hunter (Cambridge: Cambridge University Press, 1980), 39–50.
4. *King Lear*, 1.1.62.
5. *Ben Jonson*, ed. C. H. Herford and P. and E. Simpson, 11 vols. (Oxford: Clarendon Press, 1925–52), 8:625; 11:272.
6. See further in my "Shakespeare and the Healing Power of Deceit" in *Shakespeare Survey 31* (Cambridge: Cambridge University Press, 1978), 115–25.
7. The text of this passage is from my edition of *Hamlet* (Cambridge: Cambridge University Press, 1985).
8. I argue the case for irony in *Sea-Mark: The Metaphorical Voyage, Spenser to Milton* (Liverpool: Liverpool University Press, 1997), chapter 4.
9. *Ben Jonson*, ed. Herford and Simpson, 8:597.
10. Quoted by Inga-Stina Ewbank, "Shakespeare and Strindberg," in *Shakespearian Continuities*, ed. J. Batchelor, T. Cain and C. Lamont (London: Macmillan, 1997), 342.
11. 2.6.24–34. On this, see M. M. Mahood, *Shakespeare's Wordplay* (London: Methuen, 1957; reprinted 1979), 13–14.
12. *All's Well that Ends Well*, 4.3.333–34.
13. *Measure for Measure*, 3.2.277.
14. *De Natura Rerum* (Cambridge, Mass.: Loeb Classical Library, 1975), 3:57.
15. *The Advancement of Learning*, Book II (New York: Modern Library, 1955), 247.

The First Performances of Shakespeare's *Sonnets*

E. A. J. HONIGMANN

MAY WE SPEAK OF THE FIRST "PERFORMANCES" OF SHAKESPEARE'S *Sonnets*? I think we may. The first performances of a poem, as of a play, take place in the theatre of the mind—the writer's, then the reader's—and plays and poems designed for a particular occasion or person will usually function within restricted parameters, which will be visible or semi-visible in the written text, taking account of known tastes and expectations (the distinctive style of a theatre, the preferences of a patron). If we speak of the first reading not of a single sonnet but of a sonnet sequence, the drama of on-going relationships—the Poet, Young Man, Rival Poet, Dark Lady—again underlines the similarities of the first "performances" of the *Sonnets* and of a play. I believe that we should be able to see the *Sonnets* more clearly, and to understand their many extraordinary "scenes" more fully, if only we knew more about their first performances—that is, if the individuality of the principal characters were as sharply defined as in one of Shakespeare's less private tragi-comedies.[1]

A fine sentiment and a hopeless ambition? Not necessarily, for I do not propose to pull new rabbits from the conjuror's hat (a William Hatliff, a Sir William Harvey), but rather to press the case for the Young Man who has emerged as the front-runner in our century. I want to suggest that when all the old arguments for William Herbert, the later Earl of Pembroke, are assembled, and are reinforced by several new ones, we are dutybound to ask how *this* Young Man would be expected to "perform" the *Sonnets*, and how our understanding of the *Sonnets* will be modified, perhaps modified quite radically, when we relate what we are told of the Young Man to contemporary accounts of Herbert's character.

E. K. Chambers announced in 1930 that the case for William Herbert "was elaborately argued by Thomas Tyler and others thirty years ago, and I think that it was mishandled."[2] Hyder E. Rollins and Samuel Schoenbaum and many more also favored William Herbert as the Young Man, and now Katherine Duncan-Jones, in the new Arden edition of the *Sonnets* (1997),[3] has restated and strengthened the case for this candidate. My paper is offered as a pendant to the Arden edition, and I begin with a summary of its argument (52–69). It should be noted that together with Duncan-Jones (86) and many critics since A. C. Bradley,[4] I assume that the Poet of the *Sonnets* speaks for Shakespeare, even if Shakespeare "dressed up" for a special literary purpose.

Let me summarize several of Duncan-Jones's arguments. (1) Like Chambers, she was "struck by the fact that, although Southampton was still alive, it was not to him, but to Herbert and his brother that [the First Folio] was dedicated." (2) Yet "there is some danger that Mary Fitton's candidature for the role of 'dark lady' may confuse the case for Herbert, so it requires to be disposed of." (3) "The chief bearing of Mary Fitton on the case . . . lies in the fact that she was at least the fourth well-born girl whom Herbert resolutely refused to marry." (4) "It was not that Herbert was lacking in sexual passion: indeed, according to Clarendon's later testimony, 'he was immoderately given up to women'. It was to marriage, specifically, that he was strongly averse." (5) Duncan-Jones assumes that "Mr. W. H." is the Young Man of the *Sonnets,* since "the most obvious connotation" of begetter ("To the only begetter") is "inspirer." (6) The financial aspect of patronage must not be overlooked: "his well-documented generosity to writers makes William Herbert . . . a powerful candidate"; according to John Aubrey, "he was the greatest Maecenas to learned Men of any Peer of his time." (7) "Shakespeare was not alone in celebrating [Herbert's] beauty as well as his high birth and munificence." (8) "Two further documents, while not clinching the case, suggest strongly that some degree of unconventional intimacy between Pembroke and a celebrated playwright and actor is at least within the bounds of possibility." (a) An eyewitness account of the coronation of James I mentions that "the Earl of Pembroke, a handsome youth, who is always with the King, and always joking with him, actually kissed his Majesty's face, whereupon the King laughed and gave him a little cuff." (b) On 20 May 1619, Pembroke wrote to Viscount Doncaster that "even now all the company are at the play, which I being tender harted could not endure to see so soone after the loss of my old acquaintance Burbadg" (who died on 9 March). Duncan-Jones states that "the important point here is that Pembroke was prepared to receive and express affection in an individual and somewhat unconventional way." (9) "It appears that Pembroke perused and responded to *Shakespeare's Sonnets.* One of his own poems . . . opens with a verbal and thematic elaboration of Shakespeare's sonnet 116 . . . and incorporates the phrase 'love is not love.' "

I begin with a comment on the fourth point. An important UCLA dissertation has argued that Clarendon was a political enemy who wished to blacken Herbert's character; Herbert, said Brian O'Farrell, was not immoderately given up to women, quite the contrary: "Apart from the [Mary] Fitton affair . . . there is not a shred of evidence that Pembroke [Herbert] was a gallant with the ladies."[5] Recent biographers, however, have shown that Clarendon was correct: a family chronicle of the Herbert family records that the third earl "had two natural children by the Lady Mary Wroth," his cousin.[6] So Herbert resembled the Young Man both in his reluctance to marry and his womanizing.

Clarendon, indeed, also deserves our attention when he goes on to explain that Pembroke "was not so much transported with [female] beauty and outward allurements, as with those advantages of the mind as manifested an extraordinary wit and spirit and knowledge, and administered great pleasure in the conversation."[7] The Dark Lady seems to have attracted Shakespeare (and, we may take it, the Young Man) not so much by her conventional beauty as by her spirit and wit—why else did Shakespeare write Sonnet 130?

> My mistress' eyes are nothing like the sun;
> Coral is far more red than her lips' red;
> If snow be white, why then her breasts are dun;
> If hairs be wires, black wires grow on her head.

Duncan-Jones thinks that

> there could surely be no question of the woman described in *Sonnets* either reading or understanding what is said about her, let alone receiving any pleasure from it. Shakespeare's speaker seems . . . to brag to other men . . . that he can make satisfactory sexual use of a woman too stupid to realize that she is also being set up as the butt of his wit. (48)

This seems to me not only unlikely in itself but to contradict Duncan-Jones's statement that Shakespeare sought to "redefine the genre, rejecting the stale conceits of mistress-worship" (49). Some of the most outrageous sonnets are actually addressed to the Dark Lady, not to the Young Man: Shakespeare pays her the compliment of assuming that she will have the "wit and spirit" to appreciate his inversion of clichés—in short, he assumed that she, endowed with "advantages of the mind," was exactly the kind of woman who, according to Clarendon, attracted Pembroke. So we are indebted to

Clarendon for two vital facts: that Pembroke was immoderately given up to women, and that Pembroke was particularly attracted to women such as the Dark Lady. And we may add in passing, is it not inherently probable that Shakespeare would also be attracted by "extraordinary wit and spirit" rather than by the "stupid" creature favoured by Duncan-Jones?

As for her sixth point above, Duncan-Jones quotes Aubrey, and mentions Pembroke's gift of £100 "for the purchase of books to the newly founded Bodleian Library." Since we know from other sources that Pembroke extravagantly supported "learning," as well as men of letters, let us observe that the Rival Poet's learning appears to give him a significant advantage over "unlettered" Shakespeare, and that not every Young Man respects learning as did Pembroke.

Next, I want to ask a question: who knew the *Sonnets* before they were published, these "sugared sonnets among his private friends," and who was the central personage of this circle, if it was a circle? There are at least five possible candidates.

1) Francis Meres had certainly heard of the *Sonnets* in 1598, and his adjective, "sugared" sonnets, may imply that he had seen them, or some of them, for "sugared" suggests their melodious sweetness.
2) John Weever's *Epigrammes* (1599) contains about 150 poems, most of them between 4 and 20 lines in length. "One, and only one, is fourteen lines long, and takes the form of a Shakespearian sonnet," the epigram addressed "*Ad Gulielmum Shakespeare.*" As I argued in 1985, "adopting the form of Shakespeare's still unpublished sonnets, Weever signals to those in the know that he is one of the privileged few who have read them."[8]
3) John Donne's *Farewell to Love*, like Sonnet 129, compares a man's attitude to love before and after sexual intercourse, as others have noted.[9] First, Sonnet 129:

> *Had*, having, and in quest to have, extreme;
> A bliss in proof, and proved, a very woe;
> *Before*, a joy proposed; *behind*, a dream.

Now Donne:

> Being *had*, enjoying it decays:
> And thence,

> What *before* pleas'd them all, takes but one sense,
>   And that so lamely, as it leaves *behind*
> A kind of sorrowing dullness to the mind.

I do not know whether anyone has noticed that the same sonnet, 129, seems also to be echoed in Donne's *The Progress of the Soul* (1601). The sonnet begins, "*Th'expense* of *spirit* in a *waste* of shame / Is lust in action*"; Donne wrote, "*Th'expense* of brain and *spirit*, that my grave / His right and due, a whole *unwasted* man may have." Neither of the Donne passages can be called an indisputable echo, nevertheless, since they both point back to the same sonnet, I think we may say that Donne had seen this sonnet, whether or not he knew the rest of the sequence.

4) John Davies of Hereford appears to refer in *Microcosmos* (1603) to Sonnet 111 and its complaint that Fortune had not provided better for the poet than a career in the theatre, which brands his name like an infection.[10] Here is the relevant portion of Sonnet 111:

> O for my sake do you with *Fortune* chide,
> The guilty goddess of my harmful deeds,
> That did not *better* for my life provide
> Than public means, which public manners breeds;
> Thence comes it that my name receives a *brand*.

The branded name is a "strong *infection*." Davies wrote as if to console Shakespeare for his hard fortune, saying that

> fell *Fortune* cannot be excused
> That hath for *better* uses you refused.

He conceded that a career in the theatre may seem to be infected but added that some actors are nonetheless "generous" (i.e., gentlemen):

> And though the stage doth *stain pure gentle blood*
> Yet generous ye are in mind and mood.

In the margin he placed the letters W. S. and R. B., usually taken to stand for Shakespeare and Burbage.

5) Another poet who seems to have known the *Sonnets* is Michael Drayton, as Thomas Tyler explained in 1890[11] and Duncan-Jones confirms (23–24).

Meres, Weever, Donne, Davies, Drayton: these are the only writers I know of who might qualify as the "private friends" acquainted with Shakespeare's *Sonnets* before their publication in 1609 (though I do not doubt that there may have been others). Is it a pure coincidence that just these men appear to have known the *Sonnets*, or could these five men have been connected in some way?

Francis Meres, in his survey of English writers published in 1598, first identified twelve of Shakespeare's plays, was the first person to refer to the *Sonnets* in print, and "shows a special regard for Drayton, whom he mentions again and again."[12]

John Weever, I assume, came to know Shakespeare through the Hoghtons of Hoghton Tower, the family to various members of which his *Epigrammes* were dedicated.[13] He also addressed flattering poems to Drayton and Shakespeare, and to Jonson and Robert Allott.

The possibly significant link between Donne and Davies is this—that they both had a long-standing relationship with William Herbert, the Earl of Pembroke. We can date it back, in both cases, to just after the turn of the century but as it continued, in both cases, for many years, we may assume that these relationships could well have begun before 1600, since the start of a relationship is not easily dated after 400 years. Moreover, Lady Pembroke—"Sidney's sister, Pembroke's mother"—became, after her brother's death, a focal person in the literary life of her time, and her son would therefore have met many leading writers at Wilton and elsewhere, from his earliest years. Indeed, Mary Sidney may well have been at the center of the circle of "private friends" referred to by Meres, and could be another character in the "drama" of the *Sonnets* if, as others have conjectured, the first seventeen were written at the behest of the Young Man's family, more interested than he seems to have been in "succession":

> Thou art thy mother's glass, and she in thee
> Calls back the lovely April of her prime.
>
> (3.9–10)

My suggestion that Ben Jonson was the Rival Poet supports the Pembroke hypothesis, insofar as Jonson and Donne were close friends for many years, and Pembroke's patronage of Jonson is well attested. In addition, Jonson and Donne were protégés of Lucy, Countess of Bedford, and friends of Sir Henry Goodere, and the Countess and Goodere were also friends and patrons of Drayton (Drayton, however, is not known to have been patronized by Pembroke).

Meres, Weever, Donne, Davies, Drayton, Jonson: these six writers were linked by many threads, and, I suggest, while some were closer to Pembroke than others, appear to have been the circle of "private friends" first invited (by the Young Man?) to read the *Sonnets*. Is it surprising that, in such tightly-knit circles of influence and patronage, the enthusiasm of the Young Man (probably a youth of sixteen or seventeen) for a new poet, a recent arrival, would seem so fickle and hurtful (Sonnets 85, 86)?

Here I would like to make a more tentative suggestion. Not only did Pembroke patronize Donne, Davies, Shakespeare and Jonson, he may also have echoed the dedication to the *Sonnets* in a letter dated 2 September 1601, in which he wrote "I will ever *wish* you *all happiness.*"[14] Compare the dedication:

> TO. THE. ONLIE. BEGETTER. OF.
> THESE. INSVING. SONNETS.
> Mr. W.H. ALL. HAPPINESSE.
> AND. THAT. ETERNITIE.
> PROMISED.
> BY.
> OVR. EVER-LIVING. POET.
> WISHETH.
> THE. WELL-WISHING.
> ADVENTVRER. IN.
> SETTING.
> FORTH.
>   T.T.

Is it significant that the phrase "wisheth . . . all happiness" is also found in the dedication of *Lucrece* ("To whom I wish long life still lengthned with all happinesse"), and again later in *Cymbeline* (3.2.45)? It may well be a Shakespearian phrase, for I know of only one other occurrence, in Robert Allott's *Wits Theater of the little World* (1599), where R. A. "wisheth all happines" to "Maister *Iohn Bodenham.*" (Allott, also the recipient of verses in Weever's *Epigrammes*, seems to have been a fringe-member of the Pembroke-Shakespeare circle).[15] If the phrase was not widely used—and I confess that I am not sure about this—we could deduce (1) that Shakespeare may have had a hand in preparing the dedication for *Sonnets*; and (2) that Pembroke in 1601 had already seen Shakespeare's dedication (although it is also possible that he remembered the *Lucrece* dedication).

And now let me offer a second tentative speculation: noblemen and state officials employed secretaries to write their letters, and sometimes no doubt to draft important letters. Is it not likely that a professional writer might be asked to help out as a secretary, especially one as close as Shakespeare to the dedicatee of *Lucrece* or to the Young Man of the *Sonnets*? Is it possible that some of the letters of Southampton or Pembroke or Essex were drafted, or written to dictation, by William Shakespeare?

Are the two preceding paragraphs too speculative? I would like to suggest as a possible scenario that many if not all the *Sonnets* were brought together in a single manuscript by 1598, when Meres referred to them, and that it would have been appropriate to dedicate this manuscript to the Young Man—who, I have argued, is most likely to have been William Herbert. My scenario differs from that proposed by Duncan-Jones when we move on to the role of the publisher, Thomas Thorpe. She writes:

> My conjecture is that when Shakespeare left London for Stratford in some haste at the end of May 1609 he left instructions with Thorpe to use this form of address to Herbert, and to set out the dedication in pointed capitals. Though the initials of "T.T." are at the bottom, and the over-rhetorical wording is evidently Thorpe's, the dedication, like the text itself, had Shakespeare's authority. (59)

I think it more likely that, while Thorpe acted in good faith and printed from an excellent manuscript, he had neither Shakespeare's nor Pembroke's authority in "setting forth." Like others, Duncan-Jones struggles to explain "Mr." W. H. Why "Mr"? This form of Herbert's name, she says, "alluded to the period before his father's death in January 1600/1," when Herbert was "not yet either an earl, or of age, or married." Why then drop his courtesy title, "Lord William Herbert"? And, a more awkward question, was it not usual to identify dedicatees by their full title or titles, or even to include expected future titles ("son and heir of Henry Herbert, Earl of Pembroke"), rather than to strip them of their legitimate titles? To repeat: why did Thorpe call him "Mr" W. H.? Now a related question: how usual was it to identify a dedicatee only by his initials? What could be the motive for suppressing W. H.'s full name? That there might be a motive we may infer from the textual tampering in the second edition of 1640, when some male pronouns were changed to female, for, even before that, "Jonson may have been one of the first of many readers to feel that Shakespeare's sonnets are morally compromising" (Duncan-Jones 64). Might William Herbert's father not react like the later Marquess of Queensberry, whether or not the "Hellenism" of the *Sonnets* should be equated with Oscar Wilde's? In my scenario the dedicatee's full name and title were therefore suppressed by Shakespeare himself, in case the manuscript fell into the wrong hands, and the inscription read roughly as follows: "To the only begetter of these insuing sonnets, W. H., all happiness, and that eternity promised by them, wisheth W. S." (or some such phrasing); and, years later, Thorpe appropriated and adapted these words (cf. Duncan-Jones 59).

Schoenbaum thought it "doubtful that the obsequious Thorpe would insolently address a noble lord by the unhonorific 'Mr.' "[16] In my scenario this could easily have happened *if Thorpe did not know that the dedicatee was a lord*, and only knew him from the MS. dedication as "W.H." For surely Thorpe would have had second thoughts about issuing the *Sonnets* had he known that W. H. was the twenty-nine-year-old Earl of Pembroke, a rising star at court (a Privy Councillor at 31, Lord Chamberlain at 35).

I move on to the Rival Poet. Duncan-Jones (65) thinks that Francis Davison, John Davies of Hereford, Samuel Daniel, George Chapman and Ben Jonson are all "plausible candidates for the role of 'rival poet.' All were protégés of Pembroke." Yet, we need to ask, were they all equally formidable as rivals? Shakespeare, after all, felt sick, defeated, and "struck dead" by the Rival Poet (e.g., Sonnets 78, 80, 85, 86), and implied that this man was not merely a very good poet but also an overpowering personality. How many rivals are known from other sources to have competed with Shakespeare? Only Jonson could be described, throughout his career, as a formidable competitor; no one disputes that Jonson saw himself as Shakespeare's rival over a period of many years, and that contemporaries were aware of this. For instance, (1) Thomas Fuller stated:

> Many were the *wit-combates* betwixt him [Shakespeare] and *Ben Iohnson*, which two I behold like a *Spanish great Gallion* and an *English man of War;* Master *Iohnson* (like the former) was built far higher in Learning; *Solid*, but *Slow* in his performances. *Shake-spear*, with the *English-man of War*, lesser in *bulk*, but lighter in *sailing*, could turn with all tides, tack about and take advantage of all winds, by the quickness of his Wit and Invention.[17]

Fuller (born 1608) could just have witnessed a wit-combat but, as others have noted, more probably "beheld" the ones he described in his mind's eye. What gave him the idea? Could it have been Sonnet 80?

> O how I faint when I of you do write,
> Knowing a better spirit doth use your name,

> And in the praise thereof spends all his might,
> To make me tongue-tied speaking of your fame.
> But since your worth, wide as the ocean is,
> The humble as the proudest sail doth bear,
> My saucy bark, inferior far to his,
> On your broad main doth wilfully appear.
> Your shallowest help will hold me up afloat,
> Whilst he upon your soundless deep doth ride;
> Or, being wracked, I am a worthless boat,
> He of tall building, and of goodly pride.
> Then if he thrive, and I be cast away,
> The worst was this: my love was my decay.

It has been said of Fuller that he described the wit combats "in terms reminiscent of the stock description of the Armada battle."[18] True: yet the coincidence that Shakespeare and Fuller both resorted to Armada imagery needs further consideration. How many other rivals in wit had been compared to warships, one that could "tack about" and the other "built far higher in Learning," solid and slow? The Rival's learning and Shakespeare's "rude ignorance" had been contrasted in Sonnet 78, and the Rival's pride, his polished verses and competitiveness all point to someone very like Jonson. In addition we must keep in mind that, while the identities of the Young Man and Rival Poet are now lost in the mists of time, Fuller was in touch with literary gossip and is therefore likely to have known, where we can only guess. Fuller's story of wit combats, so close to Sonnet 80, quite simply assumed that Jonson was the Rival. Of course, Fuller could have been mistaken: I think, though, that we disregard him at our peril.

It should also be emphasized that other seventeenth-century anecdotes depict Shakespeare and Jonson's relationship very much as the *Sonnets* depict that of the Poet and Rival Poet. (2) Thomas Plume recorded that Jonson composed the first line of an epitaph for himself and asked Shakespeare to finish it: "Here lies Ben Jonson who was once one [or: one's son]"; Shakespeare added, "Who while he lived was a slow thing / And now he's buried is nothing." Jonson's slowness, about which we hear from Fuller and others, is implied by Shakespeare's image of a galleon "of tall building and of goodly pride" (Sonnet 80.12), compared with a "saucy bark."

(3) At the christening of one of Jonson's children, Shakespeare "being in a deep study, Jonson came to cheer him up, and asked him why he was so melancholy." Shakespeare explained that he had been thinking about a present for his godchild: "'Faith, Ben, I'll e'en give him a dozen good latten spoons, and thou shalt translate

them." The pun on latten, a worthless metal, and Latin, the dead language, ridicules Jonson's oppressive learning, of which we hear again in the *Sonnets* and in Fuller. It is a curious coincidence, by the way, that Jonson misinterpreted Shakespeare's silence ("asked him why he was so melancholy") and that in Sonnet 86 Shakespeare's silence, provoked by the Rival Poet, was also misunderstood. As I have argued elsewhere,[19] Jonson characteristically thought of himself as the stronger and Shakespeare the weaker, and Shakespeare seems to have been aware of this, as the *Sonnets* again appear to confirm.

(4) Sonnet 86 describes the Rival Poet's overbearing behavior, which reduced Shakespeare to silence:

> Was it his spirit, by spirits taught to write
> Above a mortal pitch, that struck me dead?

Jonson's own writings, and his notorious remark "that Shakespeare wanted art," identify him as the most overbearing poet of his time, and his characteristic bullying was not reserved only for Shakespeare.[20]

(5) In *The Return from Parnassus* (?1599–1600), Kempe says, "O that Ben Jonson is a pestilent fellow . . . but our fellow Shakespeare hath given him a purge that made him beray his credit."[21] This confirms Fuller's wit-combats and the rivalry described in the *Sonnets*. Kempe here refers to the War of the Theatres, in which Shakespeare and Jonson supported opposite sides; the War, of course, was either an exact contemporary of the writing of the *Sonnets* or followed shortly thereafter.

The portrait of Ajax in *Troilus and Cressida*, which others have seen as a satire on Jonson, perhaps Kempe's "purge," gibes at Ajax's insolence, pride, emulation, surliness (Jonsonian qualities, amply confirmed by his other opponents in the War of the Theatres), and includes the mocking lines "I'll let his humour blood," "Fam'd be thy tutor, and thy parts of nature / Thrice fam'd beyond, beyond all erudition" (2.3.200–201). Jonson's pride in his famous tutor, William Camden, was expressed in a neat epigram, in his dedication for the Folio version of *Every Man in His Humour*, in his *Conversations* with Drummond and, we may guess, on other occasions, as an oblique way of congratulating himself on his own learning. If Shakespeare already thought this conceit insufferable when he first encountered Jonson, perhaps whilst he was writing the *Sonnets*, would that be so very astonishing?

(6) And here let us recall that even after Shakespeare's death Jon-

son could not resist remarking on his great contemporary's "small Latin and lesse Greek," a tactlessness very similar to the Rival Poet's attitude to Shakespeare's "heavy ignorance" (Sonnet 78).

Nevertheless, I have to admit that there are weaknesses—or at any rate uncertainties—in the thesis that Jonson was the Rival Poet. First, what poems by Jonson could Shakespeare have meant when he referred to "the proud full sail of his great verse" (Sonnet 86.1)? The truth is: we don't know. Yet we do know that Jonson chose not to preserve some of his early work, dating from before 1598. Second, is it likely that Jonson, who told Drummond that he would not flatter though he saw death, could be described by Shakespeare as guilty of gross flattery, which is how I interpret the charge of "gross painting" of Sonnet 82? The answer is: despite Jonson's disclaimer, many of his occasional poems and dedications are unblushing exercises in patron-pleasing. Third, how can we explain the Rival's "affable familiar ghost / Which nightly gulls him with intelligence" (Sonnet 86.9–10)? The answer is: Jonson told Drummond that, when the plague raged in London, he—in the country—"saw in a vision his eldest son . . . appear unto him with the mark of a bloody cross on his forehead"; he heard the next day that his son had died in London. Jonson believed in supernatural visitations.

In sum, the portrait of the Rival in the *Sonnets* fits Jonson's very unusual character both as a man and as a writer. The Rival is learned, proud, composes polished verses "by all the Muses fil'd," is a gross flatterer, makes Shakespeare feel "unletter'd," puts pressure on him to give way and, by his overbearing, highly competitive behavior impresses the Young Man. The "weaknesses" in the case for Jonson are not really weaknesses, they are merely blanks in his biography, no more surprising than the blanks in Shakespeare's biography before 1592, when Shakespeare was older than was Jonson in 1598.

And if Jonson now emerges more clearly as the Rival Poet, this in turn supports the case for William Herbert as the Young Man. Even if we cannot date the beginning of Jonson's friendship with Herbert, its continuance over many years, and the fact that Shakespeare and Jonson were Herbert's most significant poetical protégés, gives added weight to these identifications.

As for the identification of Mary Fitton as the Dark Lady, although I hold no brief for her, I want to clear up some misunderstandings. To begin with, she was pregnant in February 1601, Pembroke being the supposed father of her child. Does that disqualify her as the Dark Lady, since Meres referred to the *Sonnets* in 1598? Not necessarily, for Meres did not say that all the *Sonnets* were written by 1598, and a Herbert-Fitton relationship could have continued for some time before 1601. Also, it has been said that Fitton was not a brunette. This objection was challenged by Arthur Marlowe,[22] who pointed out that at least one portrait, exhibited at the National Portrait Gallery in 1972, depicts her as a brunette. Perhaps we should conclude that surviving portraits of Fitton, as a blonde and as a brunette, suggest that, at a time when black was not beautiful, she dyed her hair, like Queen Elizabeth. Next, Duncan-Jones assumes that the Dark Lady's "bed-vow" (Sonnet 152.3) must be a marriage vow, hence that she is married (Sonnet 53). But the nonce word "bed-vow" could refer to her vow to be "true" to her lover (cf. *Troilus and Cressida*); "thou are twice forsworn to me love swearing" then means "you promised to be faithful to me, and you were unfaithful with the Young Man; you swear again to love me, and I know that you will be unfaithful again." Her bed-vow, in short, belongs to the same class of vow as the Poet's, who admits "I break twenty" (Sonnet 152.6). Lastly, two years older than Herbert, fourteen years younger than Shakespeare, Fitton suits the age differences implied in the *Sonnets*. I have the impression that the Dark Lady was older than the Young Man, and sexually more experienced: a two-year gap would do, if he was 16 or 17 and she 18 or 19 (in 1596 or 1597), and Shakespeare 32 or 33.

The identifications proposed in this paper may be graded, in my view, as follows: Herbert as the Young Man, very probable; Jonson as the Rival Poet, probable; Fitton as the Dark Lady, possible. How, finally, would Herbert have "performed" the *Sonnets*, how did Shakespeare expect this particular Young Man to react and what signs of his performance do we detect in the poems themselves?

We must assume, for a start, that when the Young Man first encountered the *Sonnets* he read them not as we do, as a sequence, but singly, when he received them one by one (or occasionally in small groups of two or more). Also, he seems to have been in close contact with the Poet, leaving aside some absences (Sonnets 27–28, 51, etc.) in the three years or more (Sonnet 104) covered by the sequence: the Poet therefore had the opportunity to observe the Young Man's reactions and to take these into account in writing his next sonnet.

Shakespeare being Shakespeare, we may be sure that he would have observed the Young Man's reactions with some care in any case. But the son of a glover from provincial Stratford, addressing a future peer of the realm and putting so many different kinds of emotional pressure on him, had to be exceptionally careful. I think we may take it that Shakespeare knew exactly what liberties he might permit himself, and that the Young Man reacted encouragingly (but see below). In other words, the Young Man's "performance" fed into the sequence and helped to shape it: we could almost say that he collaborated in the writing of the *Sonnets*.

He did not collaborate in publishing them. Why not? If the first seventeen were written to please the Young Man's parents,[23] I cannot believe that those that followed would be expected to have the same effect, for, to quote Duncan-Jones again, they could have been thought morally compromising. Some or all were composed by 1598 and the sequence remained unpublished until 1609: may we explain this gap by saying, as others have done, that "sonnets were no longer fashionable"? In the period 1598 to 1609 the stationers learned that Shakespeare's name on a title-page could sell any book, even books he had not written—is it conceivable that they would not have fought for the right to publish the most splendid sonnet sequence in the language? I conclude that steps must have been taken to ensure that these "sugared sonnets among his private friends" remained very private indeed.

While the Young Man found it exciting to be celebrated in the *Sonnets*, neither he nor Shakespeare seems to have wanted them to be widely known in their life-times. Quite apart from their love— whatever that may signify—the Poet inches towards an ever closer relationship with his lovely boy, and this is bound to make readers uncomfortable.[24] He may be perfectly sincere, but he and the boy must have been aware that it might be greatly to the Poet's advantage to cultivate someone so far above him socially. The relationship is unflattering to both: the more the Poet praises the more conscious we become of a campaign to take advantage of the boy's vanity. When he delivered the *Sonnets* one by one this would not have been so noticeable; once some or all were brought together in a single manuscript, the Poet's campaign and the Young Man's willingness to be flattered become embarrassing.

It was a permitted campaign, this very unusual declaration of love. Having established his position the Poet even dares to express negative feelings, rebuking his young friend for favoring an inferior poet (Sonnets 78–86, etc.) or for betraying him by sleeping with the Dark Lady (Sonnets 35, 134). This last episode demonstrates, more clearly than any other, that the Poet wrote under special constraints—that he could only say what the Young Man might be expected to permit him to say. So the Young Man and Poet, I repeat, were locked together in their "performances." How else can we explain the extraordinary self-torturing tactfulness of "Take all my loves, my love; yea, take them all" (Sonnet 40)?

In the *Sonnets* we hear only one voice but we are conscious of two principal performers (and several minor ones as well). There are moments when we almost hear the second principal's voice—"I grant thou wert not married to my Muse" (Sonnet 82),[25] apparently picking up the Young Man's impatient retort when he thought the Poet had gone too far in his reproaches. This reminds us that there are two sides to the story, and that the Poet's version could be misleading.

Many readers have been puzzled that Shakespeare, a shrewd judge of character, seems to have been so enchanted by his Young Man. Northrop Frye thought that "Shakespeare has lavished a century of the greatest sonnets in the language on an unresponsive oaf as stupid as a doorknob and as selfish as a weasel."[26] Once again the inherently improbable notion that Shakespeare might be attracted to his closest friends by, or in spite of, their stupidity! Is it really so, or is it possible that, because large sectors of the story remain invisible to us, we misjudge what appears to be visible? If the Pembroke theory is correct we now see that the Young Man's unworthiness, so memorably described by Frye, must be exaggerated by our angle of vision, and by the fact that Shakespeare tells only one side of the story to a reader who needs no help to be fair to the other side.

What else becomes more clearly visible? Take the Poet's daring when he stresses the Young Man's wasteful indifference to what he is so richly endowed with, his beauty (Sonnets 4.5–8, 9.9–11, etc.). This surely glances in passing at Herbert's wasteful generosity with money (he received more dedications than any English contemporary, except for Queen Elizabeth). Even after he succeeded to the earldom, in 1601, Herbert remained heavily indebted to moneylenders.[27] "Unthrifty loveliness" (Sonnet 4.1) indeed!

To pursue the "other side of the story" for a moment, there is very little evidence in the *Sonnets* that the Young Man had a sense of humor, and yet it seems inconceivable that Shakespeare would choose to have a close relationship, such as that described in the *Sonnets*, with someone lacking in humor: it is therefore reassuring to hear of Pembroke "always joking" with the king. There are few signs of the Young Man's intelligence, as Frye observed, though Shakespeare mentions "the beauty of thy mind" in passing (Sonnet 69.9), for, writing to the Young Man, Shakespeare did not feel the need to describe him to himself.

The Young Man's "performance," therefore, must have differed quite radically from the modern reader's. He first read the *Sonnets* singly or in small groups, in Shakespeare's own handwriting, and his reactions will have influenced the tone of those that followed; we, by contrast, see the completed sequence, in impersonal print, and our modern reader-response cannot affect the outcome. He knew what happened "off-stage," between sonnets, and would have no difficulty in decoding every allusion—the "sad augurs," the "canopy" (Sonnets 107, 125), etc., not to mention the Dark Lady and Rival Poet; we are not so privileged. When he first perused the Sonnets as a sequence, however, he may have realized belatedly that a whole may differ from the sum of its parts. We, too, four hundred years on, will see the *Sonnets* more clearly if we keep in mind not only that there will have been two sides to the story and two phases in the Young Man's "performance" but, no less important, how completely William Herbert fits the role of the Young Man. This explains the social distance between the Poet and his patron, the poet's social and emotional daring as also his seeming obsequiousness. When we see "the other side of the story" by recalling Herbert's early life at Wilton surrounded by rival poets, his affectionate and easy-going nature, his extravagance, his perhaps excessive respect for learning (and hence for learned men like the Rival Poet), his susceptibility to witty and highly sexed women (and hence to the Dark Lady), his unwillingness to marry—we are rewarded with a better understanding of a fascinating relationship. The "other side of the story" becomes even more visible when we take into account what is known of Herbert's later career—as a stylish letter-writer and minor poet; a theatre lover, the friend of Burbage and of a host of literary men. In the words of Clarendon, a political opponent, Herbert was "the most universally loved and esteemed of any man of that age"; he had "a disposition affable, generous and magnificent." Despite his faults, he was probably worthy of Shakespeare's love. Heminge and Condell, dedicating the First Folio to him, said that he had "prosecuted" the plays and their author "with so much favor" that "the volume asked to be yours." And, to conclude, do we not now have good reason[28] to believe that Shakespeare served Herbert's father as one of Pembroke's Men in the early 1590's?

Notes

1. In this essay I develop ideas from my two previous discussions of the *Sonnets*: see *Shakespeare's Impact on his Contemporaries* (London and Basingstoke: Macmillan, 1982), 104–8, and *Myriad-minded Shakespeare* (London and Basingstoke: Macmillan, second edition, 1998), 7–9, 11–14, 128–19. In *Shakespeare's Impact* I examine Shakespeare's relationship with Jonson in greater detail: 35–45, 93–103, 109–20, etc.

2. E. K. Chambers, *William Shakespeare: A Study of Facts and Problems*, 2 vols. (Oxford: Clarendon Press, 1930), 1:566.

3. *Shakespeare's Sonnets*, ed. Katherine Duncan-Jones (Walton-on-Thames: Thomas Nelson, 1997). All quotations from the *Sonnets* are from this edition.

4. A. C. Bradley, "Shakespeare the Man," in *Oxford Lectures on Poetry* (London: Macmillan, ed. 1950), 327. Cf. Duncan-Jones, "Introduction," *Shakespeare's Sonnets*, 86.

5. Brian O'Farrell, *Politician, Patron, Poet: William Herbert, Third Earl of Pembroke, 1580–1630* (Ph.D. dissertation, UCLA, 1966), 22.

6. Cf. Andreas Gebauer, *Von Macht und Mäzenatentum: Leben und Werk William Herberts, des dritten Earls von Pembroke* (Heidelberg: Carl Winter, 1987), 76; Michael Brennan, *Literary Patronage in the English Renaissance: The Pembroke Family* (London: Routledge, 1988), 156–57.

7. Edward, Earl of Clarendon, *The History of the Rebellion*, 6 vols. (Oxford: Clarendon Press, 1888; reprinted 1969), 6:120.

8. E. A. J. Honigmann, *Shakespeare: the 'lost years'* (Manchester: Manchester University Press, 1985, 1998), 54.

9. Cf. Giorgio Melchiori, *Shakespeare's Dramatic Meditations: An Experiment in Criticism* (Oxford: Clarendon Press, 1976), 144–45.

10. Cf. Bradley, "Shakespeare the Man," 336 fn.

11. See Tyler's edition, 1890, 41–42.

12. Bernard H. Newdigate, *Michael Drayton and his Circle* (Oxford: Basil Blackwell, 1941), 96.

13. Cf. *Shakespeare: the 'lost years,'* 52–53; Honigmann, *John Weever* (Manchester: Manchester University Press, 1987).

14. *Historical Manuscripts Commission* (Hatfield House, Part XI; London: H.M.S.O., 1906), 376.

15. For Allott's connections with Meres and Weever see *England's Helicon*, ed. Hyder E. Rollins, 2 vols. (Cambridge, Mass.: Harvard University Press, 1935), 2:47–49.

16. Samuel Schoenbaum, *William Shakespeare: A Documentary Life* (Oxford: Clarendon Press, 1975), 219.

17. Thomas Fuller, quoted by Chambers, *William Shakespeare*, 2:245. W. R. Alger in 1862 seems to have been the first to see that Fuller's story of wit-combats must be connected with Sonnet 80; see Hyder E. Rollins, *The Sonnets*, 2 vols. (Philadelphia: Modern Language Association, New Variorum Edition, 1944), 2:283.

18. I. A. Shapiro, " 'The Mermaid Club': An Answer and a Rejoinder," *MLR* 46 (1951), 58–63.

19. Honigmann, *Shakespeare's Impact on his Contemporaries*, 17.

20. Cf. Jonson's *Conversations* with Drummond, in *Ben Jonson*, ed. C.H. Herford, Percy and Evelyn Simpson, 11 vols. (Oxford: Clarendon Press, 1925–52.): "Samuel Daniel was a good honest Man . . . bot no poet"; "that next himself only Fletcher and Chapman could make a Mask"; "he . . . knew more jn Greek and Latin, than all the Poets jn England" (1:132, 133, 149).

21. For the anecdotes quoted in my second, third and fifth examples, cf. Chambers, *William Shakespeare*, 2:247 (Plume), 243 (Shakespeare as godfather), 201 (the purge).

22. Arthur Marlowe, *Shakespeare: Digging for the Truth* (Market Harborough: Green & Co., 1978), 34. The identification of Mary Fitton in early portraits may be open to challenge, but there is no dispute that ladies dyed their hair and made use of other cosmetic aids.

23. If Shakespeare's role as a go-between, enlisted to urge a young man to marry, seems farfetched, it should be remembered that he played a similar role when the

Mountjoys wanted to persuade Stephen Belott to marry their daughter (Chambers, *William Shakespeare,* 2:90). For Lady Pembroke's initiatives in arranging her son's marriage see Gebauer, 28.

24. See Gerald Hammond's account of the teasing, even rebellious, subtext of the *Sonnets (The Reader and Shakespeare's Young Man Sonnets,* [London: Macmillan, 1981], 13–14).

25. Compare Sonnets 57.9–10, 58.1–14.

26. Northrop Frye, "How True a Twain," (in *The Riddle of Shakespeare's Sonnets,* essays by Edward Hubler, etc., [London: Routledge, 1962], 27).

27. See O'Farrell, 54.

28. See Andrew Gurr, *The Shakespearian Playing Companies* (Oxford: Clarendon Press, 1996), 270–77.

II
Shakespeare Performed in Our Time: Theatre, Film, Text, and Interpretation

II

Writing about Shakespeare's Plays in Performance

John Russell Brown

Believing that Shakespeare set down words so that a company of actors would perform his plays before very varied audiences, readers have sought to respond to the texts as if in performance and have taken whatever opportunity arises to see them in the theatre. In both efforts they are often frustrated, but critics and scholars provide further assistance by reporting on reviews and records of earlier productions and writing detailed accounts of performances they have witnessed. They also listen to actors, directors, and designers talking about their work and then try to distinguish between intention and achievement. Writing about performances of Shakespeare's plays has become such an accepted and often industrious academic pursuit that it may be profitable to stop to consider exactly what the "theatrical dimension" in Shakespeare studies entails.

The basic questions are: "To what are we giving our attention, and what do we bring to this experience?" Neither "hearing" nor "seeing" a play are satisfactory words for this activity, because attending a performance involves far more than sight and hearing, and more than simple cognition of fixed signs. All our senses, instincts, and memories may be involved and will interact with each other. Both words and everyday actions can be given unexpected and exceptional powers in the theatre, so that any full account of performance must go beyond mere quotation or factual description and call upon impressionistic and very personal reconstruction. Two other questions arise immediately: "How can we best describe or report on a theatre experience, and what do we gain by this exercise?"

In recent years, the study of what constitutes performance has occupied many scholars in university Departments of Theatre, Anthropology, Linguistics, and Sociology. In 1980 Keir Elam's *The Semiotics of Theatre and Drama* was the first book to provide analyses of speech-acts and so demonstrated the interweaving of many modes of perception and reception involved in the performance of a dramatic text.[1] Later critics have built on this, giving more emphasis to the physical and corporeal elements of performance, to the actors' modes of preparation, to social and political contexts for performance, and to all the reactions and interactions that occur among individual members of an audience as they share the occasion and, in some measure, help to create it. It must seem strange to scholars in this new discipline of Performance Studies that so little writing about Shakespeare has made use of the distinctions and terminology that are now available. Perhaps one reason is that so much cannot be assimilated rapidly, especially at this time when new forms of literary, as opposed to theatrical, criticism are already busying the more adventurous minds. Another reason for neglecting this new form of study may be that "Performance," as Marvin Carlson has put it, "by its nature resists conclusions, just as it resists the sort of definitions, boundaries, and limits so useful to traditional academic writing and academic structures."[2] To consider Shakespeare's plays in the light of recent Performance Studies is to enter forbidding territory in which perception must always be open to question.

The critical challenge, nevertheless, remains: we should respond to the plays as works for performance and therefore need to know how best to do this. Shakespeare's imagination was not simply full of words or speeches, but of men and women in action; his art was to write down what actors should speak while representing those invented individuals as if they were fully alive in continuous action on a stage before an audience. Necessarily such a performance is more difficult to comprehend than any number of written words. Much of it will contain a great deal which Shakespeare cannot have foreseen and, even when he was alive, could not control. Moreover every single performance will be different from all others, even if the same actors are involved and use the same theatre building. Faced with describing such complex and ever-changing phenomena, a critic must decide, consciously or unconsciously, to which incidents on stage and to which impression made upon him- or herself—and on other critics—should be given most attention. To notice everything is impossible but, even if it were, the task of describing and assessing everything would remain. The critic's own mind and personal history are of crucial importance because they will control both the selection of material for study and the perception of it. The best person to describe performances could be someone of strong sensibilities but without conscious predilections or foreknowledge of the play's stage history; such a person might give attention to the show, entirely and openly, as it evolves moment by moment, seeing clearly and responding wholeheartedly and imaginatively. Yet, on the other hand, another person who is experienced enough to be on the lookout for what is new and what has been achieved with special power or in closest accord with Shakespeare's words might be the more useful, if more biased, critic.

Among the wide range of methods used in writing about Shakespearian performances some may be considered provocative rather than essential, because they fasten on modern stage techniques that would have been impossible in Shakespeare's day or are interpretative in ways alien to thought and perception at that time. So, for example, Jay L. Halio's volume on *A Midsummer Night's Dream* for the *Shakespeare in Performance* series has a concluding chapter which details the innovations of Robert Lepage and his designer, Michael Levine, in a production for the National Theatre in London in 1992:

> A large circular pool of water, about 25 mm deep over an area of 120 square metres, surrounded by a bank of mud (made of Bentonite mixed with lignite and water), dominated the set from the first scene to the last ... [T]his *Dream* was meant to take us back to the beginnings of life and to suggest connections between the primitive world and the civilised one; hence, the primordial mud, a violent coupling between an androgynous Puck and a blue-faced fairy ... , the "group sex" in muddy water, and the "noisy rutting" of Titania and Bottom.³

The critic is objective for the most part, noting, almost in passing, that Titania "does not lie asleep in her bower but hangs above it, upside down suspended by a rope" (121). However he also allows himself a few marks of approval, so he describes "some very nice touches ... that somewhat softened the effect of the 'mud-wrestling' " (122–23). These are comparatively simple actions that might have been found in almost any twentieth-century production.

This review gives reasons for recounting so much that has little direct connection to the dialogue which Shakespeare wrote:

> the theatre often resorts to new, hitherto unimagined—even unimaginable—ways of presentation ... : "what works" [on stage] translates into what illuminates for us things we did not see or hear or feel, and therefore did not comprehend as fully in previous productions. (26)

The critic recounts and marvels at new devices of theatre production and the results of long, idiosyncratic, and painstaking rehearsals because his imagination had been aroused and had jolted his previous perceptions of the play. The result was that he was able to sense the "ghosts of Freud and Jung inhabit[ing] the production" and to find a "liquidity in the text" that Shakespeare wrote centuries before (119).

One thought must occur to any reader: could not these perceptions have derived as well from a present-day reading of the text by someone who was familiar with the same books and had had much the same "lived experience" as this director and his designer? We shall never know, but the production had given their ideas a palpable quality, a "local habitation and a name" for those who witnessed it without too much resistence to its innovations. Theatre is a place for seeing and Halio is claiming that this production showed its audience qualities that have always been inherent in the text and had illuminated it for them at this time.

The very new, especially in scenic and extravagantly non-realistic stage activity, is the easiest part of any production to document and critics often give most attention to it, even when they disapprove of its treatment of a text. As chronicles of Shakespeare's plays on the stage in our time, such writing about performances has its value, even at the cost of considerable length as its words limp behind the spectacle they try to describe. Of course, a stubborn question remains: is this, indeed, "our" *Dream* or is it, less interestingly, that *Dream* which a few theatre people had judged appropriate for themselves and their particular kind of theatrical pleasure? The critic cannot sufficiently answer that question by asserting a personal interest in the contrivance. The task of writing about performances of Shakespeare is not complete until the critic has taken into account these performances' effect on audiences. Any striking invention should be judged according to its particular value as entertainment or as an illumination of life or thought outside the theatre.

Other critics are wary of new and obviously contrived stage effects and take refuge in fixing their attention on the words of the text, noting what the actors make them "mean" for a hearer, as if reference to a printed edition provided sufficient understanding of any effect and was a mark of authenticity in their description of performance. Others try to "look" beyond words at what the actors do, pretending that they are performing on some unlocalized Globe-like stage, without twentieth-century embellishments and trickery. They pay heed to the "presence" of actors and assess the individuality and interactions of the play's characters. Both kinds of discourse have a great deal to document and many small details to compare between one production and another. So extensive and so various is the material to be dealt with, that criticism of this kind can never be complete and, therefore, seems incidental, governed by accident in choice of what it considers and, consequently, in any judgement that it makes. Not surprisingly, these critics tend to write at length and in conclusion are liable to note the "infinite variety" of interpretation that Shakespeare's "characters" give rise to in performance, forbearing to express any preference between them. This does not take their readers very much further than a slow and thoughtful reading of the text itself might achieve, although descriptions of actual behavior can awaken sense-responses and so be a spur to fresh perception.

Any writing about how a performance deals with the words of Shakespeare's text is an endless task, always limited by its means and its author's selectivity. Even Marvin Rosenberg's huge accumulations of careful detail in his books about four of the tragedies are limited in scope, as he has been the first to confess. As the volumes followed each other over the years from 1961 to 1992, comparisons were supplied ever more generously and scrupulously, as frequent and minutely careful reference was made to Shakespeare's texts. But their principal shortcomings are those of selectivity and not incompleteness: Rosenberg is star-struck and so pays attention only to leading actors or, for present times, to what directors have encouraged their actors to do. His scope includes star performers from all ages since Shakespeare's and from theatres other than the English-speaking, but he does not give to any one performance of a play the attention that follows its entire action, and so he is unable to consider its overall shape and impact. He tells readers what his chosen performers have done to bring their roles alive on stage but only at one moment and then at another. While he uses every possible means to say how they spoke particular words of the texts and what they did while doing so, much is inevitably missing. The more ground he has been able to cover in his studies of single plays, the more inadequate has become the engagement with any single performance as a response to the whole play in one unique time and place, his concentration on the leading actors notwithstanding. Because his method is to create a patchwork out of small observations, he has no scope to consider either the material substance, shape, or impact of any one of the productions from which the shreds and patches have been taken.

Rosenberg's latest volume on *The Masks of Hamlet* is exemplary of much other writing about performance when it centers attention on the actors of the principal characters of a play. The "Prologue" tells us the reason for undertaking this task:

the words [of the text] were written to be clothed in the unmistakably physical, recognizable human forms of Shakespeare's players. Live people. Hamlet is only part of himself on the page; he is complete only as real-ized on stage or in the imagination.[4]

In line with this approach, the book's last section spends thousands of words on how various Hamlets have, or might have, said "The rest is silence" and, possibly, the Folio's "O, o, o, o." as well. An earlier section considers the other figures on stage in this scene, but briefly, and mostly in their relationship to Hamlet. The focus of the book is unmistakable: "What may Hamlet be trying to convey?" (924). That the critic cannot answer with any certainty is the message that he reiterates time and again; for example:

> All the words about Hamlet, almost three centuries of words, and as many of stagings, and the adventure into the depths of the play has hardly begun. (924)

But we should remember that this play has width as well as depth because it mirrors life as Shakespeare lived it and thought about it in the context of an entire nation and among people in all their variety of mind, feeling, and activity. These social and political concerns are expressed in narrative, action and interaction, dramatic structure and timing, stage images of all kinds and in many combinations, whole casts of characters and supernumeraries, and the entire text of each play—which all together needs a "fellowship" of actors to perform and not just a few star actors. Rosenberg's star-centered observations about moments of performance do not take his readers very far towards an understanding of these essential aspects of the plays.

This form of study—the creation of a patchwork from details about how Hamlet and others around him behave—has other shortcomings. Because no one performance is considered as a continuous action, description always lacks an important ingredient: the actor's response to his or her whole journey through a play, which involves changes in relationship to other characters and actors, and in self-awareness. How any one moment is arrived at will always be part of that moment in theatre performance. In outwardly visible and audible signs, the past is always marked indelibly in the present on the bodies and minds of the performers and so no moment can be fairly judged in isolation. Moreover, as expectation changes, so does the actor's very being and the audience's attention. From manifestations of these facts stems much of the excitement of performance—an excitement which falls through the net of those descriptions of performance that focus on single moments. But perhaps the greatest difficulty of this form of writing about Shakespeare's plays is to know what to choose to emphasize in any brief description. Often it is only those details that the critic finds to be unexpected and also describable that find their way into the reckoning, and these details may not always represent the full force of a production or the reasons for its appeal or failure.[5]

Hamlet's encounter with Ophelia in Act 3, scene 1, may serve as an example of Rosenberg's detailed accounting, as he piles up conflicting "treatments" of "Ha, ha, are you honest?":

> Calvert assumed that the laugh indicated that Hamlet was to put on the "antic" role here—he suspects the plot. . . . With the tense Kainz who had turned his back to Ophelia, " . . . [it] is an attempt to regain composure: laughing nervously, he suddenly turns round. . . ." Warner "falls back shocked and fumbling" . . . Kachalov's subtext [was]: "I want to show her to her face that I know all." Booth took the gifts in his left hand, but with his right he seized Ophelia's wrist, and gripped it even though she cried out; Olivier stared at her; Evans seized her and held her before him; Gielgud grasped her by the hands; McKellen held her face, and studied it—she had to turn away. (507–8)

From this bombardment of "facts," a dazed reader will gather little more than many incomplete and conflicting impressions.

The effect of a critic's predilections can be seen most clearly when he or she writes at much shorter length, as in the accounts of performance included in many recent one-volume editions of the plays. In his Oxford edition of *Macbeth*, Nicholas Brooke heads the relevant section of the Introduction "Staging," which is as revealing as Rosenberg's repeated use of the plural "Masks" in the titles of his books. In a Preface, the editor explains more: during a visit to Munich long ago, in the church of St. John Nepomuk he

> experienced a conversion, not of a religious kind, but to a perception of baroque art. What was most strange was that it was *Macbeth* which came so powerfully into my mind: for better or for worse, my debt to that occasion will be obvious in this volume.[6]

So, it would seem, the attention to "performance" provided in other volumes of this edition is replaced here by a care for "staging." Brooke gives a high proportion of his four or five thousand words to operatic versions of the play. He notes that the Folio edition has numerous calls for music and quotes Frances Shirley's opinion that when the text speaks of "horses' hooves, the mew, croak, and whine of the witches' familiars, the owl's screech, the bell, and more certainly thunder," these sounds were all heard in the play's first performances. He records how the supernatural episodes were staged over succeeding centuries and the text reduced accordingly. He notices that Lady Macbeth came to have more sway in the theatre than her husband, but quotes Mrs. Inchbald to the effect that "spectators return again to their childish credulity, and tremble, as in the nursery, at a witch and a goblin" (43).

Coming to the present century, Brooke seeks to explain why "though quite often played, the play has so seldom been successful in modern theatres" (47). He notices Laurence Olivier's Macbeth at Stratford-upon-Avon in 1955 as remembered "chiefly (it seems) for his resemblance to Edmund Kean in dynamic presence and blazing eyes, together with his own characteristically eccentric locutions" (47)—an opinion that can easily be countered by the recorded effect of this performance in the minds of other theatre-goers, actors, and numerous writers about Shakespearian performances.[7] No other twentieth-century production gets more than glancing attention, except Trevor Nunn's at the intimate Other Place theatre in Stratford (1976):

> The odd stress on religious rituals which had been tedious in the main theatre [in Nunn's earlier version] was neutralized here because it seemed to be a convenient device to organize the play in what was very nearly a round space; Ian McKellen and Judi Dench gave fine performances, but they were not what made the play so memorable. (47)

Here, with the almost endless "evidence" of a film to choose from, this editor gives no more than this generalized, and consequently dismissive, appraisal of "fine" acting.

Gary Taylor's *Henry V*, also for Oxford University Press, gives attention to more of the multitudinous facts of performance and adds some weight to the stage-history by splicing his account of it into the general critical Introduction of the play. But his focus is narrow and he refers to the theatre only when wishing to debate some problematic intention of the dramatist. His writes as if very sure of his own opinions, so that reference to performances is primarily a way of reasserting previously-held views. One actor catches the attention of this critic when he presents a dogged and pugnacious Henry the Fifth, "shorter and less impressive physically than many of the other actors around him," and another when he "may have exaggerated Henry's own uneasiness with his role." Judgement follows decisively:

the demotic, complicated Henry of these recent productions takes us closer to the play than has any production since the Restoration.[8]

Taylor makes no apology for selectivity and no attempt to give a comprehensive account when judging performances but, at his best, he uses stage-history shrewdly, showing how the play's minor characters have made a greater mark in the theatre than is obviously indicated by the words they speak (59–62) and how the theatricality of the Chorus has been vindicated in many very different ways (56–57).

By virtue of their small scale, accounts of performance in editions of the plays cannot demonstrate all the ways of writing about performance. They do however exemplify the most common methods in relation to other forms of study and criticism. When two new editions of the same play are published simultaneously, as happened when the Oxford and New Cambridge editions of *Measure for Measure* appeared in 1991, comparisons between them can illuminate their different usage of identical material. The very strategy of writing about performances when presenting a text is different in these two cases. In N. W. Bawcutt's Oxford edition, the section on "The Play in Performance" precedes that on "The Play," as if such matters are to be dealt with before giving attention to the main task in hand. In Brian Gibbons's edition for Cambridge, "The play on the stage" is promoted to be the concluding section of the Introduction.

These editions have much in common, most notably the inclusion of many undebatable facts about the various cuts and additions that have, at various times, been made to the text. However, when acting is their concern, they are very different. Naming the actors in principal roles or describing specific pieces of stage business is usually as much as the Oxford provides—although the "real, sombre splendour" of John Emery's "depraved, abandoned" Barnardine gets a long descriptive quotation from 1846—while the Cambridge seldom cites any performer without being precisely descriptive of some element in performance and attempting to characterize its style. While Bawcutt comments that Sarah Siddons was forty years of age in 1795, Gibbons notes that in 1811–12 at Covent Garden, she was "so weakened by age that when she knelt in the last scene before the Duke she could only get up again with his help."[9]

The Cambridge edition is also more ambitious in trying to put each piece of information into its context. While both editors retell the story of William Poel placing an "Elizabethan stage" within a picture-frame stage, it is Gibbons who notes that, in 1908 at Stratford-upon-Avon, Poel's actors were playing "constantly to the front" and that the stage projected "beyond its usual limits" (59). While both note the long pauses that have variously been introduced in modern productions, it is the Cambridge edition that is the more helpful in showing the effects that have been obtained. The silence that Peter Brook asked his young Isabella to hold before pleading for her brother's life is noted by both, but only Gibbons tells how, afterwards, her "words came quiet and level, and as their full import of mercy reached Angelo, a sob broke from him" (64). Whereas, for Keith Hack's production at Stratford in 1974, the Oxford edition notes that, at the beginning of act 5, the Duke "descended from the flies on a bar labelled 'Deus ex machina' " (40), the Cambridge explains that the director was an admirer of Brecht and had conceived the play as a "fable of social oppression." His Duke was the actor-manager of a jaded and underpaid company of actors:

> For the final scene the Duke with golden hair descended on a ramp labelled "deus ex machina"; his over-acting was intended to undermine the audience's belief in the happy ending. (70)

"It was ironic," the editor adds, "that this production failed to give the low-life characters substance: [they] were mere caricatures without conviction."

While the Oxford edition describes performances in moments, leaving the reader to think of the consquences, its Cambridge rival attempts a wider and more sustained view and gives attention to a production's physical and ideological context. The concluding paragraph of the former begins, dutifully: "Outside the British isles the play has had a rather limited stage-history"; that of the other edition:

> The play's rhythms, the scale of emotion and the texture of the language, the development of thought and argument, can be damaged or obscured by unsuitably dominant settings.

Writing about performances of Shakespeare's plays should not be limited to a collection of momentary details about what individual actors have said and done so that they can be used to support, without defending, the writer's own critical views. Nor should it be guided solely by an uncritical acceptance of the writer's own predilections. The pleasures of recounting a number of new and amazing stage inventions or a wide range of unexpected on-stage activities should also entail some adjudication of their interest and value. These are some standards that could usefully be applied and would be in keeping with recent developments in Performance Studies.

By asking what is entailed in any performance in a theatre before an audience, scholars in this new discipline have come to recognize certain basic elements that are often neglected by writers about Shakespeare. First, a performance provides a progressive experience for both actors and audiences. The passage of time should be involved in any description of a theatrical event: sequence, development, growth, and possibly change is happening at every moment in a play. Neither actor nor audience remains the same throughout a performance. Secondly, during a performance, the actors as the persons in a drama pass through various imagined, and sometimes partly realized, locations and so arrive at a conclusion or, occasionally, come to a stop. On stage, the play is like a journey in which various places are visited and so, to describe its performance, space as well as time must come into question. The journey needs to be noticed, at least its beginning and its end, and what gets lost in the process, and what is retained, newly discovered, or created. Describing both these basic features of performance, and so involving time and space, should encourage critics who write about any play of Shakespeare's to keep its whole effect in view and dissuade them from dealing only with momentary perceptions.

Performance Studies insist that what happens on stage is only one part of a theatrical performance. In theatres within European traditions, audiences are usually kept sitting comfortably in the dark, their attention held by what happens in the bright and other "world" on the stage. But even under these un-Shakespearian conditions, the actors, if not the audience, know how much they are affected nightly by the behavior of the audience and how, in consequence, what they do changes as well. This effect is heightened when performances are given in close contact with an audience that is free to move and talk in the same light as the actors. Under those conditions, many more of Shakespeare's lines can be addressed to the audience than may at first appear to a reader and, it will also be found, the audience is likely to respond with surprising freedom. A critic who wishes to view the plays on stage in something like the conditions for which they were written, should seek out performances in which the actors and audience are not kept apart from each other by lights or the physical conditions of staging and where the imaginations of neither party are confined by restrictive predetermination. Yet even with minimal contact between stage and audience, theatre is a social occasion and the nature of that meeting is part of what the enactment of a play achieves at any moment. A performance has not been fully described if its audience has not been given careful attention.

A writer who wishes to study Shakespeare's plays in the theatre—for whatever reason—should remember that each performance is unique. Not only does it include much that could never be under a dramatist's control because of the many other agencies at work and the complexity of the human participators on stage and in the audience, all of which will change from one occasion to another, but a performance will not be the same for every member of an audience, no matter how fully shared is the pleasure that is given. Writing about performance, it is prudent to remember Marvin Carlson's advice that its nature is to resist conclusions, definitions, boundaries, and limits. In a theatre we view Shakespeare's plays as they give rise to an endless series of new manifestations in which each instance has unique qualities. Descriptions should be specific about date and place; their writers should be aware that the finer details of any one moment may well be ephemeral and their wider significance open to doubt. On the other hand, insofar as the plays become the mirrors of our age and of ourselves, those unique and temporary qualities, dependent as they are on the lives outside of the theatre of all participants, may well be among those that are most worthy of attention.

Writing about performances of Shakespeare's plays is a complex task, but worth attempting because each three or so hours in the theatre are like a glass through which we are able to see Shakespeare's imagined creation coming to life in more or less its full context. We also witness the play's effect as performance draws upon the experience and sensibilities of actors and audiences of later ages, including most revealingly, our own.

Notes

1. Elam, *The Semiotics of Theatre and Drama* (London: Methuen, 1980).
2. Marvin Carlson, *Performance: a Critical Introduction* (London and New York: Routledge, 1996), 189. Another introduction to this field of study is Elaine Aston and George Savona, *Theatre as Sign-System: a Semiotics of Text and Performance* (London and New York; Routledge, 1991).
3. Halio, *A Midsummer Night's Dream* (Manchester: Manchester University Press, 1994), 118–19.
4. Rosenberg, *The Masks of Hamlet* (Cranbury, N.J.: Associated University Presses, 1992), xiii.

5. The present writer had prolonged experience of two of the productions referred to in Professor Rosenberg's study, directing one and being present at many rehearsals of Peter Hall's with Albert Finney at the National Theatre in London, and can report that neither account mentions any details from the scenes which he would chiefly speak about in assessing the achievements and failures of these productions. This is not to argue that closeness to a production will give a truer view of its qualities, but to illustrate how far one judgement may vary from another.

6. Brooke, Preface, *Macbeth* (Oxford: Oxford University Press, 1990), vii.

7. See, for example, Gareth Lloyd Evans, from a careful account of the performance, in *Focus on "Macbeth,"* ed. John Russell Brown (London; Routledge, 1982), 97: "Olivier created an overwhelming sense of growing spiritual fatigue in a man haunted by some of the very questions the play leaves us wondering at" or Dennis Bartholomeusz in his comparative stage history, *Macbeth and the Players* (Cambridge; Cambridge University Press, 1969), 259: "Olivier seems to have caught unerringly the sensitiveness intermingled with the evil in Macbeth."

Samuel L. Leiter, in the compendium he edited, *Shakespeare Around the Globe: a Guide to Notable Postwar Revivals* (New York; Greenwood Press, 1986), writes of Olivier's "momentous performance" as Macbeth (356) and brings together the testaments of numerous critics, such as "that rare Macbeth who was outstanding both in speaking the poetry and conveying the sense of a dangerous warrior" or, more briefly, a Macbeth who was "strenuous, lurid, unforgettable" (368–69).

Perhaps the most affirmative review was by Harold Hobson in *The Sunday Times*, concluding: "Macbeth is notoriously one of the most treacherous parts in the entire realm of drama; but Sir Laurence's performance is such that I do not believe there is an actor in the world who can come near him." The value of this review is considered in the context of Sir Harold's other reviews by Dominic Shellard in *Shakespeare Survey 49* (Cambridge: Cambridge University Press, 1996), 225–34.

8. Taylor, Introduction, *Henry V* (Oxford: Oxford University Press, 1982), 51.

9. Gibbons, Introduction, *Measure for Measure* (Cambridge: Cambridge University Press, 1991), 29, 56; Bawcutt, Introduction, *Measure for Measure* (Oxford: Oxford University Press, 1991), 29.

Unfolding and Cutting: *Measure for Measure* at the Old Vic in 1957–58

G. R. PROUDFOOT

IN THE OPENING SCENE OF *MEASURE FOR MEASURE*, VINCENTIO, DUKE OF Vienna, assures Escalus that it would be superfluous and impertinent on his part to unfold the properties of government to so learned and experienced an exponent of them. He also assures Angelo that he is an open book, that his history is unfolded to the beholder by his visible behavior. The ensuing action is much concerned with the unfolding both of the Duke's view of government and of what may be concealed beneath Angelo's visible austerity. Faced with the play's Gordian ironies and complexities, theatrical directors frequently prefer to cut the text rather than to let it unfold to its full length.

In a review of Michael Boyd's 1998 production of *Measure for Measure* at the Royal Shakespeare Theatre, Stratford-upon-Avon, Peter Holland takes note of some cutting of the text:

> For the most part, Boyd's cuts are aimed at simplification. Directors and actors playing the Duke usually have to come to an understanding of why the Duke chooses not to tell Isabella that Claudio is alive, trying to make their own sense of his explanation that he "will keep her ignorant of her good, / To make her heavenly comforts of despair / When it is least expected." Boyd cuts the lines and, with them, the difficulty. Such a cut removes the play's density in favour of an easier comprehension of character. But, in any case, Boyd's overdetermined work militates against the actors' subtle explorations of role. (*TLS*, 22 May 1998: 23)

Holland characterizes the production as "At times maddeningly crass" but "just as often, piercingly brilliant." Among Boyd's more radical cuts are the suppression of all references to Vienna and the removal of the Duke from the opening scene before Angelo enters—"his appointment of Angelo is left as a message on a cylinder dictaphone after he has rushed out on the verge of collapse . . . close to a nervous breakdown."

In the cyclic debate between text and performance—or at least between the rival impulses of the challenge to animate the words of the received text and the temptation to include reshaping of those words in the interests of a favored, selective interpretation—we would seem to be back in a phase of directorial tyranny. The situation curiously recalls the 1950s, when illuminating productions, especially of plays then not much in favour with audiences, were hailed as discoveries in productions—most famously those of the young Peter Brook—which achieved their power and impact, among other means, by wholesale and tendentious reshaping and cutting of the text. Among the plays so reshaped was *Measure for Measure*, not only by Brook himself in 1950 but by other producers in his wake. What Brook chose to play down at the end of the action was any explicit association of the Duke with divine power or prescience; he also cut the first of the Duke's two tentative proposals of marriage to Isabella, thus increasing the shock of incongruity of the second.[1] Some years later, Margaret Webster, producing the play for the Old Vic company, chose rather to emphasize the Duke's role as spiritual mentor. My aims in this essay are to draw attention to her production, which has received less than its due of comment, and to reflect further on the ways in which cutting the text can not only damage "the play's density" but even militate against "an easier comprehension of character."

In the 1950s, Michael Benthall undertook a five-year program of staging every play in the First Folio at the Old Vic. The fifth year—the season of 1957–58—included a number of plays which were not often performed and had presumably been postponed until late in the project. Among these were the three parts of *Henry VI* and *Measure for Measure*. Margaret Webster, who was invited to tackle *Measure*, had left London in the 1930s to make a career in the U.S.A., where she was well known by 1957 both as a Shakespearian producer and as author of *Shakespeare without Tears* (1942). She returned to England to direct *The Merchant of Venice* at Stratford-upon-Avon in 1956. Her views of *Measure* were already highly developed, and her enthusiasm for it showed clearly in her book.

Her production opened on 19 November 1957. Critical reactions were overwhelmingly positive (on the evidence of some fifty newspaper and magazine reviews and articles). The play's theatrical fortunes had been in the ascendant at least since Peter Brook's Stratford production in 1950: now it was hailed as exciting, topical and gloriously funny; as "one of Shakespeare's liveliest plays" (N.D. in *The Scotsman,* 25 November); even as "one of the very top ones, way up with Lear and the Tempest" (*Tribune,* 29 November).

One reason for its success was the outstandingly strong cast. Even the smallest parts were played by such future stars as Judi Dench (Juliet; she was also Ophelia to John Neville's Hamlet), David Waller (Barnardine, reduced by cutting to a single scene and played as a drunken circus clown), Barbara Leigh-Hunt (Francisca) and Margaret Courtney (Mistress Overdone). A further source of strength was that the Duke and Isabella were not new to their roles: Anthony Nicholls had been the Duke at Stratford in 1956 while Barbara Jefford had made a notable debut as Peter Brook's Isabella in 1950. John Neville's young, attractive Angelo was innovative by contrast with such mature earlier performers as John Gielgud or Charles Laughton.

The producer regarded the play as a challenge, but one that she had been confronting in theory for many years. She approached *Measure* with clear ideas about the play, some of which she had already expressed in her book. Classing it among Shakespeare's "Plays Unpleasant," she revealed her awareness of it as a "problem play" in the 1890s sense. She was also aware of its theatrically problematic character: "the balance of the play's second half swings dangerously away from the Isabella-Angelo story toward the comedy of the prison scenes. Lucio, Pompey, and Abhorson threaten to carry it away, with their pungent vitality"; "There are inconsistencies of a minor nature in the text, which skillful staging will easily smooth out"; "Shakespeare is not even sure, I think, that this spiritual regeneration [of Angelo] can take place; but the artificial devices of the happy-ending plot have at least opened the way for it, and the whole play must be motivated not to the finality of a last-act curtain, but to this speculative conclusion."[2] Interviewed for the *Daily Telegraph* (18 November 1957), she revealed her plan for the production. " 'I have always thought,' she said," that it is a difficult " 'play to tackle and I had to find a formula on which to work.' " Her conclusion was that " 'Measure for Measure' is built on the lines of the medieval moralities and calls for a highly stylised setting. . . . the somewhat arbitrary emotions in 'Measure for Measure' call for various levels: almost the Heaven, Earth and Hell of the old plays."

The practical realization of these ideas began as the spectators took their seats. "Neatly labelled for us to read on the drop curtain at the Old Vic last night were all the ingredients of Shakespeare's 'Measure for Measure'—justice, authority, lust, charity, frailty, lechery, vice, trust, allegiance and law" (Felix Barker, *Evening News,* 21

November 1957). The labels appeared within silhouetted forms identifiable with the characters, "like a dust-jacket for a handsome edition of *Everyman*" (Philip Squire, *Plays and Players*, January 1958). The drop curtain was displayed before and after the play and during the interval.

It rose to reveal a stage very full of actors. On a high platform at the back stood the Duke, with four attendants, two bearing large banners, against a grey-blue backcloth of radiating sunbeams, shadowed at right and left by the dark outlines of a large, spiky wheel and of a gibbet, emblems of mortality in Vienna. Steps led up past the wheel to the wings right and down from either end of the platform to the level of the main stage. On the steps at stage right stood, in descending order, Escalus (ready to step up in answer to the Duke's first word), the Provost, the Justice, and Friar Peter. The upstage area beneath the platform was fitted with heavy, studded double doors which, when shut, could suggest convent or prison. Now they were open to reveal Lucio, Froth, and the two gentlemen standing directly under the Duke. Four pike-bearing soldiers lined the stage, in front of the stage-left steps that Angelo would soon ascend to receive his commission from the Duke. A low rostrum raised the stage level within the semicircle described by the platform and its two descending sets of steps. An apron stage extended beyond the proscenium arch, which was walled at the sides by flats and supplied with a down-stage entrance door at each side. The apron went as far as the orchestra pit, into which it descended by three broad steps, converting the pit into the lower reaches of the prison. For the opening scene, this large space was empty except for Elbow and Abhorson. The Duke was above (some nine feet above stage level), his benign authority pictured in the radiating sunbeams; Escalus and Angelo rose to join him; the lower rostrum was occupied by the middle of humanity, Lucio and friends; the pit—hell, perhaps, as much as dungeon—remained untenanted.

The main effect of this staging was to assert the importance of ducal authority and of its insignia and ceremony. It also presented most of the characters to view, placing them as parts of an overall picture of the Vienna in which Angelo was to exercise his powers of "Mortallitie and Mercie" (1.1.44: TLN 50). The on-stage audience was large enough to allow the theatre audience a degree of detachment, to let them see the opening of the play as an animation of the drop curtain (if with a few important gaps). The director here contrived to compromise between introducing an invented mob of extras, such as Peter Brook had used to much effect at Stratford in 1950, and delegating the role of witnesses of the opening action merely to the Folio's "Lords" and to the theatre audience. The compromise involved one awkwardness. To fill the stage for this scene with characters remote from the ducal court must rob the Duke's professed dislike of public occasions and of staging himself to the view of his people of much of its force and diminish the secrecy and enigma of his sudden departure.

The principal characters were strongly defined by costume and make-up. Anthony Nicholls was a powerful, middle-aged Duke, on whom authority sat easily; John Neville an icy Angelo (in a much-deplored short blond wig) but, beside the Duke, a slight and youthful figure, and so potentially an object of sympathetic understanding. Daniel Thorndike as Escalus represented an older generation: heavily white-bearded and bespectacled, he might easily be derided as "olde father Anticke the law,"[3] yet he looked substantial enough to validate the Duke's commendations of his wisdom and experience. These three, sharply distinct from each other, embodied three types of governor as well as three ages of man and—in the terms of the drop-curtain—three abstractions, though just how the labels "Justice," "Authority," "Law," "Allegiance" and "Trust" might best be distributed was, and would remain, debatable.

While audiences might not have identified most of the other characters on stage in 1.1, they could be in no doubt that Lucio was to play a prominent role. Derek Godfrey, dressed in lurid shades of "pantomime-demon green" (*Daily Mail*, 20 November), flaunting cuffs, hat and codpiece, and in a dazzling ginger wig, had the strongest position on stage, leaning negligently on the central support of the platform. His retreat when Angelo first appeared completed the definition of a force of anarchy, or at least an exponent of license, strongly opposed both to Angelo's austerity and to the harmonious dignity of the Duke.

This production of the scene raised little curiosity about the motives or intentions of the Duke: rather it gave a powerful picture of his departure. The next three scenes are in any case much concerned with the Duke's motives and the director had already indicated that in her production the Duke's authority would receive more emphasis than his personality. Eight attendants and soldiers were no doubt readily available in a company whose repertoire for the season included *Hamlet* and all three parts of *Henry VI*, but their presence gave the Duke's public role unusual importance.

The opening of this production revealed much of what was to follow. Webster was concerned with the play's moral argument, which this opening set forth with great clarity, and with the context of spiritual values and sanctions within which the human drama would be acted out. The drop curtain, with its invitation to see the characters as morality-play abstractions, might seem oversimplifying, but its identifications were unclear enough for its full effect to include involvement of the audience in the moral debate. The pictorial style of production and the availability of a large company supplied a well-manned stage for the play's opening and closing scenes, but the main effect was to build up the ceremony surrounding the Duke's only public appearances in his symbolic role as a figure of unquestioned power and authority. The sense of ceremony predominated, but the initial questions about Angelo were strongly posed.

The set, which attracted much comment, was crucial to two dimensions of the production: its insistence on hierarchy, whether temporal, spiritual, or moral, and the rapidity of the playing, unimpeded by more than a few movements of large properties and the opening or closing of the gates.

Hierarchy was never more strongly asserted than in the public scenes with which the play begins and ends. The final condemnation of Lucio was especially memorable. After his ironic unhooding of the Duke he was, of course, arrested: a guard snatched his flamboyant green hat from his head—"his elegant, golden hair proved to be a wig which came off, revealing a bald and scabrous skull."[4] Thus shorn, it was a ratlike Lucio who was consigned to the Hell of the orchestra pit. For act 5, Isabella was no longer in the nun's habit she had worn hitherto (in familiar defiance of the text's insistence that she is "yet vnsworne" [1.4.9; TLN 359][5]). Now she wore her hair loose and was enveloped in a full-length, light-hued cloak. It was in this guise that she brought the play to a close as she climbed the stage-left stair towards her ducal partner in an exact visual echo of the movement of Angelo to receive his commission in 1.1. That partner was still in his friar's habit, merely unhooded by Lucio, not defrocked. We were left to assess whether it was a heavenly bridegroom or an earthly one towards whom Isabella ascended.

The dawning celebrated by the Duke with "Looke, th'vnfolding Starre calles vp the Shepheard" (4.2.196–97; TLN 2068–95), and by the producer with the rapid fade-in of a glorious sunrise, was no false one. Angelo's salvation might have remained a dubious proposition, but even the much-criticized wig could do nothing to abate Mariana's enthusiasm for "no other, nor no better man" (5.1.423; TLN 2816). It was Angelo, not the absent Barnardine, whom the Duke admonished to "take this mercie to prouide / For better [*Webster*: fitter] times to come" (5.1.481–2; TLN 2883–84).

The success of the production was summarized by the *Bristol Eve-*

ning Post (20 November 1957) in terms which other reviewers echoed:

> Margaret Webster's production of 'Measure for Measure', . . . brings off something of a miracle by making sense of the two apparently irreconcilable halves of the play. . . . This production eases gently into a pastoral beauty which enfolds all the characters in a compassion that transcends the direst of their griefs. All here depends on the Duke, Angelo's master, and Anthony Nicholls speaks the part with unfailing depth and nobility. . . . all in all, a memorable production of this mysterious and wonderful play of Shakespeare's maturity.

It is at this point that I should reveal that it was at the Old Vic in December 1957 that I saw *Measure for Measure* for the first time. As a final-year undergraduate who had recently tussled with the play on the page and found much bafflement and confusion among such critics as I had read, Margaret Webster's production seemed to make all difficulties easy, to transform Tillyard's broken-backed play into a coherent and gripping experience and to allay the intensities of Wilson Knight[6] with a life-giving shot of bawdy humor (several reviewers seemed bemused by the rare experience of having laughed spontaneously at Shakespearian clowns).

In the early 1980s, I had occasion to consult the documentary record of this production in the archive of the Old Vic. The company's archivist, Molly Sole, kindly gave me access to the promptbook, the publicity photographs and miscellaneous papers relating to the production.

Margaret Webster's promptbook was a marked-up copy of M. R. Ridley's New Temple edition (1935). This edition belongs to a period when the Folio text of *Measure for Measure* was still conventionally (and mistakenly) thought of as unreliable and supposed to be as full of unresolved textual cruces—many of them designated by Ridley with an editorial dagger in the margin—as was the Duke's Vienna of corruptions. Though cutting was generally light, not only cruces but obscure jokes or difficult phrases were excised or simplified, either by substitution of modern synonyms or by rearrangement of phrase order. The producer's most radical alteration, evidently related to her fear of the play's falling into two halves of unequal interest, was to move a passage of nearly two hundred lines back from act 3 into the middle of act 2. In the Folio, the scenes of confrontation between Isabella and Angelo (2.2 and 2.4) are separated by a short scene in which the Duke makes his first appearance in the costume (and role) of Friar, visiting the prison and interviewing the pregnant Juliet. 3.1 opens with Claudio, first reconciled to his imminent death by the Duke and then thrown back into confusion by his sister's offer of uneasy "comfort," and ends with the Duke's meeting with Isabella. Shakespeare then steps aside from Angelo and Isabella. 3.2 comprises a series of encounters between the disguised Duke and his subjects: first Elbow, Pompey, and Lucio; then, after a short soliloquy, Mistress Overdone and Escalus.

It was the first section of 3.2, up to the Duke's soliloquy on slander, that was moved back, to stand between 2.3 and 2.4. The rest of 3.2 duly followed after 3.1, except that the rhyming soliloquy which concludes it, "He who the sword of Heauen would beare, / Should [*Webster*: Must] be as holy, as seueare" (3.2.249–70; TLN 1746–67), was also transposed. In the middle of 4.1, Isabella leaves the stage with Mariana to tell her, in private, of Angelo's attempt on her honor and of the "Friar's" plan to offer Mariana the role of understudy for her in Angelo's garden-house. This gap in the action, which need not be long, is covered in the Folio by six lines for the Duke on the vulnerability of great men to slander—lines which most editors recognize as belonging, not here, but to the soliloquy on the same topic in the middle of 3.2. Webster chose to insert the rhyming soliloquy, reduced to a mere eight lines (3.2.249–50, 255–60; TLN 1746–47, 1752–57), at this point, simultaneously asserting the Duke's control of the situation and keeping the audience's attention on Angelo during the imagined off-stage revelation of his iniquity and of the "falshood" with which the Duke proposes that it should be paid.

The move forward of the Duke's exchanges with Pompey and Lucio from 3.2 to before 2.4 had several results. The most significant was to allow for the placing of the single interval, usually taken after 3.2, at the end of 2.4. The first half thus ended on the strong shock of Isabella's "Then *Isabell* liue chaste, and brother die; / More then our Brother, is our Chastitie" (2.4.184–85; TLN 1198–99). This left the anticipated interview with Claudio as an equally strong opening for the second half. Though the rearrangement thus allowed the impetus of the Isabella-Angelo plot to be sustained into the second half, it also had the less helpful effect of disturbing the sequence of the "Friar's" encounters with his people. By reducing the interim between the Duke's discovery of Angelo's evil-doing and their final confrontation, it also reduced the buildup of expectation towards that moment. A further effect was the prominence afforded Lucio, who thus became the first character to be revealed to the Duke in his true colors. His refusal (3.2.39–81; TLN 1531–74) to bail Pompey (Paul Daneman) was a show-stopping success—understandably, as it brought together the production's two outstanding comedians—but the intrusion of such comedy between 2.3 and 2.4 dissipated tension and blurred the implicit comment of Juliet's one scene of dialogue on the contrasting portrayal of Isabella in the scenes between which it is placed in the Folio.

After the interval, things moved in a more predictable sequence. 3.1 led into the scene between the Duke, Escalus, and Mrs. Overdone which concludes 3.2. Despite heavy internal cutting, act 4 had only one major adjustment. The transposition of Pompey's soliloquy at 4.3.1–18 (TLN 2078–94) back to the start of 4.2 made it a kind of prologue to the long prison scene. The cutting of 4.5 (TLN 2306–22) was standard, though it removes Shakespeare's only clear indication that Friar Peter is privy to the Duke's designs in the final scene of the play. The Duke's dialogues with the Provost in 4.2–3 were severely curtailed, at the cost of much significant detail including the Duke's expression of concern for the spiritual state of Barnardine, and the Provost's report of the "vndoubtfull proofe" of Barnardine's guilt "now in the gouernment of Lord Angelo" (4.3.133–34; TLN 2002–3). As in most productions, the circumstances of the arrival of Angelo's messenger (4.2.82–97; TLN 1945–62) were greatly simplified. Friar Peter in 4.6 turned out—again as usual—to be the same man as the Folio's "Frier Thomas" from 1.3 (this conflation has an obvious convenience, and Shakespeare may merely have been careless about a name, though a case can be made for granting superior authority within the monastery to Friar Thomas, the Duke's confidant, and making Friar Peter a junior brother).

The last scene (5.1) was trimmed of some dozens of lines, mainly where it may seem too slow, as in the lengthy complaints of Isabella against Angelo (ll.43–67; TLN 2398–425). More substantial was the removal of Barnardine from the final entry direction and the transposition of lines properly addressed to him to a speech addressed by the Duke to Angelo (ll.495–96; TLN 2893–94). Here, as in some other details, Webster was taking her cue from Peter Brook, but many directors have found the presence of Barnardine at the end unaccountable. Some have removed the difficulty by cutting him. Others, more patiently attentive to the text, have found good reason to retain his entry here to confront Angelo, condemned to death, with a fellow inmate of Death Row and with an embodiment of the fallen humanity he has attempted to transcend or deny in himself, and to raise for one final time the question of the Duke's definitions of justice and mercy.

The discernable aim of most of the internal cutting was to sharpen and clarify issues. A few further examples must suffice: the Duke did not number fear of slander among his motives for appointing Angelo (1.3.42–43; TLN 334–35), nor did he offer "the doublenes of the benefit" as a sanction for the deceit of the bedtrick (3.1.257; TLN 1477–78), and he was spared the embarrassment of his first, muffed, proposal to Isabella (5.1.488–89; TLN 2890–91). The heaviest cutting came in acts 4 and 5, where to the motive of simplifying the plotline was added that of keeping the second half down to a tolerable length. Angelo and Isabella lost the fewest lines, but much direct and oblique comment on Angelo was trimmed from scenes in which he doesn't appear—again with simplifying effect.

Though the presumptive evidence for cutting afforded by the parallel texts of a number of Shakespeare's plays may be taken to signify that his company was as ready as another to cut without much sensitivity when occasion arose, certain passages in his plays have become traditional targets without any strong reason. Margaret Webster's *Measure for Measure* had its fair share of such traditional cuts. I would like at this point both to narrow and extend my discussion by giving a close account of three such cuts. My narrow point will be to indicate what seem to me to be good reasons for retaining the cut passages, and my wider one will be to suggest that impatience with what may seem to be longeurs or clumsinesses in the verbal text may often be our cue for seeking non-verbal explanations of that text. Here I am happy to acknowledge my own cue, in the form of J. W. Lever's note on the puzzling passage which immediately precedes the interview of the Duke/Friar with Isabella at 3.1.172–75 (TLN 1394–97):[7]

> *Duke.* *Prouost*, a word with you.
> *Pro.* What's your will (father?)
> *Duk.* That now you are come, you wil be gone.

Lever's note reads: "This summons leaves Claudio alone with Isabella for a mimed reconciliation. The Duke's call is intentionally fatuous, and would be understood as such between the two older men." We may or may not agree as to how Claudio will use his opportunity, or Isabella respond to it, but what is of interest is that the seemingly nonsensical dialogue may have a significant theatrical function. Similar considerations may affect other familiar cuts adopted by Margaret Webster.

Shortening the outcries of Isabella against Angelo in act 5 (20–119; TLN 2370–88) has two obvious attractions: time will be saved at a late moment in the play, and the performer will have her job simplified by the reduction of a passage in which the character can hardly fail to forfeit some measure of sympathy from an audience that is given ample time to reflect, during her outcries, that although her indignation is righteous, her charge against Angelo is, in her own particular, false. Part of the effect intended may indeed be to subject Isabella herself to the public shame imposed on Claudio and Juliet in 1.2, and to reduce the feasibility of her ever returning to take her vows as a Clare. But the length of her tirades has also a simpler function. Though Angelo is silent most of the time, we, the audience, should share with the Duke the knowledge that what is going on constitutes his trial, and that Angelo's silent reactions (or lack of them) to what is said to and about him are the focal point of the scene. Everything the Duke says or does is sharply calculated in terms of Angelo's response and is designed both to keep him on tenterhooks between hopes of bluffing his way to safety and fears of exposure, and to keep his conscience under relentless pressure, with the aim of moving him to confession and penitence. The technique resembles that of Portia in her treatment of Shylock in act 4 of *The Merchant of Venice*. Abbreviation of Isabella's speeches can only relax the pressure on Angelo.

My other examples have more to do with staging and reflect the difficulty of performing Shakespeare in theatres much unlike those he wrote for. In 4.2, the climactic night of the action is mediated to us through the reactions of the Duke and the Provost (as well as through thematic on-stage jesting about loss of heads timed to coincide with the off-stage loss of a pair of maidenheads). As they wait in the prison, the Duke is confident that, however late, a pardon for Claudio will arrive, while the Provost is as confident that it won't. When the Duke arrives (4.2.69; TLN 1929), his entry is heralded by the knock on the prison door that habitually precedes such entries in this play. The knock interrupts a short dialogue between the Provost and Claudio, thus easily motivating the Provost's misinterpretation of it: "I hope it is some pardon, or repreeue / For the most gentle Claudio" (68–69; TLN 1927–28). The misinterpretation carries its own irony: seeing the Duke enter, we know that the Provost has spoken truer than he can be aware. The dialogue which ensues is one of Shakespeare's nightpieces (compare *All's Well that Ends Well*, 4.3.1–70). Though very brief, it is also slow and it changes direction inconsequentially, creating in a few lines a strong sensation of waiting, whether for Angelo's messenger, or for the inevitable arrival of Isabella. The Provost's unguarded "It is a bitter Deputie" (75; TLN 1938) moves the Duke to loyal, if white-washing, support of his deputy, imaginably prompted in part by the hope that the pardoning of Claudio may begin to set Angelo's own account straight. This leads up to a second round of knocking.

Then comes the puzzle. We expect the Provost simply to admit the newcomer, as he has just admitted the Duke. Instead, he leaves the stage, to return, a moment later, with a comment on the insistent and reiterated knocking: "There must he stay vntil the Officer / Arise to let him in: he is call'd vp" (87–88; TLN 1950–51). Nine more lines about Claudio's pardon follow (with no hint that this round of knocking may herald its delivery), before the messenger enters and is recognized by the Provost as Angelo's man. On a Jacobean stage with two doors in its tiring-house wall, the staging must have been more or less as follows: the Duke enters through one door, unlocked for him by the Provost and thus identified (as in earlier scenes) as the outer door of the prison; the Provost subsequently leaves and re-enters by the other door, implying that it leads into the further recesses of the prison. It is by this second door that, in his turn, the messenger enters. The reiterated knocking, that is to say, must be understood to be at a side or back door of the prison, not in regular use, at least at night. Angelo's messenger approaches with surreptitious urgency—expressed by sustained knocking at a door, a favourite device of Shakespeare's[8]—and by a devious route, entailing the special unlocking of a door—details which implicitly link this moment with Angelo's instructions to Isabella for the midnight assignation at his garden-house (4.1.27–35; TLN 1799–1806). Before we learn what message Angelo has sent, we are reminded of its irregularity. But all may yet be well—a last-minute pardon would certainly be irregular enough to warrant secret delivery, if only to save Angelo's face, and we have just heard the Provost confirm Angelo's refusal of a pardon:

> vpon the verie siege of Iustice,
> Lord *Angelo* hath to the publike eare
> Profest the contrarie.
> (4.2.95–97; TLN 1960–62)

Shakespeare evidently wanted the delivery of Angelo's message to be the climax of about two minutes of speculation and buildup of tension created by the conflicting convictions of the Duke and the

Provost and intensified by the insistent, though perhaps rather distant, knocking. He stretches tension farther, first by the messenger's courteous speech, with its false hope of dawn, "Good morrow: for as I take it, it is almost day" (103; TLN 1970); then by the Duke's unfoundedly optimistic aside while the Provost reads the message. We may expect Angelo to break his promise to Isabella—if we know the story, we must do so—but Shakespeare does all he can to challenge that expectation by giving full expression to the Duke's optimism before he proves us right.

One further passage which is often cut comes at the end of the long double soliloquy for Angelo which opens 2.4. He describes his excitement as the approach of Isabella is announced:

>   oh heauens
> Why do's my bloud thus muster to my heart,
> Making both it vnable for it selfe,
> And dispossessing all my other parts
> Of necessary fitnesse?
> So play the foolish throngs with one that swounds,
> Come all to help him, and so stop the ayre
> By which hee should reuiue: and euen so
> The generall subiect to a wel-wisht King
> Quit their owne part, and in obsequious fondnesse
> Crowd to his presence, where their vn-taught loue
> Must needs appear offence.
>
> (19–30; TLN 1022–33)

The lines from "and euen so" to the end of the speech are obvious candidates for cutting, as Angelo descends into elaboration of an anticlimactic simile, which slows the rhythm of excitement and seems, by its very deliberation, to call in question his claim to be in danger of loss of control. In 2.2, the arrival of Isabella to see Angelo (2.2.25; TLN 757) is announced some eight lines before her entry: here the gap is twelve lines long. If Angelo is downstage center for these lines, a likely position for self-revealing soliloquy, Isabella's entry, by one of the tiring-house doors, will leave her still as much as twenty feet away from him.

When Angelo turns to her after the lines just quoted with "How now, faire Maid?" where should she be? Still at the door, or at some nearer point between it and Angelo? If the latter, has she moved during a pause after "offence," or has her entry been placed a little earlier, giving her time to move, visible to the audience, though not yet to Angelo, during the final words of his speech? Of course she will not overhear him, but there is dramatic force in her full visibility to the audience as he says the words "vn-taught loue / Must needs appear offence." Her presence lends these words a terrible appropriateness, far indeed from their sense to Angelo in the context of his speech, but very close to the main concerns of the play. The Folio's stage direction is no help: it follows "faire Maid," which cannot be right, but conjures the vision of tidy-minded Ralph Crane, or Compositor C, bringing down a direction that lay a line or two higher in his exemplar. Whether or not authority can be invoked for the effect produced by an earlier entry for Isabella, it is a powerful one, as was demonstrated at the St George's Theatre, Tufnell Park, in 1978, where the early entry of Isabella (Anna Carteret) was above and she had a long stair to descend in full view of the audience during the lines in question and before Angelo (Alan Dobie) turned to address her.

My general argument is, of course, familiar, but less critical attention is often given to the cutting of texts as a method of constructing or directing significance than the results warrant. Indeed cutting can play a crucial part in the interpretation of some plays and characters (how often is Shylock allowed—or constrained—to retain his first long and hostile aside about Antonio at 1.3.41–52 of *The Merchant of Venice*?) The instances I have cited from the 1957 *Measure for Measure* vary from the radical to the barely perceptible and my strongest contention can hardly be more than that minuscule trimmings and verbal substitutions which seem individually innocuous, or even beneficial, can have the cumulative effect of sandpapering the interrogative text of the plays in the interests of supposed clarification or acceleration. Few plays can be so easily slanted towards tendentious interpretation by surreptitious cutting as *Measure for Measure*, a text of moderate length that needs no trimming to reduce playing time and can be played uncut and at an intelligible pace in little over two hours. The ending of Webster's production gave unequivocal evidence of a desire to vindicate the Duke and Isabella within a Christian scheme of things. It did so at the expense of other voices, most significantly those of Angelo and Lucio.

What suffered most was the complexity of relations between Angelo and Isabella. A succession of cuts, including those I have considered, was apparently designed to remove much of what might either qualify the guilt of Angelo or diminish sympathy for Isabella. There were plenty more. Much of the commentary of Lucio and the Provost which intersperses the first interview of Isabella with Angelo was removed, and with it the equivocal effect of Lucio's advocacy of her plea. Isabella's innocence was subtly underlined by a small cut late in her second dialogue with Angelo: "Women? Helpe heauen;

men their creation marre / In profiting by them" (2.4.127–28; TLN 1138–39).

Reviewers who mentioned Angelo at all (whether or not they found John Neville convincing in the part) emphasized act 2. Philip Hope-Wallace (*Manchester Guardian*, 21 November 1957) simply saw the Duke and Isabella as the "two main characters," commenting that "Angelo's collapse in the second half shows him up for what he is, a quite secondary figure," but, he added, "The big scenes went well." R. B. M. (*The Stage*, 21 November 1957), having found Neville's Angelo "highly effective . . . . vivid, forceful, and utterly convincing" in the first half, reflected that "it is probably not his fault that in the final scenes, when he seeks forgiveness and redemption, he is less convincing; here Shakespeare is particularly sudden in his alteration of mood" (and Webster particularly ready to supply Angelo with subtextual motivations). The suddenness can only have been accentuated by the cuts which had moved Angelo further from our minds by greatly reducing reference to him in the scenes of acts 3 and 4 in which he does not appear. Margaret Webster, commenting retrospectively on her production, had this to say of Angelo:

> I thought . . . that the play was concerned with triple identity: every man is three people—the man he would like to appear, his public image; the man he himself likes to think he is; and the man he *really* is, the basic stripped essence. . . . We tried to follow out my triple-identity theory visually. Angelo, for instance, first appeared dressed soberly in a scholar's black gown; was invested with the robes of office; and, in the last scene, stripped of them, leaving the unadorned "man". (I have since thought that today's permissive nudity could have made a valuable statement here; except that for an actor to wriggle out of a pair of tights onstage in view of the audience would not have been either dramatic or impressive.)[9]

Theatre, a pragmatic art, has always recognized that meaning is constructed in performance. A more recent theoretical diffidence in texts has accompanied the wider claim that meaning is always the construction of the reader or spectator. That diffidence has changed our questions, and has diminished our readiness to dismiss as simply wrong or mistaken interpretations, on stage or page, which do not harmonize with our own constructed meanings. I enter my observations as a caution against too total a capitulation to relativism, but I do so in no fundamentalist or restrictive spirit. If Margaret Webster might seem, in forty-year retrospect, to have got *Measure for Measure* wrong, it was by pushing the play too resolutely towards a major cadence at the end (despite her stated awareness that matters were not so simple). In my view, a more patient attentiveness to the play would have found in it a spirit of skeptical questioning rather than convinced judgement—which is to say no more than that I have lived through four decades since 1957, in the course of which my familiarity with the play has increased while critical and theatrical interpretation has veered to the secular and politically troubled extreme exemplified by Michael Boyd's Stratford production in 1998. My own debate with the play nevertheless began with and will continue to include the experience of *Measure for Measure* as an exciting, coherent and, above all, funny play—an experience which I owe to having seen Margaret Webster's production of it.

Notes

1. See Richard Proudfoot, "Peter Brook and Shakespeare," in J. Redmond, ed., *Themes in Drama* 2: *Drama and Mimesis* (Cambridge: Cambridge University Press, 1980), 159–62.

2. Margaret Webster, *Shakespeare without Tears* (New York: McGraw Hill, 1942), 253–54.

3. W. Shakespeare, *1 Henry IV*, 1.2.61. Line numbers for works of Shakespeare other than *Measure for Measure* are those of *The Riverside Shakespeare*, ed. G. B. Evans (Boston: Houghton-Mifflin, 1974).

4. Margaret Webster, *Don't Put Your Daughter on the Stage* (New York: Knopf, 1972), 304. I am grateful to Dr. Elizabeth Schafer for drawing my attention to the references to *Measure for Measure* in this book.

5. Quotations of the text of *Measure for Measure* are from the *Norton Facsimile* of *The First Folio of Shakespeare* (New York: Norton, 1968) with act, scene and line numbers from the New Penguin edition of the play, ed. J. M. Nosworthy (Harmondsworth, U.K.: Penguin Books, 1969).

6. E. M. W. Tillyard, *Shakespeare's Problem Plays* (London: Chatto & Windus, 1950); G. Wilson Knight, "*Measure for Measure* and the Gospels," in *The Wheel of Fire* (London: Methuen & Co. Ltd., 1930).

7. *Measure for Measure*, ed. J. W. Lever, (London: Methuen & Co., Ltd., 1965), 77.

8. E.g. *1 Henry IV*, 2.4.491; *Macbeth*, 2.2.54.

9. Webster, *Don't Put Your Daughter on the Stage*, 303–4.

The Performance of Text in the Royal National Theatre's 1997 Production of *King Lear*

Grace Ioppolo

In the last twenty years, the text of *King Lear* has either become far too real or not real enough, depending on which set of scholars has attempted to rescue it from its dangerously intermediate status. For the "new revisionists" who argue that Shakespeare revised the play after composition, *Lear* has yet to become real; for some more traditional editors, including those pondering whether their role is to serve as mediator or even author, *Lear* is already real but has begun a metamorphosis into something illusory. In 1997, R. A. Foakes lamented this preoccupation with the transubstantiated *Lear* in his warning that "there has been a fashion in criticism for claiming that the 'real play is the performance, not the text,' or that a play is a 'communal construct.' " He shrewdly concluded that "the 'real play' is as much the text we read, and perhaps act out in the mind, as the performance we watch; and scripts are what directors and actors make for the stage out of the reading texts provided for them by editors."[1]

In this essay I want to explore what directors and actors make of *King Lear* for the stage when they reject the "reading" texts provided by literary editors, such as Foakes, and instead act as the play's editors by producing their own theatrical texts. While Shakespearian critics have struggled amongst themselves for control of the "real" *Lear*, they have yet to consider the ways in which a theatre director can more immediately, powerfully, and expertly realize and thus serve as mediator and as author of *Lear* than a literary editor can. Some new revisionist editors may be adamant in theory about not conflating the Quarto and Folio texts, but, in practice, many have had to make concesssions about conflation and in editing out possible "corruptions," even in presenting a facsimile text of the play.[2] They usually fail to consider who else faces such considerations, particularly a theatre director.

I will look at what decisions and concessions the distinguished director Sir Richard Eyre and his Royal National Theatre company made in our post-revisionist age in performing this same function of deliberately attempting to "unedit" a text, by choosing the Folio text as the basis for their highly acclaimed 1997 production, and then re-edit it through conflation to bring it closer to their conception of the author. In other words, I want to examine what happens *in practice* to "theory," or what happens when, as Harley Granville-Barker might put it, Eyre deliberately chose to replace "more Shakespeare" with "less Shakespeare."[3] I am especially curious to see whether Eyre's conflated acting text, expertly and movingly performed, demolishes in practice the theory that the two separate texts of the play should *not* be conflated, or whether his acting text supports in practice the theory that one conflated text of the play cannot represent Shakespeare's play. But let me offer a brief history of the modern literary controversies about editing the texts of *King Lear* in order to assess the tremendous impact of Eyre's theatrical choice to unedit and then re-edit them.

The 1608 Quarto 1 text of the play (written by 1606) contains about 300 lines (including the mock-trial episode in 3.6 and the entire scene of 4.3) that do not appear in the 1623 Folio text; the Folio contains about 100 lines that do not appear in the Quarto. Rather than seeing these major variants as resulting from censorship, playhouse adaptation, printing errors or another non-authorial agency, the new revisionists, including Michael Warren, Gary Taylor, Steven Urkowitz, Stanley Wells, and myself, have argued that they provide evidence that Shakespeare revised his first version of *King Lear*, represented by Quarto 1, into the later version, represented by the Folio, for his own artistic reasons.[4] Therefore we have argued that there are two distinct versions of the play, each with its own focus, shape, and form. For example, Warren, the first to reopen in 1976 this centuries-old debate about authorial revision, concludes that due to revision, "the ample, relatively loose structure of the Quarto is tightened in the Folio; passages of moral commentary are removed, some speaking parts are eliminated, particularly characters with no identifiable name; the whole movement of the play is streamlined and sharpened, and the action concentrated."[5] One of the major results of these alterations is that in the Folio, Lear "has proportionately more dialogue" and his "presence is increased especially in the later acts, where most of the cuts were made."[6] Others have since agreed with Warren that Shakespeare revised the play in strategic and carefully planned ways in order to intensify Lear as the major figure of attention, emotion, and performance.

Such an argument for authorial revision may have been the natural result of what Foakes sees as a major cultural shift in the mid-twentieth century in which literary critics substituted *King Lear* for *Hamlet* as Shakespeare's preeminent play and cultural representation and commentary. Foakes argues that "the main tradition of criticism up to the 1950s had interpreted the play as concerned with Lear's pilgrimage to redemption, as he finds himself and is 'saved' at the end, but in the 1960s the play became Shakespeare's bleakest and most despairing vision of suffering, all hints of consolation undermined or denied."[7] This important shift in both literary criticism and performance gave rise in the next decade to a highly focused examination into the varying degrees of the intensity of Lear's despair and suffering, most notably, and controversially, through textual scholars' focus on comparing or "collating" these variant Quarto and Folio texts.

Many of us contend that the editorial practice begun in the eighteenth century of conflating the best parts of each text into one text, in an attempt to reconstruct an imaginary, lost original *Ur*-Lear, destroys Shakespeare's self-insistence on creating more than one version of his play. Instead, we have argued that the two plays should not be conflated but reprinted, studied and performed in their original, separate texts with an individual integrity and scholarly and theatrical value and validity.[8] As Randall McLeod notes, "subtleties of interpretation can scarcely come to us from the conflated *Lear*. Neither are they likely to occur to us from reading either text in isolation. They can reveal themselves readily, however, if we engage in differential readings of whole texts."[9] It is this insistence on two *whole* texts that has caused the most dissent and controversy among other Shakespearian critics, including those trained in and practicing the "New Bibliographical" methods passed down by R. B. McKerrow, W. W. Greg, and Fredson Bowers, among others.

The conflation of the Quarto and Folio texts has been editors' standard practice largely because the Quarto text, although longer than the Folio, was badly printed and therefore considered a "pirated" or stolen and surreptitious text deriving no authority from Shakespeare or his acting company, the King's Men. The Folio text, on the other hand, was considered to have derived from the acting text, or playbook, used by the company, at least immediately before its printing. Thus twentieth-century editors, for example, chose the Folio as their base text (or "copy-text") to print their editions, importing into it the major Quarto variants, including the mock-trial passage and the missing scene of 4.3. This type of conflated text can be seen in *King Lear* editions in the Oxford and second Arden series.

Collected editions such as *The Riverside Shakespeare* and David Bevington's edition of *The Complete Works of Shakespeare* also used conflated texts. The result has been that, as Granville Barker disapprovingly remarked of the play early in this century, "editors, considering only, it would seem, that the more Shakespeare we get the better, bring practically the whole lot into the play we read."[10]

Yet, Quarto 1 is no longer seen as a surreptitious text. In 1980, Steven Urkowitz argued that it was printed from an authorial manuscript, and in 1982, Peter Blayney meticulously demonstrated that Quarto 1 was badly printed not because it derived from a corrupted, stolen, or memorially reported or "pirated text" but from a manuscript that was difficult to read. He stopped short of claiming it was Shakespeare's original draft or "foul papers," although others have since used his study of Quarto 1 to argue that it was printed from Shakespeare's original text of the play.[11] In addition, Gary Taylor and T. H. Howard-Hill separately argued that the Folio was printed from an annotated copy of Quarto 2, a 1619 reprint of Quarto 1, corrected against a theatrical manuscript, possibly a playbook.[12] Therefore, both texts could be seen as authoritative representations of different stages of the text, immediately after its original composition and some time after its first performance.

Thus the new revisionists have attacked in theory if not in practice the modern insistence on conflation, now seeing it as unnecessary or obsolete, at least in the case of *King Lear* which offers so much possible or probable evidence of Shakespearian revision. Yet conflated editions have continued to serve as the bases for acting scripts of the play. Twentieth-century scholars, students, readers, directors, actors and theatregoers have written about, studied, used, acted in or seen and heard a *King Lear* that many new revisionists would now argue never really existed or even derived from Shakespeare, but instead is an apocryphal creation deriving from a heavily intrusive editor who serves more as author than Shakespeare.

In 1986, Taylor and Stanley Wells, the editors of *William Shakespeare: The Complete Works*, published by Oxford University Press, tried to make the play unapocryphal by refusing to print a conflated text of the play, and instead they printed two separate, edited texts of the Quarto and Folio, as did Jay Halio in his separate New Cambridge editions in 1992 and 1994. In 1990, the Royal Shakespeare Company used the Folio text as the script for their production directed by Nicholas Hytner.[13] Yet such theatrical insistence on non-conflation has been rare, even though Granville Barker recommended as early as 1930 that the two texts should not be conflated because "where Quarto and Folio offer alternatives, to adopt both versions may make for redundancy or confusion." He therefore advised the producer to "found himself on the Folio. For that it does show some at least of Shakespeare's own reshapings I feel sure."[14] And these reshapings quicken the pace and focus of the play significantly, as Michael Warren has noted, and, like McLeod, he has argued that it is these sorts of distinctions which disappear in a conflated and editorially "mediated" text.[15]

However, some editors have continued to see it as their duty to produce a conflated, "reading" or "acting" text, free of the non-authorial corruptions which had crept into the texts of the Quarto and Folio and which would suit a wide variety of modern audiences. As editor of the third series Arden Shakespeare *King Lear*, Foakes spoke for many of his predecessors when he advised in 1997 that "readers should be free to make up their own minds, just as actors and directors will see the text(s) as the basis for a script they can use." He offers variants marked by superscript letters within the text rather than in the textual notes, but he does not apologize for offering a conflated edition which generally prefers Folio readings but "that seeks to give an idea of the work, while making the major differences between the versions easily recognizable; it then becomes the decision of readers, actors, and directors whether to prefer Q to F, F to Q, or to take readings from both."[16] I want to use Foakes's reminder in 1997 that directors and actors can *choose* to accept or reject literary editors' choices as the basis for my argument that directors and actors can also *choose* in 1997 to act as literary editors, textual critics, and partial authors of a Shakespearian play.[17]

In March of that year, London's Royal National Theatre produced a *King Lear*, directed by Eyre and starring Ian Holm, based on a conflated text primarily using the Folio but interpolating the mock-trial scene in 3.6, most of 4.3, and occasional single sentence or even one-word substitutions into the Folio from the Quarto. The production was almost unanimously hailed as "exceptional" and "deeply moving" and Holm's performance as "timelessly classical, harrowingly modern and unforgettable" and "possibly the greatest King Lear of the century."[18] Eyre, who adapted the text in collaboration with his actors, was especially praised for offering a production that was "admirably fluent and lucid" and for hacking out "a clear, consistent and rationally planned path through a play that is essentially an untamed moral jungle."[19]

Although Holm received most of the attention in the reviews, his interpretation clearly depended heavily on Eyre's textual shaping of the play, for, according to one critic, the "marvel" of Holm's performance "is the way it lives in the line—the way it makes you feel anew the surprising developments of Shakespeare's thought in every word, and yet makes these sound spontaneous, new-minted."[20] Eyre's shaping of every word seemed to re-create the play, so much so that Sheridan Morley raved in *The Spectator,* "Never have I seen a production of Shakespeare's most demanding play which was more willing to accommodate itself to our understanding and involvement, and less inclined to distance its hero whether on the throne or on the heath."[21] Alastair Macaulay echoed this reaction in his claim in the *Financial Times* that "the barnacles of theatricality, style and interpretation seem to fall away from *King Lear* in the National Theatre's new staging. I envy anyone for whom this is his or her first *King Lear.* Often, wonderful to say, I felt as if it were mine."[22] Thus, even though most of the twentieth-century productions of the play performed before Eyre's used some type of conflated text, this production seemed particularly remarkable for its conscious attention to the two individual texts' provenance and power. Eyre intended to use the Folio text but eventually found himself conflating it with the Quarto, partly because he could not resist using Quarto-only material.

Eyre had written a general foreword to the reissue of Granville Barker's *Prefaces to Shakespeare* in 1993[23] and seemed heavily motivated by Granville Barker's textual commentary, including his preference for the Folio text, in adapting the play for theatrical performance (Eyre adapted the play once more, mostly by making major cuts, in the television production aired in March 1998 in the UK and several months later in the United States). In a television interview, Eyre outlined his vision of *Lear* as "a play about a family" which focuses on "the relationship of father to children, children to fathers," and which demands that you see all parenthood and fatherhood as "potential tyranny." He summarized the play in contemporary terms as "the archetypal dysfunctional family, a widowed father with three daughters."[24] Eyre's intent was missed by Michael Billington, the only critic who disparaged the production, and who claimed that "if there is a governing idea behind Eyre's production, it is of the play as a moral and political anatomy lesson that tears off masks, clothes and disguises to show humanity as it really is."[25] Actually, Eyre seemed more interested in a particular family than in general humanity.

Eyre staged the play in the small and intimate setting of the Cottesloe Theatre, using a traverse stage which acted as both barrier and pathway for the audiences seated on either side of it on the ground floor as well as for the two levels of upper galleries. The set consisted of a large council table bounded by plain walls; by the beginning of the heath scenes, the table had been removed and the walls fell away with a large crash, leaving a bare stage. Sets and properties were minimal because, as he explained in his television interview, Eyre wanted to use the council table as focal point to emphasize that the play is about a family, not the court, and "family business is conducted round a table, generally at meals."[26] Thus, the opening scene of the division of the kingdoms took place with everyone seated around the table. But the table was also used threateningly by an elevated monarch: Lear, for example, when angry at Cordelia's response of "Nothing" and at Kent for his defense of her in 1.1, leapt onto the table and strode panther-like back and forth on it, occasionally cracking his whip, his main prop, at those scurrying away from the table, including his daughters.

In terms of the play's language, Eyre's production seemed unique in modern memory in its insistence that actors use dialogue as stage directions and thereby act out the literal meanings of the words. Eyre explained these literal interpretations, stating in the television interview,

> Every scene of the play we approached as extreme rationalists from the point of view of saying, "What is our evidence?" Our evidence is what is written down. "What do these words actually mean, what do we know of the characters from what they say, what they do up to this point? What can we extrapolate from that?"

His extrapolation came from the words' most literal meanings; for example, at Lear's comment, "Off, off, you lendings" in 3.4, Holm stripped off his clothes and remained naked or huddled beneath a blanket throughout the heath scenes. According to one reviewer, the language was demystified at this literal level, demonstrating a play "uneasy with period bravado or the verse beautiful, eager to analyse itself and forever twisting and turning our reactions."[27] Most of the reviews echoed this fascination with Eyre's successfully literal re-interpretation of the language.

In a personal interview with me on 16 June 1998, Richard Eyre elaborated on his focus, intent, interpretation, and textual shapings of *King Lear*, a play he recognized to be some critics' central example of and test case for Shakespearian revision. In establishing his text, he had carefully considered some of the new revisionists' arguments but was not convinced that Shakespeare was responsible for the major revisions between the Quarto and Folio. He granted that "there's a certain amount of evidence" for revision and that "you can argue that there are improvements" but that "equally, no playwright would ever cut the trial scene; it's just simply implausible . . . because it's one of the most wonderfully inventive pieces of writing, *playwriting*, in the play." Eyre seemed irritated with what he saw as a contradictory attitude among Shakespearian literary scholars that Shakespeare was at the same time the greatest playwright and the most incompetent. Eyre argued that you have to start from the assumption that Shakespeare is a highly accomplished playwright, but at the same time, the scholars say, " 'O the world's greatest playwright,' and then treat him as if he's some sort of holy fool." Eyre saw it as his role to accept Shakespeare simply as a working man of the theatre.

Yet, at least one other prominent director, John Barton, has complained that the mock-trial scene and two other mad scenes serve to "suspend the action unhelpfully; it's very difficult for actors to sustain dramatic momentum," and he recommended cutting them.[28] In addition, Roger Warren has argued that Shakespeare cut the mock-trial scene as part of a pattern, as he "abridges those features of the Quarto scene which look backwards, like Edgar's mock-possession and the Fool's jokes, while emphasizing those which look forward." Warren concludes that the author places greater emphasis on Lear's mad scene in 4.6 by cutting his mad attack on his daughters in 3.6, tightening the Folio focus on Lear internalizing rather than externalizing his madness.[29] Eyre's production was highly commended for offering a Lear who manifested his madness externally with continued momentum and who left very little internalized, in part because Ian Holm seemed physically incapable of keeping Lear's suffering below the surface.

Eyre began the process of creating an acting text by examining the separate Quarto and Folio texts of the play in the Wells-Taylor Oxford University Press edition of *William Shakespeare: The Complete Works* (ironically, these texts are not facsimiles but are lightly edited, hence Eyre did not begin with unmediated Shakespeare). Eyre admitted that he chose the Folio as his base text because it was the more "theatrical." He claims to operate from "the pragmatic view of someone making a piece of theatre" who is working with "the work of a consummate playwright." Therefore he rejected parts of the text which he considered "theatrically dubious." Ultimately he asked himself, " 'Who cares which text it is?'. . . I mean, one or the other is more or less authentic or neither. I think I did start with the Folio because I felt it to be the more, as it were, 'cleaned-up' text." Although Eyre began with this single text, he re-authored it because he developed the acting text during read-throughs with the entire cast, who served as his collaborators. He felt no compulsion to enact every line in the Folio or the additional lines of the Quarto, arguing that there are two kinds of theatrical cutting: no cutting and "strategic" cutting; in the former you do the entire play, but he finds this "a slightly pedantic view and it's slightly sort of saying, 'I'm not going to intervene.' " He chose the latter method, thinking,

> "I'm going to shape this play a bit more and I can distill it, compress it a bit," and so then you have to take a number of . . . painful decisions. Do you let Lear [go uncut], do you ever touch Lear, do you cut the subsidiary characters? Are you in danger of some sort of star cutting; you know, the higher the billing you are, the less lines you lose?

However, Eyre stated that ultimately he cut to maintain and strengthen the narrative line of the play, his main concern.

Eyre depended on his actors to create and finalize the text, arguing that they must contribute because they have to take possession of their text. He noted that when he cut a speech,

> the actors would say, "But I can't really make this work; if I don't have that line, how can I make it work? It doesn't really make sense," and I would say, "You can *make* it make sense." "Yeah, but you've changed the meaning" [they'd say], so we would barter, you know, and that's also a good process because it means the actors are really immersed in the text and they're compelled to make it work.

Thus the remarkable attention to each word with which Eyre was credited in reviews resulted from his collaboration with the actors:

> Every single word at some stage would have been weighed up and discussed and debated, and the meaning of it would have been explored, and quite often you'd say, "Actually this simply doesn't make sense—what does the Quarto say, what does the Folio say? Well, of course, it means that . . . How could anybody argue that it meant otherwise?"

Eyre emphasizes that an acting text is not fixed but fluid and would "evolve" throughout the play's run. However, he dismissed the idea that changes had been made during preview performances solely because the audience seemed disturbed or confused by particular lines. As it is the director's and the actors' job to "make sense" of what they're playing, a skilled director and actors should do so without modernizing or simplifying dialogue for modern audiences.

Eyre cut numerous small and large passages of dialogue, most of which appear in both the Quarto and Folio texts. But he did not treat the Folio text reverentially, as he occasionally cut Folio-only passages, including the Fool's prophecy at the end of 3.3. These cuts strongly altered the shape and focus of the play. Most interesting were the lines which were cut and then reinserted after the script had been finished.[30] However when importing Quarto variants, Eyre did not let them stand alongside Folio dialogue, as at least some modern editors have done,[31] but *substituted* them for the Folio variants. Thus Eyre did not allow *any* juxtaposed Quarto and Folio variants in his conflated acting text. (The Quarto passages that Eyre substituted for Folio passages and the Quarto-only passages that he added to his Folio-based script are listed in the Appendix below.)

Clearly some of Eyre's one-word substitutions from the Quarto correct errors, inconsistencies or difficult readings in the Folio, but others seem to reinforce a Quarto pattern that Eyre has recognized and wants to reinsert: the primacy of Cordelia as a sympathetic and loving daughter and a powerful foreign monarch and military commander. Eyre cogently explained that he retained 4.3, a scene often cut in performance and criticized in scholarly study as boring, too long or too hagiographic to Cordelia, because he saw it as the necessary result of and succession to the blinding of Gloucester in 3.7. Eyre argues that if 3.7 is retained, 4.3 must also be retained; in 3.7 Shakespeare presents "the most violent scene in the whole of dramatic literature" and which is "the distillation of the most violent feelings of a family" and then follows it with "a succession of scenes that are all . . . forms of love," including the love of the child for the parent (Edgar-Gloucester), the subject for the king (Gloucester-Lear), and sexual love (Goneril-Edmund; Regan-Edmund). Thus "the sort of apotheosis of these series of scenes, which are symphonic variations on the theme of love, is the extraordinary demonstration [in 4.3] of the selfless love of Kent for the daughter of his best friend." Eyre argues that if you recognize this pattern, Shakespeare's "scheme is very, very simple." Eyre insists on the emotional quality of 4.3 and insists that a director retain it, arguing that it's "an immensely touching scene," and that once "you see that shape [symphonic variations on love] to it, then it would be extremely perverse, in fact, damaging, to take out that element."

Eyre's argument also implies his post-revisionist understanding that Cordelia's role in the Quarto has been reduced and demoted in the Folio.[32] Gary Taylor has argued that in the Folio Shakespeare cut most of the Quarto's references to a foreign war with France in order to substitute for it the civil war within the country which intensifies Lear's internal struggle.[33] Such a pattern is particularly evident in the changes in Cordelia's role from Quarto to Folio from act 3 onward, not only in the dialogue of Kent, the Gentleman, Gloucester, and Cordelia herself but in some stage directions. For example, in 5.2, the stage directions for her entrance during the battle read in the Wells-Taylor Quarto, "The powers of France pass over the stage [led by] Queen Cordelia with her father in her hand"; in the Wells-Taylor Folio the same directions read, "Enter with a drummer and colours, King Lear, Queen Cordelia, and soldiers over the stage." Thus Cordelia enters as the commander of the French army and of her father in the Quarto but as merely her father's companion in the Folio.

Eyre implicitly recognizes and maintains this pattern, for his retention of 4.3 required him to use the Quarto reading in the Gentleman's speech in 3.1 regarding the coming invasion from France rather than the Folio reading of the increasing civil war between Lear's English sons-in-law. Eyre's production presented Cordelia as a strong, martial leader through her near-canonization in the discussion of Kent and the Gentleman in 4.3. In fact during the scene, Eyre had the actress playing Cordelia march across the stage dressed in armor and holding a sword upright, with the short hair and bearing reminiscent of Joan of Arc. Thus the 3.1 passage in the Quarto beginning, "From France there comes a power," sets up the arrival of Cordelia from France with her army supporting her, resulting in a foreign invasion of England. The substitute passage in 3.1 in the Folio sets up the civil war only between Albany and Cornwall, internalizing the martial struggle without outside interference, so Eyre chose selectively to reinsert the Quarto's reading into his Folio text. He continues this pattern in his reinsertion of Goneril's warning in 4.2 that "France spreads his banners in our noiseless land." Other Quarto substitutions in Eyre's Folio-based text also emphasize his main focus of the "dysfunctional family" and concern all of the major characters of Lear, the Fool, Kent, Edgar, Edmund, Goneril, and Albany expounding on the cruelty and perversity of family relationships, as in 4.3.35 in which Albany chastizes Goneril and her absent sister for behaving as "tigers, not daughters" to Lear and for being "most barbarous, most degenerate."

Eyre's linkage of text to action and of word to gesture demanded in his mind the use of a traverse stage. He believes that the text is only seamless if the action is. He was "absolutely determined" that the play would be presented "in the most accessible, immediate way possible—that you simply wouldn't be able to detach yourself from it, and it was high risk," yet he wanted "the thing to be seamlessly fluent." He argues that a writer uses verse to "set up this pulse, the iambic [pentameter], and the pulse never breaks." For these reasons, each scene flowed into the next with no music between acts or scenes and with the last set of actors moving off one end of the stage with the next set moving in from the other. The traverse stage is meant to act both as highway and as barrier for actors and audience to emphasize that the play is a journey for both.

In the personal interview, Eyre was hostile to recent post-structuralist concepts of a text being "theory-driven," which imply that a text exists only when the critic as audience creates it. He insists instead that a text is author-centric and that it exists without an audience. He argues, "It's like Dr. Johnson refuting Bishop Berkeley, isn't it? You know, 'I refute it thus,' when he kicked a stone. I refute it thus: here is a text; you know it exists." So, Eyre's direction and Holm's performance produced a *King Lear* that exists for but not because of an audience, yet it is clear from Eyre's stated concerns with collaboratively creating his text that his production of *King Lear* was neither "theory-driven" nor "author-centric."

In the end, what is clear is that Eyre's text of *King Lear* is *his* text; he has authored it and is its creator. In his mind he may be clarifying it or, to use his words, "making sense" of it, but it is as mediated as any other edited text. He and the actors serve as editor, acting a text no closer or more original to Shakespeare than any that we have, except Quarto 1 if it is printed from foul papers. So, far from questioning or dismissing the new revisionists' complaints about conflated texts, Eyre's production of *King Lear* demonstrates that a conflated text becomes a more mediated text than an original text of the Quarto or Folio, and that mediated texts remain for modern reading and theatre audiences, who have become accustomed to them, the real, "original" Shakespearian texts.

Eyre's *Lear* is one that begins with a "more theatrical" and "cleaned-up" Folio text but then imports into it many Quarto passages that in fact expand and slow the play's focus and movement at particular points and speed it up at others. He reintroduces the verbal moral imperatives and judgements of the Quarto, offering a play that both internalizes and externalizes Lear's decline into madness. What seems most clear is that Eyre's text adds the most actable of the Quarto's lines, speeches, and scenes while recognizing particular strategies and patterns unique to the Quarto. Sheridan Morley may be correct in his assessment that this production's title character "seems to defy all the preconceptions about the King as he pads about the stage, mannered and mad and majestic by turn, but always letting us into the inner workings of his increasing self-destruction, always inviting us to share in his downfall and side with him even when he is at his most cruel or curmudgeonly."[34] If so, then it is due to Eyre's textual reshapings. The play has no *final* form but always an intermediate one, dangerous or not. In this, Eyre validates the ideas of theatrical and textual revision expressed by the new revisionists, but he also demonstrates that literary editors and critics are not the sole or even primary constructors, purveyors or interpreters of a Shakespearian text.[35]

Appendix
A Complete list of Eyre's interpolations of Quarto variants into his Folio-text of *King Lear*

I use the spelling, punctuation, and line numbers as given in the texts that Eyre used: *The History of King Lear* (Quarto text) and *The Tragedy of King Lear* (Folio text) in *William Shakespeare: The Complete Works*, ed. Wells and Taylor, 1027–98.

1.1.68 Our dearest Regan, wife of Cornwall? Speak] Speak *Q, not in F*
1.1.79 Although our last not least] not *Q*; and *F*
1.1.96 To love my father all] *Q; not in F*
1.1.163 Revoke thy doom] doom *Q*; gift *F*
1.1.173 To shield thee from diseases] diseases *Q*; disasters *F*
1.3.16   Idle old man,
That still would manage those authorities
That he hath given away! Now, by my life
Old fools are babes again, and must be used
With checks as flatteries, when they are seen abused.] *Q; not in F*
1.4.95 Why fool?] *Q*; Why, my boy? *F*
1.4.137 Fool's song and following dialogue:
That lord that counselled thee
To give away thy land,
Come, place him here by me;
Do thou for him stand.
The sweet and bitter fool
Will presently appear,
The one in motley here,
The other found out there.
LEAR: Dost thou call me fool, boy?
FOOL: All thy other titles thou hast given away. That thou wast born with
KENT: This is not altogether fool, my lord.] *Q; not in F*
1.4.235 O sir, are you come?] *Q; not in F*
1.4.285 Is't come to this?] *Q; not in F*
1.4.290 thou shalt, I warrant thee] *Q; not in F*
2.2.79 With every gale] gale *Q*; gall *F*
2.2.197 LEAR: No, no, they would not.
KENT: Yes, they have.] *Q; not in F*
3.1.13 But true it is. From France there comes a power

Into this scattered kingdom, who already,
Wise in our negligence, have secret feet
In some of our best ports, and are at point
To show their open banner. Now to you:
If on my credit you dare build so far
To make your speed to Dover, you shall find
Some that will thank you, making just report
Of how unnatural and bemadding sorrow
The King hath cause to plain.
I am a gentleman of blood and breeding,
And from some knowledge and assurance offer
This office to you] *Q*;
Who have—as who have not that their great stars
Throned and set high—servants, who seem no less,
Which are to France the spies and speculations
Intelligent of our state. What hath been seen,
Either in snuffs and packings of the Dukes,
Or the hard rein which both of them hath borne
Against the old kind King; or something deeper,
Whereof perchance these are but furnishings—*F variant that Eyre deleted in favor of Q*
3.6.16 EDGAR: The foul fiend bites my back.
FOOL: He's made that trusts in the tameness of a wolf, a horse's health, a boy's love, or a whore's oath.
LEAR: It shall be done. I will arraign them straight.
Come, sit thou here, most learned justicer.
Thou sapient sir, sit here.—No, you she-foxes—
EDGAR: Look where he stands and glares. Want'st thou eyes at trial madam?
Come o'er the burn, Bessy to me.
Her boat hath a leak,
And she must not speak
Why she dares not come over to thee.
[deleted lines]
KENT: How do you, sir? Stand you not so amazed.
Will you lie down and rest upon the cushings?
LEAR: I'll see their trial first. Bring in the evidence.
Thou robed man of justice, take thy place;
And thou, his yokefellow of equity,
Bench by his side. You are o'th'comission,
Sit you, too.
EDGAR: Let us deal justly.
[deletions]
LEAR: Arraign her first. 'Tis Gonoril. I here take my oath before this honourable assembly she kicked the poor King her father.
FOOL: Come hither, mistress. Is your name Gonoril?

LEAR: She cannot deny it.
FOOL: Cry you mercy, I took you for a joint-stool.
LEAR: And here's another, whose warped looks proclaim
What store her heart is made on. Stop her there.
Arms, arms, sword, fire, corruption in the place!
False justicer, why hast thou let her scape?] *Q* [but with deletions noted];
  not in F
3.6.55 KENT: Oppressed nature sleeps.
This rest might yet have balmed thy broken sinews
Which, if convenience will not allow,
Stand in hard cure. Come, help to bear thy master.
Thou must not stay behind.
GLOUCESTER: Come, come away.
EDGAR: When we our betters see bearing our woes,
We scarcely think our miseries our foes.
Who alone suffers, suffers most i'th'mind,
Leaving free things and happy shows behind,
But then the mind much sufferance doth o'erskip
When grief hath mates, and bearing fellowship.
How light and portable my pain seems now,
When that which makes me bend, makes the King bow.
He childed as I fathered. Tom, away.
Mark the high noises, and thyself bewray
When false opinion, whose wrong thoughts defile thee,
In thy just proof repeals and reconciles thee.
What will hap more tonight, safe scape the King!
Lurk, lurk.] *Q; not in F*
4.2.32 GONORIL: No more. The text is foolish.
ALBANY: Wisdom and goodness to the vile seem vile;
Filths savour but themselves. What have you done?
Tigers, not daughters, what have you performed?
A father, and a gracious, aged man,
Whose reverence even thee head-lugged bear would lick,
Most barbarous, most degenerate, have you madded.
[deletions]
If that the heavens do not their visible spirits
Send quickly down to tame these vile offenses,
It will come,
Humanity must perforce prey on itself,
Like monsters of the deep.] *Q* [with deletions as noted] *not in F*
4.2.35 GONORIL: Where's thy drum?
France spreads his banners in our noiseless land,
[deletion]
Whiles thou, a moral fool, sits still and cries
"Alack why does he so?"] *Q* [with deletion as noted]; *not in F*
  4.2.37 ALBANY: Were't my fitness

To let these hands obey my blood,
They are apt enough to dislocate and tear
Thy flesh and bones] *Q; not in F*
4.2.37 GONORIL: Marry your manhood, mew—] *Q; not in F*
4.3 Entire scene [beginning with line 10; cuts at 4.3.25–33, 4.2.37–50] *Q; scene is not in F*
4.5.83 they cannot touch me for coining] coining Q; crying F
5.1.24 EDMUND: I shall attend you presently] *Q; not in F*
5.3.37 CAPTAIN: I cannot draw a cart,
Nor eat dried oats. If it be man's work, I'll do't] *Q; not in F*
5.3.46 EDMUND: At this time
We sweat and bleed. The friend hath lost his friend,
And the best quarrels in the heat are cursed
By those that feel their sharpness.
The question of Cordelia and her father
Requires a fitter place] *Q; not in F*

Notes

1. Foakes, Introduction to his edition of *King Lear* (Walton-on-Thames: Thomas Nelson and Sons Ltd, 1997), 4.
2. See for example the types of editorial decisions made by Gary Taylor in his Oxford edition; also Michael Warren's rationale for his facsimile texts (*The Complete 'King Lear,' 1608–1623* [Berkeley: University of California Press, 1989]) and those of René Weis in his *King Lear: Parallel Text Edition* (London: Longman, 1993) and Jay Halio in *The Tragedy of King Lear* (Cambridge: Cambridge University Press, 1992) and in *The First Quarto of King Lear* (Cambridge: Cambridge University Press, 1994).
3. Granville Barker, *Prefaces to Shakespeare: King Lear* (London: B.T. Basford, 1958), 1:328–29.
4. See for example, Michael Warren, "Quarto and Folio *King Lear* and the Interpretation of Albany and Edgar," in *Shakespeare, Pattern of Excelling Nature*, eds. David Bevington and Jay L. Halio (Newark, Del.: University of Delaware Press, 1978), 95–107; Steven Urkowitz, *Shakespeare's Revision of King Lear* (Princeton: Princeton University Press, 1980); the individual essays in *The Division of the Kingdoms: Shakespeare's Two Versions of King Lear*, eds. Gary Taylor and Michael Warren (Oxford: Clarendon Press, 1983); my book, *Revising Shakespeare* (Harvard University Press, 1991). Also see R. A. Foakes, "Textual Revision and the Fool in *King Lear*," in *Essays in Honour of Peter Davison*, *Trivium*, 20 (1985), 33–47; although not a new revisionist, Foakes discusses the impact of limited revision in the play.
5. Warren, "The Diminution of Kent," in *The Division of the Kingdoms*, 62.
6. Thomas Clayton, " 'Is this the promis'd end?': Revision in the Role of the King," in *The Division of the Kingdoms*, 121.
7. Foakes, *Hamlet versus Lear: Cultural Politics and Shakespeare's Art* (Cambridge: Cambridge University Press, 1993), 3–4.
8. Stanley Wells summarizes the new revisionists' views about *King Lear* in his essay, "The Once and Future *King Lear*," in insisting they are opposed to the general opinion "that Shakespeare wrote one play about *King Lear*; that this play is imperfectly represented in both the Quarto and the Folio texts; that each of these

texts contains genuinely Shakespearian passages which are missing from and should have been present in the other; that comparison of the variant readings of the two texts must form the most important basis for the correction of errors of transmission; and that conflation of the two texts, along with such correction, will bring us as close as we can hope to get to the lost archetype which each is supposed imperfectly to represent" (*The Division of the Kingdoms*, 8–9).

9. McLeod, "No more, the text is foolish," in *The Division of the Kingdoms*, 170.

10. Harley Granville Barker, *Prefaces to Shakespeare: King Lear*, 1:328–29.

11. Urkowitz, *The Revision of 'King Lear,'* 129; Blayney, *The Texts of King Lear and their Origins*, vol. 1: *Nicholas Okes and the First Quarto* (Cambridge: Cambridge University Press, 1982); some authors of essays in *The Division of the Kingdoms* cite Blayney's book as making this claim.

12. See Taylor's arguments in relation to Howard-Hill's in Stanley Wells and Taylor's *William Shakespeare: A Textual Companion* (Oxford: Clarendon Press, 1987), 529–32; also see Howard-Hill, "The Problem of Manuscript Copy for Folio *King Lear*," *The Library* 6th ser. 4 (1982), 1–24, and "The Challenge of *King Lear*," *The Library* 6th ser. 7 (1985), 161–79.

13. Hytner did, however, import Quarto variants into his text. For his comments on authorial revision between the Quarto and Folio, see "A Stage for Second Thoughts," *The Times* (London), 30 June 1990, 25.

14. Barker, 329, 332.

15. Warren, "The Diminution of Kent," 64.

16. Foakes, Introduction, *King Lear*, 119, 143; he argues that "it is possible that the additions in F were written by Shakespeare, who may also have been responsible for, or at least assented to, the cutting of nearly three hundred lines" (126) but is otherwise non-committal about assigning all or most of the variants between Quarto and Folio directly to Shakespeare.

17. Foakes's edition was not yet published when Richard Eyre prepared his production script of the play. It would be interesting to consider what Foakes's nearly synoptic edition might have contributed to Eyre's textual reshapings of the play. However, Stanley Wells did write a brief essay for the RNT program for Eyre's production on the Quarto and Folio texts and defended the argument for authorial revision in the play, concluding of Shakespeare, "As a working man of the theatre, he would probably not have understood the concept of a definitive text, but would have sympathised with performers who, from his time to ours, have, like Bottom and his crew, adjusted their texts to the needs of the performance."

18. Reviews, Alastair Macaulay, *Financial Times*, 1 April 1997; John Peter, *Times* (London), 6 April 1997; and Damian Whitworth, *Times* (London), 29 March 1997.

19. Reviews, Benedict Nightingale, *Times* (London), 29 March 1997; Michael Billington, *The Guardian*, 29 March 1997.

20. Macaulay, Review.

21. Morley, Review, *The Spectator*, 5 April 1997.

22. Macaulay, Review.

23. See Harley Granville Barker's *Prefaces to Shakespeare: King Lear* (London: Nick Hern Books, 1993).

24. Eyre, Interview in "Love, Tyranny and Madness," broadcast on BBC2, 21 March 1998.

25. Billington, Review *The Guardian*, 29 March 1997.

26. Eyre, BBC2 Interview.

27. Morley, Review.

28. Cited by Gary Taylor in "*King Lear* and Censorship," in *The Division of the*

Kingdoms, 97. Taylor argues that "the Folio abridement of 3.6 not only improves the structure of the play; it also improves the structure of 3.6 itself." He insists that whatever reasons caused the omission of the mock-trial scene, censorship was not among them (97, 101).

29. R. Warren, "The Folio Omission of the Mock Trial," in *The Division of the Kingdoms*, 48. Numerous other essays in this collection argue that the Folio shows cutting for "streamlining and simplification," to use Roger Warren's words.

30. The most consistent and thorough cutting was in the lines of Edmund.

31. See for example, Kenneth Muir's juxtaposition of Quarto and Folio variants in the Gentleman's speech in 3.1 in his Arden edition of the play (London: Methuen, 1972).

32. See my discussion of Cordelia's roles in Q and F in *Revising Shakespeare*, 167.

33. See Taylor, "The War in *King Lear*," *Shakespeare Survey* 33 (1980), 27–34.

34. Morley, Review.

35. I wish to thank Sir Richard Eyre for granting me an interview and the staff of the Royal National Theatre for allowing me to consult their promptbook for this performance. Material from his interviews and from the RNT promptbook and program is used by permission.

Possessing Edgar: Aspects of *King Lear* in Performance

Michael Hattaway

How do we read and locate Edgar in Shakespeare's *King Lear*? The critical task may be intractable, given that Shakespeare himself seems not to have made his mind up about him, and this son of Gloucester occupies different spaces in the two versions of the play. I want to begin with some very old-fashioned "character criticism," and then use it to question some large ontological claims about the fraudulence of theatre. These were made by Stephen Greenblatt when he was attempting to historicize the references to devils in the play. He argued that *King Lear*, and indeed the theatre of early Jacobean London, had been emptied of meaning as the reformation had "evacuated" the significance of papist rituals.[1] My argument is laced with readings of images from productions, because part of my project is to argue that Shakespeare, as anyone writing in the post-modernist period is bound to claim, gives us the impression that he *read* what he wrote and imagined for the playhouse even as he wrote and imagined it. The poet, as Sir Philip Sidney reminds us, "nothing affirms and therefore never lieth,"[2] and I am loath to agree with Greenblatt that the devils conjured by Edgar in *King Lear* are figures that invoke an antique pageant, evacuated of meaning, which is paradigmatic of the nature of theatrical experience. Instead, I would submit, the borrowings from Harsnett—the names of devils (who, of course, do not actually *appear* on stage)—are a way of dramatizing the inwardness of Edgar.

It may be, however, that the character of Edgar is not a "person" at all but a dramatic device, his nature defined by his role, the antagonist and opposite of Edmund. Edmund seems so obviously "the bad guy" that Edgar must be a figure of the good.[3] This makes the character a kind of sketch that a director might color in—as was done by Jonathan Miller for the BBC television version of 1982. His Edgar (Anton Lesser) bore thorns that did not pierce his arms but were set on his head: Edgar wore a crown of thorns, so becoming a

Christ figure. Was he taking upon himself the sins of the world? The production, worryingly, did not attempt to answer its own question.

Obviously such an approach is simplistic: Edgar is *not* simply the "good guy" (nor is Edmund merely a baddie), although it is interesting to think about the older brother's role as a hero—a problematic role which I shall later describe for Edgar's case. That moralizing approach through the familiar structure of the *Psychomachia* is not adequate: we must at least consider Edgar's position or rank, and note the contradictory things that are said about him. These demolish any simple opposition between virtue and vice.

First, rank. In early modern England, primogeniture, the habit of giving all to the first born, disempowered younger sons. In Edmund's case his misfortune to be "some twelve or fourteen moonshines Lag of a brother" (1.2.5–6)[4] is compounded by his illegitimacy. Edgar, the senior brother, was heir to an earldom, godson to King Lear. The dynamics of the relationship between the brothers, sharing a father but unequal by birth, were nicely enacted at a production of the play in November 1997 by Deborah Paige at the Crucible Theatre in Sheffield. Bunk beds were thrust up through a stage trapdoor at the beginning of 1.2. Edmund lounged on the top one for "Thou, Nature, art my goddess" (1.2.1). When the brothers appeared together, Edgar was lying with languid superiority on top, Edmund relegated to the bottom. Anyone who has siblings and remembers having to share a bedroom will recognize the symbolic hurt done by that.[5] So we remember differences in rank, and remark, in some productions, the unlikeable superiority or disdain that comes from rank. Edgar assumed he was *born* to authority and the respect that goes with it—perhaps he has to *earn* it. (Compare King Lear.)

Next, how is Edgar read by other characters in the play? Here is Regan to Gloucester:

> REGAN   What, did my father's godson seek your life?
> He whom my father named, your Edgar?
> GLOUCESTER   O lady, lady, shame would have it hid.
> REGAN   Was he not companion with the riotous knights
> That tend upon my father?
> GLOUCESTER   I know not, madam; 'tis too bad, too bad.
> EDMUND   Yes, madam, he was of that consort.
> (2.1.91–7)

Is Regan, with Edmund to back her, a reliable witness? The Peter Brook production of 1962 revealed that the king's all-licensed retinue of knights might, very tellingly, be *portrayed* as riotous on the stage. (It could even be decided that Edgar should appear among Lear's retinue in 1.4.) If the director decides to suggest that they *are* riotous, then it is totally reasonable—if not right—for Goneril and Regan to take the line they do. This is crucial: before Brook the knights were not much noticed. Brook had them overturn tables on stage. Yet Shakespeare's company may have decided that, at court, this would be dangerous, given that King James's favourite sport—like that of King Lear—was hunting.[6] Whatever the degree of riot that is fixed upon, a crucial production decision turns out to be how to get Lear's retinue into the play. Extras are expensive: at Sheffield a load of old boots was dumped from the flies before Lear entered from hunting. The women had to clear them up and put them away. The play's action is, as it were, tossed by the waves this sea of knights makes.

Now if it is decided that Edgar *is* of their companionship, he is at best thoughtless, careless of the space of others. Edgar may have to grow up, stop being a man who behaves badly or who colludes in thoughtless behavior. But, contrariwise, perhaps no "growth" is necessary. Although he later supports her, Edmund had earlier described a very different man from the one evoked by Regan:

> A credulous father, and *a brother noble*,
> Whose nature is so far from doing harms
> That he suspects none—on whose foolish honesty
> My practices ride easy.
>
> (1.2.157–80; emphasis added)

Is Edmund any more reliable than Regan? The jury remains out, and will always remain out. Any personality that we find for a dramatic character is something we ourselves have made. There is no essential Edgar, only a range of possibilities that actor and director arrange into a coherence that is "true" only for the historical moment of their production and which is constrained as much by its *mise en scène* as by the text.

We are justified in singling out Edgar for attention by at least one piece of historical evidence: the "blurb" on title page of Q (1607) reads:

> M[aster] William Shakespeare: his true chronicle history of the life and death of King Lear and his three daughters. With the unfortunate life of Edgar, son and heir to the Earl of Gloucester, and his sullen and assumed humour of Tom of Bedlam. As it was played before the King's

Majesty at Whitehall upon St Stephen's Night in Christmas holidays. By his Majesty's servants playing usually at the Globe on the Bankside.[7]

Now there is no evidence that any of this reflects Shakespeare's thinking about the play. It is, however, reasonable to conjecture that there may have been a bravura performance by the first actor to play Edgar. Jay Halio notes that Robert Armin may have taken this part rather than that of the Fool.[8] It is also important to remember that Edgar's original in Sidney did not "assume madness"—that antic humour is Shakespeare's invention, but we need not follow the blurb and assume that it is voluntarily and consciously assumed.[9]

Concentration on Edgar generates an interesting adjustment of perspective. *King Lear* has a subplot, and from one vantage point we see *Gloucester*'s story as the main parallel to that of Lear, two men "sinned against" by children. However, the blurb invites us equally to compare Lear's story, and in particular his madness, with that of *Edgar* (and the Fool). Both are conspired against, both go mad, both have to sound the base string of humility, expose themselves to what wretches feel. Both Lear and Edgar are detached from their possessions and, as a materialist critic writes, "removing what a person *has* simultaneously takes away what a person *is*."[10] This double structure based on both symmetrical and asymmetrical father-child relationships is one of the many disconcerting things about the play.

Where then, and how, does Edgar appear? Many directors have given him a "silent entrance" in 1.1: in Kosintsev's film he exchanges nods with his father on "I have a son, sir, by order of law, some year older than this" (1.1.18–19). Much could be established there, especially by way of signifying Edmund's dis-ease. There are brief appearances in 1.2 when he is duped by Edmund, and in 2.1 when Edmund wounds himself (Edgar has only one line). It would be legitimate for the half-brothers to begin a fight on stage here, or at least make a din, prefiguring the final duel, just as in the previous scene Edmund's line "My cue is villainous melancholy, with a sigh like Tom o' Bedlam" (1.2.135–6) prefigures Edgar's role.

In 2.2 we have Edgar's soliloquy that includes the following:

> My face I'll grime with filth,
> Blanket my loins, elf all my hairs in knots
> And with presented nakedness outface
> The winds and persecutions of the sky.
>
> (2.2.180–3)

Implicit in this is a stage direction that seems to call for Edgar to strip off his clothes, a central emblem for the play as a "naked wretch," a Bedlam beggar. We also remark the paradox of taking off clothes to create disguise. Yet we must be careful, because "nakedness" in the period can mean "destitution" (*OED*, 2), "houseless poverty." In Kozintsev's film Edgar steals a scarecrow's castoffs.[11] Yet there is no doubt but that the fashion in modern productions to offer a near-naked Edgar creates a powerful stage image, perhaps because again there is a parallel to Lear—"off, off, you lendings" (3.4.106).

We could compare Hamlet to Edgar, in particular the way character is built by costume. Hamlet dons "solemn black" for the beginning of the play and then is set "naked" in England. Moreover it is possible to argue that, a bit like Hamlet, Edgar may find a kind of therapy or cure in playing a mad role, a license in his antic disposition to vent his repressed confusion or anger. It is fruitless to conjecture whether or not Hamlet was definably mad—his antique role "suits" him at key stages of the narrative. But perhaps we should try to define what makes Edgar mad as well as the kind of madness he enacts.

We may think ill of Edgar as we may do of Hamlet. D. J. Enright wrote, "Edgar plays the part with what seems excessive zest, or doggedness. It is as if he were trapped inside his disguise, unable to reveal himself, or simply unwilling to."[12] There is little sign of conscience: unlike Hamlet—who does have a conscience,[13] Edgar acts upon compulsion. We wonder whether he moves towards self-knowledge in madness: has he, like Lear, "taken too little care of this"? Or is madness just a disguise?

Alternatively, one might argue, Edgar gives the impression of being possessed by devils just as Hamlet may have been possessed by his father's ghost. This character may be, *pace* Jonathan Miller with his Christ-like figure, a "goblin damned" rather than a "spirit of health" (*Hamlet,* 1.4.21).[14] The critical and moral question is, was he himself possessed, or did he adopt this "humour" as way of telling his father and Lear that they are possessed, not by devils but by faults or sins?

Putting the matter this way enables us to question the assertion of Stephen Greenblatt, made in a celebrated essay about the relationship of the play to one of its acknowledged sources, Samuel Harsnett's *A Declaration of Egregious Popish Impostures* of 1603, that the play is about a world emptied of significance. (Harsnett was chaplain to the Arminian Bishop of London, John Bancroft. His pamphlet sought to expose exorcisms conducted in Buckinghamshire by Jesuits.) Greenblatt characteristically reaches his conclusion by arguing by analogy, on this occasion between Shakespearian theatre and the conceit of an empty pageant which is Harsnett's rhetorical device for the exposure of papist exorcisms. "The sense of the theater's tawdriness, marginality, and emptiness—the sense that everything the players touch is thereby rendered hollow—underlies Harsnett's analysis not only of exorcism but of the entire Catholic Church."[15] Greenblatt then gives a very reductive view of Edgar and his motives, arguing with seeming assurance that Edgar is merely *disguised*, "no more possessed than the sanest of us,"[16] and that "the playwright finds in Harsnett . . . the inauthenticity of a theatrical role."[17] Doubling back (by what seems an illegitimate route) to *King Lear*, Greenblatt writes that this is a "post-Christian" play, "haunted by a sense of rituals and beliefs that are no longer efficacious, that have been *emptied out*."[18]

Greenblatt's essay is full, but I think he is guilty of a kind of cultural determinism: "Who knows if Harsnett has not already, in a deep sense, borrowed from Shakespeare's theater what Shakespeare borrows back?"[19] The implication is that all lines of cultural force exhibit the same polarities.[20] One fundamental problem is that Harsnett had earlier exposed *Puritan* exorcisms as impostures:[21] Harsnett seems to have been concerned above all with the purveying of false miracles, and his theatrical *topos* is the tool rather than the object of his invective. Although Greenblatt notes that *King Lear* was performed in 1610 in a recusant household in Yorkshire, an indication of the strong hold of the old religion, he offers a mechanistic and absolute model of cultural change: "At the *moment* [emphasis added] when the official religious and secular institutions were, for their own reasons, abjuring the rituals they themselves had once fostered, Shakespeare's theater moves to appropriate this function." Contemporaries did use the metaphor of "evacuation" to describe the replacement of papistry by Anglicanism, and Greenblatt mimes the confidence of contemporary "Anglican"[22] polemicists: this is Richard Hooker, writing perhaps just before Harsnett, in a passage cited by Dr. Johnson in his *Dictionary*: "Popery . . . hath not been able to re-establish itself in any place, after provision made against it by utter *evacuation* of all Romish ceremonies."[23] And yet there is much testimony of the prevalence and popularity of public exorcisms conducted by Catholic priests from the 1580s to the 1620s,[24] and the spectators in Yorkshire may have read the exorcisms in a manner very different from the manner imputed by Greenblatt to London audiences.

Are there really, moreover, "moments" in cultural history, and can we use "literary" texts to capture them in this manner? Literary forms and figures of speech are possessed of a *longue durée* and it may be impossible to fix their meaning at or for one historical moment. One could also charge Greenblatt with intentionalism. It is not a case of Shakespeare believing or disbelieving in demonic possession and exorcism, it is a question of his using these topics and Harsnett's vocabulary as a set of exploratory images. (I have more on Harsnett later.) Whatever Shakespeare did, he surely wrote heuristically. This point is crucial: fictions are not *determined* by lines of cultural force. The overlaying of papistry by Protestantism was far from complete in the period. Fictions are ways of reading the world, and themselves contribute to the making of a culture—which is why the theatre could appear so seditious. The vocabulary of Edgar's possession may have been appropriated from a dissident culture, but the notion of possession was, I submit, fully resonant in the years in which Shakespeare was writing *King Lear*.[25]

Shakespeare, I would like to think, did not "believe in" the narratives, the ideas, the theatrical images, that came his way: even as he recreated them, represented them, he *read* them.[26] Indeed Greenblatt argues that the play was written at a very specific moment when, because of the "evacuation" of reformation—to use the vocabulary of Hooker—words that once had a literal now have a metaphoric or literary meaning.[27] But it is not possible to gauge the currency of these critical terms, or the kinds of response they would have gathered. The distinction between the "literal" and the metaphoric cannot hold in the playhouse where everything on stage is a sign. The notion of demonic possession was part of a cultural heritage and must have been interesting to Shakespeare, not as an orthodox or blasphemous opinion, but as a topic by means of which societies and individuals represent themselves to themselves. Moreover, we need to entertain the notion that certain stage Edgars may have played their role as though they *were* possessed, which restores the "literal" meaning.

Here I need to return to theatrical practice and move regressively from a reading of a modern performance to the kind of reading of performance possibilities that Shakespeare may have engaged in. At Sheffield there was a stage trap, up through which basic props were thrust: a table, a brazier, those bunk beds and into which, after his soliloquy, by a piece of directorial invention, Edgar leapt. Down and out, into a kind of hell? Or purgatory—but, wait a moment, purgatory had been "evacuated" by the reformers! Edgar's jump prefigured Gloucester's leap—a necessary act, away from ease and "accommodation." A kind of purification? An attempt to recover psychic equilibrium? Maybe. Marvin Rosenberg wrote of this scene: "He is being born again, naked, into a harsh world, where he learns anew strange wawls and cries. He has a long way to go."[28] I think the resonance of that Crucible stage image is appropriate, and suggests no mere change of appearance but a passage into a new mode of being that involves self-discovery as well as the exposure of others.

We can sharpen the focus by looking at the way Nahum Tate "improved" the play for a socially exclusive, "accommodated" audience in his *The History of King Lear* (1681). Tate significantly changed the language of a passage where Edgar is *reading* his society, and it is interesting to see what he thought might bring a blush or a frown to the face of a genteel spectator. Tate "censors" any suggestion of visible flesh: where Edgar describes his "basest and most poorest shape [costume]," he gives Edgar a motive for self-preservation in love for Cordelia:

> How easy now
> 'Twere to defeat the malice of my trail,
> And leave my griefs on my sword's reeking point.
> But Love detains me from Death's peaceful cell,
> Still whispering me Cordelia's in distress.
> Unkind as she is I cannot see her wretched,
> But must be near to wait upon her fortune.
> Who knows but the white minute [opportunity] yet may come
> When Edgar may do service to Cordelia;
> That charming hope still ties me to the oar
> Of painful life, and makes me, too, submit
> To th'humblest shifts to keep that life afoot.
> My face I will besmear and knit my locks.
>
> (2.2.122–34)

Moreover, clothes were proportionately more expensive in this period than they are now because fashion or costume was a kind of self-definition: if Edgar rips his clothes, this is not only a recognised sign of madness[29] but a demonstration that rank is not something essential, innate, but something just "put on." Tate also rinses out the colour of Edgar's social criticism: Edgar's evocation of "low farms, Poor pelting villages, sheep-cotes and mills" is reduced to "sheep-cotes, villages, and mills" (2.2.139). Shakespeare always reminds us of what is base: the word designates the lowest, but also the basis upon which the luxury of the privileged rests. Edgar seems to see the world clearly, but does he understand himself?

It is in 3.4 (his mad scene) that Edgar encounters first King Lear. Perhaps the sight of this Bedlam is what tilts Lear into full madness after his wits have begun to turn. "Didst thou give all to thy two daughters?" (3.4.48), Lear asks. Notice how Lear had delivered his noble speech of recognition "Poor naked wretches" (3.4.28) just *before* he encountered Edgar/Tom. He *had* achieved moral social recognition before the image of suffering is presented to him. Notice too how Edgar offers no hint of comfort to the mad king: is this cruelty? Does he "infect him with fiends"?[30] When he appears as the poor man, not Poor Tom, to rescue his father from "the bottom of Dover cliff" he says of himself that he is one "Who, by the art of known and feeling sorrows, / [Is] pregnant to good pity" (4.6.218–19). There is no sign of this kind of "pregnancy" in his encounter with the king.

The role of the devils becomes crucial at the end of his long speech in 3.4: "There could I have him now, and there, and there again, and there" (3.4.60–61). Is Edgar here fighting an imaginary "foul fiend," the moment prefiguring his duel with Edmund at the end of the play? Might this suggest that he is possessed, and that the foul fiend has to be exorcised? Shakespeare borrowed the fiends' names from Harsnett.[31] We might argue that Edgar is guilty of very bad faith in that he is suggesting that evil comes from devils rather than from man's inhumanity to man (the topic of his soliloquy), or from excess. This may make us very uncomfortable as we witness Edgar's "performance."

This sequence generates another of Lear's great recognition speeches: "Unaccommodated man is no more but such a poor, bare, forked animal as thou art" (3.4.105–6). Notice the ambiguity of this: here is the horror of discovery but also a statement of essence. Maybe man does not need more. The rest is superflux. Then Edgar's father appears:

Enter GLOUCESTER *with a torch*
. . . .

EDGAR   This is the foul fiend Flibbertigibbet: he begins at
          curfew and *walks till the first cock*; he gives the web and
          the pin, squinies the eye and makes the harelip;
          mildews the white wheat and hurts the poor creature
          of earth.
               Swithin footed thrice the wold;
               He met the nightmare and her nine foal,
               Bid her alight and her troth plight,
               And aroint thee, witch, aroint thee.
                              (3.4.107SD-120; *emphasis added*)

It is commonly assumed that "Edgar's disguise was meant to bring home certain home truths to Lear."[32] But, under the "counterfeiting" of disguise, Edgar can mouth these imprecations against his *father* as well, identify *him* with the devil, the source of all evil. Inevitably we remember the Ghost in *Hamlet* who "faded on the crowing of the cock" (1.1.138) as well as the madness of the hero which allows him to sound off against his mother and his philandering stepfather (father figure).

If we think that these hints amount to a case against Edgar, was Edmund perhaps right? Did he sense a repressed Oedipal hatred in his older brother, perhaps all too eager to seize power from his old father?[33] There is more evidence:

EDGAR   Poor Tom, that eats the swimming frog, the toad, the tadpole, the wall-newt and the water—; that in the fury of his heart, when the foul fiend rages, eats cow-dung for salads; swallows the old rat and the ditch-dog; drinks the green mantle of the standing pool; who is whipped from tithing to tithing and stocked, punished and imprisoned—who hath had three suits to his back, six shirts to his body,
   Horse to ride, and weapon to wear.
   But mice and rats and such small deer
   Have been Tom's food for seven long year.
Beware my follower. Peace, Smulkin, peace, thou fiend.
GLOUCESTER What, hath your grace no better company?
EDGAR   The prince of darkness is a gentleman. Modo he's called, and Mahu.
GLOUCESTER Our flesh and blood, my lord, is grown so vile
   That it doth hate what gets it.
EDGAR   Poor Tom's a-cold.
                              (3.4.125–40)

Is Edgar speaking about being possessed himself, or implying that his father is possessed by devils? Or, that his father is a devil who "possesses" women? The ambiguity comes from a wonderful piece of stagecraft by Shakespeare. Gloucester is speaking about Lear's children, Goneril and Regan, who have thrust the old King out. He does not respond to Edgar. We could read this as a kind of chorus. Or do the lines suggest that Gloucester sees through the disguise and is speaking of his sons, one of whom stands before him?

We require a bit more detail: Modo or Modu was associated with sexuality in Harsnett. This devil had possessed a chambermaid called Sara Williams: "He had been in Sara by the space of two years . . . I [Harsnett] cannot much blame the devils for staying so long abroad, they had taken up an inn much sweeter than hell, and an hostess that wanted neither wit nor mirth to give them kind welcome."[34] When he was finally exorcised, Mahu ("muster-master over the captains of the seven deadly sins"[35]), is said "to have chosen such a strange part in Sara for his passage out as I dare not name: and yet devils, comedians, and their reporters may have license in all courts to call all things by their name."[36] Edgar is accusing his philandering father of being "the prince of darkness." Moreover, although he lists some of Harsnett's comparisons between exorcism and theatricality, Greenblatt makes no note of this remarkable reference to the truths that may be revealed by acting. Shakespeare, by license, is calling all things, mental as well as physical, by their (metaphorical) names.

Frateretto, Flibertigibbet, Hoberdidance[37] were also possessors of Sara Williams: "She, poor wench, had all hell in her belly."[38] They appear later in Q along with Modo and Mahu (in lines cut from F) when Edgar is babbling before his blinded father:

> Five fiends have been in Poor Tom at once, of lust, as Obidicut; Hobbidi-
> dence prince of darkness; Mahu, of stealing; Modo, of murder; Flibberti-
> gibbet, of mopping and mowing, who since possesses chambermaids and
> waiting-women. So bless thee, master. (4.1.61–66)

The lines gain Edgar the reward of Gloucester's purse: Flibbertigibbet was Edgar's first devil-name, obliquely applied, as we have seen, to his father. Was Edgar's mother a chambermaid?

In the latter part of the sequence of madness, in Edgar's presence, Gloucester says to the disguised Kent:

> I'll tell thee, friend,
> I am almost mad myself. I had a son,
> Now outlawed from my blood; he sought my life,
> But lately, very late. I loved him, friend,
> No father his son dearer. True to tell thee,
> The grief hath crazed my wits. What a night's this?
> (3.4.161–66)

Note that Gloucester is still deluded, but we might judge that Edgar could have taken this moment to reveal himself to his father. Rather he suggests revenge:

> Childe Roland to the dark tower came,
> His word was still "Fie, foh and fum,
> I smell the blood of a British man."
> (3.4.178–81)

In 3.6 Edgar again comes in with oblique sexual charges against his father: [To Lear] "Frateretto calls me, and tells me Nero is an angler in the lake of darkness. Pray, innocent, and beware the foul fiend" (3.6.6–7). His riddling is like Hamlet's:

> Soft, now to my mother.
> O heart, lose not thy nature! Let not ever
> The soul of Nero enter this firm bosom.
> Let me be cruel, not unnatural.
> I will speak daggers to her, but use none.
> (3.2.362–66)

Nero, of course, murdered his mother Agrippina, whose womb Nero "slitte to biholde / Wher he conceyved was,"[39] and Edgar's "lake of darkness" is not just the Stygian Lake of the classical underworld, but the "pudend-pond of a woman."[40] As Howard Mills describes Hamlet's riddle, this is "a little more than overt and a little less than covert."[41] It is notable that in this scene Edgar empathizes with Lear in a way he never does with his father, first weeping and then taking his side, implicitly, in the trial sequence, which of course is cut from the Folio text.

The scene is problematic: here the Fool speaks his riddling last line and Edgar does not respond in F to Gloucester's long speech at the end wherein he makes arrangements for Lear to be conveyed to Dover. But in Q he is given another soliloquy in couplets:

> EDGAR When we our betters see bearing our woes,
> We scarcely think our miseries our foes.
> Who alone suffers, suffers most i'th'mind,
> Leaving free things and happy shows behind.
> But then the mind much sufferance doth o'erskip,
> When grief hath mates, and bearing fellowship.
> How light and portable my pain seems now,
> When that which makes me bend, makes the King bow.
> *He childed as I fathered.* Tom, away;
> Mark the high noises, and thyself bewray
> When false opinion, whose wrong thoughts defile thee,
> In thy just proof repeals and reconciles thee.
> What will hap more tonight, safe 'scape the King.
> Lurk, lurk.
> (3.6.99–112; *emphasis added*)

Halio calls the cutting of this "artistically defensible."[42] Maybe, but again I would reflect upon *Hamlet* and the way the protagonist projects all of his discontent onto his father (in Hamlet's case his stepfather).

It is in 4.1 that Edgar encounters the blinded Gloucester. Blinding is symbolic of new vision:

> I stumbled when I saw. Full oft 'tis seen
> Our means secure us and our mere defects
> Prove our commodities. O dear son Edgar,
> The food of thy abused father's wrath,
> Might I but live to see thee in my touch
> I'd say I had eyes again.
>
> (4.1.21–26)

So although Gloucester thus hints at repentance, Edgar does not reveal himself but prepares to guide his father to Dover.

One of the purposes of the difficult Dover Cliff scene (4.6), I consider, is metatheatrical: Gloucester's "leap" may be a visualization of the central metaphor of a tragic fall.[43] We may read it as a penance that Edgar forces upon his father, and we may think it cruel. After Gloucester's fall Edgar both confesses to "the enormous risk [he] is aware he is taking"[44] and justifies a kind of killing of the old man:

> And yet I know not how conceit may rob
> The treasury of life when life itself
> Yields to the theft. Had he been where he thought,
> By this had thought been past.
>
> (4.6.43–5)

He then doffs his antic disposition and adopts a simpler role of "a most poor man, made tame to Fortune's blows" (4.6.217).

Greenblatt sees at the centre of the scene a fake exorcism, performed by Edgar upon his father. Edgar claims that "a thing . . . parted" from his father:

> As I stood here below methoughts his eyes
> Were two full moons. He had a thousand noses,
> Horns whelked and waved like the enraged sea.
> It was some fiend. Therefore, thou happy father,
> Think that the clearest gods, who make them honours
> Of men's impossibilities, have preserved thee.
>
> (4.6.69–74)

But I resist Greenblatt's generalizing tendency to see this as a key to the mode of the whole play, composed of empty histrionic rituals.

This is not a metatheatrical image, but a specific one. And perhaps it is sexual: those "whelked horns" are twisted like seashells, deformedly phallic,[45] and covered with pustules or "whelks." Moreover if we do see exorcism as central here,[46] we could argue that it is efficacious, not an "empty ritual."

Edgar is becoming the champion of the play, like Henry Richmond or Fortinbras, and, like both, not necessarily totally attractive. He appears in 5.1 to deliver his challenge to Edmund. There ensues the battle in which Lear and Cordelia are defeated, and in 5.2 Edgar leads in Gloucester. He comforts him with "Ripeness is all" (5.2.11), perhaps an echo of Hamlet's "The readiness is all" (5.2.160). Edgar's urging of his father to submit to providence[47] is a corrective to Gloucester's fatalism but also a refusal to acknowledge that he is playing God with his father's life. As Enright noted of Kenneth Muir's claim that Edgar's epigram is "the dramatic answer to Gloucester's cry" in 4.1,

> As flies to wanton boys, are we to th'Gods;
> They kill us for their sport.

Surely it is more a counterassertion than an answer."[48]

In 5.3 he emerges to do battle with Edmund. When he reveals himself, Hamlet-like, he dwells on the criminous sexuality of the father figure:

> Let's exchange charity:
> I am no less in blood than thou art, Edmund;
> If more, the more thou'st wronged me.
> My name is Edgar and thy father's son.
> The gods are just and of our pleasant vices
> Make instruments to plague us:
> The dark and vicious place where thee he got
> Cost him his eyes.
>
> (5.3.164–71)

The lines recall the antic injunction of Edgar as Poor Tom to Lear: "Keep thy foot out of brothels, thy hand out of plackets" (3.4.94–95). Are they repugnant, "cheap moralising," as H. A. Mason described them?[49] For we must remember that Gloucester was punished not for philandering but for treason, sending letters to France and arranging for the king to go to Dover. Or, we might say, for the humane feelings he reveals to Regan:

> . . . I would not see thy cruel nails
> Pluck out his poor old eyes; nor thy fierce sister

> In his anointed flesh stick boarish fangs.
> The sea, with such a storm as his bare head
> In hell-black night endured, would have buoyed up
> And quenched the stelled fires.
> Yet, poor old heart, he holp the heavens to rain.
> If wolves had at thy gate howled that stern time,
> Thou shouldst have said, "Good porter, turn the key;
> All cruels else subscribed"; but I shall see
> The winged vengeance overtake such children.
>
> (3.7.55–65)

There are other explanations, perhaps merely ingenious: we might think about what Freud, in his essay on "The Uncanny," says about the relation of blindness to castration in psychoanalysis as punishment for Oedipal crime,[50] and remember how eyes are identified with testicles in the *Sonnets*.[51] Medical lore associated blindness with lechery,[52] and "blind cupid" is Lear's name for Gloucester (4.6.134). We might want to argue that Regan's blinding of Gloucester is a sort of castration of the father figure.[53]

But had Edgar redeemed himself in a traditional manly way by protecting his father from Oswald who lights upon a "proclaimed prize" in 4.6? Then he kills Edmund in a fight to the death. This was very brutal at Sheffield, not a formal duel. They were brothers out to savage each other—there was no question of a rite of justice. Edgar confesses his "fault" for not revealing himself to his father, and narrates the death of Gloucester. So, is he a hero at the end? Q gives a sequence to Edgar that narrates the death of Kent: his "strings of life began to crack." Jay Halio comments:

> F's omission of Edgar's seventeen lines describing his meeting with Kent does more than reduce the inexplicable delay between Edmund's announced intention to do some good and the actual attempt to save Lear and Cordelia. It also modifies the role of Edgar as "the immature, indulgent man displaying his heroic tale of woe"[54] in the face of Albany's desire not to hear anything "more woeful." Edgar thus emerges as a man worthier of the responsibility that becomes his at the close, certainly as F fashions it.[55]

It is to Edgar that final lines are given in F: in Q they had been given to the more high-ranking Albany—in Tate, of course, Lear survives and rewards Edgar with the hand of Cordelia.

In Shakespeare was Edgar a hero? Is this old-fashioned character criticism adequate to channel the excesses of new historicism? Did Edgar send himself to a state of wretchedness to purge the spirits of riot and excess that may have possessed him at the beginning of the play? Did he act as a tough and unrepentant mentor, unpregnant of good pity, to his father and the king? That's for Shakespeare to have asked and us to decide.

Notes

Versions of this essay were delivered as papers at Sofia on 2 October 1988 and at the Shakespeare Institute in Stratford-upon-Avon on 11 March 1999. I am grateful to Professor John L. Murphy who generously sent me off-prints and whose conversation stimulated me into carrying my argument forward.

1. My "as" reproduces the ambivalence of Greenblatt's argument, pointing either to an analogy or to a chain of cultural cause and effect.

2. Philip Sidney, *An Apology for Poetry*, ed. G. Shepherd (Manchester: Manchester University Press, 1965), 123.

3. For the idealizing of Edgar in this century, see R. A. Foakes, *Hamlet versus Lear: Cultural Politics and Shakespeare's Art* (Cambridge: Cambridge University Press, 1993), 50–52.

4. Quotations are taken from William Shakespeare, *King Lear*, ed. R. A. Foakes (London: Thomas Nelson, 1997).

5. "In [Peter] Brook's [1962 production] Edmund—who lounged on the scene's central chair during his soliloquies—was up and busily dusting about when Edgar came in to take his ease" (Marvin Rosenberg, *The Masks of "King Lear"* [Berkeley: University of California Press, 1972], 91).

6. For a discussion of the issues involved, see Rosenberg, 98–99 and 192–93.

7. Foakes, ed., *King Lear*, 112; "sullen" means "melancholy" or "obstinate"; from about 1676 its meaning turns to "baleful," "malignant" (see *OED*).

8. William Shakespeare, *The Tragedy of King Lear*, ed. Jay Halio (Cambridge: Cambridge University Press, 1992), 35 n.

9. Geoffrey Bullough, ed., *Narrative and Dramatic Sources of Shakespeare*, 7 vols. (London: Routledge and Kegan Paul, 1957–73), 7:299.

10. Margreta de Grazia, "The Ideology of Superfluous Things: *King Lear* as Period Piece," *Subject and Object in Renaissance Culture*, ed. Margreta de Grazia, Maureen Quilligan and Peter Stallybrass (Cambridge: Cambridge University Press, 1996), 17–42, at 21.

11. Compare Foakes, *Hamlet vs. Lear*, 196–97.

12. D. J. Enright, *Shakespeare and the Students* (London: Chatto and Windus, 1970), 43.

13. I argue this in my book *Hamlet, The Critics Debate* (London: Macmillan, 1987).

14. Quotations from other Shakespearian texts are taken from *The Norton Shakespeare*, ed. Stephen Greenblatt et al. (New York: W.W. Norton, 1997).

15. Stephen Greenblatt, "Shakespeare and the Exorcists," *Shakespeare and the Question of Theory*, ed. Patricia Parker and Geoffrey Hartman (London: Methuen, 1985), 163–87, at 172; for a full study, see F.W. Brownlow, *Shakespeare, Harsnett, and the Devils of Denham* (Newark, Del.: University of Delaware Press, 1993).

16. Ibid., 177.
17. Ibid., 175.
18. Ibid., 177.
19. Ibid., 165.

20. Michael Hattaway, "Describing and Explaining: New Historicism and its Metaphors," *Histoire et secret à la renaissance,* ed. F. Laroque (Paris: Presses de la Sorbonne nouvelle, 1997), 59–72.

21. S. Harsnett, *A Discovery of the Fraudulent Practices of John Darrell* (London, 1599); see Keith Thomas, *Religion and the Decline of Magic* (Harmondsworth: Penguin Books, 1978), 578.

22. The word in this modern sense is cited by *OED* only from 1635.

23. Richard Hooker, *Of the Laws of Ecclesiastical Polity,* 2 vols. (London: Everyman, 1907), 4:9 (2:389).

24. Thomas, 582–88; John L. Murphy, *Darkness and Devils: Exorcism and "King Lear"* (Athens, Ohio: Ohio University Press, 1984), 19–20.

25. "How long hath this possession held the man?" (*The Comedy of Errors,* 5.1.44) is the first citation of the word in this sense in *OED;* compare "If . . . Legion himself possessed him, yet I'll speak to him" (*Twelfth Night,* 3.4.77–79).

26. In Jacobean and Caroline comedy images of demonic possession and exorcism serve as commonplaces in the discourse of love and are not associated with papistry; see, for example, Robert Davenport, *The City Night-cap* (1624), act 4; James Shirley, *The Bird in a Cage* (1633), 5.1; Richard Brome, *The English Moor* (1637), 5.1; James Shirley, *The Cardinal* (1641), act 2. George Ruggle's Latin comedy *Ignoramus* acted at Trinity College Cambridge in 1615 uses exorcism as a satirical device in act 4.

27. Greenblatt, 182.
28. Rosenberg, 153.
29. De Grazia, 25.
30. Rosenberg, 218.
31. A facsimile edition of the relevant passages is to be found on http://www.library.upenn.edu/etext/furness/lear/harsnett/045.html.
32. H.A. Mason, *Shakespeare's Tragedies of Love* (London: Chatto and Windus, 1970), 203.
33. Foakes, *Hamlet versus Lear,* 6.
34. Bullough, 417.
35. Ibid., 426.
36. Ibid., 420.
37. Ibid., 417, 420.
38. Ibid., 418.
39. Geoffrey Chaucer, "The Monk's Tale" 2484–85, *Works,* ed. F. N. Robinson (London: Oxford University Press, 1957), 195.
40. Eric Partridge, *Shakespeare's Bawdy* (London: Routledge and Kegan Paul, 1968), 95.
41. Howard Mills, *Working with Shakespeare* (Hemel Hempstead: Harvester, 1993), 79.
42. William Shakespeare, *The First Quarto of King Lear,* ed. Jay L. Halio (Cambridge: Cambridge University Press, 1994), 25; see also Foakes, *Hamlet vs Lear,* 107–8.
43. Michael Hattaway, "The story of Gloucester in *King Lear,* or, how not to do it," *The Show Within: Dramatic and Other Insets. English Renaissance Drama (1550–1642),* ed. François Laroque, 2 vols. (Montpellier: Publications de l'Université Paul-Valéry, 1992), 2:217–33; for other readings, see Foakes, 202–3.
44. Foakes, *King Lear,* 329 n.
45. *OED* cites R. Niccols, *Beggers Ape,* 1627, "He with . . . shaggy beard And whelked horns, so Satyr-like appeared" (Sig. A4).

46. Foakes, *King Lear,* 332 n reads the devil figure as one who tempts men to suicide.

47. For a review of interpretations of this line, see Foakes, *King Lear,* 363–64 n.

48. Enright, 46.

49. Mason, 223.

50. Sigmund Freud, "The Uncanny," *The Standard Edition of the Complete Psychological Works of Sigmund Freud,* 24 vols., (London: The Hogarth Press, 1953–74), 217–52, at 231.

51. Stephen Booth, ed., *Shakespeare's Sonnets* (New Haven: Yale University Press, 1977), 470, 535.

52. De Grazia, 25, 29.

53. See also De Grazia, 25.

54. Michael Warren, "Quarto and Folio *King Lear* and the Interpretation of Albany and Edgar," *Shakespeare: Pattern of Excelling Nature,* ed. David Bevington and Jay L. Halio (Newark, Del.: Associated University Presses, 1978), 95–107, at 104.

55. Halio, *King Lear,* 276–77.

Designs on Shakespeare: Sleeves, Gloves, and Helen's Placket

CAROL CHILLINGTON RUTTER

"Soft, here comes sleeve. . . . Hold thy whore, Grecian! Now for thy whore, Trojan! Now the sleeve, now the sleeve!"
—*Troilus and Cressida* (5.4.18, 24–25)

"In the past, critics reviewed actors; more recently, directors. Today one reviews the designer."
—Ralph Berry

"Modern dress is one thing. Fancy dress another. With modern dress we know where we are. With fancy dress we might be anywhere, which means anything goes."
—Eric Shorter

"The designer, like the writer and director, may flatter or disturb the dreams of spectators."
—Michael Ratcliffe

"All art is political."
—Michael Bogdanov

Designs on bodies

I CAN DATE WITH SOME PRECISION THE MOMENT I LEARNED WHAT A DEsigner does in the theatre: it was twenty minutes past seven on 11 July 1977, the opening night of the Royal Shakespeare Company's revival of Terry Hands's *Henry V.* For the first twenty minutes, the production had been played on a bare stage by actors in rehearsal gear. When the French ambassador arrived in sumptuous court costume, though, the under-dressed English began to shift uneasily. And when the Dauphin's sportive gift of tennis balls, sarcastically presented in a gilded coffer, was opened, King Harry's crooked, boyish smile froze: "This mock of his / Hath turned his balls to gunstones." Behind him, the Chorus, armed with his "muse of fire," put his rhetorical touch paper to the nation's fervor. It was then that the scene exploded. Out of the flies dropped a massive canopy designed by Farrah that caught the air with a roar like flame seeking oxygen. It billowed open to hang over the action: a gorgeous, terrible mushroom cloud. Farrah's canopy literalized imperial ambition; it made politics explicit. Blazoned in red, blue, gold, in lions rampant and fleur de lys, it presented, literally *and* figuratively, the arms of France and England, and held out to the aspiring conqueror's reach the "crowns imperial . . . / Promis'd to Harry and his followers." "Now sits Expectation in the air," crowed the Chorus. The canopy reified Expectation. Later, though, the guy wires sagged. The canopy fell, covering the stage in a vast expanse of grey canvas underbelly, the mud of Agincourt: here was adventurism turned bleakly unheroic-side out. The effete French, camped center stage and longing for the dawn that would bring the battle, lounged in a circle of light, glimmering in cloth-of-gold tunics, stroking their plumed crests, flaunting their polished, high-gloss armor, while around them, in the shadows, the wretched English in filthy battle fatigues, their St. George crosses faded to the color of dried blood, hugged the canvas mud and tried to sleep.

Designers are interpreters who translate Shakespeare into visual languages that reimagine him in material terms. Their business is to *wright* the play, like Prospero in partnership with Snug the joiner, fashioning for the poet's "airy nothings" a "local habitation and a name" that "turns them to shapes," invents a physical world, and locates the play's "nothings" in that world among functional objects. Designers *see* words. They structure the audience's looking (closing down or opening up the scenic aperture; blocking the view or giving access to seeing; framing the scene; ordering or distorting perspective; creating visual parallelisms or superimpositions; foregrounding; distancing). They offer a repertoire of visual images to make Shakespeare's text legible in performance: in 1983, for example, *Measure for Measure* at the RSC opened in front of a full-length ormolu mirror where "seemers" narcissistically played to their own appearances; in 1991, in Freud's Vienna, in a room with an analyst's couch; in 1978, in Hogarth's Gin Alley, beneath an icon of blind Justice, armed with sword and scales; in 1987, in Thatcher's Soho, among rent boys and kerb crawlers cruising a set that looked like the gents' loo off Leicester Square.[1]

A designer's images work intellectually, cerebrally; also, emotionally, affectively. Always, they work politically: in 1987, Venice from one angle was rendered in high-Renaissance art, a Madonna and Child in gold and lapis lazuli mosaic, from another, in graffiti, a Star of David in yellow paint daubed on a wall[2]; in 1993 Prospero's island was packed inside a theatre skip: Ariel was the first thing to emerge from it. Later, imagining the masque, he brought out a miniature Pollock toy theatre to serve as the prototype for the life-sized version that instantly arrived, "magicked in," from the flies.[3] In 1984, Richard Gloucester swung his deformity along on crutches like a spider; in 1977, Henry VI perched on a throne several sizes too big that made him look like a child; in 1976, Juliet stretched from a balcony so high that only the lovers' fingertips touched.[4]

Working in space, designers make the stage a world, a notional "wooden-O" that can be dressed as a claustrophobic "cockpit" or "the vasty fields of France." The stage may replicate reality (when spectators walked into the theatre for *As You Like It* in 1989 they saw on stage an exact copy of the RST foyer) or burst reality expressionistically apart (the map that covered the *Lear* stage floor in 1993 was ripped up piecemeal; the globe that hung surreally over the heath split like the Fool's proverbial egg, spilling the sands of time into a Beckettian heap for the Dover scenes, a bizarre pre-play of *Happy Days*).[5] In 1989 Hamlet roamed an open-plan Elsinore in striped pajamas; in 1997 he retreated to a cramped attic boxroom littered with half-read books and crusted milk bottles.[6] In 1987, High Street Padua was set at such a steep rake that everyone coming into shrewtown was thrown off balance.[7] In 1985, Celia and Rosalind fled the "court": an abandoned nursery covered in dust sheets. Arden was through a green-framed looking glass, and the exiles trudged into banishment pulling over their shoulders out of the center of a winter sun lengths of parachute silk that spread out behind them, covering the world in white.[8] In 1962, Lear staggered across a wilderness of grey stretched canvas—the heath—where perspective had disappeared; in 1990 he spun inside a revolving cube that simulated both the enclosure and the turmoil of his mind.[9]

Designers also work with style. One convention is to put Shakespeare into period dress (his, ours, or something in between) where the conceit operating is that the design constructs a whole world: the illusion simulates reality and the aesthetic depends upon consistency, coherence, historic accuracy, and density. Period design is layers deep in detail. In 1975, *The Merry Wives* was played in "authentic"

Elizabethan ruffs and farthingales and set against a replica Windsor skyline, circa 1595; in 1985—updated to England's *second* Elizabethan age—"Mrs." Ford and "Mrs." Quickly sat on "authentic" 1953 linoleum under hair dryers in pedal pushers.[10] In 1991, *Romeo and Juliet* was dressed in Veronese doublet, hose and rapiers; in 1987, Verona's punks cruised on roller skates among gangs in black leather, armed with flick knives and bicycle chains, and Tybalt and Mercutio lunged at each other over the bonnet of Tybalt's new Alfa Romeo.[11] Putting Shakespeare into modern dress makes him our contemporary, tells us to read domestic comedy, adolescent tragedy off the front page of today's *Guardian*, *Daily Mail* or *Sun*. Putting him into another period's costume requires us to historicize, to place the story in a past that is a "foreign country" where "they do things differently."[12] One design strategy reproduces a contemporary world in archival detail: *Richard II* (1986) was set in a medieval Book of Hours; *Richard III* (1984), among table tombs copied from the Beauchamp Chapel.[13] Another strategy makes aptness of analogy the stylistic issue: the play is set in a place or time—*Much Ado* in the British Raj (1977); *All's Well*, during the Crimea (1981); *Henry VI*, in Bosnia (1994)—that the audience recognizes, that makes the play's issues accessible, but that also locates the production in a world that registers the play's original rules of engagement, that makes sense of its social organization and caste system (particularly gender hierarchy), its political rivalries, religious and ethnic antagonisms.[14]

Since the 1960s the design style that has come to dominate at the RSC as designers have moved away from consistency and scenic decoration toward non-illusion is what the theatre critic Michael Billington calls "eclecticism," design for a post-modern stage that works by pastiche, assembling jarring visual images from disparate places and periods that inform and confound each other, that interrogate or critique the politics—private, public, sexual, national, gendered, racial—the play is projecting. Eclectic design deconstructs Shakespeare's play-as-myth to reject the notion of the self-contained playworld, its fiction of aesthetic coherence, its illusion of moral and political consistency. It mixes fantasy with realism, nostalgia with the avant garde: the play becomes a palimpsest of its previous productions. Eclectic design is disintegrationist and so takes pleasure in fissures: cracks that run down characters' faces (like the faultline through the Fool's face in *Lear*, 1982, or the red gag slashed across his mouth in 1993)[15] or through the stage picture.[16]

For actors, designers construct a play space that is also a work room. They furnish it with apparatus: "stuff" for performance; costumes that are working gear but also identity, expression, an intimate scaffold to hang characterization onto. Designers write bodies: they use the body as material; they put material onto the body to make its meanings variously legible. Like set design, costume design is significant design, never merely "fancy dress." It works toward a political construction of the body in play. Portia, in 1993, was trapped in a black mourning dress so tightly corsetted she could scarcely breathe; so heavy, she moved like she was dragging chains; so massively skirted, her suitors stood at bay. But headed for Venice, she kicked up her heels in a skirt short enough to aim the blow that kicked over Belmont's traces.[17] In 1985 Desdemona staggered the Venetian council when she came to them dressed as a Moorish bride.[18] In 1997, Gertrude wore orange; in 1992, more shocking, white: a wedding dress.[19] Celia went "native" in sheepskin in Arden in 1985; Rosalind was a bowler-hatted Chaplinesque clown. Helena in *All's Well* (1981) changed from buttoned-up dependent, chatelaine hanging from the waist of her serviceable black dress, to stunning court creature, in miles of blue satin, jewels in her hair, a partner for a king. Across the *Henry VI* trilogy (1977) Queen Margaret metamorphosed from lissome girl (stepping fastidiously through smoke and battlefield carnage in figure hugging velvet) into harridan hag, her body made over in chain mail that, moulded to the curves of her female form, monstered her sexuality.[20]

The first designer of Shakespeare was, of course, Shakespeare himself.[21] Like his subsequent designers who follow "the oblique imperatives of [his] dialogue,"[22] Shakespeare began with the material of the body, and he made that material signify in radical ways. He worked from the skin up: from Othello's blackness and Edgar's nakedness; from Coriolanus's scars (those wounds that map Rome's triumph on his martial body); from Richard's (and Caliban's) deformity; from Falstaff's corpulence. Making the body signify, he required his audience to read it, and not just one way: the fat knight's mountain of flesh is Good Cheer, but it is also Gluttony; Commonwealth, but also Riot. His great belly tropes him both as "cannibal" (consuming not just "some" but "all") and "female": he is the "sow that hath overwhelmed all her litter" whose "womb undoes me"; a travesty Doll Tearsheet ("pregnant" with a cushion up her skirt) or Mother England, devouring her off-spring, daubing her lips "with her own children's blood" as her new recruits are exhorted to civil war, "On, bacons, on! Young men must live." Set against him are the kingdom's Slenders and Shallows; coming after him, the Fangs and Snares who, embodying Lenten leanness, bring in the new regime's ascetic reformation: the end of carnival.

The body as Shakespeare writes it demands to be read as "thing itself" (like Poor Tom, naked on Lear's heath) or as inscription: "Was this fair paper, this most goodly book / Made to write 'whore' upon?" (4.2.73–74) asks Othello of Desdemona, defaced—as he thinks—with pornographer's graffiti. Trying to read bodies, King Duncan laments human inscrutability: "There's no art to know the mind's construction in the face" (1.4.11–12). So does Leontes. Unable to decipher his wife's gravid belly, he turns to his son's face instead: "They say it is a copy out of mine . . . /Art thou my calf?" (1.2.124, 129). On Shakespeare's stage, "Look there, look there!" draws attention time and again to the body, to its multiple signification; to its plural or contradictory interpretation; or maybe to its indecipherability. Everywhere in Shakespeare the body is politic: Cressida's "foot speaks" (but what *language* does it speak?); so does Juliet's. Menenius's belly smiles. Phebe's eyes wound. Bottom's head wisely confirms him an ass. Or maybe not: for these bodies simultaneously construct and contest the interpretations fixed upon them. Without question, though, bodies reproduce: twins double cross their plays; children "print off" their parents. Polixenes and Hermione stand before Leontes a second time, copied in Florizel and Perdita.

Putting costumes on bodies, Shakespeare, like every early modern theatre wrighter, had to hand a semiotics of dress regulated by cultural practice and legal constraint in the Tudor sumptuary laws, a code—elaborated in the mind-numbingly "tedious brief" style of a Polonius—whose object was to illustrate each scrupulous gradation of social hierarchy by assigning every cloth, every buckle, every stocking (silk, woolen, worsted) its right sartorial station in life. So, beginning at the top, the statute of 1597 commanded "that None shall weare in his Apparell":

Cloth of gold or siluer tissued, Silke of colour Purple, vnder the degree of an Earle, except Knights of the Garter in their purple Mantels onley.

Cloth of gold or siluer, tincelled Sattin, Silke or cloth imbrodered with Pearle, Gold, or Siluer, woollen Cloth made out of the Realme, vnder the degree of a Baron, except Knights of the Garter, Privey Counsellors to The Queenes Maiestie.

Veluet in gownes, cloakes, Coates, or other vppermost Garments, embroderies with silke, Netherstocks of silke, Under the degree of a Knight, except Gentlemen in ordinarie Office, attending vpon her Maiestie in her house or chamber; Such as haue bin imploied in Ambassage to foreine Princes. The sonne and heire apparant of a knight. Captaines in her maiesties pay: and such as may dispend CC.li [£200] by the yeere for terme of life in possession aboue all charges.

Sattin, Damaske, Grogeran, Taffata in Hose, Doublet, Under the degree of a Gentleman bearing Armes. . . . And such as may dispend xx.li [£20] by the yeere.[23]

The one clause in this frequently re-issued proclamation that was never amended was the one regulating the bottom rung on the social ladder: "no Seruyngman in husbandrye, or Jurneymen in handycraftes, takyng wages, shall weare in his doublet any other thyng than fustyan, Canuas, leather or Woolen cloth."

Theoretically, at least, this statute meant that a person's rank, profession, family, position of precedence in that family (the heir to a title was allowed a dagger forbidden to his younger brother), even annual disposable income were displayed in the cut, cloth, color, insignia and ornamentation of his gown, a sign system that operated on the street *and* on the stage. (How convenient for the play writer that such a visual shorthand be common parlance.) We know from the company accounts in Philip Henslowe's *Diary* how lavishly the players spent on costumes. £6 was their standard payment to a playwright for a new "book"; they might disburse many times that amount to dress a play in costumes that designed expectation: "cottes for gyantes" in *Brutus*; "a grey gowne for gryssell" in *Patient Grissell*; £20 for "taffataes & sattyns" for *The Seven Wise Masters*; "A canves sewt & Lame skenes" for *The Black Dog of Newgate*; £2 10s "for mackynge of crownes" for *Mahomet*; £21 for "ij pylle velluet of carnardyn" (plus another £17 "for tynsell & tyffeney & lynynge & other thinges") for *Cardinal Wolsey*; "blacke buckrome to macke a sewte for a fyer drack"—a dragon—in *Tom Strowde*.[24]

Like bodies, then, costumes on Shakespeare's stage were legible, freighted with significance that is both iconic and performative: Osric's hat, Shylock's gaberdine; Caesar's assassinated toga; Macbeth's armor; the popinjay's snuff box wafted in Hotspur's battle-grimed face; Coriolanus's "gown of humility" (or rather, his "wolvish toge" that bizarrely reverses the fable to make him both the sacrificial lamb and the scapegoat in wolf's clothing). When Isabella, the probationary nun, is invited to "put on the destined livery," the "livery" Angelo has in mind is the one that constructs all women "whore." When Lady Macbeth, her mind pestered, walks in her sleep, she is wearing the dress of innocent sleep, the nightgown she told her husband to put on to alibi his innocence in act 2. In all these instances, "Apparel . . . proclaims the man," but it simultaneously interrogates him, for if a man is what he wears, a change of clothes is a change of role, character, identity. "Which is the justice, which is the thief" when clothes can lie, when clothes—on stage, *always*—are "usurp'd attire," disguise, a cover-up; when "robes and furr'd gowns hide all"? Who is the hypocrite in *Hamlet*? The sable-suited Prince, obstinately affecting condolement? Or Claudius, the spruce bridegroom? How are the politics of gender exposed in Rosalind's transvestism, or the politics of marriage in Kate's wrecked wedding dress? And what about the politics of politics as England's crown goes the rounds as fashion accessory to a string of self-promoting "wannabe" kings: it is fashioned in paper for dogged York; in "brass impregnable" for Richard II. But it is always hollow. It can be bored through "with a little pin" by antic King Death.

Costume, I'm arguing, writes an entire level of theatrical meaning for Shakespeare. In *Lear*, for example, the King's costume changes demonstrate a life coming apart and mark the stages of his transformation with a savage, ironic visual commentary. Grief is finally redressed at the end—Lear wakes in new robes—but the effect is to alienate comfort. "Oh reason not the need," cries the child-changed father before the storm breaks over his head. But in that storm, Lear learns to reason the need inflicted by deprivation. In act 1, he asked, facetiously, "Doth any here know me?" That question of knowing by reading externals is a serious one, though, for what is a king when regiment is gone? Having metaphorically stripped his daughter to her smock and banished Kent from all he possesses in scene 1, Lear's journey is toward equivalent self exposure, a literal process of stripping away—"What need you five and twenty, ten, or five?"; "What need one?"—that razes Lear's likeness to King Lear as implacably as Kent defaces Kent to play servant Caius or Edgar ruins Edgar to travesty sanity in the savage grotesquerie of naked, mad Tom. The costume changes of *King Lear* materialize a terrifying spectacle: authority, reduced to "unaccommodated man," stands naked in the storm, teeth chattering. "Is man no more than this?" wonders the grief-wilded King. But is *authority* no more than this? That is what the play-stricken audience has to wonder as it is required to look at a king whose crown is "idle weeds," whose chief courtier is a squinney-eyed Cupid blinded by love. Shakespeare's design for this play constantly projects ways of seeing that teach a radical politics. Given such a vocabulary of costume, how is it possible to leave *King Lear* with an ideology of authority intact?

As a designer, Shakespeare made costume work both literally and figuratively: to identify and decorate, but also to dismantle (as in "undress," "expose") and so, by theatrical seeing, to dismantle (as in "take apart") cultural practice. Costumes tell stories in Shakespeare's performance text that were never written into his playtext. Consider Vienna's Duke in *Measure for Measure*, interested to see "what our seemers be," becoming a "seemer" himself. He puts on a friar's habit and so "passes" in disguise for four acts of the play as the un-selfconscious embodiment of the hypocrisies he is discovering endemic to his regime. What complicated visual story does his costume tell, then, in continuous counterpart to the lines the Friar/Duke speaks?

Or consider Cressida and her change of clothes. Like Romeo and Juliet, but with a world of difference (for starters: in *this* warped world, Pandarus plays the Nurse), Troilus and Cressida spend one night together. The morning after (4.2), early, while the dawn is still cold, Troilus makes to leave: "night will hide our joys no longer."[25] He sends Cressida back to bed: "To bed, to bed"; "Sleep kill those pretty eyes. / I prithee now, to bed." Is Cressida in her nightgown?[26] Or—more nearly naked—her smock? Troilus fusses over her, "You will catch cold and curse me." But to her, his concern sounds like a brush-off: "Are you a-weary of me?" she asks anxiously. "Prithee tarry . . . / O foolish Cressid! I might have still held off, / And then you would have tarried." But the intimacy of her un-dress mocks as vain her strategy of holding off. Pandarus comes bustling in, as always, salacious and officious ("How now, how now, how go maidenheads?"), feigning incomprehension as he pointedly asks Cressida to her face, "Where's my Cousin Cressid?" For last night's Cressida—virgin Cressida—is gone; *this* Cressida is unrecognizable as *that* one; Cressida's changed. It is a profound point, made grossly. Two virgins went to bed together the night before. This morning, only one of them is physically inscribed with the act they mutually consummated. Cressida *is* changed, and Pandarus's joke enjoys the cultural discrepancy his mockery depends upon: Cressida's "privates" are somehow publicly legible. She is now irreversibly—and what is more, to the practised eye, *visibly*—the "deed's creature." So what has the deed created her?

A knock at the gates interrupts Pandarus's banter; the lovers withdraw, but Troilus (alone) re-enters when it is clear Aeneas knows he is there. Troilus receives the message: Cressida is to be handed over to the Greeks, exchanged for captured Antenor. "Is it so concluded?" asks the prince and exits with Aeneas. "Twill be his death; twill be his bane; he cannot bear it." That's as Pandarus sees it. But the phlegmatic Troilus who left with Aeneas did not seem inclined to "go mad or die." Not so Cressida. When she re-enters, discovers Troilus gone, and finally prises the news from her uncle—

demanding "What's the matter?" four times in twelve lines clotted with Pandarus's wailing *non sequiturs* ("Would thou hadst ne'er been born. I knew thou wouldst be his death. O poor gentleman")—she calls upon the gods to witness her resolve. "I will not go" from Troy:

> I will not uncle. I have forgot my father;
> I know no touch of consanguinity,
> No kin, no love, no blood, no soul so near me
> As the sweet Troilus! O you gods divine,
> Make Cressid's name the very crown of falsehood
> If ever she leave Troilus! . . .
> . . . I will not go from Troy.
>
> (4.2. 99–112)

Shakespeare takes Cressida off stage for twelve lines (4.3). When she returns, in 4.4, she is changed. She is dressed for going. She has her gloves: she gives one to Troilus at line 70. Her costume tells a story the lines withhold. The lovers swear constancy. The clothes dismantle constancy. The lovers exchange tokens. They give what they have to hand in the extremity of the moment, suddenly: Troilus, his (heraldic) sleeve, Cressida, her glove.[27] These piecemeal tokens of absent bodies are loaded with the promise of metaphor, for hands pledge hearts, and chivalric arms defend female honor. But the tokens are likewise cruelly ironic, for they are, literally, emptied out of meaning. The sleeve comes without the arm, the glove, without the hand. Again, four scenes hence (5.2), Troilus's sleeve will change hands yet once more when Cressida hands it over to Diomedes to pledge a new vow, "token for the surety of it."

What is this "it" Diomedes wants sworn? "It" remains unuttered, inexplicit, but Troilus, looking on, sees Cressida first offer the token—*his* pledge: had she nothing else to commit perfidy with?— then take it back, and with it the faith-breaking vow she has just made to Diomedes. But then Diomedes grabs it out of her hands—he wins at "snatch"—and Troilus sees Cressida surrender languidly to the compliance the sleeve signifies and she, finally, does not resist. The "it" Troilus sees is betrayal: "False, false, false."

After this, Cressida is literally written out of the story. She sends a letter back to Troy and Troilus the next morning. What does it say? Like the "it" of the night before, the message is undisclosed. Troilus reads it silently—"Words, words, mere words, no matter from the heart"—then tears the paper and throws it to the promiscuous "wind, to wind: there turn and change together" (5.3.108, 110). Meanwhile the sleeve that Diomedes flaunts in his helmet taunting the Trojan who owned it to combat is no longer "the thing itself" but reconstituted, in Thersites's interpretation, into a portable emblem—"Hold thy whore"—and synecdoche for Diomedes: "Here comes sleeve." Women are excluded entirely from the exchange of meaning the token now tropes: the testosterone-driven combat for the doubly evacuated sleeve is about male bonding in death's *passo doble*.

Designs on Shakespeare

To see how Shakespeare's subsequent designers interpret Shakespeare and how, through their interpretation, they interpret Shakespeare to us, I want to use *Troilus and Cressida* as a case study, for this is a play whose crises are written as moments that are peculiarly vulnerable to design to construct, mediate, and interpret them. Designers tell us what this play is about. And we use this play to tell ourselves what *we* are about, for *Troilus and Cressida*, uniquely in Shakespeare's canon, is a *modern* Shakespeare play. (Its performance history begins postwar—post, that is, Vietnam war: no record survives of any production—Elizabethan, Jacobean, Georgian, Victorian—before 1894; Stratford saw it first in 1913 and only three more times in the next fifty years. Since 1960, though, there have been eight RSC productions.)[28] In a very immediate sense, then, this play is ours, our invention; the theatre images we have to think it through are modern images. No wonder we use it discursively to reflect ourselves to ourselves. But there is something more that makes this play immediate (and explains its former neglect): its tone, its take on heroic Homeric epic, is tuned to our own disillusioned, dissident postmodernism. Michael Billington calls *Troilus and Cressida* "a cynic's Iliad."[29] It is peopled, says Paul Taylor, with "big shots" on both sides who "fail, with embarrassing frequency, even to recognise the opposition VIPs." This is hardly surprising since "there is a farcical discrepancy between the glamorous 'press' these figures have received in legend and the collection of machiavels, geriatrics, sulking narcissists and slippery self-deceivers the play actually presents."[30] For Benedict Nightingale, it is "a play for an anxious generation in a pluralist society":

> Past ages found it bewildering, offensive, or ridiculous, an affront to every Aristotelian virtue; we find it only too lucid. Where else in our literature do we get so sustained an assault on the romantic values, honour, military glory, "pure" love? Indeed, the play goes further than this, and

calls the whole concept of an established and orderly social system into question. Self-willed and reckless of "degree," its people seem about to stumble over the brink into what Shakespeare would regard as anarchy and confusion.[31]

Bleak, reductivist, corrosively comedic, the play's vision is utterly familiar to its late-twentieth century spectators, to a culture that invented "smart bombs" and "post-traumatic stress syndrome," that laughs at Scarfe and Doonesbury and transmits HIV. It is not just the debunking of heroes, of romantic idealism we recognize; it is the politicking, the ethical relativism in a world void of absolute values, the indeterminacy of actions in a doldrum-ed narrative that seems to be all middle, where the muddled, unresolved ending has both sides claiming victory in a war we know is only half fought and everybody loses. The play stages the end of heroics: Troilus, metamorphosed overnight from mooning calf to murderous thug; Hector, pursuing golden fantasies—troped in golden armor—rotten at the core; Achilles, roused from lolling in his tent clapping Patroclus's cheap theatricals, slaughtering Hector ignominiously. And productions since 1960 have gazed unflinching at heroism's deglamorized trashing in this play: Shakespeare's mood on militarism is our own. We can watch the death of heroism impassively. But what about the death of fidelity?

That is a different story. For we're much less certain of Shakespeare's mood on love and faith in this play, the way it strips idealism—and, worse, both wonder and pleasure—from what, under greenwood trees in the Forest of Arden or behind box hedges in walled gardens in Illyria, were wooing and wedding games, but here are commodified exchanges of variously valued merchandise managed by variously situated "broker-lackey[s]": blue-chip Paris; shyster Pandarus. In this commodities marketplace (which speculates on futures and residuals and doubles as a battlefield), Helen may be "a pearl / Whose price hath launch'd above a thousand ships, / And turn'd crown'd kings to merchants" (2.2.82–84). She may, that is, be worth a Cressida: "a pearl," says Troilus, whose "bed is India . . . / Ourself the merchant" [1.2.100, 103].) Or she may be, as Hector argues, "not worth what she doth cost the keeping" (2.2.52), being no more "dear" than "every tithe soul 'mongst many thousand dismes" (2.2.19) slaughtered in war's body brokering. Maybe, like them, she is only so much dead meat, "carrion"—a carcass in the flesh trade—for "every scruple" of whose "contaminated . . . weight / A Trojan hath been slain" (4.1.72–73). (Troping love and war is no surprise in Shakespeare. What is different here is that the combatants—all of them—are mercenaries, and vows are not eternal pledges but interim bargains on the lookout for better deals.)

This is a discrepancy that interests me. The same productions that pull no punches when Achilles betrays Hector, that play out his betrayal to its appalling, brutal consequences (observe: men who betray men in Shakespeare are called traitors; that's politics), duck, weave, and backpedal when Cressida betrays Troilus (observe: *women* who betray men in Shakespeare are not called traitors: they are called whores).[32] Cressida's betrayal makes them nervous. There is no model for it elsewhere in Shakespeare to teach them how to play it, and no performance history to refer to. In the event, they "design" their way out of their confusion.

One recourse is to reconstruct Cressida's betrayal as something else. (That was John Barton's strategy in 1968: Timothy O'Brien's design wrote Cressida a voluptuary from the start and kept her that one thing, in the same costume, throughout. She was a slapper; Troilus, a twerp not to have noticed. What she did was not betrayal. It was "natural." Misogynist history saw it coming.) Another recourse is to motivate it. That was the story Tom Piper's design told in 1998. Troilus betrayed Cressida *first*. It was the suitcase that did it. Dragged kicking and screaming in Pandarus's grasp toward the hostage exchange, Cressida managed to tear her valise out of his hand, wrench it open, and yank out her clothes. Then she watched—appalled, bereft—as Troilus (stumbling, tense) retrieved her scattered bras and cardigans, folded up her excruciating self-exposure, packed it all away, and handed her over, reminding her, as he did, to be "true." A third recourse is to extenuate it. (So Liz da Costa, 1985, designing costumes for Howard Davies's Crimean *Troilus*, sent Cressida to the Greeks in her nightgown. What Cressida experienced—a lone woman hemmed in by soldiers—when the greatcoat Troilus had draped protectively over her shoulders for the journey—his uniform, not insignificantly, marking her both "of Troy" and "of Troilus"—fell away, exposing her to their hungry eyes, was gang rape. It was better, then, to accept Diomedes as "guardian" and be visited in "particular" than used "in general" by the "general" camp.)

All of these versions were ultimately conservative (not so say reactionary) and clichéd in making Cressida a whore. That is, they confirmed what Barton's production premised, that Ulysses's reading (and writing: Ulysses, remember, wants his verdict "set . . . down" for "every ticklish reader") of Cressida was right: she *was* "sluttish spoils of opportunity," a "daughter[] of the game" (4.5.61–63). Additionally, Davies's version made her a victim before it made her a whore. And all of these versions recruited to their interpretation the powerfully legible images the designer invented to make their Cressida explicit: Cressida was as she was designed. And the design ironed out her contradictions.

But did they get it right? Is Ulysses, chief machiavel and spin doctor (see, for example, his management of Achilles's public image), to be trusted as the play's authority on Cressida? Who *is* Cressida? *What* is she, given that she provokes not just contrary valuations ("pearl"; "spoils") in Troilus and Ulysses, but in herself, a conflicted sense of her self as constitutionally double? She is, she says, *two* Cressidas: she has "a kind of self resides with" Troilus, but another "unkind self, that itself will leave / To be another's fool" (3.2.146–48). Is duality premised as constitutional in this play? (See the attempt Hector makes in 4.5 to separate Ajax into his Greek and Trojan selves.) Elsewhere in Shakespeare the collection of conventions we call "character" proposes something we recognise theatrically as an essential self. It may develop, transform; go into hiding behind a disguise; be betrayed. But it is (mostly) coherent, (mostly) continuous. In Cressida, though, the self is aware of a lived doubleness: that is, duplicity. Is duplicity constitutional? Is it biological, not moral or ethical? Troilus, ending his voyeurism on Cressida with Diomedes in 5.2, observes in the flat tones of a clinician, "This is, and is not, Cressid." To this, another voyeur on the sidelines snorts, incredulously, "Will a swagger himself out on's own eyes?" (5.2.135). For Thersites, Cressida is one thing only. But perhaps Troilus is right. Perhaps the challenge Shakespeare constructs for this play is to put before us two Cressidas, a genuine contradiction.[33] Is it possible to play this two-ness in the theatre? How do you "design double"?

Ubiquitous, Absent, Iconic Helen

To try to answer my questions I need to shift my sights from Cressida to Helen, the play's other problematic woman, a role Shakespeare quite consciously constructs as Cressida's distorted twin. I see Helen as Shakespeare-the-designer's design coupe for this play. And it is Helen—as I want to show by remembering three versions of her in performance—who cuts Shakespeare's subsequent designers free from caution and cliché into risk, transgressiveness, radicalism. With Helen they find the visual language Shakespeare scripts, but which they miss, for Cressida. They understand Helen both as icon and iconoclast.

Helen is what this play is about. "Ravish'd Helen"—the Prologue tells us—"that's the quarrel." Her name tropes war; also, love: "the mortal Venus, the heart-blood of beauty, love's visible soul" (3.1.31–32). She's everyone's "matter," everywhere discussed, her image continuously re-formatted as it is appropriated to the political business at hand. So, when Troilus needs it, she is

> . . . a theme of honour and renown,
> A spur to valiant and magnanimous deeds . . .
> And fame in time to come . . .
>
> (2.2.200–203)

This is when he is urging the Trojans to keep their "pearl," their "prize," their "worthy" "theft," "stol'n" by "crown'd kings" turned "merchants"—his words. He sees the "Grecian queen" whom his brother Paris abducted as "inestimable": her "youth and freshness / Wrinkles Apollo's, and makes stale the morning" (2.2.79–80). (When he is not in the "urging" vein, Helen is hideous, the cosmetic that lays the blush on her cheek, blood: "Helen must needs be fair / When with your blood you daily paint her thus" [1.2.90–91].) To others she is "mad idolatry," "will . . . infectiously . . . affected" (Hector); "woe" (Cassandra); "a flat tamed piece" (Diomedes); "a deadly theme" (Menelaus). Most memorably, for Thersites, she is "a placket," that is, reductively, the slit in a woman's petticoat that gives access to her privates: so the whore-war for Helen is a "war for a placket."

Helen is also a set up. She is framed as Cressida's alter ego. To begin with, it merely seems odd that they happen to keep turning up in the same conversations together. Later, it looks less like accident than policy. They are constantly compared, troped with the same metaphors ("pearl"; "merchant"), crossed in identities, and, most bizarre of all, fantasized as rivals. "And her hair were not somewhat darker than Helen's—," sighs Pandarus, hyping his niece, "Well, go to, there were no more comparison between the women." Later, when the hype is on the other foot and Paris's servant is wire-drawing the metaphors—"the mortal Venus, the heart-blood of beauty . . ."—Pandarus affects to interrupt and name this paragon: "Who, my cousin Cressida?" "No, sir. Helen" (3.1.33–35). Helen, Pandarus tells Cressida, loves Troilus "better than Paris"; Cressida, he tells Helen, "is horribly in love with a thing you have, sweet queen," but it is not Paris: "He? No, she'll none of him: they two are twain" (3.1.95, 98). Still, Cressida remains Paris's "disposer" (3.1.84). At significant moments Helen's narrative inserts itself into Cressida's. In 4.5, when Patroclus steps between Menelaus and Cressida to filch his superior's kiss, he mocks the cuckold—"thus popp'd Paris in his hardiment." One abducted woman stands in allusively for the other: "Paris and I kiss evermore for him" (28, 34). In the same scene, Ulysses, too, remembers Helen in Cressida: "give me a kiss / When Helen is a maid again" (49–50). Not insignificantly, Cressida ultimately fetches up at Helen's old address: her "traitor" father Calchas "keep[s] / At Menelaus's tent"; Diomedes and Troilus find her there. It is as though Helen constitutes the master narrative of women's history, the bedrock layer, that keeps surfacing through the palimpsest of individual women's histories. Does she ground those histories, or contaminate them, or perhaps determine them?

Helen and Cressida never meet. (Women don't in *Troilus and Cressida*. Shakespeare makes a point of it. Cassandra and Andromache are the only women ever on stage together—in 5.3, for some forty lines. Nor do women talk to each other. In the 3500 or so lines of this play, women exchange exactly one line.) Helen is just disappearing around the corner when Cressida makes her first entrance inquiring, "Who were those went by?" (1.2.1) This tantalizing absence turns out to be the play's in-joke, for Shakespeare, making Helen the entire matter of the play, keeps her entirely off-stage, out of sight; except for one, single scene, 3.1, placed smack in the center of things, the play's axis.

Pandarus goes to Paris to deliver a message: its burden, Paris is instructed to make his excuse if Troilus is missed at dinner. There is tedious chit-chat with a servant (delay as foreplay?) that serves to remind us that Helen proxies Cressida, and then, finally, forty lines—more delay!—into the scene, Paris enters with what, by now, anticipation has roused us for, "the face that launched a thousand ships / And burnt the topless towers of Ilium"[34]: Helen! What do we get? Disconcertingly, longueur. Unbelievably protracted puns on "fair" and "broke" that delay the message (the alibi, in any case, is so inept that Troilus's "cover" is transparent: "I spy," says Paris). There is some odd stage business (suggested by the text; indeed, suggestive *in* the text; but opaque): Pandarus seems to be fending Helen off ("Sweet queen, sweet queen, that's a sweet queen, i'faith. Nay that shall not serve your turn...." [70, 72].) She wants a song: "You shall not bob us out of our melody" (67). He delivers, but only to deflect further interrogation ("You spy? What do you spy?— Come give me an instrument" [90]). The song is about love; really about sex: the "generation of vipers." When it is over, news is traded, as if out of Filofaxes: "Who's afield today?"; "I would fain have armed today, but my Nell would not have it so" (130, 132).

Pandarus exits (144). Ten lines later, so do Paris and Helen: he wants her to use "these your white enchanting fingers" to "unarm our Hector"; she will be, she says, "proud to be his servant." "Sweet," answers Paris, "above thought I love thee." The scene ends as desultorily as it began. We see no more of Helen.

Is that it? Is that all there is? It feels so vapid and aimless, so vacuous; routine, as if going through the motions, even in the nudging and winking. ("Tickle" is a favourite word in this play: in the Prologue "expectation, tickling skittish spirits . . . / Sets all on hazard" [20, 22]; in Pandarus's song, "love's . . . shaft" "tickles . . . the sore" it "wounds" [111, 115]. "Tickling": is that what this scene is doing, but wearily, as if the ritual of arousal is enervated? It is all so pointless, and rhetorically, unpointed: what, for instance, does Helen mean when she says "this love will undo us all"? What is her tone? What is her level of awareness? Is this a staggering insight or banality? And what about Paris's "I love thee"?)

My protest—is that *it*?—is, I take it, precisely the point. Shakespeare's strategy is to withhold Helen, to starve our sight of her, ratchet-up her mystique by circulating her reputation while preserving her self incognito, an elusive mystery. When he finally does bring her on, fame materializes in a body, mystique registers in what we see. The icon is made flesh. And anticipation is wrecked in a spectacular anti-climax. It is inevitable. The "thing itself" cannot match expectation's idealization. As Shakespeare-the-designer understands it, there is nothing for Helen to do in this play. She must simply *be*. She must "image." And the image—we only need to see it once; it remains on our retina for the rest of the play—both delivers and deconstructs Helen as icon.

It is this double work of simultaneously delivering and deconstructing Helen —"pearl" *and* "carrion"—that three of Shakespeare's subsequent designers have registered spectacularly to our understanding of this play. In 1990, Anthony Ward designed a world for Sam Mendes's *Troilus and Cressida* that was littered with the junk of every post-Trojan conflict in history. Costumes made characters walking palimpsests. Agamemnon, in a slack, moth-eaten cardigan worn over his vintage breastplate, had to rifle the debris—screwed up briefing papers, scummy coffee mugs, an anglepoise lamp—on the generals' map table to find his name plate to shake under Aeneas's nose when the Trojan asked incredulously, "Is *this* the great Agamemnon's tent?" Achilles, dangerous, hooded-eyed, his hair greased to outshine his leather trousers, his muscles on display under his black string vest, sat propped in the entrance to his tent, munching popcorn. Ulysses looked like Ulysses S. Grant.; Ajax, like what lurks in the sadomasochist's basement in *Pulp Fiction*.

In 3.1, Pandarus, in white flannels and striped Henley blazer (how did he manage to keep up such "Hooray-Henry" appearances in Troy after seven years' siege?) played straight man—for once—to an even camper servant whose lines on the "mortal Venus" ushered in four bearers, carrying onto the darkened stage a palanquin, on it, a figure seated like a Buddha, wound round and round in a cloth-of-gold shroud. Paris presided over a choreography that was half ritual, half strip tease. He gave the impression of daily worship at a shrine to "love's visible soul." Holding the end of the gold cloth, walking in languid, mesmerizing circles, he unwrapped the parcel to Pandarus's goggle eyes. It was Helen. In kitsch red chiffon, as darkly voluptuous as Jane Russell, as dangerously desirable as her weight in dark chocolate. But the spectators' disappointment was audible. We were crushed. Was this the face that launched the thousand ships? It wasn't that she wasn't beautiful. It was simply that she wasn't enough. And that was the point. The design image contained its own interrogation and subversion. Was *any* woman worth this war? No. Was "Helen," then, merely a legitimating fiction for the violence men intended to commit any way? Yes. Helen-the-woman was made over as totem, packaged by the politicians' PR-men like some Golden Calf designed by Cadburys. As Sally Dexter played her, Helen was ripe, full-blown; her slow groping of Pandarus was, like lava flowing, a natural force. But her sudden insight that "this love will undo us all" was as prophetic as any of Cassandra's visions, and as tragic, in being, like hers, ignored.

In 1998, Tom Piper (in Michael Boyd's production) took the ritualization of Helen—and the troping of the erotic with the sacred that Ward's design suggested—further, much further. In Piper's world, worship of the "mortal Venus" was the national religion; she was the divine whom men knelt to; but she was also the icon who fronted their political Cause: the Cause that made war religion. And both the icon and the Cause were debased. Piper set *Troilus and Cressida* in a spare, whitewashed room—just across the Irish border, into the IRA badlands; or perhaps in the Balkans, Bosnia, say. (The Trojans had Irish accents; the room looked like it had survived Sarajevo.) The walls were bullet scarred, blackened with shelling; the stained glass fanlight was blown out over the altar in the corner—all that was left of any furniture in the room—where a life-sized statue of the Blessed Virgin stood, a permanent spectator on human atrocity, presiding over and inciting sectarian slaughter, her palms turned serenely outward, distributing balm. Mostly everyone ignored her (though clearly this was the "doll" these "guys" were "doin" it for"). But when Pandarus—a lank-haired Dublin clubman, alcoholic-gaunt—came looking for Paris in 3.1 he found black-shawled women kneeling in front of the Virgin, keening. There was something odd about the devotion, though: the priest was out of Hieronymous Bosch, a Rumpilstiltskin transvestite in a surplice and skull cap who punned leering profanities under the statue's holy gaze. Pandarus was clearly thrown by this walking oxymoron. He turned to go. But when he moved, so did the statue. The head swivelled. Out from under her skirts, Paris somersaulted backwards, wiping his pleasure off his lips and landing, sprawled, at Pandarus's astonished feet. The "Virgin" descended from her plinth. Her votresses cackled. Here was Helen.

The body swap was more than a *trompe l'oeil*. The gag worked in two directions: retrospectively, to re-inform the audience's reading of the Virgin who sanctifies slaughter as holy cause; pre-emptively, to stand Helen (played by Sara Stewart) in the place of "worship," as Virgin substitute, then to write that worship as blasphemy. The moment released a whole repertoire of reactions. It was the stuff of farce: outrageous, impudent, carnivalesque; also offensive, iconoclastic. In representing a "war for a placket" as a religious conflict, it extended its reference beyond the play's local disputes to register all war as a version of lechery, and war's "sacrifice" as sacrilege.

Thirty years earlier, in 1968, the iconic—and iconoclastic—bodies John Barton's production was interested in were male. Censorship was still in force in England; the Lord Chamberlain, still in office (he would fall, as censor, in September; Barton's *Troilus* opened in August). The pressure, however, that theatre practitioners had been putting on censorship for years had reached a crisis: *Oh! Calcutta!*, Ken Tynan's erotic revue—devised to include everything from transvestite strip tease and erotic tableaux ("a nun being raped by her confessor") to documentary (a history of underwear) and sex sketches (John Lennon, David Mercer, Joe Orton contributed)— opened in New York: lesbianism, simulated sex, "all kinds of fetishes and sexual ambiguities" were in. But male homosexuality was out: Tynan specifically excluded it. Was homosexuality a taboo too far?[35]

If so, Barton, back in provincial Stratford, and under the Lord Chamberlain's nose, used Shakespeare to represent it on Establishment theatre's holiest stage. His designer, Timothy O'Brien, inspired by Attic vase painting, created "friezes of bare-torsoed warriors in tiny kilts and huge, bird-like helmets": Achilles was "overtly homosexual, a high-camp posturer in tight gold braids"; Hector and Ajax were stripped in combat "like wrestlers to minuscule breech-clouts, buttocks and biceps straining"; Trojans encountered Greeks in a perverse iron mating dance like "metallic crested cock-birds."[36] Combat was voluptuous, a form of homosexual seduction, and both sides desired it.

Women in Barton were marginalized. Helen, modeled on late-60s icons (Diana Dors, say, imitating Jean Shrimpton: two brands of sex object instantly recognisable to the consumer market in 1968) lounged on a litter in 3.1, her platinum blonde hair cascading down her back. It was later, in a return invented by Barton, that she made her really spectacular entrance. Hector's sportive combat with Ajax (4.5) was done; now, Greeks and Trojans were pursuing sport indeed, half-drunk from Agamemnon's conviviality, invited to Achilles's tent for the serious "sport" to ensue. A flurry of movement in the direction of Troy turned attention. Servants entered, carrying that litter which everyone recognized. Menelaus sprang forward, to claim—his wife, the reclining figure whose blonde hair could be seen under her veil. It was Helen! But then the veils parted to reveal not Helen, but Achilles in drag, in a look-alike Helen wig, inviting Hector to mount him, enticingly opening his woman's gown, showing himself naked. Later, as the midnight party scene reached its orgiastic climax, Thersites ("a jigging carcass of syphilitic sores with a phallic red tongue lolling from a snoutish mask over his groin") was beckoned toward the prostrate Achilles, who seemed to invite him to sexual intercourse.[37]

All of these designs on Helen collaborated with Shakespeare's political narrative in *Troilus and Cressida*: they understood at a deep structural level how violence appropriates the erotic in this play, how blood is the warrior's keenest aphrodisiac. Male politics in *Troilus and Cressida* needs the woman, needs her, mystified, to legitimate its practices; needs her, objectified, to serve its objectives. In short, it needs Helen's discursive body. So it produces her as object, but in such a way that her performative body "reduces" to mere mortality, demystified. Indeed, these designers were canny in showing how the "real" Helen recedes, blocked by her images—the golden parcel, the statue—so that, finally (in Barton as in Euripides' and Herodotus's tellings of Troy, centuries earlier), Helen was not even on the scene. (When Barton returned to this play for a *third* time, in 1976, Paris kept Helen on a golden leash; the Trojans, in council, represented her as a golden mask. But the Greeks possessed Helen, too: their "Helen" was a life-sized doll. She made her way through the action, observing things from a balcony, exiting over Diomedes' shoulder. What was he, the bitterest of Helen's detractors—"she's bitter to her country"—going to do with her? He carried her to Calchas's tent and propped her up against a pillar where she could watch his seduction of Cressida. So not only did Troilus, Ulysses, and Thersites eavesdrop on 5.2; so did "Helen.") Helen in Shakespeare, as in these productions, is a pretext, a male fantasy, a trope for male violence. When men really get down to the business of violent copulation in war's iron mating dance, it is male bodies they desire.

For Cressida, though, Helen's appearance in 3.1 serves a different purpose. It is the curtain raiser, the pre-text to her meeting, her *first* meeting, in the next scene with Troilus. There, in the orchard, he, like Paris, will make some such declaration as, "Sweet, above thought I love thee." Is Helen, then, the "book of sport" that teaches us to read what's "set down" for Cressida in the next scene?

Notes

All citations of *Troilus and Cressida* refer to the Arden edition, edited by Kenneth Palmer (London: Methuen, 1982); Berry, quoted in Peter Holland, *English Shakespeares* (Cambridge: Cambridge University Press, 1997), 14; Shorter, review of *Measure for Measure*, *Birmingham Post* 13 November 1987; Ratcliffe, quoted in John Goodwin (ed.), *British Theatre Design: The Modern Age* (London: Orion, 1998), 24; Bogdanov, quoted in "The state of theatre—a symposium," *Times Literary Supplement*, April 28 1995, 15.

 1. All the design work I survey in this essay appeared in Royal Shakespeare Company productions, most of it originating in Stratford upon Avon. *Measure for Measure*: 1978: directed by Barry Kyle, designed by Christopher Morley; 1983: Adrian Noble/Bob Crowley; 1987: Nicholas Hytner/Mark Thompson; 1991: Trevor Nunn/Maria Bjornson.

 2. Bill Alexander/Kit Surrey.
 3. Sam Mendes/Anthony Ward.
 4. Bill Alexander/William Dudley; Terry Hands/Farrah; Trevor Nunn/Chris Dyer.
 5. John Caird/Ultz; Adrian Noble/Anthony Ward.
 6. Ron Daniels/Antony McDonald; Matthew Warchus/Mark Thompson.
 7. Jonathan Miller/Stefanos Lazaridis.
 8. Adrian Noble/Bob Crowley.
 9. Directed and designed by Peter Brook; Nicholas Hytner/Mark Thompson.
 10. Terry Hands/Timothy O'Brien and Firth Tazeena; Bill Alexander/William Dudley.
 11. David Laveaux/Alison Chitty; Michael Bogdanov/Chris Dyer.
 12. I am, of course, remembering the opening of L. P. Hartley's *The Go-Between*.
 13. Bill Alexander/William Dudley; Barry Kyle/William Dudley.
 14. John Barton/John Napier; Trevor Nunn/John Gunter; Katie Mitchell/Rae Smith.
 15. Adrian Noble/Bob Crowley; Adrian Noble/Anthony Ward.
 16. *Troilus and Cressida* in 1985 was holed-up in a shelled mansion—in antebellum Virginia, or was it Chekov's Crimea? There was a samovar on the table; a battered honky-tonk piano; rebel uniforms, a ticker tape machine. A wide staircase

swept up in a curve designed for a culture used to making grand entrances. But exploding shells had shuddered the window frame to a crazy angle, and below, the mosaic floor was split. Here was a culture literally coming apart at the seams. Howard Davies/Ralph Koltai and Liz da Costa.

17. David Thacker/Shelagh Keegan.
18. Terry Hands/Ralph Koltai and Alexander Reid.
19. Matthew Warchus/Mark Thompson; Adrian Noble/Bob Crowley.
20. Terry Hands/Farrah.
21. Some years ago, Anne Pasternak Slater made *Shakespeare: The Director* (Sussex: Harvester Press, 1982); I am extending her suggestive anachronism. It is, of course, a commonplace of theatre history that there were no directors or designers on Shakespeare's stage, but what is Peter Quince doing if not directing *Pyramus and Thisbe*? And Prince Hamlet is certainly more John Barton than the tragedians of the city might wish. It must have been standard playhouse practice before a new playbook was copied into parts, and parts distributed, to hold a company read-though so that the players could hear the whole play. (Players, it must be remembered, learned a play piecemeal: they held only their own lines, not copies of the entire script, pasted, with their cue lines, into a scroll). Philip Henslowe's *Diary*, edited by R. A. Foakes and R. T. Rickert (Cambridge: Cambridge University Press, 1961), 88, records one such occasion:

> lent vnto the company ....
> .... for the boocke called
> th*e* famos wares of henry th*e* fryste & the prynce
> of walles the some of ....   iiij li v s
>
> lent at that tyme vnto the company for to spend
> at th*e* Readynge of that boocke at the sonne in
> new fyshstreat*e* ....   v s

Who did the reading? The likeliest candidate, in my guess, is the playwright who, as he "told" the play, would have been "directing" it. It is clear from the company accounts quoted below that players had a developed sense of production design. But the first real design team we can identify was undoubtedly the Ben Jonson/Inigo Jones partnership.

22. Slater, 1.
23. Extracts from the Proclamations of Apparel, 6 July 1597, 39 Elizabeth I, are reprinted in Carol Chillington Rutter, *Documents of the Rose Playhouse* (Manchester: Manchester University Press, 1984), 233–34. The statute in full appears in P. L. Hughes and J. F. Larkin, eds., *Tudor Royal Proclamations 1588–1603* (New Haven: Yale University Press, 1969). I emphasize the statute's theoretical power: given that Elizabeth's government found it necessary to reiterate the Act nine times during her reign, it may be supposed that it was regularly flouted. Jacques's quillet about the "city-woman" who "bears the cost of princes on unworthy shoulders" (*As You Like It*, 2.7.75) clearly hit a target: abuses of apparel by the "unworthy" were regularly satirized by the "Jacks" of the day. For more on costumes and their legibility see Slater, 137–70, and Peter Stallybrass, "Patriarchal Territories: the body enclosed" in Margaret Ferguson, Maureen Quilligan, and Nancy J. Vickers (eds.), *Rewriting the Renaissance* (Chicago: Chicago University Press, 1986), 123–42, and "Worn Worlds" in Margreta de Grazia, Maureen Quilligan and Peter Stallybrass (eds.), *Subject and Object in Renaissance Culture* (Cambridge: Cambridge University Press, 1996), 289–320.

24. These accounts pertain to Worcester's Men at the Rose and the Admiral's Men at the Fortune; see Rutter, *Documents*, 156, 180, 182, 209, and Foakes and Rickert, 178,179. An inventory, now lost, of properties and costumes belonging to the Admiral's Men at the Rose itemizes a variety of design effects, large and small: "a gown to goe invisible," "the sitte of Rome," "Harey the fyftes vellet gowne," "Kentes woden leage," "j dragon in fostes," and "j frame for the [be]heading in Black Jone." See Foakes and Rickert, 317–25.

25. Textual differences between the *Troilus and Cressida* Quarto (1609) and Folio (1623) need to be observed at this point. Neither F nor Q contains act or scene divisions; the standard organization of the text was introduced by Nicholas Rowe in 1709. The Arden, New Penguin, New Shakespeare (Cambridge), Alexander, and Riverside editions follow Rowe in making 4.2 the "morning after" scene; 4.3 the "knocking up Cressida" scene; and 4.4 the "rail and farewell" scene. Wells and Taylor, in the Oxford edition, and after them, Greenblatt et al. in Norton, follow Q and F in marking a general Exeunt at 4.2.76; they then indicate a new scene (4.3 / sc. 12) with the subsequent entrance of Pandarus and Cressida. This throws off the traditional scene-numbering for the remainder of the act. In order to clear the stage at 4.2.76, however, Wells et al. require Pandarus to obey Aeneas's order to "go fetch [Troilus] hither." They have him exit, an exit not in Q or F; and they place the exit at l. 58 rather than l. 76 to avoid turning him around like a top to re-enter with Cressida at l. 77. If Pandarus goes at l. 58, though, instead of being pre-empted from going by the entrance of Troilus, how does Pandarus know the burden of Aeneas's message which he then retails to Cressida when she enters asking, "What's the matter?"

26. Shakespeare's contemporaries, if they were men, slept in their shirts; if women, in their smocks. Nightgowns—made of woollen or worsted fabrics, sometimes with a hood, were not for sleeping; they were worn, says Janet Arnold in her excellent and comprehensive *Queen Elizabeth's Wardrobe Unlock'd* (Leeds, Maney: 1988), "as an informal gown during the day" (139). It was seen as an intimate garment. When the French Ambassador from Henri IV gained an audience with Queen Elizabeth in December 1597 he recorded that "She excused herself because I found her attired in her night-gown [sa robe de nuit], and began to rebuke those of her Council who were present saying, 'What will these gentlemen say'—speaking of those who accompanied me—'to see me so attired? I am much disturbed that they should see me in this state' " (quoted in Arnold, 7).

27. Cressida's glove, like Troilus's heraldic sleeve, is certainly anachronistic. The Greeks and Trojans of this play are end-of-reign Elizabethan makeovers of Chaucerian originals. Cressida, like Cleopatra, is in a farthingale. Like many of his subsequent designers, Shakespeare is an eclectic, as is shown in the Peacham drawing of *Titus Andronicus* (1595) in which R. A. Foakes sees "Goths dressed like Romans, Titus as an ancient Roman [in tunic, toga, and sandals, his head wreathed in laurel] but his sons or followers in variations of contemporary costume of the Tudor period. Tamora wears a loose gown with elaborate puffed and embroidered sleeves, which again belongs to the sixteenth-century rather than to ancient Rome" (*Illustrations of the English Stage 1580–1642* [London: Scolar, 1985], 48). Where gloves are represented in early modern English portraiture—as in portraits of Elizabeth—they are usually held or worn on one hand only (see Arnold, pp. 126, 136, 140, 148). Gloves were tokens of public dress, frequently ornamental, but—and this is the key point for Cressida—essential gear for the traveller . So Arnold: "gloves were absolutely essential for protection on horseback, in summer as well as winter" (p. 217). If, then, a playwright wanted to signify a character in transit, giving her a pair of gloves would make this instantly legible.

28. A "Prefatory Letter" to the 1609 Quarto—of which R. A. Foakes gives an account in his New Penguin edition (1987) of *Troilus and Cressida*—famously describes the published play as "never staled with the stage, never clapper-clawed with the palms of the vulgar," "not . . . sullied with the smoky breath of the multitude." The play's history, says Foakes, was "a blank" until John Dryden reworked it, changing the ending drastically by adding a scene in which Cressida commits suicide. Dryden's version held the stage from 1679 until 1734. A production directed by William Poel, which transferred to Stratford from London for two performances only in the 1913 festival season, was the first full scale *Troilus and Cressida* ever recorded. Ben Iden Payne's 1936 production at the Shakespeare Memorial Theatre (later renamed the Royal Shakespeare Theatre) was described as a "museum piece" by reviewers. Anthony Quayle directed the play in Stratford in 1948, Glen Byam Shaw in 1954. Six years later, John Barton, co-directing with Peter Hall, made his first attempt at the play, a production revived to tour in 1962. then came productions at the RST in 1968 (directed by Barton, designed by Timothy O'Brien); 1976 (Barton with Barry Kyle, designed by Chris Dyer); 1981 (Terry Hands/Farrah); 1985 (Howard Davies/Ralph Koltai with Liz da Costa); 1990 (Sam Mendes/Anthony Ward); 1996 (Ian Judge/John Gunter with Deidre Clancy); and 1998 (Michael Boyd/Tom Piper).

29. It is a phrase he has used regularly in reviews of this play in the *Guardian*; see, for example, 19 August 1976; 8 July 1981; 26 July 1996.

30. *Independent*, 30 April 1990.

31. *New Statesman*, 16 August 1968.

32. Except for Cressida, women in Shakespeare accused of betrayal are wrongly accused—Hermione, Desdemona, Cleopatra, Diana; everywhere, their alleged betrayal (whether political or not) is sexualized: Cordelia, Goneril, Regan; Gertrude; Ophelia. For the move that turns the female "traitor" into the strumpet, see Iago accusing Emilia, "Filth, thou liest" and "Villanous whore" in *Othello* (5.2.238, 236).

33. I am reminded here of Eve Sedgwick's observations on the fair/dark lady of Shakespeare's Sonnets whose "contagious self-division," which registers as "false plague" or "plague of falseness," seems, in the sonnets, to be what defines femininity. "To be a woman" is "to be oxymoron militant." Eve Kosofsky Sedgwick, *Between Men: English Literature and Male Homosocial Desire* (New York: Columbia University Press, 1985), 44.

34. These are, of course, Marlowe's mighty lines in *Dr. Faustus* (5.2.97–98). It is inconceivable that Shakespeare did not know (and glance at?) Marlowe's seductive, subversive Helen—Helen as succubus—when he created his own "mortal Venus."

35. Quoted in Kathleen Tynan, *The Life of Kenneth Tynan* (London: Phoenix, 1995), 278–79.

36. Ronald Bryden, *Observer*, 11 August 1968.

37. Bryden, *Observer*, 11 August 1968; Harold Hobson, *Sunday Times*, 11 August 1968.

Australian Shakespeare
Alan Brissenden

IN FEBRUARY 1998, TWO HUNDRED AND TEN YEARS AFTER GOVERNOR Arthur Phillip landed at Sydney Cove, Australia made a firm commitment to cutting its familial ties with the United Kingdom; it held a convention of 152 elected and appointed delegates to discuss constitutional changes needed for the country to become a republic. The sentiment which led to this convention had been around for over a hundred years, but it had begun to gather real strength only during the previous three decades, a period which also saw a decline in the study of Shakespeare in schools and universities but a resurgence of Shakespeare as popular entertainment. Films helped to foster this resurgence, among them Kenneth Branagh's *Much Ado About Nothing*, Ian McKellen's *Richard III* and, even more, Baz Luhrmann's *Romeo + Juliet*, produced in Hollywood with American actors, but with an Australian director and design team. Luhrmann's first film, *Strictly Ballroom*, gave him world fame but he was also one of a clutch of young directors who had brought a new audience to opera by presenting classic works in modern settings with slim, good-looking singers who were, as well, naturalistic actors with splendid voices. Luhrmann's 1990 Australian Opera production of *La Bohème* had the highest box office in the history of opera in Australia, the videotape became a top seller in the United States, and his 1993 production of Benjamin Britten's *A Midsummer Night's Dream* repeated its initial success when it had soldout performances at the 1994 Edinburgh Festival and was revived again back in Sydney in 1996.

The lavish production values of Luhrmann's *Midsummer Night's Dream*, which was set in the India of the British Raj, were less in accord with ideas on current presentation of the plays themselves than with those of a previous era. From the early 1970s directors turned increasingly to relatively unadorned stages, concentration on the text, and actors speaking with natural Australian tones instead of the hitherto necessary accents of the English stage. To try to discover why it took so long for this revolution to take place, we can take a journey from the beginning, since it's not so very long ago—the first recorded evidence of a Shakespeare performance in Australia is a playbill advertising "the favorite play Henry the Fourth" at Robert Sidaway's theatre in Sydney on 8 April 1800; as Hotspur and Douglas are in the list of characters, we can add "Part I" after the title, but we don't know whether or not the play was in fact performed. We hope so. It is significant that the theatre management did not think it necessary to include the playwright's name on the bill, an indication of the general acceptance of Shakespeare as part of the essential cultural baggage brought to the new colony.

Sidaway's playhouse, like Burbage's called simply "The Theatre," opened in January 1796 and was closed by order of the Governor, Captain John Hunter, in 1800. Plays were considered by the authorities to be unsuitable fare for a convict settlement, and it was not until 1832 that Barnett Levey, who had been trying for several years to get a license, was given permission to present plays, not just concerts and balls, and then only plays which had been presented at one or other of the two licensed theatres in London. And so what can be claimed as Australia's first professional Shakespeare performance— *Richard III* in Colley Cibber's version—took place in the recently completed Theatre Royal in Sydney on 26 December 1833. During the next ten years fourteen Shakespearian plays were given; all initially had two or more performances, and *Macbeth, The Merchant of Venice, Hamlet, Othello,* and *Richard III* were performed many times.[1] The general fare was melodrama, comedy, farce, and musical variety; audiences for the infrequently played Shakespeare were at first assured by mounting the plays for benefit nights and other special occasions. Later, a star actor such as Conrad Knowles would draw both crowds and press coverage; in June 1834 Knowles was the first Othello to be seen on an Australian stage, and in August the first Hamlet.

A year later, 700 kilometres to the south the site of Melbourne was established on Port Phillip Bay, and in September 1843 Knowles again staged *Othello*, the town's first Shakespeare play, "in a wooden shed . . . which seated 500 and was called the Pavilion."[2] Audiences of the time were composed of all social strata, and in 1853 at a performance of *Hamlet* in the Queen's Theatre, "an enthusiastic member of the audience was so 'impressed' by 'the jolly-good-fellowness' of Claudius, that he sent him down a bottle of brandy from the gallery by the thong of his stock whip."[3] There was no special reverence for Shakespeare, whose plays were simply another item on the bill; the text was far from sacrosanct and a play formed part rather than the whole of the evening's entertainment. John Lazar, for instance, opened the Adelaide Queen's Theatre on 11 January 1841 with

"Shakespeare's admired tragedy entitled Othello the Moor of Venice," according to the press advertisement, which continued, "*After which Miss Lazar will Dance an entirely new Pas Seul.* To conclude with a laughable farce called Our Mary Anne." Shakespearian burlesques developed as a popular genre, one of the earlier examples glorying in the title of *Shakespericonglomorofunnidogammoniae,* which titillated Sydney audiences in 1844 with its thinly veiled allusions to contemporary life in the colony. As in all the few theatres of the time, the actors were the current company of the establishment.

This changed as the gold rush began to attract overseas "stars." Among the first were James and Sarah Stark, who arrived from San Francisco in June 1853 and opened at the Victoria in Sydney with *Hamlet.* The Sydney *Herald,* while beginning its review by saying that "Mr Stark is an actor of ordinary pretensions," went on to describe various interruptions to the performance, including "some very disgraceful scenes which occurred in the boxes, wherein it is an unpleasant duty to state parties who ought to have known better, took prominent parts" and concluded that Stark's "success may be pronounced to have been complete."[4] The Starks went on to considerably greater success, and included *Macbeth, Richard III,* and *King Lear* in their repertoire; when they left for California in May 1854 on the appropriately named steamer *Golden Age,* they had reportedly made £20,000 from their tour. Edwin Booth, Laura Keene and D. J. Anderson, who arrived in October 1854, were less successful, their commercial failure being at least partly due to Booth's excessive drinking (in celebrating his twenty-first birthday he drunkenly hauled up an American flag at his hotel). More significantly, their restrained acting style was in strong contrast to the rhetorical and histrionic acting of the Starks, who had so recently preceded them. Booth appeared as Hamlet, Benedick, and Richard of Gloucester, as well as in four non-Shakespearian roles, then went on for a brief season in Melbourne. Although financially disastrous, this tour gave Booth his first chance to play roles in which he later became famous, and it strengthened the establishment of the imported star system which was to bedevil the Australian theatre for more than a century.

The combination which did more than anything to confirm the process was composed of George Selth Coppin and G. V. Brooke. Coppin was a comic actor who arrived from England in 1843 and became a gung-ho entrepreneur, making and losing more than one fortune in theatres, mining, hotels, and other ventures. Gustavus Vaughan Brooke was an Irish actor brought by Coppin to Australia, where he first appeared at Coppin's Queen's Theatre Royal in Melbourne on 26 February 1855, inaugurating a new era in colonial theatre. While he had had some success in London, particularly as Othello, the role in which he made his Australian debut, Brooke was essentially a provincial star, with an especially enthusiastic following in Ireland, Scotland, and the north of England. In his biography of the theatre critic and physician J. E. Neild, Harold Love has remarked that London critics conceded Brooke's "power to enthrall an audience but regarded him as one of the dying race of 'tragedians' rather than one of the new generation of actors who, under the influence of Charles Kean, were developing a more restrained and gentlemanly style and a greater concern for ensemble."[5] The looking back to England for the supposedly necessary standard is manifestly clear in the remarks of the critic of the Melbourne *Argus* on Brooke's Othello, a performance, he wrote, "such as on leaving our English home we never expected again to witness. It was the creation of Shakespere, but an essentially original rendering."[6] Describing his Shylock, the critic of the *Age* declared, "Manliness is the grand characteristic of his acting. Whatever is exalted, nobly ambitious, and commanding in the manly character, Mr Brooke can represent to perfection; but also whatever is stern, inflexible, unrelenting."[7] Brooke became the most admired actor in the country, appearing as Hamlet, Richard III, Macbeth, Hotspur, King John, and King Lear in his first two seasons. By the time he returned to England in 1861 he had performed in twenty-three of Shakespeare's plays, along with fifty by other playwrights. For Neild he became the touchstone for naturalistic acting in comparison to which the performance of others would be found bombastic, artificial, or aiming merely for effect.

Although Brooke was a popular idol, even he did not succeed in drawing audiences to lesser-known plays like *Cymbeline*. Nevertheless, as Dennis Bartholomeusz points out, between 1855 and 1861 more of Shakespeare's plays were performed in Melbourne than in any comparable period in the twentieth century;[8] but the influence of Charles Kean became apparent in a growing concern with spectacle and historical realism at the expense of concentration on the actor's craft and the dramatist's poetry. The actor's craft, however, was the focus of what became known as "the *Hamlet* controversy." With ninety-five performances, the tragedy became the most frequently performed play in the city between 1860 and 1869. In July 1867 a newly arrived English actor, Walter Montgomery, appeared as the Danish prince at the Theatre Royal with a portrayal much influenced by Charles Albert Fechter, who had brought to the stage the kind of Hamlet that R. A. Foakes has described as "a key figure in that shift towards an emphasis on subjectivity that began in the late eighteenth century and flowered with the Romantics."[9] When first seen at London's Princess's Theatre in March 1861 Fechter's naturalistic, meditative interpretation of the part had been revolutionary, giving rise to great argument and an overflowing box office, and he had developed the characterization further at the Lyceum in 1864. In Melbourne, Montgomery delivered the lines in a natural speaking voice and his acting was generally understated, so that his more intense moments gained strength by contrast; he drew attention to the character rather than to himself as actor. Meanwhile, James Anderson was appearing in the same role at the Haymarket. An actor of the old school, Anderson had immediate popularity, and a critical war broke out between supporters of each, enriched by an argument over whether Hamlet was mad or not. Half a dozen letters from among the many which appeared in the press were edited by F. W. Haddon and published in 1867 as a pamphlet, *The Hamlet controversy. Was Hamlet mad? Or the lucubrations of Messrs. Smith, Brown, Jones and Robinson.* Never before or since has Shakespeare been the center of so much public debate in Australia.

Montgomery had introduced a different style of acting to Australia but it was not taken up to any great extent. Indeed it is possible that the presentation of Shakespeare began to languish as it did during the next decade because the public preferred the more declamatory style; it could equally have been partly because the plays were becoming by now caviar to the general so far as the entrepreneurs were concerned. Visiting actors would usually include performances of the half dozen most popular roles in their repertoire, but it was not until the arrival of George Rignold in 1876 that a Shakespeare play settled into a solid run. Rignold was an English actor who had appeared in Charles Calvert's magnificent production of *Henry V* in Manchester four years earlier; in 1875 he took the leading role in New York and on tour when the production was sold to an American producer, then bought it himself and took it to Australia and New Zealand. He arrived with a small core of actors, hired over thirty more and placed an advertisement, "Wanted Immediately: 100 Smart Young Men," in the *Sydney Morning Herald*. Spectacular Shakespeare had arrived. The cut-down and rearranged play was presented as a series of tableaux against picturesque three-dimensional scenes, including the cathedral at Troyes for the marriage of Henry and Katherine, which Shakespeare had carelessly omitted from his text. The *Herald* reported that the battle of Agincourt "is depicted by a set scene in which the entire breadth and depth of the stage is one mass of fighting figures extending (thanks to the aid of a background painted in) apparently as far as the eye can reach. In the front King Henry and a French nobleman, on horseback [the horses were real], are engaged in hand-to-hand conflict. Upon this the curtain had to be raised again in response to the general acclamation" (30 August 1876). Somewhat ironically, it was *via* America that Australians were receiving what the *Herald* called "poetical patriotism."

Rignold's playbill is an essay in publicity for the time, appealing as it does to the moral and the intellectual as much as to the sensual:

> A GRAND HISTORICAL PASSAGE
> In English and French History
> Magnificently Illustrated,
> keeping the mind employed,
> as if in a vast picture gallery, looking at
> GORGEOUS COLOURED PAINTINGS
> of
> Castles, Baronial Halls, Kings and Thrones, Armoured Knights, Battle Fields, and Triumphs of Victory.
>
> ―
>
> And while
> these pictures are being wondered at,
> the soul is entranced with the most spirited
> MARTIAL MUSIC
> compiled from the oldest English and French Military Airs.
> Added thereto,
> the most Poetical language
> EVER PENNED BY MAN.
>
> ―
>
> It is a play
> DIVINES HAVE PRONOUNCED
> A SERMON from the STAGE.
> There is no VICIOUS or EVIL THOUGHT SUGGESTED
> from the Beginning to the End.
>
> ―
>
> SCENERY by
> Hennings, Habbe, Little, Harford, Johnston, Spong,
> GEORGE GORDON.
> 200 AUXILIARIES.
> Appropriate Costumes, Peal of Bells.
> The celebrated White Charger, Crispin, trained by and
> purchased from Mr F. Schroeder, Bligh-street.
> The whole forming a tout ensemble never before equalled in the
> SOUTHERN HEMISPHERE.
> Produced under the personal supervision of
> MR. GEORGE RIGNOLD.

The combination of spectacle, Shakespeare, and imperialism was undoubtedly successful, and Melbourne applauded as vociferously as Sydney when Rignold made his debut there in September 1878. He did not realize just how successful until he was back in England and discovered when he performed at Drury Lane the following year that the metropolis of the mother country had moved on theatrically in his absence. He returned to settle in Australia in 1884, and at the Opera House in Melbourne staged a painstaking recreation of Irving's Lyceum production of *Romeo and Juliet,* further reinforcing the view that the finest presentation of Shakespeare could come only from England. In 1887 Rignold leased Sydney's best-equipped theatre of the time, Her Majesty's, opening it with a revival of *Henry V* in September and until 1895 subsidized further lavish if infrequent Shakespeare productions with the profits from popular melodramas. Shakespearian first nights were always attended by the good and the great, the local Governor usually among them, and the plays included *Julius Caesar, Macbeth, The Merry Wives of Windsor, A Midsummer Night's Dream,* and *Othello.*

For a brief period from 1885 to 1888, however, Shakespeare seasons of several weeks again filled theatres in the capital cities and country towns—and this time there were no imported productions, not even imported stars. William John Holloway, who had arrived in Australia as a boy, formed a company in 1880 and had his first success with *The Comedy of Errors,* with himself and his brother Charles as the two Antipholuses. But it was through his stepdaughter Essie Jenyns that brilliance came. The first Australian-born Shakespearian star—and she really was a star—Jenyns was nineteen or twenty when she first delighted audiences as Juliet and the heroines of the comedies. Reviewing *The Merchant of Venice* at the Sydney Criterion, the *Sydney Morning Herald* critic wrote, "The character of Portia is endowed not only with dignity, sweetness, and a tender charm of manner, but with superior mental powers and great cheerfulness. Being an heiress to immense fortune, and having lived always in elegance and sumptuousness there is also about Portia an air of splendour and magnificence. That Miss Essie Jenyns should represent with more than average success such a character as this would be naturally concluded from her impersonations of Juliet, Rosalind, Imogen, and Beatrice" (19 December 1887). For some critics her beauty exceeded her acting ability, but she appealed to all classes, and for a time the steadily accelerating move of Shakespeare into the more rarefied air of the sacred and revered was checked. Jenyns's popularity was akin to that of today's television and film stars, and when in November 1888 she suddenly left the stage to marry a very, very rich young man (to her family's dismay—she wrote to them of her intention as the company was about to leave for London to launch her international career), thousands thronged the Sydney streets and a group of students unhitched the horses from the wedding carriage to pull it along themselves.

It is irresistible to contemplate what the course of Shakespearian production in Australia would have been had Jenyns remained in the theatre. She might, of course, have gone on to the international career her stepfather and mother, the actor Kate Arden, intended for her, and never returned. If, however, she had come back after overseas success, as her contemporary in the field of operetta, Nellie Stewart, did, Shakespeare could have been returned to the popular stage from which he had steadily been receding for the previous thirty years, and a distinctive style developed.

As it was, Shakespeare was becoming, in Richard Waterhouse's phrase, elevated "to the status of a demigod,"[10] less performed and more the subject of classroom lessons, and lectures and discussion at the Shakespeare societies which had been founded in several cities. Preeminent among these was the Melbourne Shakespere [sic] Society established in May 1884 by the newly appointed Professor of Modern Languages and Literature at the University of Melbourne, Edward E. Morris, and with two theatre critics, James Smith and J. E. Neild, on its committee. Many patrons of such groups preferred to take their Shakespeare this way rather than in the theatre. Even though George Rignold's 1887 Melbourne production of *The Tempest* was under the patronage of the Society there, for instance, few members in fact went to see it. But they turned up enthusiastically to monthly meetings to hear papers on such topics as "The physique of Lady Macbeth (petite rather than heroic)," "Caesar's wounds," "Shakespeare a republican" and "Shakespeare a royalist."

On 1 January 1901, after decades of discussion, negotiation, and political preparation, Australia's six self-governing colonies formed themselves into States of "an indissoluble Federal Commonwealth." Australians were still firmly within the British Empire, the majority spoke of England as "home," and Shakespeare could be, and was, referred to as the "national poet." With the end of W. J. Holloway's company, the decline of George Rignold in the late 90s, and the determined belief of entrepreneurs that importing "stars" and productions was the surest way to make money, there were no significant local Shakespeare productions in the first decade of the new century. In 1902 J. C. Williamson presented a "New English Dramatic Company" led by the American Janet Waldorf as Rosalind, Viola, and Portia, and the next year George Musgrove, Williamson's former partner and now arch rival, retaliated with Robert Courtneidge's lavish Manchester productions of *A Midsummer Night's*

Dream, As You Like It, and *Twelfth Night.* The Australian-born Oscar Asche returned in 1909 with extravagant productions of four plays, including *Othello,* which he considered his best Shakespearian role, though the Sydney magazine *Theatre* thought he lacked tenderness, and humiliatingly considered his Christopher Sly a more finished performance. He was back in 1912–13 with *Antony and Cleopatra* in the repertoire, and in 1922 with *Julius Caesar* as well as his greatest success, the oriental musical comedy *Chu Chin Chow,* which had run for a record-breaking five years in London.

The separation of Shakespeare from popular culture to become the preserve of the upper middle class, and consequent Anglophile attitudes, could not have been more clearly signalled than it was by "The Play," the fifth of the extraordinarily popular *Songs of a Sentimental Bloke* by C. J. Dennis, a collection of poems in a loosely linked narrative about the wooing and winning of Doreen by Bill, the bloke, first published in 1915 and never since out of print. The second verse tells us:

> Doreen an' me, we bin to see a show—
> The swell two-dollar touch. Bong tong, yeh know.
> A chair wiv velvit on the seat;
> A slap-up treat.
> The drarmer's writ be Shakespeare, years ago,
> About a barmy goat called Romeo.

A summary of the plot, in the vernacular of the time, takes the next dozen stanzas to the death of "Mick Curio"—" 'Ar rats!' " 'e sez, an' passes in 'is check"—whereupon,

> Quite natchril, Romeo gits wet as 'ell.
> "It's me or you!" 'e 'owls, an' wiv a yell,
> Plunks Tyball through the gizzard wiv 'is sword,
> 'Ow I ongcored!
> "Put in the boot!" I sez. "Put in the boot!"
> "'ush!" sez Doreen . . . "Shame!" sez some silly coot.

The Bloke's engagement with the "drarmer" is indicative of Dennis's realization of Shakespeare's power to connect with an audience as much as the "silly coot's" comment is of the reverential attitude that was the accepted, and expected, attitude to the Great Dramatist.

An experienced actor-manager was soon to arrive who would do something towards restoring Shakespeare to a popular audience, for a while at least, while also confirming the plays as an educational cornerstone and strengthening ties with the upper echelons of society, including the vice-regal set. In 1916 George Marlow, who had become an entrepreneur after acting with both Rignold and Holloway, asked his leading actor, Allan Wilkie, to form a Shakespeare company. The much-travelled Wilkie, who was born in Liverpool in 1878, had worked with Frank Benson, Ben Greet and Beerbohm Tree, and had toured his own company in India, Japan, China, Malaya and the Philippines; he now led the "George Marlow Grand Shakespearean Company" through eastern Australia and New Zealand. In 1920 he set up his own company, with the expressed aim of performing all of Shakespeare's plays. Before the Depression and the talkies, and probably his own old-fashioned style which was founded mainly on those of Benson, Tree and his great idol Irving, forced his company to close, Wilkie succeeded in playing twenty-seven of them. He toured Australia and New Zealand with a company of about thirty, persuading the government authorities to grant him free rail travel on the grounds of the educational value of his work. In June 1924 he gave the company's 1,000th consecutive performance of Shakespeare; there were still 239 to come before decreasing audiences made him include non-Shakespearian plays in the repertoire. It was an astounding achievement. Despite a successful fourteen-week season in Sydney and exemption from entertainment tax, the Allan Wilkie Shakespearean Company gave its last performance on 11 October 1930, Wilkie in his signature role of Shylock.

Eschewing elaborate sets, and generally cutting the text lightly, Wilkie staged the plays so that they moved speedily, usually had only one interval, and above all were clearly articulated. Reviewing the first production of *The Winter's Tale* in Australia for forty years, one Adelaide critic commented, "There is an Elizabethan simplicity about his productions which, while giving a fitting and artistic background to the plays, allows the audience to devote attention to the text rather than a succession of pictures which, however richly coloured and beautifully posed, are in the end mere pageantry" and, with rather too much patriotism, hailed Australia as the birthplace of "a new Shakespearean school" (*Advertiser*, 18 February 1924). Wilkie was not averse to the spectacular when it was available—in 1926 he purchased Tree's sets and costumes for *Henry VIII*—but he needed to simplify his staging when travelling such vast distances and performing such a varied repertoire. It was probably significant that his costume designer, Arthur Goodsall, had worked with William Poel.[11]

Shakespeare then virtually disappeared from the Australian commercial stage for almost two decades, apart from a tour by a company with Sybil Thorndike and Lewis Casson in 1932 which included *Macbeth*. Then in 1948 the British Council sponsored a tour of Australia and New Zealand by the Old Vic Theatre Company led by Laurence Olivier and Vivien Leigh, Olivier at the height of his powers as Richard III and also as Sir Peter Teazle and Mr. Antrobus in Thornton Wilder's *The Skin of Our Teeth*. The tour was hugely, unbelievably successful. Thousands who had never been inside a theatre flocked to see two famous film stars; theatregoers starved of first-class acting and production went again and again; the stars themselves were treated as royalty, expected to attend countless receptions during the day while performing at night. So far as Australian Shakespeare was concerned, the tour set a new, if unattainable, standard to aim for, inspired a generation of designers and directors, and massively reinforced the English style.

The rekindled taste for Shakespeare was in part met by the activities of amateur groups such as those led by Collin Ballantyne in Adelaide and John Alden in Sydney. Having returned to Australia after experience in stock companies and the Old Vic in England to become a leading radio actor during the Second World War, Alden began acting in his own productions of Shakespeare in 1948, *Measure for Measure* being the first of five of the plays presented for the Independent Theatre, Sydney's leading amateur theatre organization. The success of his vigorous production of *King Lear*, which played in a small theatre for an amazing five months to a total audience of 17,000, led to his forming a professional company, which lasted for three years. Alden headed another company in 1959, and directed a Sydney Shakespeare Festival two years later. During an eleven-year period of intermittent production, he directed and played in nine of the plays, including *Titus Andronicus, The Merry Wives of Windsor, Measure for Measure,* and *The Winter's Tale*, all, especially the first, seldom seen. If his repertoire was not always traditional, his style was, and he provided a training ground in classical acting which Australia had lacked since the demise of the Allan Wilkie Company in 1930; several of his young actors are now among the most respected seniors in the Australian theatre.

Visits by the Old Vic and Stratford Memorial companies bolstered belief that English Shakespeare was not only the best, but offered the only model. Dependence on Britain more generally had resulted in Tyrone Guthrie's spending two weeks in Australia in 1949, funded by the British Council, to report to the Australian government on establishing a national theatre. He later wrote, "Professionally my visit was not particularly exciting. There was one moderate semi-amateur production of *The Merry Wives of Windsor*, derivative in style from England [presumably John Alden's at the Independent in Sydney] . . . I can remember nothing which struck me as distinctively Australian"; but considering the quality of expatriate Australians in theatres abroad, "it was no surprise to find Australia an extraordinary mine of talent."[12] His recommendations included educating audiences in the highest standards by importing up to a dozen major British and European productions over a three-year period, sending young Australians to London for training and experience, and forming the best of them into a company in London to play the classics and eventually Australian plays with a recognizable Australian style. He felt that only by being successful abroad first would the company gain acceptance at home, but he went on in a way that would have been startling to many Australian theatregoers of the time: "The actors should not waste their time learning to speak with an English accent. . . . I believe a theatrical company, speaking well but in a recognizably and consistently Australian lingo, could succeed in England, and that this success of dialect would be an important element in the resolution of a complex that is seriously detrimental to Australian national self-confidence."[13] The Labor government that commissioned the report approved the proposals but fell at the next elections and the report was rejected by the Anglophile leader of the incoming Liberal (Conservative) party. However several actors with potential travelled overseas on scholarships after the Australian Elizabethan Theatre Trust was formed in 1954 to channel government, corporate, and private money into the arts, and named to commemorate the first visit of Queen Elizabeth II to Australia.

Under its first director, Hugh Hunt, a man of much experience in Irish and English Theatre—he had been director of the Abbey Theatre, the Bristol Old Vic and the Old Vic itself—Shakespeare was part of the general repertoire presented by the Trust: first *Hamlet* with the visiting Paul Rogers and in 1956 a lively *Twelfth Night* in the first season of the newly formed Australian Drama Company, "particularly important because it was the Company's first Shakespearian production,"[14] then in 1958 the Young Elizabethan Players were set up to tour abridged plays (45 minutes was an average length) as "Shakespeare in Jeans." This was at the time the only company in Australia giving performances in relation to school studies—for a while, in fact, separate companies were working simultaneously out of Sydney, Melbourne, and Adelaide. If Hugh Hunt's *Twelfth Night* could have arrived the day before from Stratford or London, the Young Elizabethan Players' productions provided a chance for the distinctive Australian quality which Tyrone Guthrie had hoped for.

Travelling casts as small as six, minimal sets, basic costumes, and close contact with the audience offered great opportunity for imaginative experiment and stylistic development. The enterprise lasted more than a decade, and gave thousands of country children an acquaintance with acted Shakespeare, but the opportunity was not seized; perhaps the personnel lacked the necessary inspirational spark, perhaps the constant need to get the show on the road was against it.

One of Hunt's aims as Executive Director of the Australian Elizabethan Theatre Trust was the training of young artists; after being refused by the two oldest universities, Sydney and Melbourne, his proposal for a National Institute of Dramatic Art (NIDA) was taken up by the newest, the University of New South Wales in the Sydney suburb of Kensington. The authorities were persuaded by Robert Quentin, another Englishman who had worked with the Bristol and London Old Vic companies (as a stage director), and had also directed plays in Australia during the 1940s. Quentin became NIDA's founding director in 1958, with a vision of training in the classics on the model of the Royal Academy of Dramatic Art. The first Australian institution to provide theatrical education full-time, NIDA produced over 850 graduates during its first thirty years, Mel Gibson, Judy Davis, Colin Friels, Robyn Nevin, and Jim Sharman among the more famous. The English influence of its early years gradually waned, and John Bell in particular gave an Australian orientation to the acting course in 1970–71.

Bell, the most significant person in Australian Shakespeare in the late twentieth century, acted with the Sydney University Dramatic Society, made his professional debut as Trofimov in *The Cherry Orchard* in 1963 when he was 22, and played Hamlet the same year. In 1964 he played Henry V in a tent theatre at the Adelaide Festival, and the following year went on a scholarship to the Bristol Old Vic School, moving on to the Royal Shakespeare Company and the Lincoln Repertory Company before returning home in 1970. In the same year he co-founded the Nimrod Theatre Company in Sydney and remained its artistic director, director, and principal actor until 1985. Theatre critic and historian Katharine Brisbane has remarked that "energy, colour and a certain felicitous vulgarity have characterised much of his work as a director, particularly his Shakespeare productions."[15] Along with the Australian Performing Group in Melbourne, the Nimrod, housed in a tiny building, was a prime mover in the revolutionary new wave of Australian theatre in the early 1970s, commissioning new plays and presenting the classics, especially Shakespeare, with a radical disregard for tradition. Irreverence was taken to an hilarious and successful extreme in the 1971 Christmas pantomime, *Hamlet on Ice*, in which beautiful principal boy Hamlet returns to Elsinore from Wittenberg after a sex conversion, undergone because he has fallen in love with his dumb but hunky friend Horatio. It was during the 1973 production of *Hamlet* itself that Bell noticed the actors speaking the lines with normal Australian accents, not the English pronunciation habitually adopted for Shakespeare. "As to the Oz accent thing in 'Hamlet,' " he has written, "I guess what struck me was that we never even discussed the issue, but did it unconsciously, whereas most productions then made a point of 'posh' or 'ocker' [very broad Australian], according to rather old-fashioned ideas about class. Actually it was Katharine Brisbane who brought it to my attention. (She pointed out that we were all just using our 'normal' voices)."[16] Two years later *Much Ado About Nothing* was played with Australo-Sicilian accents for several characters, to the comical enrichment of the performance.

In 1971 Jim Sharman had directed an iconoclastic *As You Like It* for the Old Tote Theatre Company, which by then had taken on the responsibilities of the state theatre company of New South Wales. Five years younger than Bell, Sharman was a NIDA graduate who had already directed a controversial *Don Giovanni* for the Australian Opera and Australian and international productions of the rock musical *Hair*; his mod Shakespeare had home-grown vocal tones, rock music, and a Touchstone on roller skates. Predictably, it pleased the young more than their elders, among whom the critic of the *Sydney Morning Herald* complained that Sharman had "turned the vintage champagne of 'As You Like It' into ginger pop" (25 January 1971). It can be seen now, however, that this was the first full professional Shakespeare production with Australian accents, invigorated by a certain brashness which it shared with the growing movement in the new Australian drama generally. A year later Robin Lovejoy set the same company's *Taming of the Shrew* in an Australian country town, with sheepdogs, fowls, Petruccio a newly arrived Irish immigrant, Katherina a squatter's (i.e., rich landowner's) daughter, Gremio and Baptista speaking with fruitshop Italian accents, and most of the other characters in broad Australian. This was a deliberately conscious, and largely successful, attempt to naturalize a text.

They were exciting, sometimes turbulent times culturally and politically, with anti-Vietnam War rallies, the hippie movement, flower power and all that went with it, the return of the Labor party, under Gough Whitlam, to power for the first time in twenty-three years, a consequent increase in funding for the arts, and after 1975, when the Whitlam government was dismissed in controversial circumstances, the upsurge in republican feeling. An efflorescence in national pride was paralleled by the rapid growth of literary and dramatic works being written and performed and there can be no doubt that the Australianization of Shakespeare was a part of this swelling enthusiasm and feeling of independence. Risk-taking replaced conservatism, experiment took over from tradition.

Rex Cramphorn, a most successfully innovative director, is a case in point. Influenced by the Polish Jerzy Grotowski (who visited Australia for workshops in 1972), by French avant-garde ideas and by Peter Brook, Cramphorn also experimented with yoga and with Asian styles of performance. His 1972 production of *The Tempest* used six actors in multiple roles, made Prospero into a guru and Miranda a flower child; it toured nationally for the Arts Council of Australia and was still being talked about twenty-five years later. In 1980 Cramphorn received a "limited-life" six-month grant to set up a Shakespeare company at Sydney University with ten mainly senior professional actors. Two plays chosen for their unfamiliarity, *Two Gentlemen of Verona* and *Measure for Measure*, were subjected to deep textual analysis and discussion; to see if the text would support unusual casting some parts were cross-gendered, and the public was invited to rehearsals as well as the final performances. Speaking about it nearly twenty years later, one of the actors, Ron Haddrick, said, "We worked on the assumption that if played truthfully, it did not matter who was playing a part; we played it straight, we played the emotions. The actors all benefited from the experiment, especially the younger ones."

Two years later Jim Sharman became Artistic Director of the State Theatre Company of South Australia, and opened his term with a landmark *Midsummer Night's Dream* which gave most in his audiences their first experience of Australian-sounding Shakespeare: the courtiers and the fairies spoke in normal educated Australian, the mechanicals with broader accents. Neil Armfield's *Twelfth Night* for the company in 1983 was given a Caribbean setting, a sparkling Viola in Gillian Jones, the previous year's Hippolyta/Titania, Rex Cramphorn's Miranda of 1973 and a future (1993) Ariel for Armfield himself. "The actors wore designer-label costumes," wrote one commentator, "and the whole convoluted love triangle of Orsino, Viola/Cesario, and Olivia was played out with a slouching sexual languor, wit, and happy comedy that despite the calypso carnival atmosphere never lost sight of the darker, subtler messages of the play."[17]

By now Shakespeare was becoming more realizably accessible to a public wider than the middle and upper class theatregoing audience. In 1981 John Tasker mounted an extravagant *As You Like It* in

Albert Park, Brisbane, for the Queensland Theatre Company; outdoor productions were presented in Tasmania by the Zootango company for several years, and in 1987 Glenn Elston produced *A Midsummer Night's Dream* in Melbourne's Royal Botanic Gardens. It was fast, athletic, raucous, and short on poetry, it had immense popular appeal, and it was revived four times; in 1993 two productions were running concurrently, one in Sydney and one in Melbourne. As Leonard Radic, critic of the Melbourne *Age*, said, "The performances are not exactly subtle . . . But while the acting is broad-humored, it is also highly accessible, being tailored for a general audience rather than the dedicated theatregoer" (21 December 1989). The first production ran for twelve weeks—a season for a single Shakespeare play that the promoter of any conventional theatre production could but dream about. The initial idea involved twelve people. By 1998 Elston's company had expanded to nine mostly Shakespearian projects involving 200 people over four states in Australia. By then he had also produced *Twelfth Night, Romeo and Juliet,* and *The Taming of the Shrew*. All were characterized by broad humor, innovative costuming, great physicality and, so far as the comedies were concerned, an inclusion of topical reference which gained ready audience response. The performance being in the open air, the audience brought rugs, cushions, picnics (the ushers obligingly sprayed on mosquito repellent), and the enjoyment was palpable. C. J. Dennis's Sentimental Bloke would have found his excited advice to "Put in the boot!" far more acceptable at Elston's 1994 outdoor production of *Romeo and Juliet* than in a Melbourne theatre of 1915.

The most important recent development in Australian Shakespeare came in 1990, with the establishment of the Bell Shakespeare Company funded initially by private benefactors and sponsors and under the leadership of John Bell, who said, "We want to evolve a way of playing Shakespeare that makes sense to Australians young and old, and to encourage actors of varied ethnic backgrounds to join our troupe so that we may truly reflect the face of Australian society."[18] The company was launched in Sydney in January 1991 with *Hamlet* and *The Merchant of Venice*, Bell playing Claudius and Shylock; the season had to be extended. During the next eight years thirteen more plays were added to the repertoire, the company toured to all states and enlarged its education program to include both Shakespearian and Australian plays. Inevitably, some productions were less praised than others, but critics consistently remarked on their clarity and accessibility. A 1996 *Much Ado About Nothing* was adjudged "a production that is clear, coherent and tells its story with verve" (*Sun Herald*, 9 June 1996). "What's so exciting about this Bell Shakespeare production [of *Pericles*]," wrote James Waites in the *Sydney Morning Herald*, "is the force with which the play's main ideas emerge. Throughout the first half, there is a palpable sense that something special is happening on stage. While still energetic and fresh, there is an aura you could describe as both mythical and sacred" (3 April 1995). Bell directed some plays, *Pericles* among them, for others engaging directors from Australia and overseas, including Londoner Steve Berkoff, whose *Coriolanus* with Bell in the title role was praised by Helen Thomson in the *Age* as "totally disciplined, physical theatre, strongly informed with ritualised gesture and visual quotations from the complex context of our modern world" (21 October 1996). Berkoff's energetic physicality suited the company, leading Tom Gilling of the *Bulletin* to say, "The result is utterly compelling, a visceral combination of action and text, spoken, spat and chanted. . . . The Bell Shakespeare Company has never looked so sure of the text and so confident in delivering it" (26 November 1996).

By the 1990s each of the Australian states had well-established subsidized theatre organizations, and most included Shakespeare in their annual repertoire, but the Bell Shakespeare Company was the only group which toured nationally; in 1993 it received some federal government funding, but it was still largely dependent on raising its own funds, through sponsorships, donations and box office. Despite vicissitudes, it had survived to fulfil its founder's hope of evolving "a way of playing Shakespeare that makes sense to Australians young and old" in what Tyrone Guthrie had fifty years earlier called "a recognizably and consistently Australian lingo." And by the 1990s Guthrie's description could be applied to most Shakespeare productions throughout Australia, from the vigorous, somewhat mannered intimate presentations of Bryan Nason's Grin and Tonic Theatre in Brisbane to Neil Armfield's deeply thought *Tempest* (1993) and *Hamlet* (1995) for Sydney's Belvoir Street Theatre to the larrikin Shakespeare of Glenn Elston.

So why did it take so long? A principal reason lay in the very idea of imperial colonization. From G. V. Brooke to Oscar Asche, through Allan Wilkie to Sybil Thorndike and Lewis Casson, from Laurence Olivier and Vivien Leigh to Anthony Quayle and Barbara Jefford, there was no escaping the belief that visitors, especially English visitors, speaking in English voices, did Shakespeare best; they provided the model to be followed. Then, Shakespeare, like opera, became more an upper-middle-class entertainment, "bong tong," as the Bloke put it, and the plays lost value as entertainment as they became essential in the education system. Virtually everyone studied them in secondary school (usually in expurgated texts, though there was not much that could be done about the closing scene of *The Merchant of Venice*), but they stayed on the page except for school productions and during the decade of Allan Wilkie.

Another major inhibitor was the insistence of theatre owners that overseas scripts and "stars" were necessary for success, that Australian playwrights could not produce serious drama, and Australian lead actors could not attract audiences. As the greater number of theatres from 1900 until 1976 were owned by the J. C. Williamson organization, known as "The Firm," and at one time the largest theatre enterprise in the world, there was virtually no chance for the development of an Australian tradition in serious drama, either in acting or writing, and this situation affected the presentation of classic drama. A contributing factor to Allan Wilkie's final difficulties was the refusal of J. C. Williamson to allow him into their theatres.

The development of government subsidies began with the founding of the Arts Council of Australia in Sydney in 1946 with the aim of taking performing arts to rural areas not served by commercial theatre interests. Funds came from both federal and state governments, and local branches. As already noted, the Australian Elizabethan Theatre Trust was set up in 1954 to foster the performing arts, one of its responsibilities being the encouragement and growth of Australian theatrical material and the presentation by Australian companies of such material. The foundation of the Trust led not only to the successful production of Australian plays, sometimes wildly successful, as in the case of Ray Lawler's *Summer of the Seventeenth Doll,* but also to the establishment of NIDA, whose early graduate actors and directors were among those who led the revolution in theatre which included the development of Australian style in Shakespeare.

It could not have happened in the way that it did, however, without the founding in 1968 of the Australian Council for the Arts, renamed the Australia Council in 1975, as the statutory body through which the federal government provides funds for the arts. Building up theatre companies in state capitals was an early priority, and innovative theatre was encouraged through special project grants, the freedom to experiment which this allowed sometimes leading to cross-fertilization between Shakespearian and other forms of theatre. A production of *A Midsummer Night's Dream* for the 1997 Sydney Festival of the Dreaming, a celebration of Aboriginals and the arts, for example, was the first staging of a classic play by an all-indigenous cast and director, Noël Tovey, who had returned home in 1991 after thirty-three years' theatrical experience abroad. Giving the play an Aboriginal context, Tovey turned the wood near Athens, for instance, into the land of the Rainbow Serpent, the Great Creative Spirit of Aboriginal lore, and Titania's bower became a waratah, a brilliant red flower which is symbolic of eternal love. Audiences and reviewers alike were generally pleased with the result, the *Sun-Herald* critic saying it was "popular, gutsy theatre for the widest audience" (21 September 1997). This appropriation did not appear to have a specifically political agenda, such as productions of *Hamlet* and *Macbeth* in Eastern Europe under Communism or *Romeo and Juliet* in Bulgaria had;[19] to some in the audiences for Neil Armfield's 1993 *Tempest*, however, the casting of an Aboriginal actor as Caliban gave unfamiliar political resonance to the role, and to the play.

The development of Australian style in Shakespeare was also due to the steady growth in Australia's self-confidence as a nation which had begun to accept itself as a player on its own terms in international culture as well as in sport. Australians win Olympic gold, but they also win dance medals in Moscow; novelists win Booker prizes and filmmakers win Oscars. There are still plenty of expatriate artists, but many return home, or travel between countries, and politically the national temper looked toward the new century as the natural time for more complete independence. John Bell remarked in an interview in 1993 that in his productions he aimed to address current Australian issues of political, social and moral concern "as we approach a republic."[20] He was speaking five years before the Constitutional Convention which gave a starting point to this paper. The productions of Bell and others like him—Gale Edwards, John Gaden, Neil Armfield, Roger Hodgman, Glenn Elston, and Simon Phillips among them—meant that in the last years of the twentieth century the plays were beginning to be accepted again as entertainment rather than as more rarefied educational or aesthetic experiences. And that meant they were entering the national consciousness as genetically Australian, not imported, experiences.

Notes

1. Eric Irvin, "Shakespeare in the Early Sydney Theatre" *Shakespeare Survey* 22 (1969), 127.

2. Dennis Bartholomeusz, "Shakespeare on the Melbourne Stage" *Shakespeare Survey* 35 (1982), 31.

3. William Kelly, *Life in Victoria* (1859), 134–35. Cited, Bartholomeusz, 31.

4. Cited, Osric [Humphrey Hall and Alfred John Cripps], *The Romance of the Sydney Stage* (Sydney: Currency Press, 1996), 148.

5. Harold Love, *James Edward Neild* (Melbourne: Melbourne University Press, 1989), 28.

6. Cited, Osric, 187.

7. Cited, Bartholomeusz, 34.

8. Bartholomeusz, 37.

9. R. A. Foakes, *Hamlet versus Lear: Cultural Politics and Shakespeare's Art* (Cambridge: Cambridge University Press, 1993), 14.

10. Richard Waterhouse, *Private Pleasures, Public Leisure* (South Melbourne: Longman, 1995), 134. Waterhouse goes on to cite Benjamin Hoare's description of Shakespeare as "Unapproachable in sublimity, ineffable in beauty, peerless in expression, matchless in world sanity" ("Shakespeare's Tercentenary," *Austral Light* 17 [1916], 352). See also John Rickard, "The Bloke and the Bard," in Philip Mead and Marion Campbell, eds., *Shakespeare's Books* (Melbourne: Department of English, University of Melbourne, 1993), 127–40, and for the view that the attitude is still current, especially in America, Michael D. Bristol, *Shakespeare's America, America's Shakespeare* (London: Routledge, 1990), 19.

11. For an account of Allan Wilkie and his company see Alan Brissenden, "Shakespeare's Australian Travels," in Tetsuo Kishi, Roger Pringle, and Stanley Wells, eds., *Shakespeare and Cultural Traditions* (Newark, Del.: University of Delaware Press, 1994), 205–15.

12. Tyrone Guthrie, *A Life in the Theatre* (New York: McGraw Hill, 1959), 280.

13. Cited, John Andrews, Katharine Brisbane, "Guthrie Report," in Philip Parsons, ed., *Companion to Theatre in Australia* (Sydney: Currency Press, 1995), 254.

14. *The Australian Elizabethan Theatre Trust: The First Year* (Sydney: The Australian Elizabethan Theatre Trust, 1957), 27.

15. *Companion to Theatre in Australia*, 84.

16. Letter to the author, 16 July 1997.

17. Peter Ward, *A Singular Act* (Adelaide: State Theatre Company and Wakefield Press, 1992), 108–9.

18. John Bell, "Review of 1991 Season of the Bell Shakespeare Company," typescript, Bell Shakespeare Company papers, Sydney.

19. See Martin Prochazka, "Shakespeare and Czech Resistance," in Heather Kerr, Robin Eaden and Madge Mitton, eds., *Shakespeare: World Views* (Newark, Del.: University of Delaware Press, 1996), 44–70, and Thomas Healy, "Past and present Shakespeares: Shakespearian appropriations in Europe," in John J. Joughin, ed., *Shakespeare and National Culture* (Manchester: Manchester University Press, 1997), 206–32.

20. Rachel Landers, "The History of Shakespeare Performance in Australia," BA Honours thesis, History Department, University of Sydney, 1993, 58.

Cutting Women Down to Size in the Olivier and Loncraine Films of *Richard III*

MARLISS C. DESENS

AT APPROXIMATELY 3600 LINES, IT IS ALMOST A FOREGONE CONCLUSION that the text of Shakespeare's *Richard III* will be cut, whether for stage performance or for film. One exception, Jane Howell's film, done as part of the BBC television Shakespeare, cuts very little and, consequently, runs nearly four hours. In commercial films, however, four hours is less common. Laurence Olivier's 1955 film, with major cuts, runs over two and a half hours. Forty years later, the Richard Loncraine film, with Ian McKellen in the title role, cuts more drastically for a running length of one and three-quarter hours. The films have some obvious artistic differences in how they approach the play and in how they translate it from stage to screen. As might be expected, each also reflects the different cultural context of its era. However, both productions agree on one significant point in cutting the text: the women's roles are of much less importance than those of the men.

The rationale for paring down the women's roles in modern films of *Richard III* might at first seem straightforward. Shakespeare's history plays are, in one widespread view, focused on the men who make history, rather than on the women who are pulled along by the actions of the men.[1] He also writes in an age where a religious, supernatural context is assumed; thus, curses, ghosts, and providence have a force that they do not have for modern audiences.[2] Closely conjoined with the supernatural context is a sense of ritual, which has far less significance in modern life. Thus, a cutting of the historical, the supernatural, and the ritualistic in modern films of *Richard III* may, on one level, make some sense, and since the women's roles are predominantly connected with all three, the women's roles are sharply cut. However, to do so means going in exactly the opposite direction from that Shakespeare took in creating the play. As Harold Brooks observes, "In *Richard III*, Shakespeare owed little to his chronicle sources for the sensational wooing of Anne" or "the "wailing royal women."[3] Indeed, if Brooks is correct about the Senecan parallels, then by using a Senecan model, Shakespeare appears to be at pains to heighten the ritualistic nature of the play in connection with the female characters.

In cutting the women's roles, Olivier and Loncraine have also, perhaps unwittingly, chosen to emphasize negative views of women, which while present in the play, particularly in connection with Richard's view of them, are also balanced by what Madonne Miner describes as "a counterprocess, one that insists upon the inherently positive value of women."[4] Olivier's and Loncraine's films of *Richard III*, by paring down the roles of Margaret, Anne, Queen Elizabeth, and the Duchess of York, not only disrupt the play's framework but also emphasize, by deleting this positive counterprocess, a far more negative view of women than in Shakespeare's text. The cuts, however, do not have the same effect in each film. In the Olivier film, the female characters are portrayed as sympathetic victims, helpless against the force of Richard's evil. Their brief moment of community centers on their victimization rather than their empowerment. In the Loncraine film, the cuts result in a depiction of neurotic women for whom we have little sympathy, and who never draw together as a community.[5] Gone is Shakespeare's close linkage of the women with the supernatural and the ritualistic, both of which Richard is attempting to subvert and destroy.[6] Ironically, the Olivier and Loncraine films manage to do exactly that by paring down the women's roles (although Olivier does add a female character, Jane Shore, the King's mistress, to Shakespeare's play, it is a non-speaking role, and it certainly does not fill the void left by excision and cutting of the female roles).[7]

Let us begin by looking at the women's characters' place within the play's historical context. Cuts to this historical context shift the play from history toward tragedy. As the role of Richard of Gloucester is close to 1100 lines, nearly a third of all lines in the play, it is tempting for directors to treat the play strictly as the tragedy of one man rather than as the tragic history of a nation. As Constance Kuriyama notes, "The removal of Margaret and the reduction of other parts forces particular attention on the psychology of Richard—who in any case dominates the play."[8] McKellen also wished to focus on Richard's psychology and does, although, curiously, he claims to have done the opposite: "Our film represents that re-assessment of *Richard III* as much more than a one man show."[9] Thus, the Olivier film, and to a greater extent, the Loncraine film, in focusing on Richard in terms of character, shift the focus away from *Richard III*'s place as the last play of the first tetralogy and, more importantly, as the play that brings to conclusion events that began nearly eighty years before with the deposition and murder of Richard II. While the three parts of *Henry VI* are plays of disorder and chaos, in *Richard III*, the movement is toward resumption of order and ceremony. It is not just the various contenders for power and the crown who have blood on their hands but England itself, torn apart by civil war, that is guilty. Expiation of sin requires a process of penance—a working through of the guilt and an acceptance of responsibility—a process for which religion uses ritual.[10] The women in *Richard III* are the expression of that ritual, played out against historical context, and Margaret's role especially underscores this connection.

Both films cut Queen Margaret's two appearances, and by doing so, automatically divorce the play from its historical context. The underlying assumption is that Queen Margaret's primary function is to remind audiences of past events from the *Henry VI* plays. Certainly, that is part of Shakespeare's dramatic strategy, especially since there is no evidence that the first tetralogy was necessarily performed in sequence. *Richard III* had to be able to stand alone. However, cutting Margaret also radically shifts the play's focus. As Dale Silviria observes, "Olivier's deletion of Queen Margaret and her curses effectively guts . . . the play's great superstructure. The lesser prophecies remain, but, without Margaret's unifying force, Clarence's dream or Anne's pronouncement . . . constitutes no more than presentiment or ironic foreshadowing."[11] Omitting Margaret thus cuts the most obvious of the women's ties to the supernatural. In the absence of Margaret, Olivier relies on Richard's evil to unify the film, an evil that is reinforced through cinematic technique, and, as Robert Hapgood observes, a "stage melodrama, updated to cool, sly black comedy."[12]

In the Loncraine film, the deletion of Margaret is more serious in that there is no attempt to replace her structurally.[13] The result is a film with intense images but no overarching structure or backbone.[14] While I do not see Margaret as a figure of divine providence, as do some critics who view the play in light of Tudor propaganda,[15] she is the voice of the wrongs that the house of Lancaster has suffered—wrongs for which the house of York must pay, just as the house of Lancaster has paid for its part in the deposition and murder of an earlier king, and in the ensuing civil wars. She also represents the elemental anger that begins to surge against Richard, and which she helps the Duchess of York and Queen Elizabeth to express. Giving some of her lines to Queen Elizabeth and the Duchess of York in an attempt to compensate for what is lost in cutting her, as the Loncraine film does, merely muddles an already unclear approach. Omitting her makes it more difficult to understand the shift that occurs in the Duchess of York and Queen Elizabeth, a shift that ultimately allows them to defeat Richard in the linguistic space he usually dominates, which is perhaps why the Olivier film omits that shift, thus leaving the women enshrined as victims.

Richard's early success on this linguistic level is best seen in his wooing of Lady Anne in 1.2. Both Olivier and Loncraine increase the difficulty of the scene for an actress, in that they show Anne with the body of her husband, rather than that of her father-in-law, Henry VI. However, by including the coffin of the murdered *king*, for the king is the embodiment of England, Shakespeare not only underscores the murder of this king but the long ago murder of Richard II and the carnage of long years of civil war. By replacing the king with his son, Olivier and Loncraine not only lose this connection but then face the challenge of showing Anne's yielding to Richard in the presence of her murdered husband's corpse. Olivier, to create some sympathy for Anne, divides the scene into two, although her husband's corpse is present in both, first in its coffin, and then encased in a marble tomb. In the first scene, Olivier keeps enough lines to show Anne's rage, although he deletes much of the verbal interplay, the stichomythia, between the two, that initially shows Anne holding her own against Richard. That scene ends when she spits at him, then orders the attendants to move on with the coffin. Yet, Olivier's Richard had moved very close to her, as if to dominate her physically, and the long look she gives him, as well as her troubled looking around as she leaves, suggests that on a dark, sexual level, Richard has made an impact.

Olivier reinforces this suggestion by immediately having Richard address the camera, "I'll have her, but I will not keep her long,"[16] thereby suggesting that he is already assured of her capitulation. When, in a subsequent scene, Richard approaches her kneeling at her husband's tomb, he begins, "Is not the causer of the timeless deaths . . . / As blameful as the executioner?" (1.2.117–19). The line is key in Shakespeare's text, for Anne's response shows Richard that she is vulnerable when the blame is turned on her. Anne, at this point, begins to lose her ability to defend herself on a linguistic level. In the Olivier film, from the look on Anne's face (she senses his presence before he speaks), and from her visible trembling, it is clear that Richard has correctly intuited her vulnerability from his first meeting with her. Olivier cuts much of the rest of the scene's text, so that Richard is not so much conquering Anne through a kind of verbal mind rape as he is through physical domination. Olivier thus translates the play's verbal text into compelling film image, but he does so by presenting an Anne who is never strong, while in Shakespeare's text we do see her initial strength. After Anne leaves, Olivier keeps enough of Richard's subsequent direct address to express his scorn for her, then he strides to her bedchamber, where his shadow engulfs the lower part of her white skirt. She becomes, at that moment, as Dale Silviria observes, "a living statue, the spiral folds of her gown distinctly resembling classical drapery."[17] The phrase is apt, for Anne's function in the rest of the film is to gaze and to speak helplessly; she has become an icon of the female victim. At the coronation, she collapses, is helped to her feet, gazes at Richard as she touches her fingers to her lips, as if in love with the man who may well be killing her. Even in her final appearance, as a ghost, a tear continuously runs down her cheek.

The Loncraine film follows Shakespeare's text in showing Richard's wooing in one scene, but the dialogue is more severely cut than in the Olivier film, and nothing is put in its place to hold the scene together. The scene is set in a morgue. Anne's dead husband's body, with a gaping head wound, is shown naked from the waist up. Anne's first words are curses against the man who killed her husband (1.2.14 in Shakespeare's text). Kristen Scott Thomas speaks the lines as if numb, as indeed she speaks most of the lines in this scene. Her Anne is obviously in deep shock. As in the Olivier film, the verbal sparring whereby Anne initially holds her own against Richard is omitted, so that the inclusion of Richard's line, "To leave this keen encounter of our wits" (1.2.115), seems odd. Whereas Olivier used Richard's physical encroachment on Anne to show visually rather than verbally how she is overcome, Loncraine puts nothing in its place. There is no sense that Richard has to work to pressure Anne, either physically or verbally. His subsequent direct address, "Was ever woman in this humor woo'd?" thus seems out of place. We do not know why Anne said yes to him, nor do we particularly care.[18]

Anne's one moment of seeming life in this film is when she enters the banquet room, either betrothed or married to Richard; we even see them holding hands at the table. However, Richard rejects her sexually in a scene shortly thereafter; as she stands enticingly on the stairs in her negligee, he walks over to her, reaches across to turn out the lights, then walks away, leaving her to turn and go up the stairs alone. Shortly thereafter, she is twice shown taking tranquilizers. On the way to the coronation, she shoots heroin into a vein in her thigh, which with its additional scars suggests that the drug has become a habit. After the coronation, she is drinking and obviously numb. The next time we see her, she is dead, a spider crawling across her face, her eyes fixed in the glazed stare she had come to wear in life. While in Olivier's film, Anne becomes the icon for the weak but innocent female victim—very much a 1950s stereotype—in Loncraine's she becomes an icon for the neurotic one—a stereotype of the 1990s.

Olivier and Loncraine also approach the character of Queen Elizabeth in very different ways, although in this case it is Olivier who cuts the role most drastically. In Shakespeare's text, she begins as a helpless woman who, despite some attempt to confront Richard, is only too well aware of her lack of power in this patriarchal context. Through her suffering—the murders of her kinsmen and her two sons—and through her interactions with the Duchess of York, Anne, and Queen Margaret, she gains a strength that allows her to confront Richard in 4.4 and, unbeknownst to him, to win their linguistic battle. Although he believes that he has convinced her to agree to his marriage to Princess Elizabeth, she never consents but uses equivocal language that he fails to penetrate. In the very next scene, Stanley announces that the queen has consented to her daughter's marriage to Richmond.

Olivier severely cuts Queen Elizabeth's role (the third longest in the play), and the effect is to render her as much a helpless victim as Anne. Her confrontation with Richard in the second wooing scene is omitted. Instead of being granted Shakespeare's scene with Margaret and the Duchess of York, in which she learns to turn her anger outward onto Richard, the appropriate target, she is given a scene with Anne and the Duchess of York in which each woman focuses on her own role as victim. Her look of scorn for Anne, as Anne describes how she gave into Richard's proposal, certainly does nothing to suggest a mutually supportive group. Queen Elizabeth's final appearance in the film is at the end of 4.1, her last words an address to the Tower in which her two sons are imprisoned. Her expressions of grief after their deaths are omitted. Although we hear later that she has agreed to Richmond's marriage to her daughter, the line carries no force because of the omission of the second wooing scene. As Dale Silviria observes, "The last time we see Queen Elizabeth, Richard has defeated her."[19]

The Loncraine film does retain the second wooing scene, and it is this scene that separates Queen Elizabeth from the other women in the film by suggesting her strength, although where that strength comes from remains unclear. In her initial appearances, however, the queen does not evoke much sympathy, perhaps because Annette Bening portrays her as shrill (and here Bening's difficulty with the blank verse is painfully obvious).[20] In addition, Loncraine and

McKellen's screenplay, by giving her some of Queen Margaret's lines to Richard, most notably "bottled spider" (1.3.241) and "poisonous bunch-backed toad" (1.3.245), give a nasty edge to her personality. Richard is making covert personal attacks at the time, but these retorts are extreme compared to his. Whereas Shakespeare's Queen Elizabeth begins the play helpless, and through her suffering grows into the ability to deal with Richard, Loncraine's Elizabeth has a hard edge to her from the beginning.

However, if initially we have little sympathy for Queen Elizabeth, Loncraine does gradually begin to build some. First, Elizabeth is told of her brother's murder; then, when denied access to her sons, she fearfully addresses the Tower in which they are imprisoned. Finally, we see a shot of her weeping, a small figure on a large empty staircase, after her sons have been murdered. As in Shakespeare's text, Queen Elizabeth confronts Richard. The second wooing scene thus allows Annette Bening's Queen Elizabeth to pour her anger and contempt on Richard, and to show her ability to defeat him. When she leaves, he thinks he has convinced her to let him marry her daughter, but is obvious to the audience that he has completely misread her. Loncraine's film gives Queen Elizabeth one additional appearance, as she stands at the interpolated wedding of the princess and Richmond. This image reinforces what is only done verbally in Shakespeare: the movement of the legitimate succession to Richmond, brought about by a woman (and historically, through his descent from a woman), but unlike in Shakespeare's text without the sense that it is because of her power as a woman—a power that the misogynistic Richard fails to grasp.

This sense of female power is also connected with the final female character, the Duchess of York, who is often easily overlooked. Here, as with Queen Elizabeth, the cutting of Margaret removes a foil for the character, thereby leaving both film directors uncertain as to what use they should make of her. What both directors miss, and indeed what editors of Shakespeare miss, is how she is integral to the play. She is the widow of a duke who died for the crown, mother to sons who killed for the crown, and now lives to see her son Richard murdering his brothers and their children for the crown. Ultimately, her life is, in miniature, the history of the civil wars, as she herself observes: "Eighty odd years of sorrow have I seen, / And each hour's joy wrack'd with a week of teen" (4.1.94–95). Editors usually add a footnote here, stating that the Duchess was only in her sixties.[21] However, Richard II was deposed and killed in 1399, and Richard III became king in 1483. Thus the eighty odd years of her life compass all the years of civil strife, and she is truly "the mother of these griefs" (2.2.80). She knows what Richard is, and she knows he murdered his brother Clarence. When she gives Richard her blessing (2.2.104–11), she omits, as Richard notes, the customary final line "and make me die a good old man" (1.2.109). Richard is mocking here, but it is possible that the omission is deliberate on her part. The blessing ritual, as Bruce Young has pointed out, is associated mainly with women, "perhaps because the authority to perform it derives from natural powers and relationships—and perhaps, too, because blessing, like cursing, is viewed as possessing supernatural power—the blessing ritual indicates women's access to a power independent of and in some ways superior to that found in the political structures within which the play's men operate."[22] Thus 4.4 becomes a pivotal scene, as Queen Margaret, Queen Elizabeth, and the Duchess of York sit together on the stage and, in expressing their suffering in choric form, express the suffering of England, so that it no longer matters to which Richard or to which Edward or to which York the speaker is referring. The Duchess of York's curse, her last words in the play, pronounce judgment on Richard, both in her role as mother and as embodiment of England's suffering.

The Olivier film greatly cuts the Duchess's role. It includes her blessing of Richard but not her curse. The film also does not suggest that she knows Richard is responsible for Clarence's death. Thus, she is tied to no intuitive knowledge. Her last appearance is in 4.1, her last words "I to my grave, where peace and rest lie with me!" (94), another woman defeated by Richard's evil.

The Loncraine film also drastically cuts the Duchess of York's role, although apparently not enough for James Loehlin, who comments that "she is given a disproportionate number of lines in the screen adaptation," and who also notes that she is given some of Queen Margaret's vengeful lines.[23] I would argue, however, that Loncraine and McKellen have taken away more than they have given, and that they radically alter the character in the process. In his notes to the screenplay, McKellen makes it clear that he is developing a psychological reading of Richard that traces his evil to mistreatment by his mother. Thus, he comments on "the emotional barrenness of Richard's childhood." He further claims: "Whatever justice there is in the Duchess of York's disaffection towards her youngest son, it is based on her disappointment and disgust at his physique. Perhaps it was from his mother that Richard learnt to hate so fiercely."[24] In the introduction to the screenplay, he goes further and suggests that the Duchess's "cursing outburst in scene 97 exemplifies the verbal and emotional abuse which from infancy has formed her youngest son's character and behavior."[25]

The film visually reinforces this interpretation. At her first entrance, arriving at the coronation ball early in the film, she seems to ignore Richard, her later blessing is given through clenched teeth, and still later, Richard is made to overhear her comments about how, with the deaths of Edward and Clarence, she has "but one false glass, / That grieves me when I see my shame in him" (2.2.53–54). Her curse causes Richard to stagger back as if she had dealt him a physical blow, and it is that curse he recalls in his nightmares before the battle. Thus, in Loncraine and McKellen's screenplay, the Duchess of York becomes the ultimate cause of Richard's evil. The woman, particularly the mother, is to blame. By relying on such a blatant stereotype, one with origins in the patriarchal context in which Freud developed his theories (theories that reflect Freud's own biases), Loncraine and McKellen present the audience with a "scientific" reason for Richard's evil, whereas Shakespeare deliberately did not ascribe a cause. Deliberate ambiguity has been recast as hard fact, a transformation which not only diminishes the Duchess's role but also that of Richard.

The cuts to the women's roles in the Olivier and Loncraine films of *Richard III* greatly diminish the women's power. They are cut down to size, and male anxiety about women who, while not powerful in the political world, wield considerable power in the emotional and intuitive realms, is thereby alleviated or at least contained temporarily. However, in paring down the women's roles, both directors have also lost the historical, supernatural, and ritualistic context that is integral to the play that Shakespeare wrote. Perhaps to compensate, both films explicitly depict the violence that Shakespeare, as Antony Hammond notes, chose to keep off stage, with the exceptions of the deaths of Clarence and Richard.[26] Olivier added the suffocation of the princes and the chopping off of Hastings's head. The Loncraine film adds the deaths of Henry VI and Prince Edward, increases the violence of Clarence's death, gives Rivers a nasty on-stage death (while he is engaged in sex), and shows the executions of Hastings and Buckingham. Violence increases as ritual is deemphasized, perhaps because ritual is a means of containing violence and a way of giving order to transitions. In Shakespeare's text, the ritualistic speaking of the women in 1.3, 2.2, and 4.4 emphasizes that the violence, while it will play itself out, is ultimately contained. Indeed, the female characters are the embodiment of that containment, even as they also embody the possibility for rebirth in this society, a rebirth symbolized by the Princess Elizabeth's forthcoming marriage to Richmond, and by the final lines that he speaks, almost as a benediction upon the land. Olivier retains those lines at the film's end; the Loncraine film inserts them earlier and chooses as its final image Richard's deliberate falling into flames below, after being cornered by a smirking Richmond. Even at the last, the Loncraine film denies the power of the women and the possibilities for rebirth.

In defense of the cuts made to the text in each film, it might be asserted that Shakespeare's plays are almost always cut in performance, and indeed there is a tradition on stage of cutting Queen Margaret's role, as well as of cutting lines from the other female roles in this play. However, Irene Dash has argued this point in a discussion of women's roles in other Shakespeare plays: "When the same sections always disappear, one begins to wonder why. And when these excisions involve women characters, as is often the case, one tries to discover what sequential arrangement of lines or scenes might have been changed, what insights into a character lost."[27] Stage tradition, which has been overwhelmingly male dominated, needs to be questioned from a feminist perspective. Dash also notes that we need to consider "the influence of the star, or actor-manager, on the women's roles, often perceived as merely complementing his."[28] Olivier's and Loncraine and McKellen's films are, to a great extent, star vehicles. Olivier was both director and star; McKellen, while he did not direct, exercised considerable influence in adapting the play for the screen.[29] In both cases, the result was an emphasis on Richard's character achieved by cuts to other roles, the women's in particular, without necessarily taking into consideration how such cuts affect the play as a whole. In no other history play did Shakespeare give female characters such prominence. It is time that directors start asking why.

In conclusion, the Olivier film is fully a part of the 1950s view of women in its presentation of stylized suffering. The Loncraine film of forty years later, with its presentation of neurotic women, is very much a part of the 1990s postfeminist backlash. The portrayal of women in both films, whatever the overt intentions, suggests a fear of women and a need to find ways of denying or containing female power. Although both films insist that the only power that matters is the political power exercised by men, it is exactly this political power that Shakespeare's play reveals as secondary to the power represented by the women. Oddly enough, it is William Shakespeare, man of the late sixteenth and early seventeenth century and certainly not a feminist, who despite the admittedly gendered approach, ultimately upholds a positive view of women in his play.

Notes

1. Norman Holland is among those who argue that the female characters have little effect on the action. In referring to the three cursing women in 4.4, he observes: "Such women were inside the action, however, impotent to change the events being created by the dominant men." See "Sons and Substitutions: Shakespeare's Phallic Fantasy," in *Shakespeare's Personality*, ed. Norman N. Holland, Sidney Homan, and Bernard J. Paris (Berkeley and Los Angeles: University of California Press, 1989), 81.

2. Constance Kuriyama makes this point in "Olivier's *Richard III*—A Re-evaluation," *Film Quarterly* 20, no. 4 (1966–67): "Margaret and her prophetic curses must necessarily seem a little quaint to modern audiences" (23). The article appears under her maiden name, Constance Brown.

3. See Harold F. Brooks, "*Richard III*, Unhistorical Amplifications: The Women's Scenes and Seneca," *Modern Language Review* 75 (October 1980): 721.

4. Madonne M. Miner, "'Neither mother, wife, nor England's queen': The Roles of Women in *Richard III*," in *The Woman's Part: Feminist Criticism of Shakespeare*, ed. Carolyn Ruth Swift Lenz, Gayle Greene, and Carol Thomas Neely (Urbana: University of Illinois Press, 1983), 52.

5. Ian McKellen, in his notes on the screenplay, suggests that there was a slight attempt to create a gathering of women in scene 73, where Anne, in an outdoor scene with the other women, speaks the lines that in the play begin at 4.1.67. The scene was an afterthought, when Richard Loncraine asked him to give Kristen Scott Thomas some additional lines. McKellen observes: "Seeing the women gathered away from the men may be a consolation for anyone expecting to hear their long, later scenes of rhetoricised grief, which I judged alien to our film." See Ian McKellen and Richard Loncraine, *William Shakespeare's "Richard III": A Screenplay* (Woodstock, New York: The Overlook Press, 1996), 180. However, there is no interaction of the women in this scene. Anne appears to be talking to the air rather than to the other women, none of whom reacts to her words. This is not the empowering gathering of women that occurs in Shakespeare's play.

6. Although Olivier deletes the relationship between women and ritual, he does maintain a ritualistic context, as Constance Kuriyama observes, by a "persistent weaving of religious references into the fabric of his film." See Brown, "Olivier's *Richard III*—A Re-evaluation," 26. Jack Jorgens, addressing this issue of ritual in Olivier's film, takes an opposite view by arguing that "Olivier showed how rituals, faced with Richardism, can no longer make the world cohere and have meaning." See Jack J. Jorgens, *Shakespeare "on Film"* (Bloomington: Indiana University Press, 1977), 139. However, I would argue that although Richard subverts ritual temporarily in the Olivier film, as in Shakespeare's play, the ritual is ultimately reasserted in Richard's defeat. Olivier understood the necessity of that reassertion of order in ritual, even if he did not perhaps grasp how the women's roles reinforce it. The Loncraine film excises the ritualistic context completely.

7. James N. Loehlin contends that despite the severe cuts, the women's roles in the Loncraine film are "in many cases expanded and developed through numerous non Shakespearean appearances." He further claims that the roles of Queen Elizabeth, Lady Anne, and the young Princess Elizabeth, "who doesn't even appear in the text—are all given prominence and in some cases additional lines." It seems to me that Loncraine and McKellen have taken much more than they have given. See "'Top of the World, Ma': *Richard III* and Cinematic Convention," in *Shakespeare*

the Movie: Popularizing the Plays on Film, TV, and Video, ed. Lynda E. Boose and Richard Burt (London and New York: Routledge, 1997), 68.

8. See Brown, "Olivier's *Richard III*—A Re-evaluation," 24.

9. See McKellen's Introduction to *William Shakespeare's "Richard III": A Screenplay*, 24. This conclusion is all the more puzzling as it follows a two page discussion of Richard's character that seeks to attribute his behavior to his social and familial context: "Studying the play reveals an opposite proposition—that Richard's wickedness is an outcome of other people's disaffection with his physique," as well as the "verbal and emotional abuse" of his mother, "which from infancy has formed her youngest son's character and behavior" (22). I shall have more to say on this blaming of the mother later in this essay. Here, I only wish to state that the idea that modern psychology can explain all human behavior is itself a literary convention not a hard scientific fact.

10. Examples of this process of penance can be found in the medieval morality *Everyman*, as well as in Edmund Spenser's *The Faerie Queene*, Book 1, canto 10.

11. Dale Silviria, *Laurence Olivier and the Art of Film Making* (Rutherford: Fairleigh Dickinson University Press, 1985), 242.

12. Robert Hapgood, "Shakespeare on Film and Television," in *The Cambridge Companion to Shakespeare Studies*, ed. Stanley Wells (Cambridge: Cambridge University Press, 1986), 281. For more detailed discussion of the film technique, see Brown, "Olivier's *Richard III*—A Re-evaluation," and Silviria, *Laurence Olivier and the Art of Film Making*.

13. In his introduction to the screenplay, McKellen notes that he resisted cutting Queen Margaret in early drafts. Theatrically, it is a powerful role, and McKellen recognizes that. However, as he sees her primarily as serving an historical purpose within the play, ultimately he did make the cut: "In the film, her powerful presence would not compensate for the time spent in explaining clearly who she is and has been.... If the action of the play often looks back, the film is centred on the living moment and then looks forward." See McKellen, *William Shakespeare's "Richard III": A Screenplay*, 17.

14. I owe this idea of a missing "backbone" to my colleague Mary Trotter from a discussion we had about Loncraine's *Richard III*.

15. For one refutation of the providential view advocated by Tillyard, see Henry Ansgar Kelly, *Divine Providence in the England of Shakespeare's Histories* (Cambridge, MA: Harvard University Press, 1970), especially the discussion of *Richard III*, 276–95.

16. William Shakespeare, *Richard III*, ed. Herschel Baker, *The Riverside Shakespeare*, 2nd edition, ed. G. Blakemore Evans and J. J. M. Tobin (Boston and New York: Houghton Mifflin, Co., 1997), 1.2.229. Further references to this edition appear in the text.

17. Dale Silviria, *Laurence Olivier and the Art of Film Making*, 235.

18. McKellen comments: "On the page, it seems incredible that Lady Anne would ever succumb to her husband's killer. In performance, the scene (1.2) is invariably convincing" (74). While that is certainly true, I think it is less so when Lady Anne's lines have been so drastically cut. McKellen also notes that Richard Loncraine was "uncertain whether Lady Anne's submission could be believable" (82). Perhaps in this instance, the director should have overruled his collaborator and star. Quotations are from *William Shakespeare's "Richard III": A Screenplay*.

19. Dale Silviria, *Laurence Olivier and the Art of Film Making*, 234.

20. One of the great mysteries in recent Shakespeare films is why directors think it charming when American actors stumble over blank verse. (Kenneth Branagh's

Much Ado about Nothing has some equally painful examples.) In the Loncraine film, there was a desire to play off the notion of Queen Elizabeth and her brother as Americans—outsiders—just as in Shakespeare's text, Queen Elizabeth obviously comes from a lower social level. Surely the same effect could have been accomplished even with the proper training in speaking blank verse. McKellen's discussion of blank verse in his introduction to the screenplay (30–35) may also be at fault, as it does not take into consideration substitutions in the iambic pentameter line, substitutions for which experienced actors, like McKellen, unconsciously adjust.

21. Herschel Baker, in *The Riverside Shakespeare*, notes: "Actually the Duchess of York was sixty-eight at Richard's accession in 1483." Antony Hammond, in the Arden Shakespeare edition, observes that she was "actually only 68 at the time." Even the Jane Howell film of *Richard III*, which preserves most of the text, cut these lines as either nonessential or as an error on Shakespeare's part.

22. Bruce W. Young, "Ritual as an Instrument of Grace: Parental Blessings in *Richard III*, *All's Well That Ends Well*, and *The Winter's Tale*," in *True Rites and Maimed Rites: Ritual and Anti-Ritual in Shakespeare and His Age*, ed. Linda Woodbridge and Edward Berry (Urbana and Chicago: University of Illinois Press, 1992), 177.

23. James N. Loehlin, " 'Top of the World, Ma'," 74.

24. McKellen, *William Shakespeare's "Richard III": A Screenplay*, 144, 236.

25. Ibid., 22.

26. Antony Hammond, introduction to *Richard III* (London and New York: Methuen, 1981), 98.

27. Irene G. Dash, *Women's Worlds in Shakespeare's Plays* (Newark, Del.: University of Delaware Press, 1997), 29. Although she does not examine *Richard III*, Dash's discussion of cuts in *All's Well That Ends Well*, *A Midsummer Night's Dream*, *Hamlet*, *Macbeth*, and *Twelfth Night* suggests that appeals to "stage tradition" often obscure a pattern of cutting in which "stereotypes tend to replace the plays' more complex portraits, and ambiguities disappear" (249). Shakespeare, she argues, while "not a revolutionary with a polemical message" was "an artist looking at the multifaceted life around him and dramatizing some of its puzzles" (24). He recognized the complexity of women's roles in society, and his plays reflect that complexity.

28. Ibid, 31.

29. In his annotations, McKellen states: "When the final screenplay was issued, it was called 'the Bible' and almost as much revered, in that every department took even the most casual of instructions as a rule of law. For instance, just because I had written that Richard wore a Rolex watch, the property department hired a genuine, vintage timepiece, worth £5,000, for me to wear onscreen" (*William Shakespeare's "Richard III": A Screenplay*, 124). Obviously the power of the "star or actor-manager" to which Dash refers is still very strong.

Film Editing
PETER HOLLAND

OPHELIA *My lord!*[1]

My concerns in this article stem from a nagging anxiety over two words in *Hamlet*, when Ophelia says to Hamlet "My lord.' The moment may seem familiar: in 4.2, after Hamlet has killed Polonius and has hidden the body, "Safely stowed" (4.2.1),[2] Rosencrantz and Guildenstern enter with others to capture Hamlet and then, just as they are about to arrest him, Ophelia rushes in saying "My lord" and Hamlet, with the wonderful line "Hide fox, and all after" (4.2.29–30), seizes the opportunity of the diversion created by her unexpected arrival and runs out. If you do not quite remember reading those two words, "My lord," at this juncture in the play, it is because they do not actually appear in any standard text of the play that I have come across. If you have a vague memory of hearing Ophelia say the words, it is because she does in Kenneth Branagh's 1996 film.

The words "my lord" or variants of the phrase come easily to Ophelia's lips. She enters in 2.1 to seek out her father, saying "Alas, my lord, I have been so affrighted!" (2.1.76). In 3.1 she responds to Hamlet's questioning of her in the "nunnery" scene, with a stream of versions of the phrase, "Good my lord," "My lord," "My honoured lord," "My lord," "What means your lordship?" "my lord" and again "my lord" (3.1.92, 95, 99, 106, 108, 111, 118), so that it is not until Hamlet says "You should not have believed me" (119) and she replies wanly "I was the more deceived" (122) that she is given a speech which does not contain the words "My lord." If Ophelia is going to speak in 4.2, then "My lord" would seem the obvious thing for her to say. The words belong firmly to her linguistic register, her idiolect; they constitute a form of definition of her self and identity in her language.

But the phrase's familiarity as an aspect of Ophelia's speech patterns will not resolve the oddity of its presence here in 4.2. For if

Ophelia does not usually or necessarily appear in the scene, her appearance in Branagh's film raises remarkable problems. I cannot find any analogue to her appearance at this point in any early printed version of the play nor can I recall seeing her enter in any production of the play I have seen.[3] It is her appearance as much as the words she speaks when she does appear that is troubling, the action as much as the spoken text that constitutes a disturbance of a normative image of textual authority that seems especially significant, given the singular approach to text that marks Branagh's film, something I shall return to later.

The published screenplay for the film makes no especial comment on the interference caused by Ophelia's entry or her two words at this juncture to the flow of textual authority that the film embodies—and I use "interference" here with its suggestion of noise interrupting the clarity of a radio broadcast, preventing us hearing the programme untrammelled. But it does contain a great deal of other kinds of interference to the reader's perception of the language spoken in the film. Branagh's published screenplay is much more than the words spoken with accompanying apparatus of performance. It is not only that the spoken text is surrounded by the appurtenances of staging, entrances, exits and speech prefixes, the kinds of minimal markers that editors are obliged to include in order to emend, round out and complete from the inadequacies of the early texts but which they add within the style of those texts. Such transformations are familiar and much analyzed. Modern editions identify act and scene in the margin, render stage directions consistent, modernize spelling, expand and regularize speech prefixes. Whatever the strength of belief in unediting a textual scholar may possess, s/he can understand the reasoning behind such formulaic metamorphosis. Branagh's screenplay necessarily adds to a version of such a transformation some of the characteristics of film-screenplay in its representation of filmic convention:

Cut to:
Interior / CHAPEL STAIRS Night
HAMLET finishes disposing of POLONIUS's body.
    HAMLET
Safely stowed.
ROSENCRANTZ AND GUILDENSTERN (O/S)
Hamlet, Lord Hamlet!
HAMLET
But soft. What noise? Who calls on Hamlet?

(115)

Text is now made up of units of editing in the screenplay's definition of transition to a new scene or set-up: "Cut to:." Film-scripts require the identification of interior or exterior, of set and of time of day, all neatly recorded in the scene heading. The additional stage direction, recording what action has just been completed, is unexceptionable in its explication of "Safely stowed," the kind of information that perhaps a school edition might record in a commentary note.

But the screenplay has also elsewhere added a kind of post-Shakespearian commentary, familiar from, say, the texts of plays by Shaw but unknown either in early modern texts or in the main tradition of Shakespeare editing or printed representation, so that Rosencrantz's response to Hamlet's description of him as a sponge and Hamlet's extension of the analogy are described as follows:

> ROSENCRANTZ can barely tolerate this so-called "wit". . . . [Hamlet] talks as if filling him in on a particularly useful piece of information. Meantime the room starting to fill up with other guards, and their dogs. (115–16)

The nearest analogue to this kind of textual addition, a commentary marking stage-business that is built into the text rather than placed in the conventional and decent distance of notes, lies in French's Acting Editions. The 1919 French's edition of *Hamlet* cuts 4.2 completely, since its "excisions . . . closely follow the version prepared by Sir Johnston Forbes-Robertson for his revival at the Lyceum Theatre,"[4] but the notes for the opening of the play are representative. It describes the lighting and the rhythm of the opening, instructing lighting designer and the actor playing Bernardo how they must effect lighting and pause: "The front of the stage, below the rostrum, is in semi-darkness. A faint steel blue light on cloth at back of C. arch. A pause at curtain rise." The position of Francisco when the curtain does rise is established: "FRANCISCO is resting on his halberd motionless, his figure silhouetted against the faint light from behind him. He stands in the archway C." The edition also defines Bernardo's[5] entrance ("from arch in wall L.") and the way his first line is to be delivered:

> An indication of apprehension in the manner of BERNARDO in respect of the apparition of the KING must be registered from the outset. BERNARDO's "Who's there?" should not be given as an ordinary challenge, but as though the man had superstitious dread. (1)

Though such editions draw on current stage practice, their commentary aims to be prescriptive for future—usually amateur—

performance. The conventions of the series necessitate the inclusion of exact props and furniture plots and a fairly detailed lighting plot. The implicit assumption with which they are working is that the editions have a just claim to authority in defining how to present Shakespeare. Hence they suggest that sets, blocking, costume, gesture and speech intonation can be fixed, even in a case where the text itself is seen as destabilized from the forms of both early textual authority (Q2, F1) and the traditions of scholarly editions. This is most apparent in the 1919 *Hamlet* in the substantial cutting in act 4. As well as 4.2, the French's edition cuts 4.1 and 4.6 and combines 4.5 and 4.7 into a single scene. As the prefatory note advises "[it] will be noticed that Act IV is arranged in three Scenes instead of seven—and that the text is, for the sake of clarity, printed for the arranged sequence." But the act could have been presented in an even more abbreviated form: it is only because of the authoritative advice of Sir Johnston Forbes-Robertson that 4.3 and 4.4 "(very frequently omitted) have been here retained" (iii). In its presentation of act 4 the French's Acting Edition is defined by its observance and representation of stage tradition, by marking possibilities for performance that go against that tradition and by its appeal to authority enshrined in the work of a distinguished contemporary actor-manager.

The 1919 French's Acting Edition edits the text in a number of senses: it both edits in the manner of conventional textual scholarship, it edits by arranging for definitive performance and it edits by abbreviating for performance. As well as the scenes that are cut completely, the text marks a number of passages "clearly bracketed for the suggested abridgments" (iii). In the context of film, the word "edit" is an act of elimination, the editing of the film into a final cut. To edit is to reduce the hundreds of hours of film that has been shot in order to generate the finished product, intercutting the different shots until the scene takes on the rhythm that the editor and/or director wish it to have. Film can, of course, be re-edited. Branagh's *Hamlet* exists in two defiantly different formats, running at 4 and $2^1/_2$ hours respectively, both derived from the same corpus of unedited film. In other cases, films can be redefined by the activity of re-editing. Ridley Scott's *Blade Runner* exists or has existed in six versions ranging from the original workprint to a version screened on American television, from the standard release print to the "Director's Cut," another marker of supposed authority over the text of the film[6].

Film as object can exist in many forms, as, for example, reels of celluloid or as video-tape or as a version broadcast on television.

Film can, in a limited number of examples, also apparently exist through the print version of screenplay. For the moment with which I am primarily concerned, the published screenplay text reads as follows:

> HAMLET ... *Bring me to him.*
> He appears to go with them willingly. They go towards the stairs as OPHELIA runs down.
> OPHELIA *My lord!*
> HAMLET *Hide fox and all after.*
> HAMLET escapes, ROSENCRANTZ and GUILDENSTERN and the soldiers begin the chase.
>
> (116)

Screenplays of Shakespeare films are not, of course, primarily representations of the Shakespeare text as an object to be read disjunct from the film to which they bear witness. Instead they are representations of forms of filmic transposition. What kind of representation they constitute will vary enormously. They may be a documentation of the completed film, a *post hoc* construction in print of what the celluloid constitutes. They may be a representation of a form of intention, a creation by the screenplay writer of the film s/he would wish to make or would wish to have made, had the finances permitted the film to be shot in the idealized way the writer wished or had the constraints of editing allowed the whole screenplay to remain in the final version rather than ending up on the cutting-room floor. To take some examples to represent something of the range, the published screenplay of Orson Welles's *Chimes at Midnight* has been constructed by the book's editor, Bridget Gellert Lyons, through watching prints of the film and creating a continuity script from it. Decisions over, for instance, the attribution of lines to particular speakers, are entirely her decision[7]. This screenplay thus represents an analytic reconstruction of that which was filmed. The published screenplay for the 1936 film of *Romeo and Juliet,* directed by George Cukor, describes itself as a "motion picture edition" and includes an essay by Irving Thalberg, the producer, on "Picturing *Romeo and Juliet,*" and a text of the play before the "scenario version." It also makes clear that the "scenario" represents the state of the film prior to release:

> If the reader finds that in certain scenes the picture shows differences from the scenario—a line or two omitted, one or more lines restored from Shakespeare's text, or some changes in business—he will under-

stand that these changes were made in the course of production, after the manuscript had been sent to press.[8]

This practice of including the originating play as well as the screenplay has occasionally been repeated, either by printing within the same volume, as for instance with Baz Luhrmann's *William Shakespeare's Romeo + Juliet*,[9] or by printing it with some reference to filming and with cuts marked, as for instance with Olivier's *Hamlet*.[10] In the case of the Luhrmann screenplay it includes a number of moments never part of the final release version and probably never filmed, for example the appearance of Father Laurence in the church before Juliet shoots herself (159–60), representing the film at a stage prior to principal photography. The Olivier *Hamlet* screenplay is derived from the finished film but deliberately avoids the forms of technical description that would have been part of the shooting script. As Alan Dent explains in introducing the text/ screenplay,

> This version should be of considerable interest even to the reader well acquainted with "Hamlet," since it has the novelty of incorporated film-directions (with technical terms deleted), as distinct from stage-directions. ("Explanatory note," unnumbered page)

Dent seeks to represent the film in a way that is both particularized to its medium and yet accessible to the presumed readership, creating a text that represents the film but which also denies the linguistic forms, the technical exactitude of a shooting-script. Where the Cukor, Luhrmann and Branagh screenplays preserve the technical language, partly to authenticate the screenplay as filmic, the Olivier screenplay replaces it with narrative description, for example, at the start:

> The camera shoots down from on high, down at the castle of Elsinore, and slowly approaches it. After about fifteen seconds a cloud settles in front of the camera, shutting out the castle from view.

It excludes the "Exterior. Castle. Night" form which constitutes the conventionalized prerequisite of formal screenplays, occupying instead a middle ground between screenplay and the capabilities of its assumed readership. Elsewhere in the same volume, Dent's essay on the editing of the play for the film includes representative samples of shooting script in more conventional film format, covering setups 168 to 200.[11] But rather than seeing the elaborate descriptions of camera position and movement as additions to the text, Dent comments, following the first few set-ups (168–71) that "what has been done with the text" in this section is that

> [t]hree unimportant words have been cut out of the second section of Hamlet's speech to the Players, and eight insignificant monosyllables out of the fourth section. That is all.[12]

As far as Dent is concerned, everything that surrounds the printed representation of spoken language is non-textual and not part of "text editing."

In their range of responses to the problems of their forms of existence, screenplays represent a particular and deeply problematic form of representation of text, a form whose precise connection to performance, that single performance which the film ostensibly constitutes, needs decoding and analyzing. Branagh's screenplay for *Hamlet* clearly represents the text prior to its final editing, close though the screenplay is to the film as released. Russell Jackson has suggested that the screenplay was in part constructed by Kenneth Branagh's personal assistant from the materials prepared prior to filming but reworked through viewing a rough cut. Photography was completed by April 1996 and the film was finally released in December 1996. The screenplay text was probably prepared at some point during the summer. Branagh's introduction defines the time of writing as "one month from complet[ion]" of the film when the "sound and music mix are in their final stages" (iv and viii). Ophelia's line did not appear in the shooting-script; in that version of the text of the film, she did not run down the staircase into the scene. Instead, she was, at that point, conceived of as watching at least part of the chase that followed "Hide fox" from a vantage point in the gallery over the main area of the court hall of mirrors.[13] The line and, indeed, the whole notion of her arrival into the scene were added during filming and hence available to be recorded in the screenplay when the alterations from the shooting script could be incorporated.

That the screenplay is neither a complete nor adequate representation of even the spoken texture of the released film is clear at this point since it makes no mention of the fact that Ophelia speaks again in this sequence, that, as Hamlet runs through a number of rooms in a self-consciously virtuoso piece of camera-work, we hear Ophelia's voice echoing after him, "My lord. My good lord Hamlet. My honoured Hamlet," followed by a series of indecipherable words whose rhythms suggest to my ears further variations of such phrases and then a series of despairing cries of "Oh." Ophelia's cries constitute here a desperate need for contact with Hamlet, as her voice recedes into the distance which defines the gap between Hamlet and Ophelia as they part for the last time in both their lives, until, that is, Hamlet will confront her corpse much later, after the film's intermission. Significantly, the spoken phrases that I can decipher from the soundtrack all come from the forms Ophelia uses in the "nunnery" scene, so that they appear to repeat the language of love between them, the forms of address prior to her line "At home, my lord" (3.1.133), the statement after which, as the screenplay puts it, "with that phrase their love is dead. We seem to see both their hearts break before us" (80).

The screenplay includes some events that do not occur in the film as released. In 4.4, the screenplay describes action absent from the release print to follow Fortinbras's line "And let him know so" (4.4.7)—"One look to the CAPTAIN which says, 'Don't even think of making a mistake'" (120).[14] But there are also misascriptions as well as omissions, perhaps the consequence of later changes during editing. The screenplay (54) ascribes to the voice of Hamlet the quatrain from his letter to Ophelia ("Doubt thou the stars are fire," 2.2.116–19) where, on the release print, the lines are spoken by Polonius in voice-over. Small examples such as these mark a gap between screenplay and film that makes the former a treacherous witness, especially since some analysis of the film already confuses film and screenplay as if the latter might constitute accurate documentation of the film. For example, the sequence of shots that accompany Voltemand's narration to Claudius of the success of the embassy to Norway is not as described in the screenplay and recorded as interpolation 18 in David Kennedy Sauer's article on the additions to the film.[15] Throughout the sequence the cuts between the shots do not occur at the points of spoken text specified in the screenplay, so that the cut from the shot of Fortinbras riding through the woods to the shot of Old Norway "reading the news of FORTINBRAS's misdemeanours" is not between "which to him appeared" and "To be a preparation 'gainst the Polack" (2.2.62–63) but between "His nephew's levies" and "which to him appeared." In addition there is a further shot of Fortinbras on horseback following the shot of the palace at Elsinore, further clarifying the meaning of Voltemand's statement "It was against your highness" and indicating from whose imagined point-of-view the sight of the palace is assumed to be taken.

Screenplay is a partial witness, a form of printed representation whose relationship to the film as made, as edited, as distributed for theatre release or for video needs analysis. If the status of screenplay as authority is questionable, so too is the balance of authority in the making of Shakespeare film between director and playwright, between, in this case, Branagh and Shakespeare, especially since the director is so often involved in the creation of the screenplay. In the examples above, Luhrmann and Welles have a writing credit. The intervention of another mode of authorship—what used in film theory to be considered as auteurism—needs consideration as a denial of the authority of the kind of text (Shakespeare's *Hamlet* as printed rather than Branagh's *Hamlet* as filmed or printed) from which the film has been generated. My analysis is concerned with the negotiations with the authority of Shakespeare which are taking place in the interventions in the process of consumption of his texts which film and video, theatre and radio, like their critical analogues of editions, articles and monographs, seek to make between that text and their consumers.

My problem over Ophelia's "My lord" relates to a particular primacy of the spoken word in our consideration of the Shakespeare text. Branagh's film includes a number of characters who are spoken of but not visible in the normative text: Old Norway, Priam, Hecuba, Yorick, each one providing a cameo appearance for a major actor (Sir John Mills, Sir John Gielgud, Dame Judi Dench, and Ken Dodd). A number of these figures are seen speaking but we do not hear their words. Hence the interpolation of such visual events is nothing more than a kind of visual illustration, a cinematic analogue to the history of Shakespeare painting, which includes numerous examples of paintings of characters unseen in performance and of events which exist solely in terms of spoken imagery, for example paintings of "pity, like a naked new-born babe, / Striding the blast, or heaven's cherubin, horsed / Upon the sightless couriers of the air" (*Macbeth* 1.7.21–23). In the film these illustrations are needed to provide the spectator with explanation, a denial of the imaginary processes on which the verbal referent of Shakespearian theatre depends. You no longer have to think when we speak of Fortinbras that you see him; now you do, for instance in illustration of Horatio's comment on him at 1.1.94, "Now sir, young Fortinbras." If this process is bound up with a certain trivialization of discourse in which speech has to be translated into sight (Branagh cannot resist—any more than almost every other director of *Hamlet* on film—showing us the drowned Ophelia, looking of course uncannily like Millais's painting), such banal visualization becomes permissible for us—even as we disdain it—precisely because it does not intrude on the sacred text, that is, the spoken text, of the Shakespearian original.

Tinkering with stage-directions—or, more properly, adjusting the received text in order to stage the plays at all—is no more than every theatre production does; tinkering with spoken language is a habit reserved primarily for non-Anglophone theatre productions, with the intriguing exception of the RSC's treatment of the Christopher Sly scenes in their productions of *The Taming of the Shrew*, sequences which are regularly rewritten. The practice of the RSC's programmes, in an example of canonicity and religious reverence for the originating text for which I have found no analogue anywhere else in the cultural world, is explicitly to state how many lines have been cut from the text being performed, as if in a state of permanent and humble apology for daring to infringe the wholeness of the text. The RSC does not usually need to record the absence of rewriting, productions of *Shrew* aside.

We are, therefore, fundamentally trapped into watching Shakespeare in a context of aural logocentrism in which the primacy of the spoken word makes us members of an audience (hearers) rather than spectators (watchers). Text, in this model of Shakespeare, is equivalent to that which is to be spoken and the other aspects of print are merely textualized ancillaries, subordinate to the overarching hegemony of voice and hearing. In the history of Shakespeare film the anxiety over disruptions to the spoken text can be traced back to the shift from silents to sound film. The first Shakespeare film made with sound was the version of *The Taming of the Shrew* directed in 1929 for United Artists, starring Mary Pickford and Douglas Fairbanks, one of the first "all-talkies" made by the company.[16] Since many cinemas were not yet equipped for sound, United Artists also released a silent version and many sequences in the film show the uneasy transition from silence to sound in their performance style. If the film is best remembered for a visual action, Pickford's wink at the end of Katherine's final speech, it also had to negotiate its relationship with a spoken Shakespeare text. Consistently mocked since for a supposed screen credit for "Additional Dialogue by Sam Taylor,"[17] the film was initially praised for its not having altered Shakespeare. E. F. M., a reviewer in the *Boston Transcript* (12 November 1929), noted,

> They have held to the Shakespearean language. Some of course has been cut. Some of the speeches have been transferred to other characters than those who had them originally. But still it is recognizable blank verse.[18]

The production company distributed information to exhibitors of the film to reassure them—and their public—about the film's fidelity to Shakespeare's language:

It will take an expert to detect any variation from the original text of Shakespeare's play. The tradition of "not changing Shakespeare" has been faithfully observed, with the exception that the marriage service is read; but even in this service Petruchio and Kate affirm their vows by nodding their heads instead of speaking. This is information for you to give to people who might try to kick about someone's attempting to write new dialogue for a Shakespeare play. [19]

What experts noticed was that some of the language was derived from David Garrick's *Catharine and Petruchio* (1756), so that, for instance, Pickford's Katherine has a brief monologue after Petruccio's exit on horseback after the wooing scene which, with minor variants, is pure Garrick:

> Look, to your seat, Petruchio, or I throw you.
> Catharine shall tame this haggard; or, if she fails,
> Shall tie her tongue up and pare down her nails.[20]

Some lines are adjusted for clarification: Hortensio will be disguised as a schoolmaster not "well seen in music, to instruct Bianca" (1.2.132) but "well versed in music, to instruct his youngest daughter" (which is therefore no longer quite "recognizable blank verse"). Other lines are garbled Shakespeare: Fairbanks's Petruccio turns "I come to wive it wealthily in Padua" (1.2.74) into "I come to wed in Padua wealthily."[21] Fairbanks was in a terrible state during the filming and never learned his lines; according to Pickford, they "had to be chalked on enormous blackboards, and I had to move my head so he could read them."[22] Other changes are the kind of minor adjustments that actors are wont to make. When Gremio turns "And unsuspected court her by herself" (1.2.135—the line was originally Hortensio's) into "And all unsuspected court her by herself," I suspect that this is the actor's alteration rather than Taylor's, since it does not significantly clarify the meaning of the line. Such alterations are on a par with the kind of changes Laurie Maguire has documented in some of the BBC television Shakespeare productions. Gremio's change is comparable to, for example, turning Polonius's "And truly, in my youth" into "And yet truly in my youth."[23]

But there is a gap between this kind of addition and some of the new lines in the film of *Shrew*. When a male servant tells Baptista, just before the first sight of Katherine, "Wait, she's stark mad," this may be Taylor's adaptation and transposition of Tranio's "That wench is stark mad" (1.1.69), but when another male servant cries "Run for your lives," there is no Shakespeare line apparent behind the desperate cry. Instead the line may represent the kind of improvised language common in silent film (when what is spoken would not be intelligible except by those able to lip-read).

Fairbanks may have stated, "We shall not presume to write Shakespearean dialogue,"[24] but the assumption that deletion was acceptable while addition was impossible is echoed in later accounts of films. Alan Dent who was responsible for the text used in Olivier's Hamlet offers this explanation for the refusal to add:

> One must therefore cut. But does one add any words?—says the innocent. The answer is—most certainly not! There is a legendary editor who said to a well-cut contributor: "Of course I can cut you—I can cut the Lord's Prayer." Your text-editor, similarly, has no compunction in cutting the hardly less sacrosanct Shakespeare when the point and purpose is a practicable film-version. But he does not presume to add words to those of the master.[25]

Dent did, however, add words to Olivier's film of *Henry V,* incorporating two lines borrowed from Marlowe's *Tamburlaine* to Pistol's role. He records his "trepidation" and Olivier's "hesitation" but

> when the film was duly presented, we noted, with a surprise amounting almost to mortification, that not a single critic appeared to have detected—much less resented—the interpolation! Eventually, many months later, a clever lady wrote from Boston, Mass., saying it was a daring thing to have done. That was all.[26]

This anxiety at such violation and the guilty relief at being undetected by all except the lady from Boston ("We, in short, 'got away' with it") could not be extended to *Hamlet*: "There could be no 'getting away' with such a piece of wantonness in the film of 'Hamlet' which is a very much more familiar play."

Yet Sauer's careful listing of the "interpolations" in Branagh's *Hamlet* does not list the textual change by interpolation that Ophelia's "My lord" constitutes; indeed, he asserts that "[s]ince the Folio is followed faithfully, the interpolations added to the text are all visual; no new lines are added" (329). But what constitutes interpolation seems peculiarly difficult to determine. For Sauer it seems to be filmic events, set-ups which are not demanded by the Shakespeare text, ranging from flash-backs, like the shots of Ophelia and Hamlet in bed together, to intercut events, like Fortinbras's attack on Elsinore. In Jill Levenson's superb analysis of the screenplay for Zeffirelli's *Romeo and Juliet* the "additions" (her term) range from words ("[But] the quarrel," 1.1.19) or lines ("Or I know not what," after

1.5.75) to repetitions (Friar Laurence's saying "I dare no longer stay" [5.3.159] four times as he hurries out) and non-verbal sounds ("Oh, aaah, hmmm, ah" etc).[27] It is, of course, the case that adding "Oh" before Juliet speaks "Where is my Romeo?" (5.3.150) alters the rhythm of the line but in a context in which the lines have been cut and re-arranged to produce a sequence of three half-lines the intrusion of an extrametrical syllabic "Oh" seems less of an addition than an actor's expression of emotion (italics are Levenson's indication of an addition):

> Friar Laurence   I hear some noise.
> Juliet   *Oh,* where is my Romeo?
> Friar Laurence   *Oh,* Lady, come from this nest . . .[28]

Levenson seems to be working within a context in which textual addition is as problematic as it was for Dent. Sauer is anxious about visual intrusion and the implications of its presence. Levenson, anxious about verbal intrusion, consistently reads the insertion of individual words as the responsibility of Zeffirelli rather than the actors so that she describes how "Zeffirelli and his assistants have sprinkled interjections as well as other monosyllables to give the flavour of colloquial expression" (111). Levenson believes that the changes to Mercutio's Queen Mab speech are deliberate alterations by "repetition and added words [to] suggest that Mercutio's phrases . . . happen extempore" to produce the following:

> *And the* collars, *ummm,* of the moonshine's watery beams;
> Her whip, *crack!* . . .
> . . . of *the* cricket's bone.
>
> (113)

But such alterations are as likely to be John McEnery's (the actor playing Mercutio) as Zeffirelli's, especially as Levenson gives no indication of having been able to consult a screenplay.

It may seem at this point that I am trying to determine responsibility for lines spoken in a film in the manner of Harold Jenkins's attack on the interference of the players in "Playhouse Interpolations in the Folio Text of *Hamlet*"[29] or Philip Edwards's astonishing statement about what happened when the play passed from Shakespeare to become "the property of these colleagues who began to prepare it for the stage":

> At this point what one can only call degeneration began . . . , for it is sadly true that the nearer we get to the stage, the further we are getting from Shakespeare.[30]

Edwards's "degeneration" and Jenkins's "interpolations" seem to align themselves, both marked as terms with fiercely pejorative overtones in their attitude to tampering with Shakespeare. That neither view now seems tenable in relation to the early texts of *Hamlet* should not obscure their implications for later uses of the text. In considering the text for subsequent performances, the ascription of responsibility—which is not the same necessarily as the ascription of blame—is part of the disentangling of the process by which an acting or performance text is created. That some part of that process involves changes to what was spoken[31] only intensifies awareness of the instability of text in the theatre, precisely the awareness that drives Edwards to seek to separate "Shakespeare's text" from the degeneration of theatre interference.

It might be appropriate to transfer terms whose meanings in traditional textual bibliography have been so much subject to analysis in recent years and to term the chance alteration of language by an actor whose memory is inexact as an "accidental" while a change introduced by a text-editor, in the sense that Alan Dent saw himself in that role for Olivier, might be seen as "substantive." Of course the line between such accidentals and substantives would be difficult to disentangle but in many cases the ascription of authority could well be definable and significant. Policing the line between Sam Taylor's changes and Douglas Fairbanks's mistakes would be well worth maintaining in their differing effects on Shakespeare's text.

But, of course, the recent revolution in Shakespeare textual theory consequent on the widespread acceptance of Shakespeare as reviser has enabled us to question the concept of "Shakespeare's text." At a point at which the Wells-Taylor Oxford edition in 1986 felt it necessary to print two *King Lears* (Quarto and Folio) and at which, ten years later, the Norton printed three (Quarto, Folio and "a conflated text"—so nominated indeed, the first time the term in textual theory has been explicitly linked to an edition), the notion of a complete text has been radically and properly problematized. Collations, that part of the printed text of Shakespeare which used to be completely ignored by critics, are now earnestly scanned for alternatives. Our evaluation of, say, Emilia in *Othello* is transformed by our awareness that her lengthy analysis of the implications for women of male behavior (4.3.85–102) is present in the 1623 Folio text but not in the Quarto of 1622. Critics, as yet, rarely conduct the same analysis for textual variants of stage directions, even though *Hamlet*, as it happens, provides a superb example of such variants: at the end of the closet scene does Gertrude stay on stage (as it were in her closet) when Claudius bursts in on her alone (as in F) or does she leave the fictive room and go to find Claudius, entering in the next scene meeting him (as in Q2)[32] in explicit denial of Hamlet's instructions to her to stay away from her husband? The Folio's form, indeed, indicates that what is normally marked as the end of act 3 is not even the end of a scene, much less an act, that the action is continuous.

The textual revolution remains unacknowledged in Branagh's text. The note in the screenplay about "the choice of text" indicates that the screenplay is based on F1: "Nothing," we are told, "has been cut from this text, and some passages absent from it . . . have been supplied from the Second Quarto" (175). The single word "absent" subsumes within it the rejection of revision, turning Shakespeare back from the working, revising, provisional, and dissatisfied dramatist of the new textual theory into the author of a totalized text of which the printed texts are imperfect witnesses. When Adrian Noble directed *Hamlet* for the RSC, in the 1992 production that starred Branagh as Hamlet, he used a conflated text, admitting that, since you don't get many chances in a professional career to direct *Hamlet*, you might as well do as much of it as possible when you can.[33] But this refreshingly honest pragmatism did not fetishize completeness. Branagh's film does.

Complete and unabridged, Branagh's film was widely hyped for its length. Indeed, though Branagh made two versions of the film, a four-hour version and a two-and-a-half hours version, the latter has rarely been used except (significantly) in non-Anglophone distribution areas. But the film was praised precisely for the revelation of the viability of the full-text; it was justified by its completeness. Terrence Rafferty compared it to Olivier's "study in 'Hamlet'": "Branagh's 'Hamlet' is no study: this is the huge unwieldy thing itself, staged with exhilarating clarity and force."[34] Rafferty added that the film "should prove beyond doubt that this tragedy, even at its full, unruly length, is anything but unplayable."[35] It was the first significant film version to include the whole of "the notoriously long playscript."[36] That now seems disturbed for Ophelia's "My lord" demonstrates that this is certainly not the whole text. Silently added to (for at no point is there any indication of such textual tampering), the film's inclusion of the two words denies the premise of completeness as an attribute of fidelity. Precisely unlike, say, the filming of Fortinbras's army's assault on Elsinore (all shot silently) or the flashbacks of Hamlet and Ophelia rolling around on a bed or Old Norway looking appropriately "impotent and bed-rid," the silent authoring of these two words and Ophelia's subsequent cries deny the authority of the Shakespearian text, redefining textual authority as in the control of the film-maker as writer (especially when, in Branagh's case, the same person is screenplay writer, director and lead actor). Branagh's concern to, as he states, "take the play into the cinema in its fullest form" stems from a recognition of the kinds of "flesh[ing] out" (his phrase) of the characters made possible in the full text. "With the full text," he writes, "the gravitational weight of the play seemed to increase" and, he goes on, "this version offered rich opportunities for the actors, particularly in the supporting roles," citing as examples how much more we understand about Polonius if we are able to see the scene with Reynaldo and how Claudius changes from "the conventional stage villain" when we see "the complexity of [his] manipulations" in the full version of the scene where he plots with Laertes (vi–vii). In interview Branagh has described how actors respond to cuts:

> You cut the play in the theatre. What happens often is that the actors just indulge a bit longer because they're somehow making a kind of silent protest against the fact that some very good piece of their text has been cut. So it seems longer anyway. And you get the effect of a lot of big scenes all being squashed together without the kind of as it were down beat Shakespeare gives you in the full-length version. And I guess you get less of the kind of epic dimension that connects a very personal tragedy concerning a couple of dysfunctional families with what's going on in the world.[37]

There has been fine work done by many theatre historians to show how the history of cutting the text has been a radical limiting of the representation of a number of roles, particularly the women in the play. But what the best work by scholars working in the light of revision theory has made available is an understanding of the incompatibilities of event revealed by the disentangling of the conflated text. More of Shakespeare is not, in this case, necessarily better and the confusions of action and of the representation of character that conflation produces is simply ignored by Branagh's decision. I offer just one example of this effect. In Q2, after Hamlet has murdered Polonius, Gertrude enters with Claudius who is accompanied by Rosencrantz and Guildenstern; Gertrude asks the others to leave so that she can tell Claudius what has happened in private: "Bestow this place on us a little while." In the Folio text, Rosencrantz and Guildenstern do not appear and Gertrude's line is also, logically, cut. It makes them appear much less like Claudius's toadying acolytes, less willing accomplices than further victims of the King's plotting. The payoff is later: when Hamlet describes how he sent them to their deaths, Horatio comments, in both Q2 and F, "So Guildenstern and Rosencrantz go to't" (5.2.57) but it is only in F that Hamlet offers the vicious pun in response: "Why, man, they did make love to this employment" (58), picking up on "go to't" as a phrase for sexual activity. The text in which Hamlet criticizes his erstwhile schoolfriends for enjoying the sexiness of conspiracy is the text in which we do not see them doing that. The conflated text goes nearer to justifying Hamlet's callousness than either Q2 or F taken separately permits.

At the same time we can recognize how deeply the claim of completeness works to underpin the cultural authority that the film seeks to annex for itself. Branagh's version of *Hamlet* becomes the true text as film, achieving something that even theatre has rarely been able to accomplish, precisely insofar as it represents itself as complete. In performing the whole text, Branagh implicitly claims, he plays the play as it should be understood and the interpretative decisions that the film makes are subsumed within the authority created by the absolute nature of its text. These decisions include precisely how we should see Claudius differing from a conventional stage villain or Polonius's nastiness revealed by the Reynaldo scene or whether Fortinbras's army does arrive at Elsinore as a deliberately planned hostile invading force or merely that Fortinbras seizes the chance to annex Denmark opportunistically. Completeness is aligned with fidelity and authenticity, whatever else may be happening in the film.

But as well as the notion of the whole text, Branagh has been concerned with the concept of the unaltered text. The text for the screenplay may conflate Q2 and F but it seeks to represent itself as accurate. Dent made a series of minor adjustments to the text for Olivier so that "vailèd lids" became "lowered lids," "beaver" became "visor" and "the general gender" became "the general father."[38] His justification was that "[i]n almost every case it will be observed, and it must be granted, that the Shakespearian word or phrase has become obsolete or has totally changed its meaning."[39] Such changes were often made in the teeth of Olivier's opposition and the clash was between a Hamlet unwilling to lose a line and the practicalities of ensuring that the "cinema-going audiences" were not confused:

> I have always borne in mind that a film of Shakespeare is not a thing primarily intended to interest a West End or London audience. It is a version intended to surprise and storm remote and un-Shakespeare-minded audiences throughout the habitable globe—not only Peru but

Poole, and Blackpool, and Ullapool, not only China but Chepstow and Chorley and Chipping Sodbury. Sir Laurence takes a higher view of humanity than I do, and wanted to keep far more of the text's obscurities than I thought advisable.[40]

Dent is arguing that in China and Peru the language would not be understood at all while in provincial Britain it would be confusing; only in the sophisticated West End would it be comprehended by an educated metropolitan audience.

Between Branagh and his textual adviser, Russell Jackson, the balance reversed: it was Branagh who was willing to contemplate change and Jackson who sought to preserve the purity of the original text. Jackson records a moment of such anxiety in his film diary:

> [C]lose in on Ken for "By heaven I'll make a ghost of him that lets me." Ken thinks of saying "stops" for "lets," anxious not to be misunderstood at this moment. Worrying, because it's a famous line and it seems a shame to compromise like this. After he's watched the first take on the monitor I hear myself almost yelling, "No, 'lets' is fine—it'll be clear enough what you mean!" . . . (We go for "lets.")   (Screenplay, 198)

The need to be understood in Ullapool is, quite reasonably, Branagh's—and Jackson's—concern. Comprehensibility can now be achieved through leaving the text intact, without contemplating or acceding to the pressure for change. It is not simply that the audience is assumed to be more "Shakespeare-minded," that understanding Shakespeare is no longer the prerogative of the West End. It may also be that the text is assumed to be equally incomprehensible in Peru, Poole and the West End and that therefore local change is unnecessary. Action now renders or seeks to render visibly explicit what the inexplicit language no longer communicates. To understand what Horatio is saying about Fortinbras it is now necessary to see him. Rather than editing the text by altering language, Branagh's film edits by adding explanatory visuals, as if to represent the play more fully.

The text can never be fully represented in performance; it cannot be consumed by, adequately fulfilled by a single exemplar since, as a transhistorical document, the play denies its own universality and can only manifest various moments of historical contingency. Irving Wardle, for many years theatre critic of the London *Times*, argued that a theatre critic should never use the word "definitive" for "if a classic could be defined once and for all it would immediately cease to be a classic: impaled on a definitive production like a moth in a display cabinet."[41] The particularities of performance are less a matter of the adequate representation of the necessary aspects of the originating text, whatever authority we might seek to appeal to in order to define that notion of necessity, than of the representation of the text in a manner adequate to its specific cultural intervention. Branagh's film needs to be tested not against our notion of the Shakespeare text but against the particular intervention a late twentieth-century four-hour multimillion dollar internationally cast Shakespeare film wishes to make—and one of those interventions is a tension with our scholastic notion of the recovery of the otherness of historical meaning. Branagh's film depends on its familiarization. Hence, the exploration of Ophelia's "My lord" involves an exploration of the particular modes of representation of female characters in late twentieth century Western culture, for it is clear that what is happening here is a small part of the film's attempt to build up the presence of Ophelia in particular ways. As Sauer notes, the visual interpolations are designed to "fill in the stories of minor characters," to give a number of them "complete stories" (329–30).

Precisely because the added words have no textual authority—that is, they cannot be justified by appeal to the authority of Shakespeare—they evade the kinds of negotiation with authority that actors—and directors—recurrently utilize as the form of justification of their work. In his exhilarating tirade, *Shakespeare and the Authority of Performance* (Cambridge: Cambridge University Press, 1997), W. B. Worthen has investigated the strategies by which actors, directors and performance critics have used "Shakespeare," an invoked authorizing presence, to explicate their approaches. The work of the actor, in particular, is often explained, by the actors themselves, as a responsibility to make manifest something they intuit as "the author's original intentions" and that is defined as being achieved by the constitution of character. That the concept of character in early modern theatre might be strikingly different, that the use of what is still almost always an essentially post-Stanislavskian method for the substantiation of the presence of character in modern production might be glaringly inappropriate, such thoughts rarely rear their awkward heads. Stanislavsky's promptbook for *Othello*, the only one of his Shakespeare productions for which the promptbook is currently available in English,[42] shows the inadequacy of such a realist psychologized method for dealing with Iago above all. But this has not dissuaded generations of actors from believing that some version of such a method must be necessary for Shakespeare because character, defined solely in terms of a coherent psychology, an inner self found in the mind and feelings of the character's existence, is seen as a constant.

The task of the individual actor is seen as the fulfilled representation of individuality located in emotion and, subordinately, thought. The character's "journey" through the play—and Worthen is particularly fierce on this concept of the journey—depends for the actor on a notion of a findable and playable inner consistency. How the actor gets from one scene of onstage presence to another is located in the offstage fictive continuities of the character. Actors worry where their characters go when they are not visible to the audience. Of course there are exceptions: when Juliet Stevenson comments that "the language tells you who the character is moment by moment, word by word. You need not, *should* not, be bound by notions of psychological consistency,"[43] she is both strikingly right and strikingly unusual.

The work of New Historicist critics has been strikingly successful in our new understanding of the otherness of notions of subjectivity and how necessary that comprehension of the difference in the meaning of subjectivity is to a proper consideration of dramatic character as historically located at the moment of the texts' production. It has taught us to understand character as socially defined, "self-fashioned" to use Greenblatt's famous term, and structurally discontinuous. Even where an actor perceives that Shakespearian character is not "psychologically coherent or consistent," the function of the discovery of character is still within a concept of inner self. Harriet Walter, for instance, recognizes that the work of the actor is to "play each scene or beat, however contradictory, or however incompatible it seems with what has gone before or comes after." She continues: "you play the moment for its integrity, for what it is. Then, by the end of the play, the character is an accumulation of all those separate moments." This sounds unfamiliar coming from an actor, though familiar as a New Historicist trope, a recognition of character as construct. But, while she asserts that "the character doesn't speak the text, the text 'speaks' the character," she also believes that what comes through is finally an internalized subjectivity:

> Through the movement of the verse, the rhythm of the speech, the confrontation with other characters, the echoing of ideas, the selection of certain words and the repetition of imagery, the mental and emotional life of the character is revealed.[44]

Social existence or structural significance is replaced here by an imagined innerness. But social existence may be the true mark of a character's structural discontinuity. This is rather effectively true for

Hamlet where the problem is acutely exemplified in the names in this play, for the word "Claudius" is never spoken in the play and the name exists solely because of its presence in stage-direction, not dialogue. Hence the character is defined in performance by a variety of social forms or moral labels—king, father, mother, more than kin, "Bloody, bawdy villain! / Remorseless, treacherous, lecherous, kindless villain!" (2.2.581–82)—but never by a particular individualized name, Claudius. We should move from that perception to seeing Claudius as the sum of these aspects of a discontinuous public performative self. Ophelia never stops being Polonius's daughter, Laerte's sister, Hamlet's love and putative bride. A posited inner emotional or intellectual consistency is irrelevant.

When Branagh chooses to bring Ophelia into a scene in which there is no justification from textual authority for her appearance, he needs a reason, something that enables Kate Winslet to play the moment. In the space between 4.1 and 4.2, between, that is, the end of Claudius's conversation with Gertrude and Hamlet's entrance having safely stowed Polonius's corpse, Branagh inserts a sequence of violent activity:

> **Cut to:**
>
> **Interior / PALACE ROOMS—MONTAGE Night**
> Soldiers on red alert. Alarms go off. The hunt for HAMLET is on!
>
> **Cut to:**
>
> **Interior /PALACE Night**
> Guards break into OPHELIA's room. She is terrified. Her bed is searched, with her still in it!
>
> (114–15)

This extraordinary breach of palace decorum is the immediate cause, we presume, of Ophelia's rushing out to find Hamlet. She runs into the next scene seeking him; he sees her, turns and runs off as her voice desperately pursues him. The film next shows her as it leaves Elsinore for Hamlet's encounter with Fortinbras's army, again a visual interpolation but also an aural one:

> The Camera still moving, this time with the body of POLONIUS as it is carried into the Chapel. OPHELIA being restrained by GUARDS. A great primal yell and then she flings herself at the body, held back by the Chapel gates. We move in on her screaming face. A scene of ugly grief. (119)

As the shot dissolves to a distant prospect of Elsinore, we continue to hear, as at a distance, the sounds of that screaming grief (again something the screenplay does not record but which the finished film makes powerfully present). The last time we see Elsinore before the film's intermission is controlled by the sound of Ophelia's pain. Her father dead, rejected by her lover (for how else can she construe his running away at the moment he sees her?), she is terrifyingly alone.

Over and over again the film chooses to enlarge the presence of Ophelia, to make her present. We will see her in her padded cell, we will watch her being hosed down (after which she will produce a key from under her tongue—Branagh providing a realist explanation of how she managed to escape from the palace so that she could drown later), we will see her drowned corpse. Earlier, in one of the film's other striking textual variants—this time of speech heading—Polonius had Ophelia read Hamlet's love letter aloud to Claudius and Gertrude; she broke down and ran out, unable to continue, as well as allowing us to see, Hamlet in flash-back speaking some of the letter to her. The flash-back both explicates the source of the letter and renders incomprehensible its existence since it fails to explain how the spoken language of the flashback came to be written. It also, in its insistence on making clear the sexual history of the relationship, explains and simplifies the reasons for Ophelia's distress at having to read the letter in public.

Far more than with any other character in the entire film, Branagh's expansion of the presence of Ophelia is an apparent recognition of the inadequacy even of the full text in the representation of character. Whatever the full text does for the actor playing Polonius or Claudius it simply seems to Branagh, it would appear, not to do enough for Ophelia. Rather than playing out that inadequacy, rather than choosing to explore the implications of her silencing by the play, Branagh seeks instead to produce Ophelia's version, to give her the space that the play denies her so that we should both be enabled to understand the processes of the character (discover the continuities, fill in the gaps) but also redefine the "gravitational weight" of the play into something with that most favored of all Hollywood filmic tropes, the requisite love story—and thereby increase the marketability of the film for that crucial teen audience. *Hamlet* will not quite become *Romeo + Juliet* but Branagh tried as hard as he could to flesh out (literally so in the nudity of the love-scenes) what Shakespeare had so signally failed to provide.

Branagh's solution is not the creation of a stronger Ophelia. Far from allowing Ophelia a space of resistance, he only increases our sense of her as victim, abused, not least, by Hamlet himself as when he presses her face hard against the two-way mirror behind which her father and his step-father are standing so that Polonius reacts with a sympathetic movement of anguish. Such a moment, of course, humanizes the father while objectifying the daughter in the structure of male power. Ophelia's resistance in this film is restricted to an act of concealment, the key with which to escape from Elsinore and the pain of living, an act that is constrained by her madness and her death. Branagh, however, ostensibly feminizes the play by increasing the presence of Ophelia while containing our vision of female behavior within a male dominant model of passivity. More Ophelia here means a lesser Ophelia but also an Ophelia whose movement from sanity to madness through grief can be, has to be, observed and traced. Where Shakespeare's text refuses to allow us any sound or sight of Ophelia from play-scene to mad-scene, from her saying, "The king rises" (3.2.253) and her exit with the court to her search for "the beauteous majesty of Denmark" (4.5.21), Branagh joins the separated dots, provides the stages of the journey, creates explication by showing Ophelia where Shakespeare only provides others' explanations of her.

The discontinuity in the role in Q2, F, or conflated text is playable but it need only be played as discontinuity. In other words, it is not a requirement that the actor playing Ophelia in the play scene enables us to anticipate the figure who appears in the mad scene, nor that the mad scene can be read back to the play scene. Rather, the two scenes concretize moments of existence whose interconnectedness does not even need to be hypothesized. Social existence is fragmentary, especially in our observation of others, and the need to explain and connect is a late-twentieth-century obsession that we can choose to resist and which the specific dramaturgy of the Shakespearian theatre can enable us to see as resistible. Ophelia is more than the sum of her scenes but also less than that, for the scenes do not add up; the part is less than the sum of the holes. Where deconstructionism has encouraged us to regard the gap, the methodology of Shakespearian characterization might encourage us to see those gaps as crucial spaces across which character cannot be turned into a modern humanist organic whole. The mad Ophelia ought to be—and in Kate Winslet's performance in the film is—unrecognizable from the earlier self, the self not disguised but reformulated and disconnected. The need to include the two words "My lord" is a direct consequence of the remapping of late-twentieth-century assumptions onto an early sixteenth-century text, the text re-edited to fit a different framework.

I find myself at this point aware of the extent to which the dramaturgical method of Shakespeare's text is thrown into sharper relief by such reworking as Branagh's, rather as the finest commentary on Shakespeare's *Troilus and Cressida* is still Dryden's adaptation. Branagh's film becomes a textual commentary as well as a text as Hazlitt saw in Kean's returning at the end of the nunnery scene to kiss the weeping Ophelia "the finest commentary that was ever made on Shakespeare." But the problem of the two words added to Ophelia's role in the screenplay also reveals something of the problem of text and its transition from the texts of Shakespeare's *Hamlet* to the texts (film, video, screenplay) of Branagh's *Hamlet*. The movement from page to script to film to screenplay is not linear. The intertwining of the textual witnesses of film reflects back on the nature of the process of editing the Shakespeare text but also on the process of creating an edited film out of the multiplicity of different shots. As R. A. Foakes writes in relation to editing *King Lear*, "[A]n editor has to juggle with all these uncertainties,"[45] but the Shakespeare editor, unlike the film editor, cannot leave text on the cutting-room floor.

Notes

1. William Shakespeare, *Hamlet*, Screenplay and Introduction by Kenneth Branagh (London: Chatto and Windus, 1996), 116. Subsequent references to this text are to "Screenplay."

2. All quotations from Shakespeare are from *The Complete Works*, ed. Stanley Wells and Gary Taylor (Oxford: The Clarendon Press, 1986), unless otherwise indicated.

3. Russell Jackson remembers Ophelia making a silent appearance in this scene to confront Hamlet in the Renaissance Theatre Company's production directed by Derek Jacobi and starring Kenneth Branagh as Hamlet in 1988. There is no manuscript witness of this entrance: neither Jackson's personal copy of the Arden 2 edition, annotated by him with the cuts and rearrangements for that production (for which he acted as textual adviser, as he did on the film), nor the prompt-book for that production, held with the Renaissance Theatre Company's archives in the library of the Shakespeare Institute, mark an entrance for Ophelia in this scene. The promptbook indicates only that "Ophelia screams off DSR" at the start of the scene, as if she has been told of her father's death or has seen his corpse. Memory of performance is necessarily fallible but so too are promptbooks and, in this case at least, I would wish to suggest that the memory of someone closely involved in the production is as likely to be accurate as any of the written evidence of a production. If the event did occur in Jacobi's production, then it may approximate to a source for the event in the film.

4. William Shakespeare, *Hamlet* (London: Samuel French, 1919), French's Acting Edition 334, iii.

5. I use here the form of the name as it appears in the French's Acting Edition,

rather than Wells-Taylor's Barnardo. Similarly, later, I use Branagh's preferred form Voltemand, rather than Valtemand.

6. See Paul M. Sammon, *Future Noir: the Making of Blade Runner* (New York: Harper Collins, 1996), 394–408.

7. Bridget Gellert Lyons, ed., *Chimes at Midnight/ Orson Welles, director* (New Brunswick: Rutgers University Press, 1988), 24.

8. William Shakespeare, *Romeo and Juliet* (London: Arthur Barker Ltd., n.d.), 139.

9. See *William Shakespeare's Romeo + Juliet. The Contemporary Film, The Classic Play* (New York: Bantam Doubleday Dell, 1996). It is described on the title-page as "The screenplay by Craig Pearce & Baz Luhrmann and the text of Shakespeare's original play together in one volume."

10. Alan Dent, ed., *Hamlet The Film and the Play* (London: World Film Publications, 1948).

11. Ibid., pages 6–19 of Dent's essay "Text-Editing Shakespeare with particular reference to 'Hamlet.' " The book is not paginated; my page references are my count within the essay.

12. Ibid., 8.

13. My gratitude, yet again, to Russell Jackson for letting me see the shooting script.

14. See also its elaborate description of Fortinbras's army with its "Close Shots of 'softly' marching feet, the set expressions, hands on weapons, the commanders on horses" (120). The screenplay text for one of the flash-backs to Hamlet and Ophelia's love-making describes them as "sitting at the piano" (54) when no piano is visible on screen.

15. See David Kennedy Sauer, "Suiting the Word to the Action: Kenneth Branagh's Interpolations in *Hamlet*" in Holger Klein and Dimiter Daphinoff, eds., *Hamlet on Screen* (Lewiston, NY: The Edwin Mellen Press, 1997), *The Shakespeare Yearbook* 8:325–48, (346).

16. I am grateful to Douglas Lanier for information on United Artists and the making of *The Taming of the Shrew.*

17. Robert Hamilton Ball argues that the credit never existed in "*The Taming of the Shrew*—with 'Additional Dialogue?' " in Joseph G.Price, ed., *The Triple Bond* (University Park, Penn.: The Pennsylvania University Press, 1975), 203–20.

18. Ball, 205.

19. Ibid.

20. David Garrick, *The Plays*, ed. Harry William Pedicord and Frederick Louis Bergmann (Carbondale: Southern Illinois University Press, 1980–2), 3:200, act 1, ll.284–86. Pickford says "Shall tie up her tongue."

21. Diana Henderson is wrong to record the error as "I come to wive in Padua—wealthily" in her otherwise excellent account of the film in her essay, "A Shrew for the Times" in Lynda E. Boose and Richard E. Burt, eds., *Shakespeare, the Movie* (London: Routledge, 1997), 148–68 (152).

22. Quoted by Henderson, 152.

23. See Laurie E.Maguire, *Shakespearean Suspect Texts* (Cambridge: Cambridge University Press, 1996), 135–46. (the example is at p.140). Compare an audience member's documentation of similar variants from the licensed playtext in 1700 when the actors at Little Lincoln's Inn Fields Theatre were prosecuted because Thomas Doggett, in a performance of Congreve's *Love for Love* on 25 December, had added "E God" before some of his lines (see Joseph Wood Krutch, *Comedy and Conscience after the Restoration* [New York: Columbia University Press, 1924], 170–71).

For a comparable later example, see Philip Gaskell's transcript of passages from Tom Stoppard's *Travesties* as spoken in two performances in his *From Writer to Reader* (Oxford: Clarendon Press, 1978), 245–62.

24. Quoted by Ball, 205.
25. "Text-editing," 3.
26. Ibid., 4.
27. See Jill L. Levenson, *Romeo and Juliet* (Manchester: Manchester University Press, 1987), 111–14.
28. Levenson, 112 (= 5.3.150–51).
29. *Studies in Bibliography* 13 (1960), 31–47.
30. William Shakespeare, *Hamlet*, ed. Philip Edwards (Cambridge: Cambridge University Press, 1985), 32.
31. For dogged documentation of such alterations, see the twelve volumes of William P. Halstead's collation of 5000 acting editions and promptbooks in his *Shakespeare as Spoken* (Ann Arbor: University Microfilms International, 1977–79).
32. Q2 does not give her an exit at the end of 3.4 but marks an entry for her at the start of 4.1. I take it that it is more likely that "exit" should be emended to "exeunt" than that the entry should be deleted.
33. Private conversation.
34. Terrence Rafferty, "Solid Flesh" (*The New Yorker* 13 January 1997), 80.
35. Ibid., 81.
36. Cary M. Mazer, "Cut! Cut!" (*Philadelphia City Paper* 24–30 January 1997) 20.
37. Kenneth Branagh in "Hamlet—To Cut or Not to Cut" (*Screening Shakespeares*, Film Education, broadcast BBC2, 12 February 1997).
38. Dent lists "the most noteworthy simplifications for words and phrases that must reasonably be considered 'caviare to the general' " in a "postscript" to "Text-Editing," 21.
39. Ibid.
40. Ibid., 20.
41. Irving Wardle, *Theatre Criticism* (London: Routledge, 1992), 41.
42. See *Stanislavsky Produces "Othello,"* translated by Helen Nowak (London: Bles, 1948).
43. Quoted in Carol Rutter, *Clamorous Voices* (London: The Women's Press Ltd, 1988), 43.
44. Ibid., 76.
45. William Shakespeare, *King Lear*, ed. R. A. Foakes (Walton-on-Thames: Thomas Nelson Ltd., 1997), 127.

Afterword
STANLEY WELLS

IN HIS ESSAY IN THIS VOLUME, JONATHAN BATE DIVIDES SHAKESPEARE critics at the turn of the twentieth century into two camps: "those whose primary interest is in ideas and those whose primary interest is performance." A reading of the remaining essays printed here, however, suggests to me an even more basic division (if division is necessary), into those interested primarily in ideas and those concerned above all with factual investigation. It is the old, often false dichotomy between scholars and critics. False because, as literary theorists constantly reiterate, the objective search for truth is a chimera, driven ineluctably if often subconsciously by ideological agenda. I once proposed to an audience of literary scholars that textual critics work aloof from the political fray in the purity of their search for truth. Sharp intakes of breath from, especially, those members of my audience who were most deeply committed to political approaches alerted me to the naivety of my remarks. Of course we cannot divide scholarship from critical thought; even the most relentless of card indexers is impelled by ideas of what is worth cataloguing, and why.

Nevertheless, it may well be that, however paradoxically, the current (if waning) emphasis on post-structuralist theory has stimulated belief in the value to literary studies of factual investigation. At a basic level, some critics of a liberal humanist persuasion have been driven in the direction of historical research out of sheer lack of confidence in their capacity to compete with the rarefied, and often inaccessibly expressed, intellectualism of their theory-minded colleagues. Reg Foakes has done more than most scholars of his generation to keep abreast of the shifting tides of critical thought without adopting the stylistic obscurantism that disfigures too much recent work. So too, to judge by their contributions to this volume, have the colleagues and students who have worked most closely with him.

More positively, increasing awareness, stimulated by theory, of the fallibility of subjectivity has resulted in a healthy retreat from dogmatism. Critics of an earlier generation often delivered their opinions *ex cathedra,* and their congregations were conditioned, notebook in hand, to adopt an attitude of docile receptivity. When the structure of society was more hierarchical than now, there prevailed a touching belief that professors and people like that would have a clearer sense of what Shakespeare meant than less academically elevated persons, that an Oxford or Harvard professor was by definition closer to Shakespeare than one from, say, Birmingham (either England or Alabama), and that although you might go to the theatre to enjoy Shakespeare, it was only by going to the professors that you could have any hope of understanding him. Now, we are less easily impressed by the "father (or mother) knows best" stance, and as Bate's emphasis on performance suggests, and as the number of essays in this volume related to staging both in Shakespeare's time and in later ages confirms, the study of performance has become central to both scholarship and criticism.

There was formerly a clearer division than now between scholars and critics. The scholars accumulated what we would now call data banks of information. Some critics drew upon them, more or less haphazardly, for facts to support their opinions; others moved in a freer air of philosophical speculation, rhapsodic imaginings, and moralistic assertiveness, telling us what the objects of their study thought, and what we should think about it. Though critical studies, such as A. C. Bradley's *Shakespearean Tragedy* (1904) and, among the work of contributors to the present volume, M. M. Mahood's *Shakespeare's Wordplay* (1957), have achieved classic status, it is on the whole the work of the scholars that has worn best. Even at the end of the twentieth century, we still need to consult nineteenth-century reference works such as E. A. Abbott's *Shakespearian Grammar* of 1869, and Alexander Schmidt's *Lexicon,* dating from 1874; and Sir Edmund Chambers's *The Elizabethan Stage* and *William Shakespeare: A Study of Facts and Problems,* dating respectively from 1923 and 1930, W. W. Greg's great *Bibliography of the English Printed Drama to the Restoration,* of 1939–59, and Allardyce Nicoll's *History of English Drama 1660–1900* (1923–46) remain indispensable. Such works continue to appear. We can be sure, for instance, that the volumes of *The London Stage* and its successor the *Biographical Dictionary of Actors* will remain invaluable to theatre historians well into the twenty-first century, and quite possibly beyond, and the ongoing volumes of the Records of English Drama series, drawn on by, for instance, Peter Davison in his essay in this volume, have established themselves as a major resource.

It is no accident that Reg Foakes, like three of the contributors to this volume—Ernst Honigmann, John Russell Brown, and Philip Edwards—was closely associated with Allardyce Nicoll in the earliest years of the Shakespeare Institute at Stratford-upon-Avon, and that Nicoll fostered among his colleagues and students close study of the non-literary as well as the literary texts of the period in which Shakespeare wrote. The gradual appearance on microfilm from Ann Arbor of the entire corpus of English printed books of every kind stimulated work on Shakespeare's intellectual and social context, and Nicoll, having persuaded the University to buy the films, made sure, in his thrifty, Scottish way, that they were put to use. As a graduate student a few years after Reg had left the Institute, I can speak feelingly of the hours that we were encouraged—nay, required—to spend on projects such as the notorious Sermon Survey, for which we all had to read a sixteenth- or seventeenth-century sermon and to report on it to the weekly gathering of staff and students, hoping against hope that we might alight upon some item of interest to students of the drama. Nicoll also encouraged as a Ph.D. topic a project known as the Books and Readers theses, which required close study of the contents of every book, whatever its subject, printed within one or two years.

Work such as this was potentially invaluable in its contribution to the detailed understanding and explication of other texts of the period, and naturally led to and fed editorial work undertaken by all the early Fellows and associates of the Institute, and by many later ones, too. Arden editions by Foakes of *Henry VIII* and *The Comedy of Errors* and by Ernst Honigmann of *King John*, along with Edwards's Revels *Spanish Tragedy* and, later, the splendid edition of the complete works of Massinger which Edwards worked on with Colin Gibson—one of the few complete editions of dramatists commissioned by Oxford University Press during this period actually to reach publication—all bear witness to the spirit of collaborative scholarship that Nicoll fostered. And such work has continued to appear from the same people. Honigmann's Arden *Othello* and Foakes's Arden *King Lear* followed forty and more years after their early contributions to the series.

Out of this environment too came Foakes's edition of *Henslowe's Diary* (1961), undertaken in collaboration with R. T. Rickert, itself an enduring work of scholarship whose continuing value is witnessed by the increasingly alarming price tags attached to the few copies that ever appear in secondhand book catalogues. Another of Reg's publications, the *Illustrations of the English Stage, 1580–1642*, has added too to the availability of material that is basic to study of the period. Work like this on the theatres and theatrical conditions of Shakespeare's time has of course gained in impetus as a result of the reconstruction of the Globe and especially the discovery of the remains of the Rose, in both of which Reg has naturally taken a keen and productive interest.

A number of the essays in, especially, the first part of this volume draw on historical research of this kind in their investigations of early performance. Peter Davison brings forward much curious information on topics as diverse as laborers' wages, the state of Elizabethan roads, meteorological conditions in 1597, and the construction of coaches in his investigations of touring by the Lord Chamberlain's Men, and shows that, however far from criticism such scholarship might appear to be, it may have editorial, and thus critical, implications. Editors nowadays are far more conscious than they were in the early days of the Arden enterprise of the need to think of plays of the period as works primarily written for performance. So Michael Hattaway, in his study of the Role of Edgar in *King Lear*, draws equally on one of the play's sources, Samuel Harsnett's *Declaration of Egregious Popish Impostures*, and on details of a recent production. Editors are also less dismissive of the potential value for research of texts deemed to be inauthentic; so for example Peter Wright, in his essay on parts 2 and 3 of *Henry VI*, shows the usefulness of a study of stage directions and of the *Contention* plays, once marginalized as "bad" but now more neutrally labelled "short" texts, and valued for the information they can give us about the way the plays were read, and possibly acted, in their own time. Textual information is used too in Alexander Leggatt's study of what used to be called "mirror scenes," an essay which skilfully interweaves awareness of the indeterminacies of Elizabethan theatre practice with critical consideration of theatrical effectiveness. Looking at staging from a different angle, M. M. Mahood draws on architectural scholarship in her study of entries and exits on the Shakespearian stage, but can also demonstrate the value to criticism of a study of staging conventions. Ian Donaldson's essay on *Julius Caesar* and *Sejanus*, too, uses historical information in its challenge to the validity of theory-based interpretation of the former play, while also practicing more purely critical technique in its appreciation of *Julius Caesar*'s aesthetic qualities as "a play of almost Mozartian formal beauty, whose themes and motifs elegantly and hauntingly return, just as its central character returns in a literal sense to haunt his murderers."

Though historical fact is central to much current work on Shakespeare and the drama of the period, that does not invalidate the fruitful exercise of informed speculation. Ernst Honigmann's work has always been notable for a combination of scrupulous scholarship with a daring willingness to espouse unorthodox opinions and to float novel ideas; though the conclusions towards which he strives are often ultimately unprovable, it is always a pleasure to travel with him in his journeys into the unknown. Whether or not we accept his views about the identity of the figures lying behind Shakespeare's *Sonnets*, we have to acknowledge that they are based on meticulous biographical research, and the insight that "the Young Man's 'performance' " of the *Sonnets* "must have differed quite radically from the modern reader's" because he first read them "singly or in small groups, in Shakespeare's own handwriting" is rich in suggestiveness. Subjectivity of reader and audience response is more to the fore in Philip Edwards's subtle investigation of "the inscrutability of language in Shakespeare's plays," and especially in his somewhat exasperated puzzling over "why some people so deeply resent the notion that Hamlet," in one of his finest speeches, is "speaking disingenuously, that he is using this fine language to mislead Rosencrantz and Guildenstern." Here we are forcibly reminded that enjoyment and understanding of literature and drama is ultimately a matter of personal response. There will always be "some people" who get it wrong. It is possible, however, as Jonathan Bate shows, to use philosophical writings of the past as a means of attempting to come to an understanding of how the responses of readers of Shakespeare's time might have differed from those of the present.

Reg Foakes has crowned his career (so far) with his magisterial Arden edition of *King Lear*, a work which demonstrates his mastery of the techniques of both scholarship and criticism. It is fitting, in view of the prominence he gives to the play's performance history on both stage and screen, that several contributors to this volume, including Jonathan Bate, Grace Ioppolo, Michael Hattaway, and (to a lesser extent) M. M. Mahood and Carol Chillington Rutter all pay special attention to theatrical realizations of that play. Editing is a demanding discipline because it calls on so many different kinds of expertise—in textual criticism, bibliography, source study, lexicography, theatre history, and critical history, as well as (perhaps most importantly) the sheer capacity to get things right. As we may see from early volumes in the Arden series, some of which pay no attention at all to the effect of the play as acted even in Shakespeare's time, let alone in later ages, the demands made on an editor have expanded as a result of increased emphasis on the significance of performance. A pioneer in the application of scholarly and rigorously critical techniques to theatre history is Reg's early colleague John Russell Brown, whose essay valuably stresses the need for a holistic approach in writing about plays as acted. It is all too easy for both reviewers and theatre historians to concentrate on star roles (as theatre photographers all too maddeningly do) at the expense of, for example, the design of the production, a subject which Carol Chillington Rutter illumines in relation both to the theatres of Shakespeare's time and to those of later ages. Editors and scholars now feel more of an obligation to acknowledge the internationalism of Shakespeare production, exemplified in Alan Brissenden's survey of Shakespeare on Australian stages.

Another recent development in Shakespeare scholarship is the study and analysis of acting editions, previously as slightly regarded as the "bad," or "short" Quartos (which, of course, may themselves be a form of acting edition.) Theatre directors share in the scholarly discipline of editing to the extent that few productions ever aim simply to project unaltered the text chosen as the basis of the promptbook. But a director's editing has very different aims and techniques from those of the textual editor. Some directors are cavalier in their treatment of text, whereas others show a scholarly concern for the problems of achieving theatrical effectiveness while interfering as little possible with what the scholar-editors have given them. Grace Ioppolo shows how a modern director, Richard Eyre, working on *King Lear* at the Royal National Theatre, validated "the ideas of theatrical and textual revision expressed by the new revisionists" while also demonstrating "that literary editors and critics are not the sole or even primary constructors, purveyors or interpreters of a Shakespearian text." The scholarly discipline of analyzing directors' treatment of text in individual productions may be put to critical use as a springboard for expounding and defending Shakespeare's stagecraft, as Richard Proudfoot shows in his study of Margaret Webster's Old Vic production of *Measure for Measure*. Film is, of course, only another branch of performance, but one that reaches far larger audiences, and remains in circulation for much longer than theatrical performance. This makes all the more relevant studies such as the two with which this volume concludes, Marliss Desens's essay on film versions of *Richard III* and Peter Holland's wider-ranging consideration of filmic treatment of Shakespeare's texts.

The requirement for thematic unity in this volume, desirable in itself, nevertheless means that it cannot reflect the full range of Reg Foakes's contribution to criticism and to scholarship, and consequently that not all of his colleagues, students, and friends who would have liked to pay tribute to him can be represented in its pages. His 1965 Revels edition of *The Revenger's Tragedy* remains, at the end of the century, the standard text of the play, even though its authorship has suffered a sea change. He has written extensively on other contemporaries of Shakespeare, on the Romantics, with especially important contributions to the study of Coleridge, and on the Victorians. His book *Hamlet versus Lear: Cultural Politics and Shakespeare's Art*, studying the critical reception of the plays over a period of two centuries, ranges widely over not only the traditional topics of literary and scholarly discourse, but also the cultural and political context in which Shakespeare's works have had their being. Over a long career of university teaching and administration he has earned the admiration and gratitude of countless colleagues and students. This volume comes as an admiring and affectionate tribute to a humane scholar-critic notable no less for self-effacing modesty and kindness than for learning and discrimination.

Selected Bibliography

Barroll, J. Leeds. *Politics, Plague, and Shakespeare's Theater: The Later Stuart Years.* Ithaca: Cornell University Press, 1991.

Bate, Jonathan. *The Genius of Shakespeare.* London: Picador, 1997; New York: Oxford University Press, 1998.

Bate, Jonathan and Russell Jackson, eds. *Shakespeare: An Illustrated Stage History.* New York: Oxford University Press, 1996.

Bentley, Gerald Eades. *The Profession of Player in Shakespeare's Time, 1590–1642.* Princeton: Princeton University Press, 1984.

Boose, Lynda and Richard Burt, eds. *Shakespeare the Movie: Popularizing the Plays on Film, TV, and Video.* London: Routledge, 1997.

Chambers, E. K. *The Elizabethan Stage.* 4 vols. Oxford: Clarendon Press, 1923.

Donaldson, Ian, ed. *Jonson and Shakespeare.* Atlantic Highlands, N. J.: Humanities Press, 1983.

Dutton, Richard. *Mastering the Revels: The Regulation of English Renaissance Drama.* Iowa City: University of Iowa Press, 1991.

Edwards, Philip. *Shakespeare and the Confines of Art.* New York: Methuen, 1981.

Foakes, R. A. *Illustrations of the English Stage, 1580–1642.* London: Scolar Press, 1985.

———. *Hamlet versus Lear: Cultural Politics and Shakespeare's Art.* Cambridge: Cambridge University Press, 1993.

Foakes, R. A., ed. *King Lear.* Walton-on-Thames: Thomas Nelson and Sons Ltd., 1997.

Foakes, R. A. and R. T. Rickert, eds. *Henslowe's Diary.* Cambridge: Cambridge University Press, 1961.

Golder, John and Richard Madelaine, eds. *O Brave New World: Two Centuries of Shakespeare on the Australian Stage.* Sydney: Currency Press, 2000.

Gurr, Andrew. *The Shakespearean Stage, 1574–1642.* 3rd edition. Cambridge: Cambridge University Press, 1992.

———. *The Shakespearian Playing Companies.* Oxford: Clarendon Press, 1996.

Holland, Peter. *English Shakespeares.* Cambridge: Cambridge University Press, 1997.

Honigmann, E. A. J. *The Stability of Shakespeare's Text.* London: E. Arnold Ltd., 1965.

Honigmann, E. A. J., ed. *Shakespeare and his Contemporaries: Essays in Comparison.* Manchester: Manchester University Press, 1986.

Ioppolo, Grace. *Revising Shakespeare.* Cambridge, Mass.: Harvard University Press, 1991.

Irace, Kathleen O. *Reforming the "Bad" Quartos: Performance and Provenance of Six Shakespearean First Editions.* Newark, Del.: University of Delaware Press, 1994.

Jorgens, Jack. *Shakespeare "on Film."* Bloomington: Indiana University Press, 1977.

Kishi, Tetsuo, Roger Pringle, and Stanley Wells, eds. *Shakespeare and Cultural Traditions.* Newark, Del.: University of Delaware Press, 1994.

Leggatt, Alexander. *Shakespeare's Political Drama.* London: Routledge, 1988.

Mahood, M. M. *Shakespeare's Wordplay.* London: Methuen, 1957.

McKellen, Ian and Richard Loncraine. *William Shakespeare's "Richard III": A Screenplay.* Woodstock, New York: The Overlook Press, 1996.

Parsons, Philip. *Companion to Theatre in Australia.* Sydney: Currency Press, 1995.

Patterson, Annabel. *Censorship and Interpretation: The Conditions of Writing and Reading in Early Modern England.* Madison, Wisc.: University of Wisconsin Press, 1984.

Rickard, John. *Australia: A Cultural History.* 2nd ed. New York: Longman, 1996.

Rutter, Carol Chillington. *Documents of the Rose Playhouse.* Manchester: Manchester University Press, 1984.

Taylor, Gary and Michael Warren. *The Division of the Kingdoms: Shakespeare's Two Versions of King Lear.* Cambridge: Cambridge University Press, 1983.

Wells, Stanley and Gary Taylor, with John Jowett and William Montgomery, eds. *William Shakespeare: The Complete Works.* Oxford: Clarendon Press, 1986.

Wells, Stanley and Gary Taylor, with John Jowett and William Montgomery. *William Shakespeare: A Textual Companion.* Oxford: Clarendon Press, 1987.

Wickham, Glynne. *Early English Stages, 1300–1600.* 2 vols. London: Routledge, 1959.

Notes on Contributors

JONATHAN BATE is Leverhulme Professor and King Alfred Professor of English Literature at the University of Liverpool, and a Fellow of the British Academy. Through the good offices of Reg Foakes, he has also been a Visiting Professor at UCLA. Among his many books are *The Genius of Shakespeare, Shakespeare and Ovid, Shakespeare: An Illustrated Stage History* (co-edited with Russell Jackson), the Arden edition of *Titus Andronicus*, and, forthcoming, *The Song of the Earth*.

ALAN BRISSENDEN is an Honorary Visiting Research Fellow at the University of Adelaide, from which he retired as Reader in English in 1994 and is a Member in the Order of Australia (AM). Among his publications are the Oxford Shakespeare edition of *As You Like It, Shakespeare and the Dance,* and the New Mermaids edition of Middleton's *A Chaste Maid in Cheapside.* Founding Vice President and subsequently President of the Australian and New Zealand Shakespeare Association, he has also been a Congress Committee member of the International Shakespeare Association. In November 1990 he took Reg Foakes to see the shell and recently excavated floor of the Queen's Theatre in Adelaide, Australia's oldest mainland theatre, now in occasional use again.

JOHN RUSSELL BROWN was, with Reg Foakes and Ernst Honigmann, one of the first junior Fellows at the Shakespeare Institute, Stratford-upon-Avon. He subsequently founded the Department of Drama and Theatre Arts at the University of Birmingham and held professorships at the University of Sussex and the University of Michigan. For fifteen years he was an Associate Director at the National Theatre in London and has directed numerous plays for professional and student theatres. His most recent book is *New Sites for Shakespeare: Theatre, the Audience and Asia.*

PETER DAVISON is Research Professor at De Montfort University, Leicester, and was a colleague of Reg Foakes at the University of Kent, Canterbury. He has also taught at the Universities of Sydney,

Birmingham (Shakespeare Institute), Wales, and Oxford. His numerous publications include seven editions of the plays of Shakespeare and his contemporaries, as well as the Facsimile of *Nineteen Eighty-Four,* and (with Ian Angus and Sheila Davison) *The Complete Works of George Orwell,* twenty volumes.

MARLISS C. DESENS received her Ph.D. from UCLA where she completed her doctoral dissertation under the direction of Reg Foakes in 1989. She is the author of *The Bed-Trick in English Renaissance Drama: Explorations in Gender, Sexuality, and Power.* She is an Assistant Professor at Texas Tech University in Lubbock, Texas.

IAN DONALDSON is Grace 1 Professor of English and Fellow of King's College, Cambridge, and a General Editor of the Cambridge Edition of the Works of Ben Jonson. He was Professor of English at the Australian National University, Canberra, from 1969 to 1991, and founding Director of the ANU's Humanities Research Centre from 1974 to 1990. From 1991 to 1995 he was Regius Professor of Rhetoric and English Literature at the University of Edinburgh. His publications include *The World Upside-Down, The Rapes of Lucretia, Seeing the First Australians, Shaping Lives,* and *Jonson's Magic Houses.* He is currently writing a life of Ben Jonson.

PHILIP EDWARDS was a fellow student of Reg Foakes at the University of Birmingham at the beginning of World War II and was later his colleague there. They have been in touch ever since. He has held chairs at Trinity College, Dublin, the University of Essex, and the University of Liverpool. His books include *Shakespeare and the Confines of Art, Threshold of a Nation, Shakespeare: A Writer's Progress, Last Voyages, The Story of the Voyage,* and *Sea-Mark.* He has edited *The Spanish Tragedy,* Massinger's plays, *King Lear, Pericles, Hamlet,* and the journals of Captain Cook.

MICHAEL HATTAWAY is Professor of English Literature at the University of Sheffield. He was a colleague of Reg Foakes while a Lecturer at the University of Kent from 1966 to 1984, and is the author of *Elizabethan Popular Theatre, Hamlet: The Critics Debate,* editor of the Revels edition of *The New Inn,* the New Cambridge editions of *1–3 Henry VI* and *As You Like It,* and (with Boika Sokolova and Derek Roper) of *Shakespeare in the New Europe.*

PETER HOLLAND is Director of the Shakespeare Institute, Stratford-upon-Avon, and Professor of Shakespeare Studies at the University of Birmingham, and formerly on the Faculty of English at Cambridge University and a Fellow of Trinity Hall. Among his many publications are *English Shakespeares* and the Oxford University Press edition of *A Midsummer Night's Dream*. He is the editor of *Shakespeare Survey*.

E. A. J. HONIGMANN was Joseph Cowen Professor of Literature at the University of Newcastle-on-Tyne until his retirement. He has taught as a Fellow of the Shakespeare Institute (with Reg Foakes), as Lecturer at Glasgow University, and as Reader at the University of Newcastle. He has also been Visiting Professor at UCLA, Tufts University and Concordia College. His many publications include *Shakespeare: "the lost years," The Texts of "Othello,"* and the Arden edition of *Othello*. He is joint General Editor of the Revels plays.

GRACE IOPPOLO is Lecturer in English at the University of Reading. She completed her doctoral dissertation at UCLA under the direction of Reg Foakes in 1989 and has published widely on the textual study of Shakespeare and his contemporaries. Her books include *Revising Shakespeare* and the forthcoming *Shakespeare and the Text*. She has taught at UCLA, American University (Washington, D.C.), and the Shakespeare Institute, Stratford-upon-Avon. She fondly remembers being a member of Reg's first class at UCLA in 1981, a graduate seminar on Shakespeare's histories.

ALEXANDER LEGGATT is Professor of English at University College, University of Toronto. He completed his undergraduate work at that College, where one of his teachers was Reg Foakes, on whose advice he did his graduate work at the Shakespeare Institute. Since then he has published extensively on Shakespeare and on English drama generally. His recent publications include *Jacobean Public Theatre, English Stage Comedy 1490–1990*, and *Introduction to English Renaissance Comedy*.

M. M. MAHOOD, who shares Reg Foakes's interests in Shakespeare and the Romantic poets, was privileged to work alongside him at the University of Kent from 1967 until her retirement. Previously, she had taught at King's College, London, at St. Hugh's College, Oxford, and at the Universities of Ibadan and Dar es Salaam. She has published books on the Metaphysical poets, Shakespeare's wordplay and the bit parts in his plays, and the literature of colonialism. She is currently engaged in a study of poet-botanists from Thomas Gray to Ted Hughes.

G. R. PROUDFOOT was until recently Professor of English Literature at King's College, London, and has also taught at University College, Toronto, the University of Durham, and, as a Visiting Professor, at the University of Virginia and UCLA. He is General Editor of the third series of the Arden Shakespeare and was for some years General Editor of the Malone Society Reprints. He has published editions of *The Two Noble Kinsmen* and *Tom a Lincoln* and is preparing the first ever Arden edition of *King Edward III*. He directed a production *Measure for Measure* at King's College in 1979.

CAROL CHILLINGTON RUTTER is Senior Lecturer in English at the University of Warwick. Her *Documents of the Rose Playhouse* is everywhere indebted to the scholarship, and friendship, of Reg Foakes. Her performance criticism likewise follows where he led: she is the author of *Clamorous Voices: Shakespeare's Women Today* and, forthcoming, *The Body in Play on Shakespeare's Stage*.

PETER M. WRIGHT did his initial graduate work at the University of Oxford and has taught for the last twenty-one years at Loyola High College Prep in Los Angeles. He worked extensively with Reg Foakes at UCLA and in 1991 completed his dissertation under him on stage directions in the Jonson *Folio* of 1616 and the Shakespeare *Folio* of 1623.

Index

Admiral's Men, 58, 62
Alleyn, Edward, 58, 60
Allott, Robert, 136; *Wits Theater of the little World*, 137
architecture: Elizabethan and Jacobean domestic, 34–39, 41
Armin, Robert, 36, 201

Bacon, Francis, 130; "Of Tribute," 103
Barton, John, 187, 228, 234–35
Beckett, Samuel: *Happy Days*, 218
Black Dog of Newgate, The, 222
Blackfriars theatre, 33
Bodin, Jean: *Method for the Easy Comprehension of History*, 18–20, 27, 29
Branagh, Kenneth, 273–96
Brecht, Bertolt, 160; *Mother Courage*, 97
Brook, Peter, 160, 165–67, 172, 199–200, 254
Brutus, 222
Burbage, Richard, 114, 119, 132, 135, 146
Burghley, Lord, 35

Camden, William, 141
Cardinal Wolsey, 222
Chamberlain's/King's Men, 56–68, 90–91, 101, 182, 302
Chapman, George, 139
Chapman, George, Ben Jonson and John Marston: *Eastward Ho!*, 99
Chekov, Anton, 34; *The Cherry Orchard*, 252
Clarendon, Earl of, 132–33, 146
Condell, Henry, 146
Cynicism, 22, 24

Daniel, Samuel, 139
Davies, John: *Microcosmos*, 135–37, 139
Dekker, Thomas: *The Wonderful Year*, 58–59

Diogenes, 22–24
Dionysus, Theatre of, 44
Donne, John, 136–37; *Farewell to Love*, 135; *The Progress of the Soul*, 135
Drayton, Michael, 135–37
Drummond, William, 93, 100, 142

Elizabeth I, 63, 90–91, 143, 145
Erasmus, 124; *Adagia*, 21, 27; *The Praise of Folly*, 18, 27–29, 31
Essex, Earl of, 90–91, 93, 138
Eyre, Richard, 181, 184–95, 304

Fair Maid of Bristow, The, 37
Fitton, Mary, 132, 142–43
Foakes, R. A., books: *The Columbia Dictionary of Quotations from Shakespeare*, 8; *Hamlet versus Lear: Cultural Politics and Shakespeare's Art*, 8, 19, 117–18, 182, 243, 305; *Illustrations of the English Stage, 1580–1642*, 8, 301; *Marston and Tourneur*, 8; *The Romantic Assertion*, 8; *Romantic Criticism*, 8; *Shakespeare: the Dark Comedies to the Last Plays: from Satire to Celebration*, 8; editions of Shakespeare: *The Comedy of Errors*, 7; *Henry VIII*, 7; *King Lear*, 8, 180, 184, 296; *Macbeth*, 7–8; *A Midsummer Night's Dream*, 7; *Much Ado About Nothing*, 7; *Troilus and Cressida*, 8; other editions: S. T. Coleridge, *Lectures 1808–19: On Literature, Coleridge on Criticism*, 8; *Henslowe's Diary*, 7; *The Henslowe Papers*, 7; Cyril Tourneur, *The Revenger's Tragedy*, 7, 304
Fuller, Thomas, 139–40

Garnier, Robert: *The Tragedie of Antonie*, 64
Globe theatre, 17, 33, 36–37, 90, 201, 301

313

314 INDEX

Hamlet (Branagh film), 273–96
Hamlet (Olivier film), 278, 284
Harington, Sir John, 64
Harsnett, Samuel, 198; *A Declaration of Egregious Popish Impostures*, 202–8, 302
Hayward, John: *The Life and Raigne of King Henrie IIII*, 91
Heminge, John, 146
Henry V (Olivier film), 284
Henslowe, Philip, 58–61, *Diary*, 222
Heraclitus, 20
Hertford, Earl of, 63–64, 66–67
Hobbes, Thomas, 23
Holinshed, Rafael, 39
Hooker, Richard, 203–204

Ibsen, Henrik, 35

James VI and I, 19, 59, 63, 66, 89, 99, 132, 200–201
Johnson, Dr. Samuel, 33, 191, 203
Jonson, Ben, 36, 60, 82, 103, 136–37; opinions on Shakespeare, 102–3; as rival poet in Shakespeare's *Sonnets*, 136, 139–43; works: *Bartholomew Fair*, 108; *Catiline*, 101, 103; *Conversations with Drummond*, 100, 141; *The Devil is an Ass*, 99; *Discoveries*, 102, 124, 126; *Epicoene*, 99; *Epigrams*, 93; *Every Man in His Humour*, 141; *Every Man Out of his Humour*, 102; *The Magnetic Lady*, 99; *Poetaster*, 99; *Sejanus*, 88–105, 302; *The Staple of News*, 103; *Volpone*, 99
Jonson, Ben and Thomas Nashe: *Isle of Dogs*, 58, 99

King Leir, 26–27, 31
Kozintsev, Grigori, 202
Kyd, Thomas, *The Spanish Tragedy*, 58, 108–9, 110, 301

Lady Elizabeth's Men, 63
Loncraine, Richard, 260–69
Lucretius, 129
Luhrmann, Baz, 240, 281

Mahomet, 222
Marlborough, as a performance site, 56–68
Marlowe, Christopher: *Tamburlaine*, 284
McKellen, Ian, 260–69, 304
Meres, Francis, 134, 136–38, 142–43

Miller, Jonathan, 198–99
Montaigne, Michel de, 181; "Apology for Raymond Sebond" (Florio translation), 23–27, 30–31
More, Sir Thomas, 31
Much Ado About Nothing (Branagh film), 240

Nietzsche, Friedrich, 19
Northumberland, Earl of, 100–101

Olivier, Laurence, 260–69, 286, 289

Patient Grissell, 222
Pembroke, Countess of (Mary Sidney), 64, 136
Pembroke, Earl of (William Herbert), 131–34; 136–38, 142–43, 145–46
Pembroke family, 63–64, 66
Pembroke's Men, 58, 62, 66, 146
Plautus, 44–45

Queen's Men, 60, 63–64

Return from Parnassus, The, 141
Richard III (Loncraine-McKellen film), 240, 260–69, 304
Richard III (Olivier film), 260–69, 304
Romeo and Juliet (Zeffirelli film), 284–85
Romeo & Juliet (Lurhmann film), 240, 278
Rose theatre, 17, 60–62, 301
Royal Shakespeare Company, 111, 183, 216–19, 226, 252, 282, 287

Seneca, 261
Seven Wise Masters, The, 222
Shakespeare, John, 63
Shakespeare,William, and: acting, 102; authorial revision, 181–84, 186–87; censorship, 88, 97; colonialism and post-colonialism, 240–58; court performances, 33, 57, 100; entrance and exit directions, 33–53; history, 88–105; music and sound effects, 72–82; performance studies, 151–162; philosophy, 20; private performances, 33, 62, 65; provincial touring, 56–68; scenic design, 216–36; treatment of female characters, 216–36, 260–69. **Works:** *All's Well that Ends Well*, 127,

129, 174, 219–20; *Antony and Cleopatra*, 72, 102, 127, 248; *As You Like It*, 20–21, 50–51, 125, 129, 218, 220–21, 223, 227, 246–48, 253–54; *The Comedy of Errors*, 43–44, 246, 301; *Coriolanus*, 36, 52–53, 72, 102, 128, 220–22, 256; *Cynbeline*, 137, 243, 246; *The First part of the Contention betwixt the two famous Houses of Yorke and Lancaster*, 72–82, 302; *Hamlet*, 19, 47–49, 110–11, 113–14, 116–20, 122–130, 155–57, 168, 182, 202, 209–11, 218, 220–23, 241–44, 251–53, 255–56, 258, 273–96; *1 Henry IV*, 128, 220, 222, 241, 243; *2 Henry IV*, 39, 41, 65–66, 115–16, 119, 220; *Henry V*, 81, 158–59, 216–18, 244–46, 252; *1 Henry VI*, 165, 168, 218–19, 220, 223, 262; *2 Henry VI*, 72–82, 165, 168, 218–20, 223, 262, 302; *3 Henry VI*, 72–82, 165, 168, 218–20, 223, 242, 262, 302; *Henry VIII*, 64, 249, 301; *Julius Caesar*, 88–105, 126, 222, 246–48, 302; *King John*, 243, 301; *King Lear*, 9, 17–31, 51–52, 113–14, 124–25, 129, 180–195, 198–213, 218–19, 221, 223, 242–43, 250, 286, 296, 301–4; *Love's Labour's Lost*, 49–50, 126–28; *Macbeth*, 34, 37–39, 40–42, 46, 53, 114, 123–25, 157–58, 222, 241–43, 246–47, 250, 258, 281; *Measure for Measure*, 46–47, 122–23, 125, 129, 159–60, 164–179, 217–18, 222, 224, 250, 254; *The Merchant of Venice*, 20, 129, 165, 174, 177, 220, 222, 241, 243, 246, 247, 255, 257; *The Merry Wives of Windsor*, 41–42, 218–19, 220, 246, 250; *A Midsummer Night's Dream*, 45, 108, 129, 153–54, 217, 221, 240, 246–48, 254–55, 257; *Much Ado About Nothing*, 21–22, 25, 49, 129, 219, 242, 246, 253, 255; *Othello*, 43, 51–52, 125–26, 129, 220–21, 241–43, 246, 248, 286, 301; *Pericles*, 36, 124–25, 256; *The Rape of Lucrece*, 98, 137–38; *Richard II*, 58, 91, 113–15, 118, 120, 126, 219, 223; *Richard III*, 56, 60, 62–65, 219–20, 241–43, 260–69; *Romeo and Juliet*, 37, 52, 127, 218–19, 221, 223, 246, 255, 258, 277, 294; *Sonnets*, 127–28, 131–46, 212, 303; *The Taming of the Shrew*, 7, 49, 129, 218, 223, 253, 255, 282–83; *The Tempest*, 118, 125, 129, 217–18, 220, 247, 256, 258; *Timon of Athens*, 22, 24; *Titus Andronicus*, 64–65, 108–21, 250; *The true Tragedie of Richard Duke of York*, 72–82, 302; *Twelfth Night*, 43–44, 49, 129, 227, 247–48, 251, 254–55; *The Two Gentlemen of Verona*, 254; *Troilus and Cressida*, 127, 141, 143, 216–36, 296; *The Winter's Tale*, 125, 221, 249, 250

Sidney, Sir Philip, 198, 201; *Astrophil and Stella*, 124
Socrates, 21, 27
Southampton, Earl of, 132, 138
Speed, John, 61
Stoicism, 22–8, 30
Strindberg, August, 127

Tacitus, 92, 100; *Annals*, 93, *Histories*, 93
Tarlton, Richard, 59
Tate, Nahum: *The History of King Lear*, 19, 205
Thomas Lord Cromwell, 37
Thorpe, Thomas, 137–39
Tom Strowde, 222

Voltaire: *Brutus*, 91–92, *La Mort de César*, 92

Webster, Margaret, 165–79
Weever, John, 136–37; *Epigrammes*, 134, 137
Welles, Orson: *Chimes at Midnight*, 277, 281
Wilde, Oscar, 139
Wilder, Thornton: *The Skin of Our Teeth*, 250
Wilkinson, Tate, 57
Wise, Andrew, 58, 63
women's domestic space, 41

Zeffirelli, Franco, 284–85